CHARACTER
PSYCHOLOGY

AND

CHARACTER
EDUCATION

CHARACTER
PSYCHOLOGY
AND
CHARACTER
EDUCATION

EDITED BY

Daniel K. Lapsley and F. Clark Power

UNIVERSITY OF NOTRE DAME PRESS   NOTRE DAME, INDIANA

Copyright © 2005 by University of Notre Dame
Notre Dame, Indiana 46556
All Rights Reserved
www.undpress.nd.edu

Manufactured in the United States of America

Library of Congress Cataloging-in-Publication Data
Character psychology and character education /
edited by Daniel K. Lapsley and F. Clark Power.
p. cm.
Includes bibliographical references and index.
ISBN 0-268-03371-4 (cloth : alk. paper)
ISBN 0-268-03372-2 (pbk. : alk. paper)
1. Moral development.   2. Moral education.
I. Lapsley, Daniel K.   II. Power, F. Clark.
BF723.M54C45   2005
155.2'5 — dc22

2005012536

CONTENTS

Orienting Themes and Issues

Daniel K. Lapsley and F. Clark Power

THE TITLE OF THIS WORK GIVES AWAY ITS PREMISE AND STRUCTURE. THE central premise is that important insights about character and character education will be forthcoming only when there are adequate advances in character psychology. How one understands the moral formation of persons must be conditioned on what we know about personality and development. How we manage the moral education of character must be conditioned on what we know about selfhood and identity. The structure of this volume follows this premise. The first half examines critical issues in character psychology, where character psychology is understood broadly to include not only psychological literatures that address moral functioning, but also recent trends in ethics that take these literatures seriously as a point of departure for ethical theory. The second half of the volume takes up the challenge of character education in several contexts, including schools, families, and sports. Our concluding Postscript identifies a number of unifying themes evident among the various chapters along with five prospects for productive interdisciplinary work in character psychology and education.

THE PRESENT CONTEXT

The present volume takes up a set of problems that are of timely significance. The role of virtues and vices in the formation of character is one of the most important issues in contemporary popular and academic discourse. Certainly the language of virtue and character has become part of the common parlance that is used to appraise political leaders and to express judgments about the source of social problems in virtually every aspect of modern society. This is particularly evident in the astonishing increase in reflection on the promise, prospects, and failings of character education in the schools. Indeed, anxiety about character formation in contemporary society has spawned an enormous popular literature on virtues, character, and character education, so much so that it has become a veritable *genre of discontent.*

Within academic discourse, virtue ethics, drawing heavily on the Aristotelian tradition (e.g., MacIntyre 1981), has returned to prominence in philosophical studies of morality, engendering vigorous debate with the Kantian deontological tradition on the role of character, traits, and reasoning in the moral life of persons. Moreover, there has been a recent discernible trend within ethics to constrain philosophical reflection on virtuous character by what is known about personality, self-processes, cognitive functioning, and development through these and other psychological literatures. According to this view the point of ethical theory is not so much to describe a normative theory that is attractive to the ideal, noumenal moral agent—the rational, impartial spectator who adjudicates instances of moral conflict—but rather to describe a kind of moral theory that is possible for "creatures like us." Modern ethical theory must possess a minimum degree of psychological realism that will require ongoing engagement with advances in psychological science (Flanagan 1991). Psychological facts about self and identity, for example, are seen to ground ethical analysis of moral character (Kupperman 1991, this volume). Similarly, Christine McKinnon (1999, this volume) has argued for a "naturalized ethics" (or what she calls "functionalistic naturalism") that takes certain facts about human nature as a starting point for virtue theory.

Hence, the emerging naturalized ethics perspective seeks to ground ethical theory by what is known about "human motivation, the nature of the self, the nature of human concepts, how our reason works, how we are socially constituted, and a host of other facts about who we are and how the mind operates" (Johnson 1996, 49). Johnson argues further that any comprehensive moral psychology must include an account of personal identity, and must be adequately grounded by the concepts, constructs, and literature of cognitive science. Hence there is an important movement within ethical theory to consider the literatures of personality, cognitive, and developmental psychology for insights about the parameters of virtue and character.

The shift from a Kantian deontological approach in ethics to an Aristotelian characterological approach has been matched in moral psychology by a shift away from moral development stage theories that paid little heed to the qualities of agents to recently proposed theories of moral self and identity that suggest new ways of understanding the development of character. Moreover, there are additional relevant psychological theories that do not yet contribute to ethical or even psychological work on the nature of moral functioning, nor do they inform contemporary educational models of character formation, although these literatures have enormous potential for providing both the "minimal psychological realism" required by naturalized ethics and ethical theory, and the foundation for new models of character education.

We are clearly at a point where important work in moral psychology and ethical theory is reaching a common juncture. Indeed, the increased attention devoted to moral selfhood, character, and identity is the result of movement from two directions. It results from the desire both to expand the explanatory reach of moral psychology beyond structures-of-justice reasoning and to ground ethical theory in a defensible account of moral psychology. Both trends, then, from within moral psychology and philosophical ethics, point toward greater interest in virtues, character, and moral identity. Moreover, it is now evident that important new insights about character and character education will only be possible when there is sustained exploration at the interface of these disciplines. We are confident that the present volume will catalyze this exploration.

INTEGRATIVE SUMMARY

The volume opens with Daniel Lapsley and Darcia Narvaez outlining the contours of what they call the "post-Kohlbergian era" of moral psychology. While acknowledging the contributions of Kohlberg's moral stage theory to psychology and education, they believe that Kohlberg's theory has become isolated from new developments in psychology and unable to meet the demands of contemporary character educators. They argue that recent cognitive and social-cognitive literatures can be a powerful source of insights for understanding moral functioning, although they are rarely invoked for this purpose. Lapsley and Narvaez use a social-cognitive account of knowledge activation to open up a new approach to the acquisition of virtue, identity, and unreflective moral behavior that bypasses some of the conceptual conundrums presented by the cognitive developmental approach.

In addition to making a concrete contribution to the "post-Kohlbergian era," Lapsley and Narvaez raise troubling questions about the proper relationship between psychology and philosophy. The breakthrough that Kohlberg achieved in moral psychology could not, in our view, have been possible without Kohlberg's commitment to certain philosophically grounded notions about the nature of morality. On the other hand, as Lapsley and Narvaez point out, Kohlberg's philosophical commitments draw the ire of many philosophers who did not share those commitments. Lapsley and Narvaez rightly question what the borders of moral psychology and moral philosophy should be and how these disciplines may fruitfully serve each other. Attacking Kohlberg's assumption of "phenomenalism" as an unnecessary encumbrance to defining the moral domain, they propose a provocative "minimalist" alternative. In their view the next phase of "post-Kohlbergian" research would do well to "psychologize morality," a perspective they claim is an analog in psychology of the naturalized ethics perspective in moral philosophy.

Christine McKinnon is a leading advocate of the naturalized ethics perspective. Her chapter, "Character Possession and Human Flourishing" provides an enticing challenge to the emerging psychology of character. McKinnon calls philosophy to cooperate with psychology and other human sciences by embracing a naturalism that entails the recognition that the ethical life is based on certain facts of human capacities and functioning. These facts ground human need and desire and allow us to understand the source of moral conflicts as well as the possibilities of resolution. Key to McKinnon's account is the metaphor of flourishing, which she explores in the contexts of plants, animals, and finally humans. McKinnon endeavors to cut through the philosophical axiom that one cannot derive an ought from an is. She notes that botanists define agreed-upon standards for plant flourishing in the areas of nutrition, growth, and reproduction and asks why the same method could not be applied to the evaluation of human flourishing. The most important fact about humans, McKinnon claims, is that they construct their own characters, and this reflective character-construction activity provides the standard for assessing human flourishing.

Through the metaphor of flourishing, McKinnon ties the construction of character to the pursuit of both personal happiness and social virtue. She embraces a naturalism that acknowledges critical reflection and social awareness as fundamental human facts. Although she consciously commits the naturalistic fallacy, she does so in a way that engages human autonomy. In this sense, she offers an alternative to

Kohlberg and his followers, who, like Kant, believed that conceptions of the good life were inherently subjective and thus focused on justice and concerns about what is morally right. In holding firm to this distinction between the right and the good, moral psychologists have dismissed the relevance of psychological indices of well-being, such as positive self-esteem or low stress. McKinnon encourages psychologists to contribute to defining in concrete, rationally defensible terms what human flourishing entails.

McKinnon's chapter serves as a philosophical bridge from Lapsley and Narvaez's attempt to rebuild moral psychology on a preconscious foundation to Augusto Blasi's attempt to develop a psychology of character focused on the will. McKinnon moves from identifying criteria of flourishing at the levels of plant and animal life that do not involve consciousness to a notion of human flourishing that consists of the self-conscious construction of one's character. Blasi's view of character has interesting similarities to McKinnon's, although Blasi does not directly engage the philosophical issues addressed by McKinnon.

Blasi sets out to provide a preliminary theoretical account of character that can provide a basis for future empirical inquiry. Beginning with a consideration of the virtues, Blasi finds one can classify the virtues on two levels of generality. The most general virtues involve either willpower or integrity. Blasi subdivides the concept of willpower into self-control, which constrains action, and desire, which motivates action. Elaborating on the psychological underpinnings for these notions of self-control, desire, and integrity, Blasi provides not only a remarkably integrated view of a highly complex system of functions but a sketch of how character develops from early childhood into adulthood. At the heart of Blasi's theory is a concept of the will as second-order desire, a concept that Blasi draws from the philosopher Harry Frankfurt (1988). Desire, a topic completely overlooked in the cognitive developmental approach to morality, provides a motive and meaning to character. Here, as in McKinnon's chapter, we see the wall of separation between the right and the good collapsing. Blasi is deeply concerned about moral desires and their place in the constellation of identity. He recognizes, however, that nonmoral desires can be every bit as influential as moral desires in ordering individuals' priorities and constituting identity.

Blasi's influence on the field of moral development is particularly apparent in Ann Higgins-D'Alessandro and Clark Power's chapter, which links character to the notion of responsibility. Encouraged by the growing popularity of the character education movement but lamenting the failure of that movement to generate a coherent theory of character and research program, Higgins-D'Alessandro and Power propose that character be understood as the responsible moral self. Such an understanding, they believe, is compatible with Aristotle's concept of character and would incorporate the contributions of moral development research in the study of the self.

Higgins-D'Alessandro and Power's main contribution to moral education theory and research was their study of the original just-community high schools. These schools were organized as small communities in which students and teachers made and enforced their own disciplinary rules through a process of direct participatory democracy. Reflecting on their original assessment of just communities and on subsequent evaluations of a second generation of just-community programs, they conclude that the most dramatic influence of the just-community approach was not the development of students' moral reasoning but the development of students' sense of responsibility. As Blasi mentions in this volume, responsibility is fostered through experiences that help students to become aware of and reflect upon their own agency. Traditional high schools rob students of such experiences by placing all of the power for legislating and enforcing rules in the hands of adults. Programs that employ the just-community approach give students a sense of ownership of the school and structured opportunities for reflection on their rights and responsibilities in the school.

The title of David Shields and Brenda Bredemeier's chapter, "Can Sports Build Character?" is a bit misleading. Although Shields and Bredemeier focus on character within the context of sport, they explore the concept of character more generally through the lens of motivation as well as the lens of moral development. Indeed, their chapter is an excellent example of how extant psychological literatures might be usefully appropriated for understanding important features of moral functioning, a theme that is prominent in the chapters by Lapsley and Narvaez. Moreover, their notion of character incorporates the perspectives on responsibility and the self advanced by Higgins-D'Alessandro and Power and directly engages Blasi's chapter on character and the will. As Shields and Bredemeier remind us, descriptions of character in a variety of contexts, including sports, include virtues, like justice, that regulate social interaction as well as virtues, like perseverance, that regulate how individuals pursue their goals. Character, however, is not reducible to the virtues that compose it. Character, according to Shields and Bredemeier, must be understood in relationship to the subject-self, a self that experiences, chooses, organizes, prioritizes, and pursues its desires. A psychological approach to character must do more than appropriate significant literatures, like moral development and achievement theory. A psychological approach to character must focus on the self and how the self constructs an identity that takes into account moral and achievement issues. A psychological approach to character development, moreover, must take into account that the self operates within a social context, which is key to the way the self develops.

Thus their answer to the question, "Can sports build character?" is a positive one, but one based on a research program in its earliest stage. Looking back on two decades of research, which they pioneered, on moral development in sports, Shields and Bredemeier find no definitive answer pro or con. Their investigations into the moral reasoning used in sports contexts suggest that the competitive game nature of sports encourages and legitimizes egocentric and sociocentric (team-centered) thinking and judgment. Sports thus appear to depress moral judgment below the level of competence, raising questions about the potential for sports to promote moral reasoning. While this may well be true, we should not dismiss the possibility that sports participation within the proper context can promote moral reasoning in very significant areas of life. For example, sports participation may lead to new insights into fair competition, which might be applied to school, business, and even international relations. As Shields and Bredemeier illustrate, sports are an exciting and relatively unexplored area for research that promises to make important contributions not only within sports psychology but within character psychology more broadly.

In chapter 6, Darcia Narvaez and Daniel Lapsley revisit the debate about the implications of phenomenalism in moral psychology that was first broached in chapter 1. Here they note that an a priori commitment to phenomenalism has served to narrow the range of behavior that can be the target of legitimate moral explanation and has isolated moral psychology from integrative possibilities with other psychological literatures. In their view, advances in cognitive science, learning, motivation, and personality cannot be irrelevant for understanding moral identity, moral socialization, and the formation of moral identity, yet these literatures are rarely invoked for this purpose. Hence this chapter attempts to steer moral psychology back to the mainstream by showing how contemporary research programs open up promising lines of research in moral psychology. Narvaez and Lapsley argue, for example, that cognitive processes that are tacit, implicit, and automatic govern much of human functioning, and that a suitable moral psychology must take account of this fact. Indeed, the authors argue that the intersection of the "morality of everyday life" and the "automaticity of everyday life" must be large and extensive.

To this end Narvaez and Lapsley show how three varieties of automaticity might play out in forms of moral behavior, and what implications these automaticities have for explaining some common features of character education pedagogy. They take up the issue of how to inculcate moral intuitions, appealing to the expertise literature as an orienting framework. Narvaez and Lapsley cite the Integrative Ethical Education (IEE) character education curriculum, which is now used by Notre Dame's Center for Ethical Education and Democracy, as an example of how an expertise approach to moral character can be applied with profit to the curricular challenges of middle school character education. They suggest that moral education should encourage students to develop multiple component skills to higher levels of expertise in order to encourage the formation and application of moral intuitions.

The emphasis in this chapter is on forms of moral cognition that are tacit, implicit, and automatic. The argument is phrased as an assault on the principle of phenomenalism, which is the cornerstone of the cognitive developmental tradition. This tradition is represented in the present volume by D'Alessandro and Power in chapter 4, and by Blasi in chapter 3. On one level Narvaez and Lapsley have come to a very different assessment of phenomenalism and its implications for moral psychology than has Higgins-D'Alessandro, Power, and Blasi. Yet the antimony need not be drawn so starkly. Higgins-D'Alessandro and Power point out, for example, that moral education must begin with the inculcation of habits and behavioral routines that are nonetheless complex activities that require reason, intention, and deliberation. In other words, what is routine and habitual, automatic as it were, implies neither simplicity nor the absence of reason. Similarly, Narvaez and Lapsley note that the various kinds of automaticity often coexist with different degrees of cognitive control; that awareness, attention, intention, and control are somewhat independent qualities of cognition that co-occur in different combinations; and that automaticity need not imply that behavior is unintended or that it cannot be brought under conscious control. Along the same lines Narvaez and Lapsley point out that just as automaticity does not rule out the possibility of intentional control, the fact that much of cognitive functioning is tacit does not mean that it cannot be the object of education, development, and training. Clearly, then, although positions are starkly drawn, there is a basis for conversation and possible integrative consensus.

The first six chapters attempt to outline the psychological features of "character possession," invoking such notions as social information-processing, motivational constructs, schema activation, self-worth, will, desires, responsibility, integrity, intuitions, and expertise. What emerges is a rich portrait of "character psychology" and a range of theories and constructs that hold promise for productive lines of integrative research. The second half of the volume takes up the problem of "character education," and, as Craig Cunningham's chapter shows, the success of character education is fundamentally tied to how adequate is one's conception of character psychology. Successful character education hinges on theoretically sound conceptions of personality and selfhood (a theme that is endorsed in several chapters in this volume). Unfortunately, these theoretical conceptions have been unavailing in the history of character education, with untoward consequences. In his view, "Unless psychology can provide a better model of human development . . . character will continue to receive sporadic and faddish treatment and the public's common school will continue to be undermined."

Cunningham shows this by a magisterial survey of the historical record of character psychology and character education in America. This record reveals a number of fascinating trends. It shows, for example, that the recent "naturalizing" tendency in ethical theory and the argument for a "psychologized morality," in fact has a long history, beginning with attempts to naturalize theological understandings of character (as "soul") to accord with emerging notions of faculty psychology. It shows that current anxiety about the sorry state of moral character of business and political leaders, let alone youth, is not a recent phenomenon. Indeed, many modern "virtuecrats" (see Nash 1997, this volume) who ardently look to a halcyon past when traditional character education was allegedly pervasive, widely embraced, and successfully implemented may be surprised to learn that the educational "tradition" of which they seek was not apparent to contemporaries. Widespread anxiety about social disintegration, and how character education might stem the rot, was as common to the early decades of the twentieth century as the latter. Both periods saw the formation of character-education pressure groups and activity by state legislatures to mandate character education in schools. Both periods saw the need for hands-on experiential (or "service") learning. Both periods saw the promulgation of widely divergent lists of urgently needed virtues, debates about direct or indirect methods of character instruction, and the proper place of coercion and democratic education in the curriculum. Moreover, the chasm between educators and researchers—between the ardent confidence of educators in their favored character education curricula and the skepticism of researchers about their value or efficacy—also has a long history in American education.

Cunningham's chapter helpfully places contemporary debates about character education and character psychology within a proper historical context. He reminds us that the "rise" of character education often accompanies periods of cataclysmic change in American society, when there are profound challenges to national identity and widespread anxiety about social cohesion, social change, and the unsettling forces of modernity, but that its "fall" is inevitable without an adequate character psychology to guide curricular intervention and instructional practice.

If Cunningham finds that the clamor for character education is heard most insistently during historical periods marked by rapid change, Joel Kupperman makes a parallel point in the chapter that follows with respect to character: genuine virtue is tested, and revealed, when faced with the moral disorientation that accompanies "rapid technological innovation, social change and personal mobility." Indeed, Kupperman argues that conformity to moral codes and habitual patterns of virtuous behavior under easy and familiar circumstances is not the real thing, is not genuine virtue. Genuine moral character is revealed in circumstances that are unusual, unfamiliar, and unfavorable. It is not simply knowledge of the moral law nor simply knowing the right answers, but involves, in addition, *good will.* It involves an internalization of volitional commitments into a sense of self that is connected with personal projects, goals, or a plan of life. Commitments that are staked to self-identity in this way will not be so easily abandoned when the winds of change shift.

So one way not to educate character is to attempt to imprint a moral code by telling, that is, to settle for knowledge of traditional pieties, stock answers, and habitual routines. These yield a character that is reliable only when circumstances are easy and favorable, when there is little social upheaval or dislocation. This "traditional" character education is perhaps serviceable, if Cunningham's chapter is any guide, when one's moral community is homogenous and change is slight. But, as Kupperman points out, we cannot foresee the special moral challenges that await us. The demands of modernity and the pace of social change may well induce moral disorientation and uncertainty. In this case, habitual routines guided by "imprinted" moral codes will be unreliable. It is perhaps no wonder, then, following Cunningham's argument in chapter 6, that during periods of cultural ferment and rapid social change, when moral disorientation and confusion is more evident, we hear the loudest cries for character education. In this case, the periodic "rise" of character education in American history might better reflect a preference for social homogeneity and a nostalgic wish for more settled times. Kupperman offers several suggestions for strengthening the sort of genuine character that reliably makes good moral choices even when faced with unanticipated moral contexts: connecting morally acceptable behavior to an agent's sense of self; cultivating certain moral emotions, such as pride and shame; and encouraging a commitment to projects that require extended effort over time.

Kupperman's chapter revisits numerous themes that resonate throughout the volume. His argument that moral character must be tied to self-identity and life projects is also reflected in the chapters by Blasi, by Higgins-D'Alessandro and Power, and by Shields and Bredemeier. His linkage of human flourishing with the emergence of a self who understands the point of morality will find resonance in the chapters by McKinnon, by Cunningham, and by Blasi. Blasi's chapter, too, takes up the question of good will and of volitional commitments. When Kupperman argues that good character requires patterns of choices that are reliably good but allows for choice to be "immediate and unreflective" and that "often people make important choices that they are unaware of making," he is acknowledging the place of automaticity in moral functioning, a view shared by Narvaez and Lapsley. His pedagogical recommendations should be read in the context of subsequent chapters by Davidson (chapter 9) and by Berkowitz and Bier (chapter 11). Kupperman's chapter, then, pulls together a number of thematic emphases of the present volume. What is particularly prized is Kupperman's claim that the life of genuine virtue is *not dull.* It is not easy, not "nice." It is, instead, challenging, dynamic, exhilarating; it is a life that engages the totality of the self in dramatic acts of construction and confronts the moral disorientation of our time. It is a life worth living.

Matt Davidson both acknowledges and replies to the often-voiced criticism of the current character education movement that it lacks both an organizing theory and a research program. Documenting the widespread popular acceptance of the movement, Davidson urges an appreciation for the movement's ideals and offers a framework for advancing its aims. Davidson adopts the Character Education Partnership's understanding of character as consisting of "core ethical values," such as respect, responsibility, justice, and caring. These, he claims, are universal values that should inform the way we treat others and the way we would want others to treat us. Why focus on core values? Davidson gives a two-part reply. First, specific values give content to character and to character education. Second, and more importantly, "the possession of such values leads to principled moral commitment." The proposition that values, themselves, are entities that lead to commitment gives them an agency that Blasi would no doubt question. In Blasi's view, the subject appropriates values in making a commitment. The agency thus resides in the subject.

Davidson is understandably less concerned about the explanatory status of values than he is about how they are acquired. Davidson provides an overview of the diverse methods and models available to character education, an overview that engages a number of psychological constructs and suggests that character education is open to diverse approaches and points of view. Values, according to Davidson and the mainstream of character educators, are "internalized" through a process of induction. Some character educators have downplayed the importance of the cognitive dimension of character. Davidson, along with Berkowitz (see chapter 11), believes that core values have a significant cognitive dimension and that, therefore, explanation, reflection, and discussion are key elements of the character education process. Relying on the work of Ryan and Deci (2000), Davidson also parts company with some popular approaches to character education that make extensive use of extrinsic rewards to promote desirable behavior. Character, in Davidson, must be based on intrinsic motivation. Virtue must be its own reward. Finally, pointing to the importance of the social environment and the need for community, Davidson challenges individualistic approaches to developing character.

In Davidson's account of character education there is a common core of ethical values that educators can confidently embrace as educational goals. "There is," he writes, "a collection of universal core ethical values that we do all agree upon." Our confidence in these core values is derived from their objective grounding and in their universality. Consequently, educators can proceed, without apology, to make these objectively evident moral values the target of educational effort. The point of character education is to encourage children to grasp, and to live out, moral truths that are otherwise objectively known by everyone else—that is, with the possible exception of *postmodernists!*

Robert Nash provides the postmodern take on character education, at least as it is practiced in the college setting. Nash does not believe it possible to establish an objective grounding for our moral commitments. There is no unassailable touchstone for our convictions, no absolute grounding, no foundation, nothing that can be made true from the "perspective of eternity." The philosophy of science has long ago abandoned any hope that the rationality of our scientific convictions can be vouchsafed on the foundations of "hard facts." As Imre Lakatos (1978) put it, all the propositions of science are theoretical propositions. Yet in moral philosophy, and in character education, the search for incontrovertible foundations of our moral convictions—the immutable moral "facts" that are objectively true—has not been given up. There may indeed be values and perspectives that contribute to human flourishing, that make intellectual sense, that command wide assent, and to which we make wholehearted commitment, but there is no "backup" argument, no certifying authority that can provide anything like an "ultimate" justification for our judgments. There is no independent standpoint from which we can determine the ultimate truth of rival interpretations of events. There is nothing to relieve us of the obligation to make up our own mind or to settle the matter with argument and reason. How much this gives comfort to relativists, emotivists, and subjectivists is a matter of controversy, although Nash insists that nothing about the form of postmodernism that he embraces prevents one from making informed choices, using reason deliberatively, taking a stand, defending a point of view, distinguishing good and evil, or doing anything else that is ordinarily expected of the moral point of view. What it does forbid is an appeal to a privileged standard external to history or social particularity, an appeal to something immutable, absolute, and outside of the web of interlocution, judgment, and interpretation, in order to justify moral claims or adjudicate conflict.

Nash rejects, then, the objectivist argument for character education in favor of a position he calls moral constructivism. In his view a postmodern alternative is necessary in character education, one that emphasizes "conversational virtues" (including civility, goodwill, reaching out, being respectful, obliging, and putting the best construction on things) and democratic dispositions (including self-discipline, obligation, tolerance, fairness, and generosity). Indeed, the point of character education, particularly in a secular, heterogenous, pluralist society that is rapidly changing, is to develop the capacity for democratic citizenship. This requires, in his view, sensitivity to the realities of incommensurability, indeterminacy, and nonfoundationalism. It requires the ability to engage in a kind of moral dialogue that is open-ended and keeps the conversation going. Moreover, Nash argues that cultivating the postmodern virtues are our best hope of bridging political and religious divides, forging consensus, encouraging reconciliation, and otherwise making liberal democracy work.

Indeed, in his discussion of various paradoxes of character education, he argues, "a character education most suitable for a democracy might not be one that teaches a bag of pre-determined dispositions but rather one that grows out of an indeterminate, democratic dialogue demanding continual compromise and consensus." This would rule out any curricula that emphasizes telling, exhortation, didactic methods, direct instruction, "assigning virtue books, requiring community service, [or] posting clever moral aphorisms on the walls." Instead, Nash advocates a pedagogy of deliberative discourse, one that demands the practice of conversational virtues, "one that fosters a spirit of respectful, open-ended moral inquiry."

This perhaps aligns Nash much more closely to Kohlberg's understanding of principled reasoning than he appreciates. Kohlberg, too, held out the expectation that moral deliberation would yield consensus, would accord with the demands of procedural justice, and would advance the cause of fair conflict-resolution. Kohlberg, too, as we see in the Higgins-D'Alessandro and Power chapter, was keen to promote the participatory educational structures (just communities) that prepare individuals to take on their responsibilities in a liberal, democratic society. These structures, too, would promote the community norms that are similar in function to the conversational virtues and democratic dispositions that drive the sort of character education that Nash describes. The cognitive developmental tradition also embraces constructivism and would endorse the curricular approaches endorsed by Nash. Although no one would call Kohlberg a postmodernist, there are elements of his work that would provide important resources to the instructional goals and pedagogy envisioned by Nash.

Marvin Berkowitz, who holds the first endowed chair in character education, has done more than any other character education leader to integrate character education concerns and mainstream psychology. In their chapter for this volume, "The Interpersonal Roots of Character Education," Berkowitz and his colleague, Melinda Bier, make a very simple but important point that character can only develop if rooted in interpersonal relationships. We tend to equate character education with a specific curriculum or set of deliberate practices, such as role modeling, which leads to the mistaken assumption that character is a product of teaching and not experience itself. Berkowitz and Bier put it nicely: "Character education comes from how people treat each other more than from what people tell each other." Character development, Berkowitz and Bier maintain, is built and maintained on a foundation of trust fostered in infancy through parental attachment and in the school years through a sense of belonging. Although children are subjected to wide vicissitudes of parental care and neglect, Berkowitz and Bier hold out hope for all children through the informed efforts of concerned teachers and effective classroom communities.

Berkowitz and Bier make a number of observations about the importance of the social environment, which can become the basis for significant psychological and educational research. For example, they move from a focus on trust and social bonding to consider other features of the school environment, such as participation in decision making and cooperative learning. Social bonding, it appears, may be necessary but not sufficient for character education. Social bonding, in and of itself, may lead to an avoidance of critical engagement and a de-emphasis on diversity. Berkowitz and Bier ask the school environment to foster a number of values that appear to involve different psychological competencies and processes: connectedness, autonomy, cooperation, and respect. How teachers are to interact with students to foster these values is indeed a formidable task, a task that Berkowitz and Bier note requires a "science of character education." Yet the task may be more difficult than informing teachers of best practices and how to employ them. Addressing the problem of involving students in decision making and classroom goal-setting, Goodlad (1984) noted that his research indicated that teachers were aware of the "desirability" of such practices (469), but nevertheless favored "time-honored practices that appeared to help maintain control" (470). Character education may well be an inherently conservative activity in the sense that character educators, whether they are parents, teachers, or coaches, are going to treat children as they were treated as children. Breaking the cycle may well require more than "expert" advice.

Berkowitz and Bier argue that effective character education must promote developmental goals, including the sense of emotional attachment to other individuals and to the school community. To pull this off may require comprehensive school reform. It requires, in their view, "a basic change in the way a school functions. It means altering policies, processes, and even structures." The chapter by Jeannie Oakes, Karen Hunter Quartz, Steve Ryan, and Martin Lipton takes up this theme as well. They argue that the history of school reform in America has oscillated between two fundamentally different visions of the purpose of public education: to promote civic virtue or individual freedom. This tension is also evident in character education. If school reform lurches from one allegiance ("individual freedom") to the other ("civic virtue"), so too will our vision of character education. Indeed, the problem of character education is the problem of school reform writ large. The traditional approach to character education championed by moral conservatives tends to emphasize moral individualism; it emphasizes traits required for making better persons. However, this approach focuses on only one side of the dichotomy. According to Oakes et al., character education "requires far more than helping individuals embrace proper values or to make moral choices for their own lives. It requires enabling participation in democratic public life that encourages citizens to collectively shape a common, public good."

Character education that aims for civic virtue, however, cannot be had cheaply, it cannot be "taught" like spelling. It is not a curriculum, a word of the week, a theme in a virtue story. Instead, character education for civic virtue requires the commitment to comprehensive school reform. It requires a commitment to transform schools into places that are *educative, socially just, caring,* and *participatory* (see Oakes, et al. 2000). The educative aspect of character education entails a commitment to thematic, interdisciplinary, constructivist curricula. Indeed, as Alfie Kohn (1997) has noted, the pedagogy behind much of traditional character education is not considered instructional best practice and would not be tolerated for the instruction of any other subject. The socially just aspect of character education requires a commitment to mainstreaming, heterogenous groupings, multicultural curricula, cooperative learning and "de-tracking." It entails a commitment to equity, inclusion, and "breaking down old hierarchies of educational advantage." The caring aspect requires locating the school as the locus of community life, as a place that cultivates community assets and is responsive to the linkages among family, school, and neighborhood. It entails a commitment to an ethic of democratic community. In their view "The school must become a place . . . where people are deeply committed to maintaining a strong and positive school community." The participatory aspect of character education requires a commitment to certain kinds of governance and consultation structures that gives stakeholders a real voice, and a real stake. It entails a commitment to make classrooms a part of life, rather than just preparation for it.

"To make society more democratic," they write, "students must participate in class-rooms that are themselves democratic societies."

The chapter by Oakes and her colleagues has resonance with several themes evident in this volume. For example, Berkowitz and Bier also endorse linking character education to comprehensive school reform. Envisioning the classroom as a democratic community is also taken up by Higgins-D'Alessandro and Power. Indeed, the general argument that schools must attend to the formation of a democratic character adequate for participation in civic life is evident throughout the volume. To echo the view of Berkowitz and Bier, Oates et al. note that ultimately "character education is not about specific curriculum or service projects; it's about membership. As students learn what it means to be a member of a thriving democratic community, they learn what it means to be part of the democratic tradition." Character education, if it is serious about its aspiration to promote civic virtue, must not shrink from the struggle for school reform.

Much of the focus of character education has been on primary and secondary school programs. Jay Brandenberger, much like Robert Nash (see chapter 10), makes a strong case that the college years can offer particularly fertile ground for character development. Drawing on a variety of literatures, Brandenberger shows that college students are developing in ways that relate to a variety of constructs associated with morality and character. Brandenberger's own notion of character has roots in Dewey's transactional approach and in more recent cognitive developmental psychology and explorations of moral imagination. Arguing that experience and reflection are the keys to fostering development, Brandenberger urges that we take a hard look at prevailing pedagogical practices in American colleges. A strong advocate of service learning, Brandenberger does not believe that higher education should rest content with providing volunteer opportunities alongside the conventional curriculum. Brandenberger proposes that the curriculum itself recognize the transformative power of experience and thus integrate the academic with the practical.

We hope the present volume will serve a number of useful purposes. It provides, in one volume, a multidisciplinary and interdisciplinary focus on moral character, insofar as the topic is addressed by diverse fields of study, such as philosophy, personality and developmental research, and educational theory. This volume also explores several psychological literatures for insights about moral character. The constructs that are of interest will have broad implications for the sort of psychological realism that is required by "naturalized" virtue ethics and for informing defensible models of character education. Finally, the volume takes up the challenge of character education in the context of schools, families, and organized sports.

REFERENCES

Flanagan, O. 1991. *Varieties of Moral Personality: Ethics and Psychological Realism.* Cambridge, MA: Harvard University Press.

Frankfurt, H. 1988. *The Importance of What We Care About.* New York: Cambridge University Press.

Goodlad, J. 1984. *A Place Called School.* New York: McGraw-Hill.

Johnson, M. 1996. How moral psychology changes moral theory. In *Mind and Morals: Essays on Cognitive Science and Ethics,* ed. L. May, M. Friedman, and A. G. Clark, 45–68. Cambridge, MA: MIT Press.

Kohn, A. 1997. How not to teach values: A critical look at character education. *Phi Delta Kappan* 78 (February): 429–39.

Kupperman, J. J. 1991. *Character.* New York: Oxford University Press.

Lakatos, I. 1978. Falsification and the methodology of scientific research programs. In *The Methodology of Scientific Research Programs: Imre Lakatos Philosophical Papers,* vol. 1, ed. J. Worrall and G. Currie, 8–101. Cambridge: Cambridge University Press.

MacIntyre, A. 1981. *After Virtue.* Notre Dame, IN: University of Notre Dame Press.

McKinnon, C. 1999. *Character, Virtue Theories, and the Vices.* Peterborough, Ontario: Broadview Press.

Nash, R. J. 1997. *Answering the Virtuecrats: A Moral Conversation on Character Education.* New York: Teachers College Press.

Oakes, J., K. H. Quartz, S. Ryan, and M. Lipton. 2000. *Becoming Good American Schools: The Struggle for Civic Virtue in School Reform.* San Francisco: Jossey-Bass

Ryan, R. M., and E. Deci. 2000. When rewards compete with nature: The undermining of intrinsic motivation and self-regulation. In *Intrinsic and Extrinsic Motivation: The Search for Optimal Motivation and Performance,* ed. C. Sansone and J. M. Harackiewicz, 13–54. New York: Academic Press.

ONE

Moral Psychology at the Crossroads

Daniel K. Lapsley and Darcia Narvaez

THE KOHLBERG PARADIGM

Until recently the study of moral development has been dominated by stage theories in the cognitive developmental tradition. In this tradition moral reasoning is said to gradually approach an ideal form of perfected operation as a result of successive accommodations that are made over the course of development. These accommodations progressively extend, elaborate, and structure moral cognition, and are described as stages that possess certain sequential and organizational properties. The most vivid example of a moral stage sequence is, of course, Kohlberg's well-known theory. Indeed, there are few theorists in the history of psychology who have had more influence on developmental theory and educational practice than Kohlberg. His embrace of Piagetian constructivism, his writings on the developmental grounding of justice reasoning, and his educational innovations have left an indelible mark on developmental psychology and education.

Kohlberg claimed, for example, that his stage theory provided the psychological resources by which to defeat ethical relativism. His cognitive developmental research program mounted a profound challenge to behavioral and social learning views of socialization, and returned morality to the forefront of scientific study in developmental psychology. The educational implications of his work are still evident in sociomoral curricula (e.g., "plus-one" dilemma discussion) and in efforts to reform the structure of educational institutions (e.g., just communities). Clearly, then, Kohlberg's research program has had a salutary influence on two generations of scholars (Lapsley 1996, forthcoming).

Yet it is also true that the authority of Kohlberg's work has diminished significantly in the last decade. This can be explained, in part, by the general decline of Piaget's theory in contemporary developmental research. Indeed, the general influence of Kohlberg's theory has always been inextricably linked to the prestige and authority of the Piagetian paradigm. The fact that Piaget's hegemony over the field of cognitive development has given way to alternative conceptions of intellectual functioning has had the effect of depriving Kohlberg's cognitive developmental approach of much of its paradigmatic support. One should not conclude, however, that the study of moral development has somehow profited from the wave of post-Piagetian theoretical and methodological innovations that swept developmental psychology in the last decade or so. Indeed, quite the contrary. While the study of cognition has changed dramatically, embracing a wide diversity of theoretical options, the study of *moral* cognition is still largely a matter of cognitive structures developing through stages.

PARADIGM ON THE MARGINS

How moral development has become insulated from theoretical and methodological advances in other domains of study is one of the issues that we explore in this chapter. We will argue that moral psychological research, at least in its cognitive developmental form, has been handicapped by an allegiance to a set of philosophical assumptions that has effectively limited theoretical growth and empirical innovation—and this quite apart from whatever empirical anomalies are associated with the research program. As a result the study of moral development is now largely marginalized within the broader context of cognitive and social developmental research. The debates and issues that once swirled around the moral stage theory, and that once provided an exciting momentum to research, now hold little interest, and not simply because all of the old scores have been settled. Rather, the structural developmental tradition does not seem very relevant to crucial contemporary concerns about the nature of moral character and the manner of its inculcation and development. It provides little guidance for parents, let alone educators, for how morally crucial dispositions are to be encouraged in young children, and, indeed, provides only a slight framework for understanding moral behavior in young children more generally.

Moreover, the cognitive developmental tradition does not provide much help in understanding how moral reasoning folds into the broad trends of development across other domains. Indeed, the cognitive developmental account of the moral agent, at any stage of development, is one that is not well-suited for integration with other domains of psychological research, largely because its core assumptions and philosophical commitments resist easy commerce with contemporary psychological research. As a result we get little sense of how moral reasoning is related to a full range of psychological processes and constructs, including memory, metacognitive, or motivational processes, either by the emergence and elaboration of self-regulation and self-identity or by mechanisms of cognitive learning. We get little sense of how moral behavior is influenced by personological and situational variables.

It is also true, of course, that researchers in these other domains rarely draw out the implications of their work for understanding moral functioning. Yet there was a time when moral development was central to research on social-cognitive development, when its implications for other developmental domains were more obvious, and when its research agenda defined the paradigm of developmental research. It is now a striking fact that so little of contemporary developmental research requires the findings or claims of the cognitive developmental approach to moral reasoning. One gets the sense, instead, reading contemporary textbooks, that the Kohlbergian tradition is now something that is covered more for historical interest rather than as a paradigm that addresses issues of crucial concern to contemporary researchers.

A NEW STARTING POINT

Yet we argue that moral psychology is at an important crossroad. In our view the evident decline of the cognitive developmental tradition opens up new opportunities for theoretical innovation, some of which are plainly evident in some recent work in moral psychology. Although this recent work has yielded important insights about, say, the parameters of domain-centered rationality (Turiel 1983, 1998; Nucci 1982, 2001) or the components of effective moral functioning (Rest et al. 1999), moral psychology is still largely defined in terms that are familiar to the cognitive developmental tradition, and, indeed, in terms that take certain cognitive developmental assumptions as a starting point (as we will see below).

We take a somewhat different starting point. In our view productive lines of moral psychological research in the "post-Kohlbergian era" will be found by searching for integrative possibilities with other domains of psychological research. In particular, we argue that certain cognitive and social-cognitive literatures can be a powerful source of insights for understanding moral functioning, although they are rarely invoked for this purpose. Indeed, the introduction of social-cognitive theory into moral psychology has enormous integrative possibilities (Lapsley and Narvaez, forthcoming). It opens up moral psychology to the theory, constructs, and tactics of social-personality research, with the potential for yielding powerful accounts of moral character, identity, and personality (Lapsley 1999). It opens up a broader array of theoretical options for conceptualizing moral rationality. It locates the study of moral functioning within a mainstream of psychological research on cognition, memory, social cognition, and information processing. It encourages researchers to look at the full range of developmental literatures for insights about the emergence of moral functioning, including those that address motivation, personality development, the formation of self, and the capacity for self-regulation.

In this chapter we show how a social-cognitive account of knowledge activation might be applied with profit to a number of issues in moral psychology. But we first revisit the longstanding problem of the proper relationship between ethics and psychology. This volume is, in some ways, a meditation on the relationship between moral philosophy and moral psychology, and it is therefore fitting that the present chapter should begin with a reflection on this problem, if only to help us diagnose the current predicament that faces the field of moral psychology.

In the next section, then, we make two points. First, we argue that Kohlberg's attempt to *moralize* psychology, that is, his attempt to transform the study of moral behavior by appealing to a set of philosophical assumptions and definitions imported from ethics, has had the unintended consequence of isolating moral psychological research from advances in other domains of psychology, effectively pushing it to the margins of contemporary psychological research. Hence our consideration of Kohlberg's solution to the "boundary problem" between ethics and psychology is diagnostic of the current state of the field. Our remedy for the marginalization of moral psychology is for *more psychology*. That is, we suggest that the next generation of research would do well to *psychologize* morality, rather than pursue the moralized psychology advocated by the cognitive developmental tradition. Second, we will argue that the movement toward a psychologized morality is congruent with the emerging naturalized ethics perspective (see McKinnon, this volume) which attempts to ground normative ethics to a defensible account of human nature. In our view a psychologized morality and a naturalized ethics point toward a common problematic, which is how to account for the "moral personality."

BOUNDARY ISSUES

One of the great stories of this century has been the astonishing rapprochement between moral philosophy and moral psychology. We have Kohlberg to thank for this. In many ways the philosophical resources of Kantian deontological ethics made the cognitive developmental approach possible. Indeed, Kohlberg argued that the study of moral development must begin with certain metaethical assumptions that define a moral judgment (Kohlberg, Levine, and Hewer 1983). Normative ethical theory is required to define the domain of justice reasoning. Armed with these ethical resources, Kohlberg could more easily wrest the study of morality from behaviorists and psychoanalysts and provide a standard by which to criticize other developmental theories.

Hence, Kohlberg's embrace of philosophical formalism not only allowed him to divest moral psychology from the clutches of alternative psychological paradigms, it also provided him a way to articulate and define the emerging cognitive developmental alternative (Kohlberg, Levine, and Hewer 1983). Kohlberg's influence was so pervasive that it is now part of the received view that in the study of moral development philosophical analysis must precede psychological analysis. As Turiel (1998) put it, one result of Kohlberg's enduring influence is that "there is greater recognition of the need to ground psychological explanations in philosophical considerations about morality" (868). Indeed, Kohlberg brought the disciplines of ethics and psychology together in such a breathtaking way that we once dared to think that we could commit the naturalistic fallacy *and get away with it!* (Boyd 1986; Kohlberg 1971).

Although there is almost universal agreement that Kohlberg's embrace of a philosophical view of morality had a liberating effect on moral psychology, in fact, *made moral psychology possible,* there is also growing anxiety about how and where to re-set the boundaries between the two disciplines. Blasi (1990) argued that moral philosophy has had a number of negative side effects on moral psychology. For example, by accepting a particular philosophical definition of morality as our starting point, we have narrowed the scope of inquiry, excluding, for example (and these are Blasi's examples): those concerns that proceed from a consideration of benevolence and affiliation, those that pertain to obedience and one's proper relationship to authority, those regarding ultra-obligation, and those relating to personal obligation. We could multiply examples of topics that have been neglected because justice is chosen as the starting point.

A second problem is that when we adopt a particular philosophical tradition as our starting point, then the terms of the debate for resolving psychological disputes becomes too easily shifted away from strictly psychological concerns regarding theory, method, and data to the coherence and adequacy of philosophical or metaethical claims. Strictly philosophical considerations become insinuated in the evaluation of psychological theory. As a result philosophical objections are improperly used to trump the empirical claims of a theory. Kohlberg's theory has been the recipient of much of this style of criticism, which Blasi calls "the mixed argument," although it might also be, called "guilt by association." So, according to this genre of criticism, Kohlberg's theory can be safely dismissed because of its affinity with Kant or Rawls or Plato, and, as everyone knows, the views of Kant and Rawls and Plato are just absurd. Apparently, if one's philosophical commitments are thought to be nonsense, then one's psychological theory is thereby guilty by association.

However, at the risk of "blaming the victim," we should also point out that Kohlberg's theory has provoked the sort of criticism that it has received, in at least two ways. One obvious way arises from the fact that Kohlberg's theory is an explicit attempt to use empirical data to resolve philosophical controversies, namely, to use psychological resources to defeat ethical relativism. It should not surprise, then, given this project, that philosophical criticism should attend the evaluation of the psychological theory.

There is a more subtle way that Kohlberg's theory has provoked or caused the mixed argument to abound in moral psychology, connected with the way that Kohlberg used the so-called "complementarity thesis" to define the relationship between normative ethical theory and psychological theory. In his view, a normative ethical theory is required to define what is to count as justice reasoning. It provides both categories that are to be used to reconstruct the moral intuitions of subjects and a conception of the *telos* of moral reasoning, the moral ideal. This conception provides the guidepost that allows one to reconstruct the moral justifications of subjects into stages of justice reasoning. This gives the normative ethical theory a role to play in the explanation of psychological stages. It helps explain why, for example, subjects prefer the perspective of higher stages—because they are more adequate, and the philosophical theory tells us *why* they are more adequate. Each succeeding stage is a better philosophical view of justice, whose adequacy can be appraised by reference to normative ethical theory. So, to say that a higher stage is *philosophically* a better stage becomes part of the *psychological* explanation of sequential stage development (Kohlberg, 1971).

The philosophical theory, then, helps us make sense of psychological data. Consequently, "our theory," writes Kohlberg and his colleagues, "requires moral philosophic as well as social scientific analysis" (Kohlberg, Levine, and Hewer 1983, 14). But there is a complementary relationship here, for the empirical theory, too, contributes to our assessment of the adequacy of the normative ethical theory. If the psychological theory is successful, if its claims are well attested, then we are entitled to greater confidence in the normative claims of the ethical theory. If the empirical claims are falsified, however, then we have grounds for doubting our normative ethical commitments (because they do not work *empirically*). Parenthetically, the claim that the empirical warrant can have implications for ethical theory is a notion that is at the heart of the naturalized ethics tradition, as we will see below.

But one may well wonder just how far complementarity goes. That is, if the normative ethical theory is found wanting on strictly philosophical grounds, should this state of affairs have any bearing on how we appraise the psychological theory? Does the incoherence of the moral ideal also corrupt the psychological claims of the stage theory? Many writers over the years have thought so, leading to numerous philosophical critiques of Kohlberg's conception of the ethical ideal that stage six is thought to represent (e.g., Flanagan 1982; Locke 1976; May 1985; Senchuk 1982; Trainer 1977). Many of these are dismissive of the stage theory just because of alleged deficiencies of the philosophical grounding of the last stage. Blasi (1990) and others (e.g., Puka 1990) have lamented this use of philosophy in psychological arguments, but, in retrospect, it was perhaps inevitable, given Kohlberg's understanding of the complementarity between moral philosophy and moral psychology.

It was inevitable, too, given Kohlberg's attempt to defeat ethical relativism with empirical data. Blasi (1990) noted that the main reason why mixed arguments are to be avoided is because psychologists should not attempt to resolve philosophical questions in the first place. For one thing, the nature of psychological inquiry becomes distorted when subordinated to answering philosophers' questions. For another, it is quite impossible to resolve the metaethical problem with empirical data. According to Blasi (1990), psychologists

> cannot resolve philosophical controversies with the tools of their discipline and following rules of evidence and adequacy that define psychology as a scientific community. When philosophical considerations become an integral part of the empirical argument, issues of methodology, data collection and data inter-

pretation cannot be isolated for scrutiny and criticism. In sum, communication becomes impossible and, as a result, the very existence of the discipline is threatened. (55)

Blasi notes, then, three negative side effects of moral philosophy's influence on moral psychology: it narrows the scope of inquiry, introduces the mixed argument into scientific discourse, and misdirects and distorts the mission of psychological inquiry.

PHENOMENALISM AND THE MORAL DOMAIN

But we think there is an additional negative side effect of philosophical assumptions on the contemporary research agenda in moral psychology. The assumption of phenomenalism is one of the distinguishing assumptions of the Kohlbergian tradition, but it is widely embraced by alternative research programs that have their roots in the cognitive developmental tradition. According to Kohlberg, Levine, and Hewer (1983, 69), "The assumption of phenomenalism is the assumption that moral reasoning is the conscious process of using ordinary moral language." The moral quality of action must be defined from the subjective perspective, judgment, and intention of the agent. It results from explicit reasoning, deliberative judgment, active decision making, and similar acts of cognitive exertion. The assumption of phenomenalism is one formalist starting point that Blasi (1990) does insist upon. For Blasi, morality "*by definition*, depends on the agent's subjective perspective" (59, our emphasis). In our view, however, the assumption of phenomenalism has contributed to the isolation of moral development research from the broad trends of recent psychological research.

The assumption of phenomenalism is thought necessary to defend the rationality of morality against behaviorists who link moral behavior to the work of external contingencies. The *cognitive* activities of the rational moral agent—interpretation, deliberation, judgment, and choice—guarantee radical moral freedom just because they free human behavior from "stimulus control." The decision-making calculus of the moral agent is our best evidence of moral autonomy. The assumption of phenomenalism is also required in order to show, contra psychoanalysis, that moral functioning is the *conscious* activity of the moral agent, which is to say that moral functioning is not driven by passions, is not emotivist, is not irrational. It is not motivated by forces outside of or unknown to reason. Indeed, "the assumption of phenomenalism implies reference to conscious processes" (Kohlberg, Levine, and Hewer 1983, 8).

Hence the assumption of phenomenalism insists that cognition, if it is to count as *moral* cognition, must be conscious, explicit, and effortful. One problem with this formulation is that much of our cognitive activity is not like this at all, but is instead characterized by processes that are tacit, implicit, and automatic. Indeed, these literatures could not possibly have much relevance for understanding moral cognition, if a philosophical starting point fixes the meaning of moral cognition to involve only controlled processes and effortful reasoning (Narvaez and Lapsley, this volume).

Hence, by opting for this philosophical starting point, the study of moral cognition becomes isolated from advances in the general study of social cognition. It instead orients moral psychology to paradigm cases that best suit its distinguishing assumptions, which is resolution of hard-case dilemmas. While typical moral lives will have occasion to wrestle with dilemmas of this sort, this by no means accounts for all of what a robust moral psychology should be called upon to explain. The search for adequate explanations of the full range of morally relevant human behavior should not be handicapped by orienting philosophical assumptions that place an unacceptable a priori constraint on legitimate lines of inquiry.

The assumption of phenomenalism also suggests that one *acts* morally only if one acts on explicit moral reasons, self-consciously and deliberatively invoked by the autonomous moral agent. Hence, according to this view, the moral status of an action can only be certified by indexing the explicit rationale invoked by the agent to justify or explain the action. According to Kohlberg, Levine, and Hewer (1983), "Moral conduct is conduct governed by moral judgment." In order to evaluate the behavior of another as moral or immoral one must be able to impute a judgment to the agent. Indeed, "the study of moral conduct and moral development per se must consider the motives and the constructions of moral meaning that are expressed in behaviors" (71).

Once again the assumption of phenomenalism gives priority to the subjective perspective of the agent in defining moral behavior (as well as moral judgment), and it is one assumption that most socio-moral researchers can agree upon irrespective of their particular theoretical allegiances (e.g., Nucci 2000; Turiel 1998). If it is true, however, that much of our social-cognitive functioning is implicit, tacit, or automatic, then the incidence of moral behavior will turn out to be rare and unusual in human affairs. Individuals who engage in morally relevant behavior are often inarticulate about their motivations, are unable to say what judgments may have accompanied an action. To first require an agent to form a judgment, to settle upon a motive, or to construct moral meaning in order to designate morally relevant behavior as distinctly moral is to relegate vast areas of human life beyond the purview of moral evaluation. Much of human behavior will simply not qualify, given the automatic and tacit nature of social cognition.

Hence the assumption of phenomenalism has an unintended consequence. It leads to an attenuation of the moral domain. It significantly narrows the range of functioning that can be the target of legitimate moral psychological explanation. In the words of Iris Murdoch (1992), it suggests that moral rationality and moral behavior are "an occasional part-time activity" (297), some "specialized isolated moment appearing in a continuum of non-moral activity" (303). But this attenuation results from adopting a certain philosophical position on the nature of moral judgment and action (and not from psychological considerations).[1]

This concern about boundary issues between the two disciplines should not obscure the obvious facts that ethicists and psychologists have much to learn from each other and that the dialogue has been enormously productive. In our view the recent interest by psychologists in character, moral identity, and moral personality was greatly influenced by the return of virtue ethics from the margins of philosophical reflection (French, Uehling, and Wettstein 1988). Virtue ethics has led the way and has given many psychologists the conceptual voice to address issues concerning the moral self, moral identity, character, and personality. Moreover, this desire of many psychologists to enlarge the moral domain in order to study issues of identity, character, and personality is now matched by a movement *within ethics* to expand ethical theory beyond its traditional focus on strictly normative concerns. There is growing recognition that normative ethics must meet minimal psychological requirements so that its prescriptions are possible "for creatures like us" (Flanagan 1991). As Flanagan put it, "Every moral conception owes us at least a partial specification of the personality and motivational structure it expects of morally mature individuals, and that conception will need to be constrained by considerations of realism" (35).

PSYCHOLOGIZED MORALITY AND NATURALIZED ETHICS

Indeed, the emerging "naturalized ethics" perspective (May, Friedman, and Clark 1996; McKinnon 1999, this volume) seeks to ground ethical theory by what is known about "human motivation, the nature of the self, the nature of human concepts, how our reason works, how we are socially constituted, and a host of other facts about who we are and how the mind operates" (Johnson 1996, 49). Johnson (1996) argues, for example, that any comprehensive moral psychology must include an account of personal identity, and must be adequately grounded by the concepts, constructs, and literatures of cognitive science. Similarly, McKinnon (1999) argues that the starting point of ethical theory should be the facts of human nature. "If ethics is to be about human lives lived well," she writes, "then certain facts about human nature must count as relevant in determining the plausibility of any ethical theory" (10). Moreover, getting the facts right in ethics "will invite cooperation with biology, psychology, ethology, sociology, even neuropsychology and cognitive science, whose findings appear promising in the task of fleshing out the details of human nature"(6). Hence an ethical theory that is *naturalized* attends to empirical realities, to actual lives and the manner in which they are lived, with the conviction that this methodological strategy

> will be more fruitful in understanding the relations between functional goodness and ethical goodness than are typical metaphysical or essentialist investigations into the nature of humans. These latter are designed so as to emphasize the rational capabilities of humans and to minimize the animal, including the social and emotional sides of human nature. The result is necessarily a very impoverished base on which to construct a story about a good human life. (7)

Hence there is an important movement within ethical theory to consider the literatures of personality, cognitive, and developmental psychology for insights about the parameters of virtue and character. Although a number of psychological literatures (e.g., social-cognitive approaches to personality, schema theory, cognitive science models of information-processing, self-constructs and motivation, etc.) are critically relevant for understanding moral psychological functioning generally, and character psychology more specifically, and although these literatures do have enormous implications for providing the "minimal psychological realism" required by naturalized ethics, they are rarely invoked for this purpose. Consequently, many relevant psychological constructs do not yet contribute to ethical or even psychological work on the nature of moral functioning, nor do they inform contemporary educational models of character formation.

In our view social-cognitive theory has resources for conceptualizing the facts and details of human nature in a way that promotes the construction of powerful, integrative moral theory, as we will see below. A social-cognitive approach also leads to a change of perspective in moral psychology that we find appealing: if the Kohlbergian research tradition brought ethics to psychology, this new perspective reverses matters and brings psychological literatures to ethics. In other words, if Kohlberg *moralized* psychology, this new perspective *psychologizes* morality. The distinction is critical.

When psychology is moralized, then philosophical considerations are smuggled into psychological arguments, or else there is a temptation to use psychological data to resolve philosophical questions. Psychological data are then conflated with philosophical categories of normative ethical theory, leading to the lamentable "mixed arguments" in the evaluation of psychological theory noted by Blasi (1990).

Moreover, a moralized psychology tends to adopt strictly philosophical models of moral rationality that constrain or forbid legitimate theoretical options in psychological research. Note, for example, how the study of "character" was simply ruled out of bounds by the Kohlbergian tradition partly on the grounds that character research does not help solve the philosophical problem of ethical relativism. However, when morality is *psychologized*, then moral functioning is addressed with the tools, theories, methods, and literatures proper to psychological inquiry. In the next section we show how certain strands of social-cognitive research can be applied with profit to address these common issues (see also Narvaez and Lapsley, this volume).

KNOWLEDGE ACTIVATION AND THE MORAL PERSONALITY

According to Tory Higgins (1999), one of the general principles of knowledge activation is *accessibility*. Accessibility can be defined as the activation potential of available knowledge. The more frequently a construct is activated, or the more recently it is primed, the more accessible it should be for processing social information. In addition, frequently activated constructs, over time, should be more easily (or "chronically") accessible for social information processing. And, because the social experiences of individuals varies widely, it is likely that there should also be individual differences in the accessibility, indeed, even the availability, of cognitive constructs.

Accessibility, then, is a person variable. It is a dimension of individual differences. Hence, one factor that influences the likelihood that some stored knowledge structure will be activated is its accessibility. And there should be individual differences in the readiness with which certain constructs are utilized. There is now a large literature that attests to the effects of chronicity on social information processing (Bargh and Ferguson 2000; Bargh 1997). Individual differences in the chronic accessibility of constructs influences the processing of behavioral information. Chronically accessible constructs are at a higher level of activation than are inaccessible constructs (Bargh and Pratto 1983), and are processed so efficiently as to approach *automaticity*. Chronically accessible constructs influence one's impression of others and memory and interpretation of social events. Hence, two individuals, each with unique and non-overlapping accessible constructs, tend to have very difference impressions and recollections of the same event.

The notion that chronicity is an individual differences variable is widely accepted in social-cognitive accounts of personality. The social-cognitive approach generally describes the dispositional "person variables" not in terms of context-free traits, but as "cognitive-affective units" or mental representations that subsume diverse content. "These encompass the person's encoding or construal of the self and of situations, enduring goals, expectations and feeling states, as well as specific memories of the people and events that have been experienced, and a host of competencies and skills particularly important for self-regulation" (Shoda, Tiernan, and Michel 2002, 317). Moreover, cognitive-affective representations are at varying levels of activation. Some units are relatively unavailable and inaccessible, while others are chronically accessible. In addition, cognitive-affective representations can be situationally primed as well, which suggests that schema activation is a process that is in dynamic interaction with contextual cues.

The social-cognitive approach to personality would appear, then, to have a number of critical advantages for conceptualizing the dispositional features of personality, along with its contextual variability, but it has not, heretofore, been invoked to account for any feature of moral functioning. Yet, when this perspective is applied to the moral domain, or, alternatively, when the moral domain is *psychologized* by this social-cognitive theory, a number of productive possibilities become evident. For one, this theory has implications for how moral personality or moral identity is conceptualized. Blasi (1984) has argued that one has a moral identity just when moral categories are essential, central, and important to one's self-understanding. Here we would add that moral categories that are essential, central, and important to one's self-understanding would also be ones that are chronically accessible for interpreting the social landscape. Such categories would be constantly "on-line," or at least easily activated and readily primed for processing social information. And, once activated, these moral constructs would dispose the individual to interpret and judge situations along moral lines.

In addition the social-cognitive perspective would suggest that traits, virtues, and other dispositional features of moral character are better conceptualized in terms of cognitive-affective units: personal constructs and knowledge structures, categories, and schemas that are chronically accessible. Virtuous individuals, by this account, would be those for whom moral categories are chronically accessible for appraising and interpreting the social landscape. Moreover, this perspective suggests a new interpretation of moral orientations or moral "voices" (e.g., Gilligan 1982). For some of us, justice issues might be chronically accessible, for others, benevolence, faithfulness, temperance, or courage. And, indeed, for a great many others there will be categories chronically accessible that have little to do with morality. Hence, not only are there individual differences in whether moral relational schemas are chronically accessible (vs. nonmoral, or even vicious schemas), but even within the moral domain there are undoubtedly individual differences in which virtues, moral categories, or orientations are accessible.

Finally, a chronicity model may provide a new perspective on our understanding of "moral exemplars." In a landmark study, Colby and Damon (1994) have shown that moral exemplars do not see their extraordinary commitments as deriving from an agonizing, decision-making calculus. They do not view their choices as dilemmas requiring protracted deliberation. Instead, they just seem to know what is the right and proper thing to do, *automatically* as it were, without the expenditure of significant cognitive resources. Interestingly, most exemplars in the study were otherwise conventional in their stage of moral reasoning. We suspect that the automaticity characteristic of moral exemplars derives from the fact that for these individuals moral categories are salient, chronically accessible, easily primed, and readily utilized.

SUMMARY AND CONCLUSION

In this chapter we have attempted to illustrate the virtues of psychologizing the study of moral functioning by showing how meaningful integration is possible between moral psychology and the literatures of social-cognitive science. In particular we draw attention to schema accessibility as a general principle of knowledge activation, to individual difference in moral chronicity, and to the tacit, implicit, and automatic features of social cognition. Moreover, the application of social-cognitive theory to moral psychology makes it possible to anticipate at least four novel facts about moral personological and moral cognitive functioning: (1) it provides a working definition of moral identity, (2) it provides a social-cognitive account of the dispositional features of moral character, (3) it provides an explanation of the diversity of moral "voices" and orientations, and (4) it provides an explanation of the automaticity of moral functioning exhibited by moral exemplars.

Indeed, the metaphor of vision seems particularly helpful in coming to grips with what it means to be a moral person. It has been said, "what we *see* depends on who we *are*" (Meilaender 1984). That is, our appraisal of the moral landscape, our moral vision, and our very ability to even notice dilemmas depend on our character. A moral personality would better *see* the problematic features of situations. What we see depends on who we are, but who we are hinges, we argue, on the kinds of social-cognitive structures (schemas, expectancies, scripts) that are easily primed, easily activated, and chronically accessible for making sense of our experience. To put it simply, a moral person, one who has a moral identity and is virtuous, is one for whom moral categories are chronically accessible for appraising and interpreting social reality, making choices, and guiding behavior. Individuals who are not known for their moral virtues, and truly vicious individuals, would undoubtedly have other schemas chronically accessible.

Finally, we also took up the question of boundaries between ethical and psychological approaches to moral functioning. We argued that the social-cognitive approach to moral personality re-sets the boundary between ethical theory and psychological theory to the extent that we move *from* a moralized psychology *to* a psychologized morality. Although this requires us to reconsider the principle of phenomenalism as a basis of collaboration, a social-cognitive perspective does provide a basis for ongoing collaboration with ethicists in the emerging field of naturalized ethics, whom we meet as fellow travelers at the crossroads of moral psychology.

Indeed, we are clearly at a point where emerging trends in moral psychology and in ethics are reaching a common juncture. For example, the increased attention devoted to moral selfhood, character, and identity in both disciplines is the result of movement from two directions. It results from the desire, within psychology, to expand the explanatory reach of moral psychology beyond structures-of-justice reasoning, and from the desire, within ethics, to ground ethical theory to a defensible account of moral psychology. Trends from within both moral psychology and ethics point toward greater interest in virtues, character, and moral identity. Psychologized morality and naturalized ethics, then, settle upon a common problematic, and our hope is that advances in social-cognitive research will pay important dividends.

NOTE

1. A weaker version of phenomenalism requires only that one is able to impute a suitable moral intention to the agent. As Kohlberg, Levine, and Hewer (1983) put it, "our actual judgments as to the moral nature of an action depend upon imparting motives and moral judgments to the actor" (71). This way of putting it seems to allow the possibility that the relevant intention, motive, and judgment are things that are clearer for observers to impart than it is for actors to articulate. It allows the possibility, in other words, for actors to have the

proper moral motive without necessarily being conscious of reaching decisions, forming judgments, or appealing to principles. It allows subjective intention to coexist with the realities of automaticity in social cognition. This is a weaker version of phenomenalism in two senses. First, it retains the importance of subjective intention, but at the expense of requiring moral cognition to be a conscious process of making judgments. Second, to the extent that it accommodates the automatic, tacit, and implicit qualities of social cognition, it becomes less reliable as a basis for defending moral autonomy. For these reasons we do not think that the weaker version of phenomenalism is the version that Kohlberg intended as the distinguishing philosophical assumption of his paradigm, its otherwise attractive features notwithstanding.

REFERENCES

Bargh, J. A. 1997. The automaticity of everyday life. In *The Automaticity of Everyday Life*, ed. R. S. Wyer, Jr. Advances in Social Cognition, vol. 10, 1–61. Mahwah, NJ: Lawrence Erlbaum Associates.

Bargh, J. A., and M. J. Ferguson. 2000. Beyond behaviorism: On the automaticity of higher mental processes. *Psychological Bulletin* 126:925–45.

Bargh, J., and F. Pratto. 1986. Individual construct accessibility and perception selection. *Journal of Experimental Social Psychology* 22:293–311.

Blasi, A. 1984. Moral identity: Its role in moral functioning. In *Morality, Moral Behavior, and Moral Development*, ed. W. M. Kurtines and J. J. Gewirtz, 128–39. New York: John Wiley and Sons.

———. 1990. How should psychologists define morality? or, The negative side effects of philosophy's influence on psychology. In *The Moral Domain: Essays on the Ongoing Discussion between Philosophy and the Social Sciences*, ed. T. Wren, 38–70. Cambridge, MA: MIT Press.

Boyd, D. 1986. The ought of is: Kohlberg at the interface between moral philosophy and developmental psychology. In *Lawrence Kohlberg: Consensus and Controversy*, ed. S. Modgil and C. Modgil, 43–64. Philadelphia: Falmer Press.

Colby, A., and W. Damon. 1992. *Some Do Care: Contemporary Lives of Moral Commitment*. New York: Free Press.

Flanagan, O. 1982. Moral structures? *Philosophy of the Social Sciences* 12:255–70.

———. 1991. *Varieties of Moral Personality: Ethics and Psychological Realism*. Cambridge, MA: Harvard University Press.

French, P. A., T. E. Uehling, Jr., and H. Wettstein, eds. 1988. *Ethical Theory: Character and Virtue*. Midwest Studies in Philosophy, vol. 13. Notre Dame, IN: University of Notre Dame Press.

Gilligan, C. 1982. *In a Different Voice*. Cambridge, MA: Harvard University Press.

Higgins, E. T. 1999. Persons and situations: Unique explanatory principles or variability in general principles? In *The Coherence of Personality: Social-cognitive Bases of Consistency, Variability and Organization*, ed. D. Cervone and Y. Shoda, 61–93. New York: Guilford Press.

Johnson, M. 1996. How moral psychology changes moral theory. In *Mind and Morals: Essays on Cognitive Science and Ethics*, ed. L. May, M. Friedman, and A. G. Clark, 45–68. Cambridge, MA: MIT Press.

Kohlberg, L. 1971. From is to ought: How to commit the naturalistic fallacy and get away with it in the study of moral development. In *Cognitive Development and Epistemology*, ed. T. Mischel, 151–235. New York: Academic Press.

Kohlberg, L., C. Levine, and A. Hewer. 1983. *Moral Stages: A Current Formulation and a Response to Critics*. Contributions to Human Development, vol. 10. New York: Karger.

Lapsley, D. K. 1996. *Moral Psychology*. Boulder, CO: Westview Press.

———. 1999. An outline of a social-cognitive theory of moral character. *Journal of Research in Education* 8:25–32.

———. Forthcoming. Moral stage theory. In *Handbook of Moral Development*, ed. M. Killen and J. Smetana. Mahwah, NJ: Lawrence Erlbaum Associates.

Lapsley, D. K., and D. F. Narvaez. Forthcoming. A social cognitive approach to the moral personality. In *Moral Development, Self and Identity: Essays in Honor of Augusto Blasi*, ed. D. K. Lapsley and D. F. Narvaez. Mahwah, NJ: Lawrence Erlbaum Associates.

Locke, D. 1976. Cognitive stages or developmental phases? A critique of Kohlberg's stage-structural theory of moral reasoning. *Journal of Moral Education* 8:168–81.

May, L. 1985. The moral adequacy of Kohlberg's moral development theory. In *Moral Dilemmas*, ed. C. Hardin, 115–36. Chicago: Precedent.

May, L., M. Friedman, and A. G. Clark. *Mind and Morals: Essays on Cognitive Science and Ethics*. Cambridge, MA: MIT Press.

McKinnon, C. 1999. *Character, Virtue Theories, and the Vices*. Peterborough, Ontario: Broadview Press.

Meilaender, G. 1984. *The Theory and Practice of Virtue*. Notre Dame, IN: University of Notre Dame Press.

Murdoch, I. 1992. *Metaphysics as a Guide to Morals*. London: Penguin Books.

Nucci, L. 1982. Conceptual development in the moral and conventional domains: Implications for values education. *Review of Educational Research* 49:93–122.

———. 2000. The promise and limitation of the moral self construct. Presidential address delivered at the thirtieth annual meeting of the Jean Piaget Society, Montreal, June 3. http://tigger.uic.edu/~lnucci/MoralEd/articles/nuccipromise.html.

———. 2001. *Education in the Moral Domain*. Cambridge: Cambridge University Press.

Puka, B. 1990. Toward the redevelopment of Kohlberg's theory: Preserving essential structure, removing controversial content. In *Handbook of Moral Behavior and Development*, vol. 1, *Theory*, ed. W. Kurtines and J. Gewirtz, 373–94. Hillsdale, NJ: Lawrence Erlbaum Associates.

Rest, J., D. Narvaez, M. J. Bebeau, and S. J. Thoma. 1999. *Postconventional Moral Thinking: A Neo-Kohlbergian Approach.* Mahwah, NJ: Lawrence Erlbaum Associates.

Senchuk, D. M. 1982. Contra-Kohlberg: A philosophical reinterpretation of moral development. *Educational Theory* 31:259–73.

Shoda, Y., S. L. Tiernan, and W. Mischel. 2002. Personality as a dynamical system: Emergence of stability and distinctiveness from intra- and interpersonal interactions. *Personality and Social Psychology Review* 6:316–25.

Trainer, F. E. 1977. A critical analysis of Kohlberg's contributions to the study of moral thought. *Journal for the Theory of Social Behavior* 7:41–63.

Turiel, E. 1983. *The Development of Social Knowledge: Morality and Convention.* Cambridge: Cambridge University Press.

———. 1998. The development of morality. In *Social, Emotional and Personality Development,* ed. N. Eisenberg. Handbook of Child Psychology, 5th ed., vol. 3, ed. W. Damon, 863–932. New York: John Wiley and Sons.

Character Possession and Human Flourishing

Christine McKinnon

THE RELATED CLAIMS I WISH TO DEFEND IN THIS CHAPTER ARE THAT character possession, because of certain facts about human nature, both permits humans to lead paradigmatically[1] good human lives and makes them better off from their own subjective perspective. I thus acknowledge, right at the outset, a methodological commitment to a form of naturalism. My account of good human lives is neither theologically based nor teleologically oriented. Nor is it reductive. Rather, it is a naturalism based in the conviction that certain facts about humans and certain capacities of humans make ethical choices both necessary and possible.

Facts about humans—including facts about their animate, mobile, self-aware, emotional, rational, social, and self-constituting nature—ground normative claims about good human lives. It is these facts which give rise to our many disparate needs and desires, which in turn form the context in which our ethical conflicts and their resolutions find their home. Endorsing this kind of methodological naturalism invites cooperation with the human and natural sciences—including biology, psychology, ethology, sociology, history, neurophysiology, and cognitive science—in the project of finding out more about human nature. It thereby distances itself from those moral philosophies committed to grounding moral principles in laws of reason, the will of God, rights and contracts, or in ultimate ends such as pleasure or happiness. In doing so, it supposes that the more we know about human nature and the more we know about kinds of human lives lived, the better will we be able to see what kinds of lives are good, flourishing ones, and why.

In the first parts of the chapter I will examine claims about flourishing in the plant and non-human animal cases, with the aims of understanding the status of these kinds of evaluative claims and of thereby seeing what an analogous naturalist strategy can reveal in the human case.[2] I will then explore what kinds of constraints the evaluations made in the process of character construction must meet. I hope to show how citing character possession as a paradigmatic feature of the best kinds of human lives can close the alleged gap between subjectivist accounts of happiness or welfare and objectivist accounts of good flourishing human lives, a gap that has sometimes been cited as problematic for virtue theorists.[3]

PLANTS

Following Philippa Foot and Rosalind Hursthouse,[4] I think it is useful to consider our evaluations of good human beings as continuous with, rather than completely distinct from, our evaluations of other kinds of living things. We can begin by looking at claims about flourishing with respect to plants. We talk about particular plants thriving or shriveling, flourishing or languishing, prospering or wilting. We also talk about species of plants faring well or badly. The former term in each of these pairs is a success term: we evaluate plants that thrive, flourish, or prosper as *better* plants of their kind or as plants that lead paradigmatically *better* plant lives than those that shrivel, languish, or wilt. In the case of plants, the dimensions along which these judgments of success are made are completely natural: a particular plant's success at its natural ends of nutrition, growth, and reproduction provides grounds for judgments about its goodness qua that kind of plant. What counts as successful functioning will, of course, differ for different species of plants: each plant species has its own standards for nutritive, growth, and reproductive success. And so too will the external conditions (including climatic and environmental conditions, as well as the presence of things like pollinating insects) under which success is likely to be achieved differ from plant species to plant species, and sometimes within plant species. Immature and mature plants of the same species may need different conditions in order to thrive; male and female plants of the same species may need different conditions for reproductive success. As well as there being different environmental factors whose presence or absence will promote or inhibit the way members of a particular plant species fare, there are also internal factors, including those that affect the systems devoted to nutrition, growth, and reproduction. The good functioning of these systems contributes to the flourishing and their poor functioning detracts from the flourishing of individual plants.

We are, of course, not interested in the details of which environmental and internal factors are required in order for members of particular plant species to flourish. We are concerned merely with the status of claims about plant flourishing and the grounds on which these claims are made. We can note several points about claims regarding plant flourishing.

First, claims about plant flourishing are based on descriptive claims about actual plants. Botanists determine, after observing very many members of the species in question, in very many different settings, and exposed to very many different kinds of environmental conditions, just what the paradigmatic way of living is for different plant species. These descriptive claims about how actual plants nourish themselves, grow, and reproduce underwrite accounts of prototypical ways of living for plants of that species, which in turn provide standards against which judgments can be made about how well individual plants of that species are faring. Empirical observations of actual members of plant species in their natural environments thus ground norms for flourishing for those species. This is not to say that the task of settling empirical, descriptive claims about what count as prototypical forms of life for different plant species is an easy one. The inexperienced may bring their own ideas of plant flourishing and of how it is achieved to their observations and may thereby mistake healthy plants for unhealthy ones, good functioning for poor functioning, or vice versa. The greater experience and expertise of the botanist are required to get the kinds of accurate descriptions of how members of different plant species live. Botanists also determine what conditions (both internal and external) conduce to the well-being of different species of plants. Again, what factors contribute to or detract from their thriving may be difficult to discern. But it is the sort of empirical task engaged in by scientists who observe various members of a given species over time and under different conditions, and at which they have met with moderate success. The botanists' descriptive claims about how actual plants live provide the evidence on which the species-relative norms for plant flourishing are based. These norms permit the botanist to make judgments about *good* or *bad* specimens of a particular plant species. Botanists cannot have preconceived ideas of what counts as success for different plant species: they can only observe how various specimens nourish themselves, grow, and reproduce, and under what conditions. These purely empirical observations ground descriptive claims about what members of different plant species *do* in terms of nutrition, growth, and reproduction. These claims then provide the standards against which evaluative judgments about good plants can be made.

The second, and related, point is that judgments about plant flourishing are objective. Assessments of plant flourishing appeal to objective criteria of success along the various dimensions of nutrition, growth, and reproduction implicit in the botanists' descriptions of plant lives. While the standards for optimal nutrition, growth, and reproduction will differ from plant species to plant species, there will be objective standards applicable across members of each species. A good specimen of a plant will be one that fares well, where the faring well is to be understood in terms of successful functioning of the plant's systems serving its three main ends. This has two implications, which will prove to be relevant later on. First, scientists do not *decide* whether a plant is flourishing. Claims about paradigmatic functioning and about typical kinds of plant life do not reflect conventional decisions or subjective preferences; instead they purport to describe the ways plants actually live. When scientists disagree about whether a particular plant is flourishing, disagreements are settled by seeing how well the plant is faring on the nutrition, growth, and reproduction scales properly calibrated for plants of its kind. These scales provide standards against which these disagreements can be settled. We will see how, in the human case, the privilege that is granted to subjective assessments of individual welfare might seem to conflict with this kind of appeal to objective standards. Second, in settling these disputes, scientists do not question whether the dimensions of nutrition, growth, and reproduction are the right ones along which to assess plant flourishing. While scientists may dispute whether *this* is an instance of, for example, successful growth or optimal exercise of reproductive capacities, they do not worry about whether optimal growth or reproductive success are indicators of plant flourishing. These are unquestioned assumptions, and they serve as part of the framework of scientists' investigations. The objectivity of evaluations about plant flourishing is not compromised by appeal to groundwork or foundational assumptions of this sort.[5] That there are background, unexamined claims at work when assessments of plant flourishing are made will be important when we come back to discuss the case of human flourishing: whereas nutrition, growth, and reproduction may seem the obvious parameters according to which to measure plant flourishing, there may seem to be no counterpart dimensions along which human well-being should be measured.

The third point regarding claims about standards of plant flourishing is that they are unknown to the plant. The fourth—and related—point is that claims about plant flourishing are not supposed to provide any motivation to the plant. These are, of course, completely trivial and vacuous claims in the case of plants. Plants are not the sorts of things that can know anything, that can desire anything, that can choose to act, or that can act. They are simply the kinds of things that live, nourish themselves, grow, reproduce, and die. We can judge them to fare well or badly, to be good or bad specimens of their kind; these judgments of ours do not affect, and are not intended to affect, the plants one way or another. While unable to do any work in the plant case, these points can still be profitably made here. They help underline the point that, at least in some cases, descriptions of paradigmatic functioning and objective standards of goodness can be derived from a thing's nature, and are, at least in some cases, completely independent of anything like *interests* or *subjective welfare* of the thing in question.

Fifth, although the plant lacks the capacities to choose to reorient its life or repair its damaged systems, *we* can take claims about plant flourishing as something akin to recipes or instructions to be followed if we want to make it more likely that particular plants or species of plants will flourish. We may not want plants to flourish, but if we do, we can try to implement the kinds of environmental and internal conditions which botanists tell us will help particular plants or species of plant to thrive.

The sixth point to note is that claims about conditions under which plants flourish are defeasible: while something like necessary conditions for plants to flourish may be specifiable, sufficient conditions are not. The fifth point made reference to recipes: following the instructions of a recipe very carefully is no guarantee that the outcome will be as hoped for. Other factors may intervene. But following the instructions offers the best chance we have of getting the desired outcome. Isolated failures are not enough to insist that the particular instructions were bad ones—or that there cannot be anything like instructions that would make plant flourishing more likely. Likewise, desired outcomes sometimes result even though the instructions were improperly followed or disregarded altogether. This is not grounds for rejecting the instructions. Ensuring that the conditions are in place under which plants are likely to flourish only makes it more likely, other things being equal, that plants will thrive. This is no doubt because of the complexity of the causal factors contributing to flourishing, and because many of the causal factors are stochastic rather than deterministic.

Finally, claims about plant flourishing are—for all this—evaluative claims. Scientists operating with the supposition that nutrition, growth, and reproductive success are criteria along which plant flourishing should be measured establish objective criteria based in empirically grounded claims that serve to specify paradigmatic ways of living for different plant species. These descriptions admit of imprecisions, the statistically based accounts of prototypical plants admit of outliers, and the specifications for success for different kinds of plants are defeasible. But what is not in question is the background belief that flourishing is to be measured along the dimensions of nutrition, growth, and reproduction. Success along these dimensions just *constitutes* plant flourishing. But, and this is an important point for any form of naturalism in ethics, these claims are—for all their descriptive content—nonetheless evaluative. They do not purport to offer injunctions or prescriptions about what ought to be done, but they do permit assessments of individual plants according to success at approximating ends. The ends appropriate for plants will be different from those appropriate for animals and from those appropriate for humans (because of the different natures revealed in the different capacities and functions, which permit the distinctive kinds of lives that members of different species typically lead). But the commitment to naturalism supposes that these evaluative claims will be generated by—and grounded in—claims about the nature of each species.

Claims about plant flourishing invoke standards for prototypical kinds of successful functioning for different kinds of plants. A *good* plant is just one that leads a paradigmatic kind of existence for its type of plant. In the plant case, there is no scope to wonder whether being a good plant (meeting the appropriate functional criteria) can benefit the individual plant itself (enhance its welfare). Given that plants are not the sorts of things that can have a subjective perspective from which their lives can be assessed as going well or badly, and cannot be thought of as having a welfare or as being able to benefit in any way other than by enjoying the internal and external conditions that make their thriving possible, it does not seem plausible to suppose that there is a problem in the plant case akin to the problem that threatens in the human case, namely, that assessments of *welfare* or *happiness* from a subjective perspective do not seem to bear any close relation to assessments of *goodness* or *flourishing* from an objective perspective. There is nothing in the plant case that could be thought of as something like its welfare distinct from the plant's performing its functions well. Hence, there is no question in the plant case of whether being a good plant of a certain kind *pays,* in the sense of conferring benefits on the individual plant. These points will be relevant when we return to consider in what ways character possession, as well as being evidence that the person is leading a good kind of human life, can be said to benefit—*from her own perspective*—the one who has a character. And they will resurface when we examine the appropriate place of motivation in claims about flourishing that appeal to successful functioning.

While not being interested in the details of what permits—or even of what constitutes—plant flourishing in particular cases, we are interested in the status of claims about good plants, claims about plants thriving or flourishing, where that means leading prototypical plant lives for their kind. We have acknowledged that the meaning of "good" in the context of assessments of plants must be sensitive to the different natures of, and the different ways the three ends of nutrition, growth, and reproduction are realized in, the different kinds of plants being assessed. "Good," like other attributive adjectives, must be responsive to the different natures of the things it picks out as good. "Small" and "large" appeal to different standards of size when applied to fleas and mastodons respectively. But the different standards are established by empirical observations of what in fact constitute norms of size for each kind of being. The norms are to be found in the nature of things—not in any interests or preferences on the part of those doing the observing or on the part of those under scrutiny. "Good" in its functional sense is just like this.[6] Our task will be to see whether a comparable functional sense of "good" can be used in the evaluation of human lives. First, though, we will look at claims about non-human animal flourishing, noting similarities as well as what seem to be discontinuities with the plant case.

NON-HUMAN ANIMALS

Claims about animal[7] flourishing are also both descriptive and objective. Just as with claims about plant flourishing, we suppose that experts can observe a multiplicity of individual members of a species under a variety of different conditions and can come to describe prototypical forms of life for animals of that species. These descriptions then underwrite objective standards or norms proper to that kind of animal, and these standards are used to make objective claims about closeness of fit to those standards. The point of insisting that these claims are descriptive and objective is to underline that they are not intended to serve—or to answer to—any human interests and to insist that they reflect norms grounded in natural facts about the animal species. They also remind us that the evaluative judgments made with reference to them are more or less true or false. Acknowledging that these claims are descriptive and objective is consistent with the fact that certain assumptions are being made. In the case of plants we saw that nutrition, growth, and reproduction were taken to be dimensions along which plant flourishing should be measured. In the animal case, the dimensions along which flourishing is measured are more complex, reflecting their more complex nature. Animals can be assessed according to criteria of nutrition, growth, and reproductive prowess; they can also be evaluated according as they live or fail to live lives that are characteristic of their species, where that includes more than considerations of how they nourish themselves, grow, and reproduce. In particular, it may include how they care for their young, how they hunt, how they communicate with one another, and how they build shelters. That is, animals are evaluated according as they perform well those *actions* that characterize their particular kinds of lives. The kind of life that a cougar typically lives is very different from that of a lobster, which is very different again from that of an owl. Zoologists and animal ethologists observe—over many instances—how the members of a particular species live; they then use these empirical observations to describe the typical life of an animal of that species. As with the plant case, they can see which environmental conditions and which internal conditions permit success along the various dimensions that characterize this kind of life. But in the animal case, unlike in the plant case, scientists will also be interested in the patterns of actions that typically characterize animals' lives, as well as the skills or traits that underwrite them. They are interested in these patterns and capacities precisely because of the kinds of things animals are: animals, unlike plants, can *act*. The causes we invoke to explain their actions appeal to their biological and social natures. Again, these can be discerned by careful observation by well-trained experts.

We noted the trivially true points that claims about standards for assessments of flourishing are unknown to the plant and are not meant to provide any motivating force. Again, given the nature of animal cognition, we could not expect animals to know anything about paradigmatic forms of life for beings of their kind or to be able to make evaluations of fit between their lives and those typical of their kind. Nor would we expect them—even if they were aware of the norms—to be able to choose to act more in conformity with them. These are not capacities animals have. The lack of this kind of rationality does not make animals inferior kinds of beings, but it does circumscribe some of their capacities. Descriptions of paradigmatic forms of life for beings of their kind establish norms for the species and thereby provide standards for objective evaluations of individual animals. They do this without at the same time purporting to embody *reasons* for the subjects under investigation to *do* anything or to *be* any particular way.

But, insofar as it is possible to understand what kinds of external environmental factors and internal genetic and physical factors and mastery of what kinds of skills make it more likely that individual members of a species will flourish, *we* can take these descriptive claims as embodying reasons for *us* to act if we want to promote the flourishing of an individual of a certain species or the flourishing of a certain species. *We* might have several reasons for wanting individuals or species to flourish, but they can be at best *our* reasons: they cannot be reasons for the animal. Again, the descriptive claims from which the objective norms are derived provide no motivation in themselves. And even when they serve to specify instructions about how best to increase the functional goodness of particular animals, they are instructions which *we* can choose to follow, not ones that the animals themselves can be thought of as following.

The sixth point above that claims about plant flourishing are defeasible can also be repeated with respect to animals: our best accounts of the conditions under which animals are most likely to thrive will capture only "normal" cases. There will be the outliers who thrive under nonoptimal conditions or against all odds. These conditions for flourishing can only specify what will make it more likely that an animal will thrive—again, either because the causal story is too complicated for our grasp or because many of the causes are nondeterministic.

Our seventh point also holds for the animal case: the empirical, descriptive claims ground the standards against which we make our evaluations of *good* and *better* animals. These standards are not conventional, in the sense of being designed to meet particular human ends or of reflecting human choices. These standards aim to reflect the way animals typically *are*. Neither do they appeal to metaphysical ends or purposes: they are grounded in facts of nature. But for all their descriptive content, they still permit evaluations of goodness.

Before we move on to consider how many of the lessons learnt from examining evaluations of good plant and animal lives can be applied in the case of evaluations of good human lives, we need to raise a complication that might already be thought to be present in the animal case and which certainly features in the human case. Much of the resistance to the idea that human lives can be evaluated along naturalistic dimensions analogously to ways in which plant and animal lives can be evaluated has to do with, first, the denial that humans have a nature and, second, the worry that even if humans do have a nature that can be specified in terms of a set of functions, the objective judgment that someone is leading a paradigmatically human life is quite a different one from the subjective assessment someone might make that her life is going well. In what follows I hope to specify the relevant aspects of "human nature" at a sufficiently formal level so as not to fall prey to the standard objections to the view that human beings have a nature, while at the same time indicating the ways in which even this account provides constraints on content. Then I will face the worry about the disparity between objective assessments of good human lives and subjective assessments of happiness by looking more closely at these subjective assessments and at what kind of subjective payoff is thought to be at stake. If having a character can be seen to contribute to the subjective welfare of persons in the sense of making them better off from their point of view, then character ethics will have an answer to critics who claim that accounts of paradigmatically good human lives do not provide *reasons* for individual persons to lead those kinds of lives.

INTERLUDE

Before we turn our attention directly to the human case, we should look more closely at what kinds of subjective assessments of happiness or welfare are meant to be in tension with objective accounts of flourishing or goodness. In the plant case we could not make sense of the notion of subjective assessments of happiness: for a plant to fare well is just for it to be leading a paradigmatic existence for its kind of plant. Animals introduce different considerations: creatures who have a subjective perspective on the world might be thought to have *points of view*,[8] and, furthermore, points of view from which their lives can seem to them to be going well or badly. Animals with subjective perspectives on the world might be thought to have a welfare distinct from their conforming to the standards appropriate to their kind. We think we can make sense of an animal that, according to scientists' standards, is leading a prototypical kind of life for its species, but whose life is beset by subjective harms which compromise its welfare. Likewise, we suppose we can imagine an animal whose life is full of subjective benefits, but which is leading a life very far removed from a prototypical kind of life for its species.

The most plausible way to understand these subjective harms in the case of animals may be in terms of pain. Sentient creatures might be thought to fare well—from their perspective—if they lead lives moderately free of pain. But paradigmatically good lives will necessarily have their share of pain:[9] we need to recognize that, given the kinds of things animals are, leading a good kind of animal life will involve enduring certain kinds of physical pain. What, then, do we say about the fact that from the animal's point of view, the pain (both characteristic and uncharacteristic) is *painful* and hence, we may suppose, unwelcome and, perhaps, an indication to them that their welfare is being compromised?

Here, again, certain natural facts about animals may be relevant. Many animals have nervous systems that may be too primitive for them to experience pain. Their bodily systems may suffer damage, but the damage may occur in the absence of any phenomenological experiences. If this is the case, whereas the damage may compromise their ability to lead prototypical kinds of lives for beings of their kind and hence be relevant to objective assessments of good lives, it can hardly be the sort of thing that contributes to a subjective assessment of welfare from the animal's point of view. The kinds of damage suffered by animals with very primitive nervous systems would be strictly analogous to the kinds of damage suffered by plants.

Some philosophers have argued that *no* animals—even those with relatively sophisticated nervous systems—are capable of consciously experiencing pain.[10] The pain they experience is never brought to conscious awareness and has no phenomenological properties; hence, the pain cannot make them worse off *from their point of view.* In the case of uncharacteristic pain, they may be worse off—leading lives further from those typical of their species—because of some damage they suffer, just as a plant might be. But because the damage is not accompanied by any phenomenological feelings, they cannot be said to have suffered any subjective harms. And subjective harms are the kinds of things that might make them worse off from their point of view.

Peter Carruthers has recently argued that we should not look to the phenomenological *feels* of pain to identify the kinds of subjective harms that we might think undermine the welfare of beings.[11] Instead, it is the awareness of desire-frustration on the part of beings that constitutes the kind of harm that makes their lives go less well from their perspective. If an animal is aware that it is in a state of having its desires frustrated, then, Carruthers argues, it must be in an unwanted mental state. Being in an unwanted mental state constitutes a subjective harm. Although this position is not without its problems,[12] it would seem that experiencing pain and awareness of having one's desires frustrated are the two most likely candidates for subjective harms for animals, and, at least initially, for humans. We should see whether either one or both of these experiences permit us to make sense in the animal case of measures of subjective harm distinct from measures of objective languishing, or measures of subjective benefits distinct from measures of objective flourishing. Can we ask, "is the animal's life going well or badly *from its point of view?*" as distinct from, "is the animal leading or failing to lead a paradigmatic life for an animal of its kind?" And if we can make sense of two distinct questions here, what follows for the human case?

It is tempting to suppose that animals' lives can be assessed as good or bad by appeal to some measure of subjective welfare distinct from standards of paradigmatic ways of being for animals of their kind. The fact that for the vast majority of us our exposure to animals is in the form of acquaintance with domestic pets no doubt encourages this view. But what would it be like for an animal's welfare to be compromised as distinct from its life not going well according to objective, functional criteria? It would seem that in order for anything to have a subjective welfare, that thing has to have a sense of self that it can assess as being benefitted or harmed. In order for it to be capable of the latter, it has to be the kind of thing that can have a sense of self, that can have beliefs about what is good or bad for that self, and that can assess certain events and occurrences as being beneficial or harmful to that self. Would the capacities to experience pain consciously or to be aware of desire-frustration be sufficient for a being to have a sense of self which it can assess as being harmed?

While these capacities may be relevant to assessments of subjective welfare, they would not seem to be the sorts of capacities that underwrite the ability to have a sense of self that has the kind of richness of content with which we are familiar in the human case. Animals of a certain level of complexity may well have subjective perspectives on the world, but that does not ensure that they have subjective perspectives on their selves.[13] In order to have the latter, reflexive, higher-order awareness of one's experiences, including one's mental states, and of oneself as the subject of these experiences is required. Our best current understanding of animal cognition seems to suggest that animals lack the kinds of capacities that underpin the possibility of a sense of self with this kind of content.[14] If one lacks this kind of self, and hence lacks an awareness of whether what one is experiencing is harmful to that self, then it would seem that the notion of subjective welfare distinct from objective flourishing does not get any purchase. One needs a subjective perspective on one's self to have one's life go well or badly *from* that perspective.

If we are right that plants and animals—because of their biological natures—cannot have a welfare that can be compromised, distinct from not flourishing according to objective standards, then it might seem that very little of what we have learnt about claims of plant and animal flourishing can be applied to the human case. But to suggest this would be to give up too readily on the naturalistic strategy. We saw that animal flourishing was assessed along dimensions that were not applicable in the plant case, because of natural facts about animals and plants respectively. The challenge here is to see whether we can provide a specification of human nature that generates objective standards for good human lives and at the same time permits a place in accounts of good human lives for subjective assessments of welfare or happiness.

HUMANS

Two common criticisms of any kind of Aristotelian virtue ethics are, first, that any functional account of good human lives is a nonstarter because humans do not have a characteristic function or set of functions, the good performance of which is constitutive of flourishing, and, second, that, in any case, no account of good human lives in terms of objective criteria of flourishing can provide *reasons* for particular humans to lead objectively optimal human lives. Unless leading a paradigmatically human life confers subjective benefits on the one leading it, so the criticism goes, we are faced with the prospect of subjective assessments of welfare being at odds with objective assessments of flourishing, with only the former being able to motivate. The challenge before us is to provide a naturalistic account of human flourishing whereby those leading paradigmatically good human lives will, other things being equal, make favorable assessments of their subjective welfare. By providing an account of good human lives in terms of successful engagement in the paradigmatically human activity of character construction rather than in terms of possession of particular virtues, I hope to avoid the criticism that virtue theories are unable to specify just which dispositions are virtues except by reiterating our commonly held moral views,[15] as well as the worry that *on particular occasions* the exercise of a given virtue may be thought to undermine the subjective welfare of an agent. I thus hope to show that constructing a character for oneself both permits one to lead a good kind of human life and makes one better off from a subjective perspective.

We have been supposing that the kind of life characteristic of a certain kind of living thing is a function of its nature and the particular capacities inherent in this nature. Plants have capacities to feed, grow, and reproduce. Animals possess, as well as these capacities, further abilities to act and, perhaps, to feel and to desire. Humans have, in addition to these abilities, further capacities of rationality and self-reflexive awareness. It is these capacities which will prove particularly relevant in the specification of a paradigmatic kind of human life. Beings with the capacity for rational thought are capable of acting for reasons; beings with the capacity for self-reflexive awareness are capable of becoming aware of the reasons upon which they act; and beings with subjective perspectives on their selves want to act for reasons of which they approve. Excellence at practical reason directed at becoming the kind of person who is moved by desires and reasons assessed as optimal in the pursuit of ends assessed as worthwhile will feature prominently in the best kinds of human lives.

Humans are social beings. This is a natural fact about them. Much of the success of their interactions with one another is predicated upon their being able to "read" the minds of their fellow human beings. While other animals need to be able to predict the behavior of the fellow members of their species as well as that of those other animals with whom they interact, it would seem that animals can and do do this without ascribing to other animals' mental states.[16] Many animals no doubt have mental states (perceptual states, states of pain, maybe even first-order states of desire and belief), but their forms of life would not seem to require a higher-order awareness of the contents of these states, either their own or others'. *We* may invoke their mental states to explain some of their behaviors, but we do not need to suppose that animals themselves have higher-order beliefs about their own or others' mental states. Lacking higher-order beliefs about mental states, animals would be unable to conceptualize mental states. Without the capacity to conceptualize mental states and hence without the ability to make inferences among mental states, animals would not be able to formulate a "theory of mind," which, many argue,[17] is required in order that they by able to mind-read. Mind-reading is essential for beings who inhabit social environments in which others' actions are done for a wide range of reasons, some of them quite unrelated to the natural ends of nourishment, growth, and reproduction, some of them related in only very convoluted ways to the natural ends of pain-avoidance and desire-satisfaction, some of them apparently not directed to the well-being of the social group, some of them nonoptimal in other ways, and some of them higher-order. Humans need to be relatively proficient at mind-reading because their well-being is intimately tied up with the behaviors of their fellow human beings, and these behaviors are ones which are done for reasons, some of which appeal to complex and often nonoptimal or higher-order desires. Fathoming the reasons other humans have for doing what they do is a characteristic human activity and one that plays a prominent role in an account of prototypical human lives.

Just as it is a fact about human nature that humans learn a language, so too does it seem to be a fact about human nature that they acquire the ability to mind-read.[18] Further, it would seem to be the kind of fact specified at a sufficiently high level of generality that it cannot properly be seen to compromise human freedom or dignity or individuality, traits that those who argue against the claim that humans have a nature are eager to defend. If the naturalistic strategy is correct, mastery of this mind-reading ability will play a central role in an account of a paradigmatically human kind of existence.[19] To what ends is this ability directed? Being a mind-reader permits humans to understand other humans and predict their actions by permitting them to access others' reasons for acting. This ability also permits humans to access their own mental states. By applying their theory of mind—learnt in a communal context—to their own case, humans come to be aware of their own reasons for acting. They come to draw connections between desires and reasons for acting on the one hand and patterns of responding on the other hand. In doing so, they come to see other humans—and themselves—as intentional systems who act for reasons in pursuit of ends. They learn to ascribe to others—and themselves—responsibility for certain kinds of actions and certain kinds of choices. Further, because reasons are the sorts of things that can be assessed as good or bad, better or worse, reasons for acting get evaluated. They get evaluated in the social context in which they are cited and in which mind-reading abilities are developed. Humans learn to evaluate others' reasons for acting, and they learn to evaluate their own reasons. Favorable evaluations of others' reasons for acting are grounds for admiring those others. The critical self-reflexive awareness directed at their own desires and reasons naturally motivates humans to want to be moved to act by reasons they have assessed as optimal. As they see how desires are related to reasons, how desires can be responsive to reasons, and how reasons are the sorts of things that apply over a wide range of similar cases, humans come to construct for themselves a self or a character comprised of those dispositions which they have endorsed and with which they come to identify. The stability of their motivational economy earned through the process of character construction helps to make them more transparent and predictable to other human beings, and often to themselves as well.

So far the sketch of human nature and characteristic human functions has been quite formal. We have noted only that, given natural human abilities and normal human processes of socialization—including those processes that encourage children to see themselves and other humans as intentional systems who act for reasons in pursuit of ends—and given the social contexts in which these reasons are assessed, children come to see other humans as kinds of persons whose reasons for acting are better or worse. Persons' reasons for acting are seen to be related to their desires and dispositions, and children learn to ascribe responsibility to other humans for being the kinds of persons they are, that is, the kinds of persons who find certain kinds of reasons compelling and others not, the kinds of persons who have and act on and endorse certain kinds of desires and not others. This is part of what it is to understand human beings as persons, as responsible agents. The maturing child comes to see himself as a human, with the potential to become a certain kind of person, one with which he hopes to be well pleased, leading a life characterized by the pursuit of certain kinds of ends, which he hopes to find fulfilling. It is against this background understanding of human nature and its connection to good human lives that the child embarks on the paradigmatically human activity of constructing for himself a character by identifying with desires and ends he has endorsed and working to inculcate optimal dispositions.

The task of character construction must be undertaken self-consciously. Infants and small children are moved to act by many desires and dispositions, some of them genetically programmed, some of them encouraged by caregivers during their early years. Infants and small children are also often trained to respond habitually to certain events. None of these patterns of response signals the kinds of traits that comprise a character in the sense relevant to this discussion. There are two major reasons for this. One is that for traits to qualify as character traits in the sense I am using the term, they have to be chosen, and moreover chosen against a background account of good human lives. The other is that these traits have to be chosen in the awareness that a decision to identify with them is a self-constituting decision. Choices of character traits are choices about what kind of person to be, about what kinds of desires to be moved by, and about what kinds of reasons to find compelling. They are choices about what kinds of preferred dispositions to instil and cultivate in the pursuit of a good kind of human life.

But, the objection goes, if we provide a purely formal account of character in terms of self-constituting choices made against background conceptions of good human lives, then we have no guarantee that the traits or dispositions with which the self-constituting human comes to identify are optimal traits, that they will contribute to his leading a good human life. Persons could be operating with background conceptions of human lives that are flawed. To say that it is a fact about human nature that humans constitute themselves by evaluating and then instilling dispositions of which they approve and that success at this ability is a central criterion for human flourishing is to leave open the possibility that humans might satisfy these formal conditions but identify with nonoptimal, vicious dispositions which will end up compromising their own good or the good of their community. They might identify with traits that in fact make them and/or other humans lead nonflourishing lives. The formal requirement of commitment to a set of endorsed traits or dispositions would not seem to rule out as good human beings those who identify with what are commonly considered vices or malevolent dispositions. Unless we can specify *which* ends and dispositions and ways of living will be deemed optimal—and *why*—by persons leading the best kinds of human lives, we will not be confident that the formal account of character with which we are operating will result in persons constructing for themselves *good* characters. Further, unless we can establish the subjective benefits of having such a character, we will have little reason to believe that persons leading good human lives according to our objective criteria will make positive assessments of their welfare. On the other hand, if the apparently requisite content is provided, so that only identification with those traits and dispositions commonly accepted as virtuous counts as the right kind of identification, we risk merely repeating our conventional views on what counts as human goodness. Respecting our naturalistic strategy means that we cannot suppose that the requisite content can be provided by simply listing a set of virtues independently claimed to be optimal.

I think there is a way between these criticisms. But first we need to say more about what kinds of evaluations are involved in the self-constituting process of character construction. We can hope to provide the requisite content by seeing along which dimensions desires, dispositions, ends, and reasons for acting get evaluated. The human capacity for higher-order awareness of beliefs and desires gives humans a subjective perspective on themselves. This capacity is directed toward the end of becoming a certain kind of person—one who is moved to act by those ends and for those reasons deemed to be valuable for the leading of a good human life. This is an end determined by human nature and the capacities inherent in it, not by some teleological or metaphysical purpose. This already means that the kinds of lives humans lead will be very different from those lived by animals lacking a subjective perspective on themselves. However, the self on which young humans have a subjective perspective is initially nothing more than a proto-self, a self that may have a minimal set of typical patterns of reacting, but not ones of which the child is aware, or which he has evaluated, or to which he has committed. Humans have to create the self with which they identify and come to be identified, and they do so by evaluating and then endorsing certain kinds of activities, ends, and ways of living, and by instilling the dispositions and traits deemed to make possible the leading of the kind of life characterized by the pursuit of these activities, ends, and ways of living.

Here we would be well advised to recall what we said about assessments of flourishing in the plant and animal cases. What counted as good functioning of the systems and, where relevant, good performance of the activities was not assessed independently of considerations of how well the functioning or the acting contributed to the kind of life paradigmatically found in that kind of being. The good functioning of the plant's systems served the well-being of the plant (and perhaps the species): nutrition, growth, and reproduction. The good functioning of the animal's systems and the good performance of the animal's actions enhanced the well-being of the animal (and the community, in the case of social animals, and perhaps the species): nutrition, growth, reproduction, freedom from pain, desire satisfaction, and the proper functioning of the group. In plants and animals, characteristic ways of functioning and acting just are those directed at the well-being of the individual and/or the community and/or the species. That is how paradigmatic—and hence good— functioning or acting is determined. The human case is enormously more complicated because human capacities for making reasoned evaluations afford humans wide-ranging abilities to choose among various possible kinds of lives. Exposing the constraints under which the evaluations about what kind of person to be and what kind of life to lead are made will help provide some content to our initially rather formal account of character.

The evaluations at work in character construction clearly appeal to something more than unexamined subjective preferences. Presumably, animals (and Frankfurt's wantons[20]) just do what they want to do: their strongest immediate desire (or instinct) just leads them to act. But animals lack both self-reflexive awareness and the ability to evaluate ends. Human lives are paradigmatically self-aware lives, and their practical reason allows them to evaluate desires, dispositions, motives, and reasons as ones that are good or bad for them, as ones that are or are not in their best interests, as ones that will help or hinder them in leading good lives. Humans making judgments about what kind of person to be must suppose that their evaluations appeal to something more than immediate and unreflective subjective preferences.

What further kinds of considerations get invoked here? And can they provide the requisite constraints on choices and criteria for good choices? The person who is constructing for herself a character must see herself as a being extended in time. Her conception of herself will be one of a being with a history and a future, as well as a present. Her evaluations of traits as conducive or otherwise to the leading of a good kind of human life are made in the awareness that the traits she works to instil will serve to constrain later desires and will provide reasons for acting at later dates. Decisions to value certain traits and to endorse and identify with certain desires are not one-off, episodic decisions. The facts that beings are extended in time and that beings with a subjective perspective on themselves are aware of themselves as beings extended in time—although banal natural facts about them—do serve to constrain character choices, which necessarily are choices that extend beyond the immediate temporal present. There will thus be requirements of temporal consistency circumscribing the evaluations that feature in character construction. Identifying with particular dispositions and endorsing certain reasons as compelling will be incompatible with identifying with and endorsing others. Requirements of temporal consistency provide some content to the relatively formal account of character with which we started.

As well as requirements of consistency across time, there are also requirements of consistency across various facets of a person's life. Humans typically engage in a wide range of pursuits with a variety of different persons, many of them making different kinds of demands on them. Traits assessed as those conducive to a good human life will not be purpose-specific, but will have to have enough built-in flexibility and adaptability to cope with many different types of situations—without generating too many internal tensions. The requirement of internal consistency reflects the fact that persons adopt a higher-order perspective on their lives: they aspire to a kind of unity of purpose as a way of providing coherence and meaning to their lives. Identifying with certain desires and pursuing certain ends will be incompatible with making other self-constituting choices. The requirement of internal consistency provides further content to the formal account of character.

The constraints imposed by requirements of temporal and internal consistency are grounded in facts of human nature: humans see themselves as extended in time, with a past and a future, and with a past that shapes the present and the future. They also see themselves as leading multifaceted and multidimensional lives; their subjective welfare is at least in part a function of the coherence of the narrative they can construct for themselves as they play their different roles. A further kind of constraint on character construction is provided by the fact that humans require—for favorable assessments of their happiness—to be moderately well-pleased with the choices they have made for themselves, both in terms of what kind of person to be and in terms of what kinds of projects to which to commit. Their lives will not be going well from their own subjective perspective unless this is the case. Because assessments of happiness from subjective perspectives are made in the context of social norms and social approbations, and because the assessments have to be sensitive to the limitations and potentialities inherent in human nature as well as to requirements of consistency across time and across contexts, they cannot be completely idiosyncratic. Subjective assessments of welfare are not made in either an evaluative or a cognitive vacuum. They measure closeness of fit between the kind of person one is succeeding in becoming and the kind of person whom one finds admirable, and such judgments are made in the context of communities in which certain kinds of persons are admirable and certain kinds of persons are despicable. They are made against the backdrop of an understanding of good kinds of human lives and of thriving human communities. They have a descriptive component, and they are grounded in empirical observations of kinds of lives and shaped by pragmatic criteria for flourishing that appeal to actual successful lives and actual well-functioning communities. They are objective judgments that can be more or less well supported. Judgments about good human lives thus express neither idiosyncratic preferences on the part of individuals nor metaphysical ends ordained for humans.

Assessments of happiness cannot express mere personal preferences either, but must reflect facts of human nature. This means that some human lives cannot be truly happy lives—despite the protestations to the contrary of the ones living them. Subjective assessments of happiness do not have absolute privilege. The prima facie authority they are usually granted can be overridden. Subjective assessments must—in virtue of the kinds of beings humans are—have rich cognitive and evaluative components. They must also be about things that really *matter* to one. Judgments about one's own happiness have to be grounded in facts about the way the world is, including facts about one's own nature. These assessments also have to be grounded in evaluative claims regarding the relative worth of various ends and dispositions. These are claims about which persons can be mistaken, and their mistakes can infect their subjective assessments. The human ability to have higher-order thoughts about mental states and to assess desires and dispositions as favorable or otherwise will mean that undergoing the mental states of experiencing pain or of desire-frustration may not be sufficient to undermine favorable subjective assessments of happiness. The benefits that are relevant to favorable assessments of happiness or welfare cannot be simply pleasurable phenomenological feels (they are too transitory); nor can they be simply maximization of first-order desire-satisfaction (for the usual reasons of happenstance and the possibility of ill-conceived desires). The real threats to happiness are those that compromise what matters most to the agent. For a self-constituting agent this will include the self she has constructed as well as those ends she has evaluated favorably and around which she is organizing her life.

Well-earned confidence that one has constructed for oneself a character with which one is well pleased and that one is engaged in pursuits which one has endorsed as worthy contributes to favorable subjective assessments of happiness. These favorable assessments can be undermined by external contingencies over which the agent has little control. But the external contingencies which pose the threats are not unwelcome instances of pain or material or emotional loss; those circumstances which force an agent to compromise one of the principles or values with which she has identified are the ones that pose genuine threats to her happiness. To have her integrity undermined because she is obliged to violate something that she holds dear, that both really matters to her and helps constitute who she is, proves a real loss and results in decreased levels of happiness for anyone who cares about her character. In extreme cases, it might result in an agent being unable to "live with herself."[21] But that possibility does not speak against the truth that constructing a character with which one is well pleased both makes one a better human and makes one happier. If objective assessments of human good are offered in terms of success at character construction, we can see how they can mesh with subjective assessments of happiness.

For humans to be happy they have to be well pleased with the things that matter to them most. And given the natural human need for favorable self-esteem and the social contexts in which judgments of admirability and despicability provide reasons for persons to identify with certain desires and dispositions, having characters with which they are well pleased will be a central requirement of any happy life. This requirement seems to stem from the natural fact about humans that their own and others' assessments of their character matter to them. This fact about them serves to constrain further the evaluations made in the context of constructing for themselves a character. Assessments of self-worth are related to assessments of admirability of others: one tries to emulate those whom one admires, and one esteems oneself more highly the more one succeeds in being like those one admires. Assessments of admirability are made in the context of the ends endorsed and the kinds of lives sanctioned by members of one's community whose judgment one respects. One could, of course, be unlucky in one's moral environment. The moral legacy one inherits could be one in which traits and dispositions and ends are wrongly valued. The assessments about worthwhile ends with which one has grown up may be distorted. This happens. And it happens most frequently in those communities in which humans are not leading flourishing lives. There may be all sorts of explanations of how communities came to be dysfunctional, and there may be all sorts of obstacles in the way of changing such communities. Those inhabiting defective kinds of communities may have a hard time persuading themselves of the merits of their own choices, given that their self-constituting identifications are not ones endorsed by the members of their community. But they will recognize, in the nonflourishing lives to which they are exposed, a failure to make the kinds of evaluations that conduce to good human lives.

The understanding of one's nature required in character construction brings with it an awareness that other persons are self-constituting in just the way one is oneself and a recognition that others require a modicum of respect, autonomy, and freedom from fear[22] in order to undertake this task. This imposes further constraints on choices about what kinds of traits with which to identify, in particular those traits often thought of as other-regarding traits. Recognizing one's own need for self-respect likewise places constraints on one's choice of self-regarding traits. My aim here is not to specify just what those traits are (and they may vary according to—pretty extreme—cultural differences); the point is that the higher-level awareness of oneself as endorsing and identifying with traits and dispositions that are optimal for one as a person (whose good functioning and earned self-respect are very much in one's interests) and for one as a member of a community (whose good functioning is also very much in one's interests) itself imports objective criteria grounded in claims about proper functioning and flourishing.

The kinds of evaluations underpinning the self-constituting that goes on in character construction constrain what kinds of traits persons can identify with. To construct a character one must be trying to construct a character. It is a task one must be self-consciously embarked upon. This means that one must understand human nature, in particular the self-constituting activities that are central to good human lives. One must understand what a character is and what the benefits of having a character are, that is, how character possession will let one lead a better human life and will make one's life go better. One must exhibit a fair degree of practical wisdom. Persons cannot identify in the requisite way with just any traits. The traits have to be the sorts of traits with which beings of their sort *could* identify, traits that are *valuable*—and valuable for beings who lead self-reflexive kinds of lives that they are constantly assessing in the context of judgments of admirable and despicable kinds of lives. It is the excellent exercise of practical reason—which is not instrumental reason—which helps identify which traits are valuable and which choices are worthwhile. Because persons naturally wish to lead lives they find meaningful and fulfilling, a person trying to construct for herself a character will be trying to construct for herself what she takes to be a *good* character, one that she thinks will permit her to lead what she takes to be a good—and meaningful—kind of human life. It is not possible for humans to identify in the manner requisite for character construction with traits that they know undermine their own good. They can, of course, make mistakes about the merits of certain traits. These mistakes betoken failures of practical wisdom, and they compromise humans' chances of leading good kinds of lives.

This makes "character possession" out to be in part a success term. This should not be taken as an objection. "Growth" and "nutrition" and "freedom from pain" are presumably success terms as well: lives are judged to be going well or badly according as the ones living them succeed or fail in pursuing these ends. This is how the descriptive claims of the naturalist come to acquire their normative force: descriptions underwrite norms relative to each kind of living thing, and these norms serve as the standards of comparison against which successful lives are measured.

Our naturalist strategy has permitted us to see a way in which human lives can be assessed as good according to success at the paradigmatic human activity of character construction. There is still the question of pay-off to the individual: will those persons who fare well by objective standards of good human lives make favorable subjective assessments of their own happiness or welfare? If we concede that those who lead good human lives by objective standards must be embarked on the task of self-consciously constructing for themselves a character, and if there are natural and conceptual constraints on what kinds of traits can be identified with and hence can qualify as character traits, then we see that, other things being equal, those engaged in the task will reap the subjective rewards of being well pleased with the kind of person they have chosen to become. This self-approval will underpin positive assessments of happiness. Being the kind of person who is motivated by dispositions one has assessed as optimal will make one happier—from one's subjective perspective—than being the kind of person who is motivated by desires and dispositions of which one disapproves. And being the kind of person who leads one's life in pursuit of ends one has assessed as worthy will make one happier—from one's subjective perspective—than being the kind of person who spends one's life engaged in pursuits one does not value. This is not to say that on each and every occasion on which the person who meets with moderate success in constructing for herself a character is confronted with a choice to act, she will always enjoy subjective benefits in terms of pleasures or desire-satisfactions, but it will mean that—on the whole—the things which matter most to her will not be compromised.

Identifying character construction as a central human function grounded in facts of human nature provides us with an objective account of good human lives at the right level of abstraction. The norms for good lives implicit in accounts of successful character construction provide reasons to individual persons to lead good kinds of human lives: leading a good kind of human life brings the right kinds of subjective benefits to the one leading it. The objection that the exercise of certain other-regarding virtues does not directly enhance (and might even compromise) the subjective welfare of the one acting, although it might enhance the welfare of others, is not worrying if we provide an account of human good in terms of character construction rather than in terms of virtue possession (or exercise). It has been claimed that, while the possession of virtues may make one a better human, that cannot provide a motivating reason for agents to acquire those traits. Further, some versions of virtue theories threaten to introduce an unwelcome teleological account of human flourishing: virtues are just those things that will permit one's life and the lives of others to approximate some end. But if we focus on character possession as the human good (with character construction the quintessentially human activity directed toward it) rather than virtue possession, we are less inclined to think that an agent's welfare has been undermined just because—on a particular instance and for contingent reasons—she has suffered some loss in terms of pains or material or emotional deprivations. This is no reason for her to think less well of herself.

With the introduction of the requirement that a person constructing for herself a character have the higher-level awareness that this is what she is doing comes the requirement that she assess those traits in a life—*her* life—and hence in a life that matters to her. This means that all character choices have an evaluative component which belies a purely formal characterization. Dispositions or tendencies or habitual responses which are merely repeated or automatic without having been evaluated as ones conducive to leading a good life do not qualify as traits that comprise a character. It is the evaluations and the context in which—and the dimensions along which—the evaluations are made that introduce the requisite content that makes plausible the claim that the best kinds of human lives are those led by persons who are engaged in the task of constructing for themselves a character.

NATURALISM REVISITED

We noted when discussing claims about plant and animal flourishing that scientists' empirical observations of many plant or animal specimens resulted in descriptive accounts of prototypical lives for members of that plant or animal species. These descriptive accounts supposed that the systems and patterns of activity found to be typical of each species were directed toward the natural ends of nutrition, growth, and reproduction, and, where relevant, pain-avoidance, desire-satisfaction, and the well-being of the social group. We have been seeking analogous descriptive claims about prototypical human lives grounded in natural facts about and natural abilities of human beings that could then provide norms for human flourishing.

According to the naturalism being advocated, if prototypical functions and patterns of activity directed at ends can be detected in the human case, then we would have grounds for saying that humans who perform well these functions and engage in these characteristic patterns of activity would be leading paradigmatically human lives. And paradigmatic human lives are good, flourishing human lives. The "goodness" here is nonmetaphysical and nonteleological. The flourishing has to do with proper functioning, which reflects human nature and the potential ways of living implicit in this nature. The most important fact about humans is that they are naturally self-constituting creatures. Their capacities for self-reflexive awareness afford them a subjective perspective on themselves and permit them to construct for themselves a self for which they are responsible and that gives meaning to their lives. The attempt to construct a character is constrained by demands of consistency and unity as well as by the need for approval (both one's own and those whom one admires). The fact that humans fare better to the extent that the communities they inhabit are populated by members who have been granted the respect and autonomy to constitute themselves further constrains what other-regarding traits can qualify as character traits. Success at the natural—and paradigmatically human—end of character construction is the measure against which objective assessments of human flourishing are made.

We have been supposing that "good" is an attributive adjective, with its meaning relative to the kind of thing it qualifies. The claim that, in order to lead, for example, a good snapping-turtle existence, snapping turtles have to be adept at nourishing themselves in the "right" way, that is, the way appropriate to snapping turtles, is not a contentious claim. The "right" kind of life for snapping turtles just appeals to the way snapping turtles characteristically do things. The claim that the "right" way for humans is the way humans characteristically do things is taken to be objectionable because it seems to make normative claims about how humans *ought* to be follow from descriptive claims about actual human lives. This is not a problem in the plant and animal case, because we do not suppose that the norms for good plants or animals *prescribe* to the plants or animals any way of living. So there are no "ought" claims that might be thought to follow illicitly from "is" claims.

This objection needs to be handled with care. Not all descriptive claims—not even all those that underpin evaluative claims of goodness—issue in prescriptions. Many such evaluative claims just do—and ought to—leave one cold motivationally, as it were. But if the descriptive claims issue from claims about good human lives, and if good human lives are those in which the ones leading them are engaged in their characteristic self-constituting function, then there will be a built-in motivation—at least for those who care about their lives. Because humans naturally have a subjective perspective on their selves, what kind of person they are will matter to them, and it will matter to their subjective assessments of how well their lives are going, of how happy they are. While claims about good plant lives and good animal lives are not supposed to motivate or to provide reasons for plants or animals to be a certain kind of way, because of the self-constituting nature of humans and because humans want to act for reasons and from desires of which they approve, claims about good kinds of human lives *do* provide reasons for humans to act. If the best kind of human lives are those in which the natural capacities of practical reason and self-reflexive awareness are directed at becoming the kind of person of which one approves, then we can see that leading a good kind of human life will confer the kinds of subjective benefits that will enhance persons' happiness or welfare. The descriptive account will thus have normative force. If, on the other hand, "good human lives" were glossed simply in terms of increasing some value—perfectionist or otherwise—or of exercising a specific set of excellences (moral and intellectual virtues), then there is no assurance that maximizing this value or acquiring these excellences will make one better off from one's subjective perspective. By specifying good human lives in terms of success at the prototypical human activity of character construction—success at which gives meaning and unity to persons' lives—we can see how accounts of good human lives can be seen to confer the right kinds of subjective benefits and hence to motivate.

A different kind of objection to the naturalist strategy is that all human lives which we have had a chance to observe to date are so miserable relative to what they *could* be that no empirical observations will expose good human lives. This is a tempting thought, although why it raises its head here and not in the case of plants and animals would need to be explained. In the plant and animal cases identifications of prototypical processes and activities serving natural ends do not presume ideal conditions. Assessments of flourishing are all sensitive to the relevant environments. Plants and animals flourish under natural—not ideal or idealized—conditions. Growth is not maximal conceivable growth, but the kind of growth required to sustain a particular kind of body. Freedom from pain is not freedom from *all* pain, but freedom from the kind of pain that interferes with proper functioning. Just as environmental factors can compromise the ability of plants or animals to flourish, so too one might think that adverse social and political conditions might compromise the ability of humans to flourish. If human flourishing requires the proper exercise of practical reason and self-reflexive awareness directed at becoming a certain kind of person, then it is the sort of thing that can be compromised if the social or political environment does not permit the conditions necessary for self-respect or autonomy or the improvement of one's practical reasoning. But there seems little reason to think that these conditions have never been met. Political or social regimes where persons are oppressed or denigrated will certainly undermine human flourishing, just as adverse environmental conditions will compromise flourishing in plant and animal cases. However, to insist that minimal external conditions must be met is not to establish that improving upon these minimal conditions will enhance flourishing.

A different kind of skeptical objection allows that humans might be able to flourish in imperfect environments, but denies that human flourishing is the sort of thing that can be detected by appealing to observable criteria. There are no natural signs like a gleaming coat or a bright eye.[23] This is to suppose that human flourishing is not something that can be specified naturally. If criteria of human flourishing were metaphysical or supernatural, we might be in some doubt in the here-and-now as to whether any given individual was flourishing. But if the criteria are natural, then it seems that we ought to be able to detect instances of flourishing human lives. Scepticism about judgments of good human lives is not consistent with the ease and confidence with which we judge particular lives to be going well or badly. We support the objective judgments we make about individual lives being good or bad ones by pointing to observable criteria, including physically grounded psychological ones like low stress-levels or relaxed demeanor. We also cite persons' own subjective assessments as evidence. Although we allowed that subjective assessments can be mistaken, the requirement of self-conscious awareness on the part of one trying to construct for herself a character means that certain constraints will be met, evaluations will be made along some of the right dimensions, and some success at the task will be assured.

The first two points about descriptive content and objective judgments made in the context of discussing claims about plant and animal flourishing would seem to apply to the human case as well. Provided they are made at the right level of abstraction, claims about human flourishing and about good human lives can be grounded in descriptive claims about human nature and quintessentially human ways of living based on observations of actual lives. Objective assessments of human flourishing can then be made on the basis of successful engagement in these paradigmatic human activities. Minimal conditions, which may be necessary but not sufficient, can be specified that permit human flourishing. Point three above that the account of flourishing would be unknown to plants and animals does not apply to the human case. If an essential part of human flourishing requires being embarked on the self-conscious task of constructing a character in directions determined by one's understanding of good human lives, then humans will need to be aware of the criteria for human flourishing. That humans, unlike plants and animals, have to be aware of criteria for flourishing in order to flourish would seem to be quite appropriate for creatures whose self-constituting, self-aware nature is implicated in their flourishing and quite inappropriate for creatures who are not self-aware. Point four above suggested that accounts of plant and animal flourishing cannot provide motivating force for plants and animals respectively because plants and animals are not the sorts of things that can be motivated, that can act for reasons. We saw that if human flourishing is specified at the right level of abstraction, with the content being provided by constraints imposed by human nature and by the kinds of lives that nature makes possible, then there are *reasons* for rational, self-aware humans to want to lead good kinds of human lives. Character possession *pays*. Even if the exercise on a particular occasion of some other-regarding virtue might seem to make one worse off, being the kind of person motivated by the kinds of traits one has deemed to be valuable in pursuit of ends one has deemed to be worthwhile cannot undermine one's welfare.

Points five and six above are related: claims about good kinds of persons or good kinds of human lives may offer something like recipes or instructions for those who wish to be good persons. But the guidance is not readily codifiable. Rather, those persons and lives we admire and esteem provide models for us to emulate. A natural extension of the human capacities to mind-read and to evaluate reasons is the human tendency to judge character types and kinds of lives. These judgments are made against background accounts of good human lives, as they are lived individually and communally. Those persons who are leading lives deemed to be good according to these judgments will serve as models to those who want to lead better human lives. Emulating those admirable persons does not offer a guarantee that one will lead a good human life or that one's welfare will be enhanced. As we noted before, certain kinds of contingencies can compromise persons' prospects for a good life and for happiness. The models provided by good persons show us the proper values of external and internal goods in flourishing human lives and expose the real threats to our flourishing and our happiness. Lives will go less well from a subjective perspective if the ones leading them are deprived of things that really matter to them; human nature constrains what kinds of things can really matter to self-aware, self-constituting beings whose self-esteem is tied up with judgments of admirability.

I have been arguing that our evaluative claims about good human lives are grounded in descriptive claims about proper functioning. These, in turn, appeal to features and capacities of human nature and to the kinds of lives made possible by their exercise. In particular, the quintessentially human function, good performance of which characterizes the best kinds of human lives, is character construction. Although, clearly, much work still needs to be done in fleshing out which dispositions would be endorsed by those who succeed in constructing for themselves a good character and, in particular, in showing *why* these dispositions and not others would be endorsed, I hope I have said enough about the constraints involved in choices of character to make plausible the suggestion that there is a route between an account of human nature that is rich in content but that compromises human freedom and individuality and an account that is so formal that it is incapable of providing normative force or guidance. Identifying character construction as central to a prototypical human life shows how objective assessments of flourishing grounded in facts of human nature are related to subjective assessments of welfare concerned with how well lives are going from the points of view of the ones living them. Human welfare is enhanced by performing well the paradigmatic human activity of constructing for oneself a character with which one is justly well pleased.

NOTES

1. "Characteristically" good human lives is really a better choice than "paradigmatically" good human lives, given that the latter might seem to suggest a single model for a good human life. But stylistic reasons appealing to excessive use of variants on "character" argue in favour of "paradigmatic" or "typical." It should be remembered, however, that it is not intended that there is only one kind of flourishing or good human life.

2. The form of naturalism to which I am committed might best be called "functionalistic naturalism": humans have characteristic functions which can be read off from their nature—though their nature is discovered by a purely natural-scientific investigation, not a metaphysical one—and the functions are not ones that appeal to purposes, either metaphysical or theological.

3. I am taking assessments of welfare or happiness to be subjective in the sense that they are made from a person's *point of view* and they are about how well a life is going *from that point of view.* This does not mean, as we shall see below, that they are incorrigible. I am taking assessments of flourishing or goodness to be objective in the sense that they can be made from an external perspective and appeal to general facts about human beings.

4. See Philippa Foot, *Natural Goodness* (Oxford: Oxford University Press, 2001) and Rosalind Hursthouse, *On Virtue Ethics* (Oxford: Oxford University Press, 1999).

5. These are just the sort of background, unquestioned assumptions that shape our investigations. It does not compromise the objectivity of these evaluations in any interesting sense to recognize that they are objective relative to these foundational assumptions. See Ludwig Wittgenstein, *Philosophical Investigations* (Oxford: Blackwell, 1952).

6. Plants (and other things) can of course also be assessed as good or bad, better or worse, along other dimensions. Depending on what human ends are adopted, different criteria of goodness will apply. Certain kinds of plants will be better than others at shading areas, at keeping away insects, at attracting hummingbirds, at adorning funeral homes, etc. My assumption here is that functional assessments of *good* plants are made in the absence of any human ends.

7. Henceforth, I will omit the qualifier "non-human" when speaking about animals.

8. Thomas Nagel, in "What It Is Like To Be a Bat," *Philosophical Review* 83 (1974): 435–50, argues that bats have subjective experiences. There must be something it is like—from the bat's point of view—to experience the world. To have a subjective perspective on the world, however, is not the same thing as having a subjective perspective on oneself.

9. See Hursthouse, *On Virtue Ethics,* 199–200, for a discussion of this important point.

10. For a classic statement, see Thomas Huxley, "On the Hypothesis that Animals are Automata" in *Collected Essays,* vol. 1 (New York: D. Appleton, 1897), 199–250. More recently, Peter Carruthers, in "Brute Experience," *Journal of Philosophy* 86 (1989): 258–69, argues that animal experiences are nonconscious and that animals do not experience painful sensations.

11. Peter Carruthers, "Sympathy and Subjectivity," *Australasian Journal of Philosophy* 77 (1999): 465–82.

12. In particular, on Carruthers's understanding, the capacity for higher-order thought makes possible the kind of conscious awareness of oneself which permits a subjective perspective on it. Without the capacity for higher-order thought and hence without a subjective perspective on oneself, it is unclear *what* is suffering the subjective harms.

13. Peter Carruthers endorses Nagel's point about animals having a subjective perspective on the world but appeals to a distinction between worldly and experiential subjectivity to deny that animals have a subjective perspective on their experiences. It is the latter that is relevant to subjective assessments of one's welfare. See Carruthers, *Phenomenal Consciousness* (Cambridge: Cambridge University Press, 2000), 127–29.

14. Ethologists are not unanimous on this matter: some argue that the apparent capacity on the part of some kinds of animals to recognize images of themselves suggests a sense of self. But it is, at best, unlikely to be more than a very primitive sense of self, somewhat like the sense of self a very young infant comes to acquire. The infant subsequently receives the kind of socialization that permits her to create a self rich in content; animals who do not share forms of life similar to humans' have no reason to move beyond the kinds of bare recognitional capacities displayed in self-identifications in mirror images. See note 16 below.

15. Hursthouse formulates this problem clearly in *On Virtue Ethics*. Having acknowledged the hazards, she then countenances a Neurathian procedure in ethics which, she concedes, does not "expect what it says to convince anyone whose ethical outlook or perspective is largely different from the ethical outlook from within which the naturalistic conclusions are argued for," 193. Likewise, I do not suppose that my arguments will be persuasive to anyone who does not care deeply about what kind of person one is.

16. Capacities to deceive others and to recognize an image of oneself are sometimes taken as evidence that some kinds of animals have abilities to mind-read. The distinction between mind-reading and behaviour-reading may not be clear-cut. See Andrew Whiten, "When Does Smart Behaviour-reading Become Mind-reading?" in *Theories of Theories of Mind*, ed. Peter Carruthers and Peter K. Smith (Cambridge: Cambridge University Press, 1996), 277–92.

17. Simulationists disagree about the need for a theory of mind, arguing that abilities to mind-read are grounded in capacities to simulate others' mental states rather than in capacities to apply a theory about mental states. But simulationists also suppose more conceptualization of—and more capacity for drawing inferences among—mental states than seems consistent with mere proficiency at simulation.

18. It is no objection that human children have to *learn* a theory of mind. Language, too, is *learnt* by human children.

19. Those who lack capacities to mind-read, whether they be very small children or humans with severe autism, might be thought not to lead paradigmatically *human* lives.

20.   See Harry Frankfurt, "Freedom of the Will and the Concept of a Person," *Journal of Philosophy* 68 (1971): 5–20. Lacking second-order volitions (that is, effective desires about first-order desires), Frankfurt's wantons cannot lead characteristically human lives.

21.   Bernard Williams's examples of Jim and George in *Utilitarianism: For and Against* (Cambridge: Cambridge University Press, 1973) are sometimes thought to provide examples of persons confronted with choices that threaten to compromise their identity and to make them into different kinds of persons.

22.   Judith Shklar, in *Ordinary Vices* (Cambridge, MA: Belnap Press, 1984), argues that cruelty is one of the worst vices precisely because it represents a deliberate attempt to undermine people's autonomy. Autonomous choices are required in character construction.

23.   Bernard Williams, *Ethics and the Limits of Philosophy* (Cambridge, MA: Harvard University Press, 1985), 46.

THREE

Moral Character

A Psychological Approach

Augusto Blasi

CHARACTER IS IN. IN NEWSPAPERS, MAGAZINES, AND TELEVISION SHOWS; in political gatherings and in Congress; in school committees and classrooms, ethical character is praised and its absence lamented, programs designed to foster it are recommended and advanced as the solution to society's ills. One would have to go back more than a century to find a similar intensity of interest. The idea of character occupied an enormous place in the ethical consciousness of Victorian people, particularly among the rising middle-classes (cf. e.g., Collini 1985; Hilkey 1997; Smout 1992). Then, this concern found its practical expression in a mushrooming of programs, experiments, and youth organizations, all aimed at educating the virtues (for the U.S., see McClellan 1999). It would be very instructive to compare the two waves of interest in character, and to examine the virtues emphasized or neglected then and now, the relative economic and industrial circumstances, and the ways the respective movements were and are appropriated, and sometimes manipulated, by political interests.

But there is one important difference. At the turn of last century the character education movement elicited an intense response in psychology. To provide only one indication, when May and Hartshorne (1925) surveyed the psychological instruments in use then, they listed more than a dozen tests strictly aimed at assessing character traits. Among these traits were: conscientiousness, honesty and dishonesty in the forms of cheating and lying, dependability, trustworthiness, sense of honor, fairmindedness, perseverance, speed of decision, and willpower. Several studies combined a number of measures into batteries to obtain a more comprehensive assessment of character; Hartshorne and May's (1928; with Maller 1929; with Shuttleworth 1930) set of measures was only the most comprehensive and the culmination of this intense effort. By contrast, this time around psychologists have been very reticent to enter the field of character and character education. The last important empirical contribution to the psychological study of character was Hartshorne and May's Character Education Inquiry. Since the end of the 1930s very little was written on this topic from a psychological perspective (see Power, Higgins, and Kohlberg 1989), even though some of the early concerns, as we will see, persisted in later years under different rubrics and within a different framework.

This sudden drop of interest in psychology is sometimes attributed to the ambiguity of the concept, the lack of a clear theoretical basis, and particularly to the discouraging conclusions of Hartshorne and May (1928–1930). These investigators' "specificist" interpretation of their data tended to deny a psychological foundation to the concepts of character and virtue, reducing these terms to convenient linguistic fictions. Their conclusions were immediately questioned (e.g., in Maller 1934) and later found to be empirically unwarranted (Burton 1963). However, more powerful factors contributing to the demise of character research in psychology had to do with the general theoretical situation of psychology as a science at that time. At one end of the field, behaviorism, by then a widely accepted theoretical perspective, tended to reduce personality to a conglomerate of habits. At the other end, Piaget's theory and research, including his work on morality, was making its entrance into the American psychological scene, bringing with it a revolutionary reinterpretation of moral functioning. From this perspective, it is not character, or even the will, that matters, but the cognitive grasp in each person of what morality is all about. The impact of this viewpoint, particularly as a result of Kohlberg's contribution, was so powerful, and, I must add, this conception of morality seemed so sensible, that earlier emphases on character suddenly appeared old-fashioned and irrelevant. It took a very long time for psychologists interested in moral development to fully realize the weaknesses of the cognitive-developmental approach, and for some of us to wistfully look back at moral character for more adequate explanations.

In this chapter I revisit the territory of moral character with psychological questions in mind and return to a long abandoned debate. In spite of uncertainties and confusions, the project seems to be worth pursuing. First, "character" and "virtue," whether we like it or not, are important, and probably unavoidable, ideas in our everyday understanding of moral functioning. Second, these terms seem to capture something that cannot be entirely assimilated to moral understanding or cognitive structures. Third, in spite of Hartshorne and May's conclusions and of later debates concerning personality traits, there is reason to believe that there are indeed relatively stable personality dispositions to feel and behave morally; the least one can say is that the issue was not settled by the early character research. My revisiting this field is strongly influenced by what I feel we have learned during the past half century of moral psychology, including a more precise understanding of the ways philosophy and psychology interact around moral issues; a better grasp of the limits of behavioral analyses, in particular of the essential role of intention in defining action, and of moral understanding in defining moral intentions; and a more secure appreciation of the limits of cognition in explaining moral functioning.

A CONCEPTUAL SCHEME

Even a cursory reading of contemporary literature on moral character education reveals that moral character is typically identified with a person's set of virtues and vices,[1] that is, with predispositions to experience certain emotions and to engage in ethically significant kinds of behaviors in response to more or less specific situations. At least in this respect, contemporary approaches to moral character are Aristotelian in spirit. Three elements in this concept need to be underlined. First, moral character involves predispositions, that is, relatively stable and general personality characteristics; moral character, then, relates morality to personality. Second, these personality characteristics are defined in terms of their relation to action. These two emphases, common to an Aristotelian understanding of the ethical life and to contemporary approaches to moral character, clearly differentiate these views from cognitive-developmental approaches to moral functioning. The third element concerns the moral significance (in Aristotelian language, the moral praiseworthiness and blameworthiness) of the actions to which a person's character is predisposed. This element should be unambiguously presented, particularly in the context of a psychological discussion: here, I take the moral attribute, of either action or character trait, in its full subjective meaning, depending, that is, on the person's moral intention and motive, and therefore on some, perhaps minimal, grasp of what morality is and involves.

These features seem to constitute the common ground, and therefore provide a convenient starting point for my present discussion. But they also involve a degree of vagueness and of ambiguity. In particular the meaning of "predisposition" has been the object of frequent discussion. Von Wright (1963), for example, pointed out its ambiguity when he wrote, "there is no current sense of the word 'predisposition,' in which the various virtues could be said to be dispositions" (142). One frequent issue concerns the nature of a virtue's relation to action. As many philosophers have noted, virtues are not related to specific activities; for example, there is nothing that is outwardly common to all courageous acts, while the observable end-results of courage could also be obtained by non-courageous acts. In psychology, we are familiar with the diversity of views and the controversies surrounding the concept of trait. It seems now clear that the nominalistic notion that trait terms are only summaries of behavioral observations, a view that used to be strongly argued by W. Mischel (1968), is not tenable, at least for moral virtues. Another issue has to do with whether any virtue can be understood as self-contained and distinct from the other virtues, or whether all moral virtues shouldn't be seen as springing from a more basic virtuous attitude (Ramsey 1997). There is no need, in the present context, to resolve these debates. We can accept, for now, that people are differently disposed to act morally, but then allow the following discussion to clarify, to some extent, the psychological nature of moral dispositions.

When one looks at the content of moral character—the various detailed lists that can be found in educational curricula, books, and a variety of studies, past and present (see, e.g., Walker and Pitts 1998)—one immediately observes that the lists frequently differ from each other, are invariably long and can be easily extended, and are largely unsystematic. It is easy to conclude, then, that it would be very difficult to engage in the psychological study of moral character by focusing on the specific virtues. In this chapter I introduce a degree of simplification and order by adopting two main distinctions as shown in table 1. First, I group the virtues in two broad categories, according to their degree of generality. Many character traits are predispositions to respond in relatively specific ways to rather circumscribed situations. Others, instead, are much broader in scope, possibly appropriate to any situation and in connection with any one of the specific virtues. It could be argued, in fact, that specific and general virtues frequently work together, each providing something special to moral char-

TABLE 1. List of Moral Virtues

Lower-order Virtues

Empathy	Obedience
Compassion	Law-abidingness
Politeness	Civic-mindedness
Respectfulness	Honesty
Thoughtfulness	Conscientiousness
Kindness	Truthfulness
Generosity	Fairness
Altruism	Justice
Friendship	Courage
Loyalty	Humility

Higher-order Virtues

Will Cluster	*Integrity Cluster*
Perseverance	Responsibility
Determination	Accountability
Self-discipline	Self-consistency
Self-control	Sincerity
Willpower	Integrity
	Principledness
	Transparency to Oneself
	Honesty with Oneself
	Autonomy

Note. This list is a brief compilation from several lists of virtues.

acter: the specific virtues seem to provide the moral meanings, while the general ones have to do with the motivational underpinning, the stability and generality of character traits. For instance, the exercise of altruism, truthfulness, or honesty, particularly in situations of conflict, seems to require either determination, self-control, willpower, independence from social pressure, or integrity. Here, I label these two categories, respectively, lower- and higher-order virtues. These terms are not meant to suggest different degrees of moral significance, but simply to reflect what seems to be a psychological fact: lower-order virtues seem to require at least one or another of the higher-order virtues in order to have stability and motivational strength.[2]

With a second distinction I subdivide the higher-order virtues, purely on the basis of conceptual similarity, into two clusters. Some virtues seem to form a network around the concept of will or willpower: here belong, e.g., determination, self-control, resistance to temptation, and courage. Others instead seem to form a network around the concept of integrity, or the tendency to maintain a high degree of internal consistency: here belong self-consistency, being a person of one's word, responsibility, accountability, transparency to oneself, resistance to self-deception, autonomy of thinking, and independence in action. To fully grasp the conceptual similarity among the traits of this second cluster may require some explanation of the meaning of integrity, which I try to offer in a later section. Finally, I subdivide the traits of the will cluster into two sets: some, persistence and determination, have to do with "moving forward," or with what I call the will as desire; the others connote negativity, "moving back," suppressing, in sum, what I call the will as self-control.

The present discussion is built around, and organized by, these distinctions. In what follows I leave completely aside the specific, lower-order virtues and focus exclusively on the higher-order ones. My main reason for doing so has to do with the wish to take the first steps toward a coherent theoretical account of moral character. It is easier to do so by concentrating on those aspects that seem to be common to, and to underlie, the many specific virtues. In addition, this move allows me to bypass entirely the complicated issues concerning the definition of morality, and to avoid having to decide which virtues should be considered as really moral and should be included in any description of moral character. The rest of the chapter is then organized into three main sections, focusing respectively on the will as self-control or willpower, on the will as desire or moral motivation, and on integrity. The importance for character of willpower and integrity has been always understood—either virtue, or both, are frequently taken as the very essence of character. My treatment of these issues is guided by a basic idea: the core of moral character, I think, is in the person's moral desires. By contrast, willpower and integrity receive their moral meaning from moral desires. All three sets of virtues are necessary for moral character, but in different ways: willpower is necessary to deal with internal and external obstacles in pursuing one's long term objectives; integrity relates one's commitments to the sense of self; and moral desires guide willpower and integrity, providing them with their moral significance.

From the perspective of psychology, we can speak of moral character both if there is evidence of a relatively general tendency to behave in ways that the agent considers to be moral and if this tendency is related to relatively permanent characteristics of the agent's personality, assessed independently of moral actions. For us, the main questions are: Is there evidence that these three factors—willpower, moral desires, and integrity—are more or less permanent characteristics, at least of some people? To what extent is each of them related to a tendency of acting morally? What is the specific contribution of each factor? I will also consider information concerning development—the origin and the qualitative changes that these factors undergo through development. The hope is that more general ideas will surface concerning the psychological foundations of moral character, providing the beginning of a general theory.[3]

WILLPOWER: THE WILL AS SELF-CONTROL

Psychology's interest in the will: A historical sketch

Psychology's involvement with the will has an odd history. Not many of us remember that, at the beginning of the twentieth century, the still new scientific discipline staged an intense debate on the nature of the will, in which the best-known theorists participated. There also was a lively research activity aimed at determining, through systematic introspection, the essential characteristics of the acts of choosing and deciding. Its methods were soon criticized, and yet this work was able to identify something basic in the phenomenology of willing: the feeling of effort or striving is not a part of it. Instead, three elements, united together, are central: the internal designation of, and mental orientation to, the chosen object; an implicit awareness of acting, through mental gestures; and the inescapable presence of the agent-self (cf. Aveling 1926). These findings, pointing to the personal, appropriative nature of the will, are important for an understanding of moral character.

This work suddenly ceased in the 1920s (important exceptions are Heckhausen's [e.g., 1991] and Kuhl's [e.g., Kuhl and Beckmann 1994] recent work). From then on psychologists focused their interest exclusively on self-control. In fact, even the term "will" was soon abandoned as old-fashioned and unscientifically subjective. The early research on character was instrumental in the shift from the positive to the negative will—from the will as desire to the will as self-control. Many in this movement argued, theoretically, that self-control and inhibition are the bases of character (an extended discussion of this idea can be found in Roback 1928). In addition, some empirical studies showed that the abilities to inhibit impulses and delay gratification account for the correlations among character traits (Burton 1963; Maller 1934; Webb 1915; this view was recently resurrected by Kochanska [e.g., 1991] and her collaborators, in their

attempt to explain moral functioning on the basis of early temperamental characteristics). The large body of research on resistance to temptation (or deviation), conducted mainly during the 1960s and '70s, should be seen as a continuation of earlier
work on ethical character (for reviews, see Burton 1976; Jones 1954; Wright 1971). But
now the emphasis on "resistance" marks a narrowing in focus: here, interest is exclusively on inhibition and impulse control, namely, on willpower in its negative forms. In
the typical experimental paradigm, children were presented with one or more practical
dilemmas, each involving a choice between conforming to standard ethical rules (e.g.,
not to steal or cheat) and yielding to the temptation to satisfy a personal wish, but, in
so doing, deviating from the ethical rule. In order to determine which factors are related to resisting temptation, all aspects of the procedure were varied: the nature of the
temptation and of the rule; the explicitness and the severity with which the rule was
presented; the authority figures involved; the consequences that would follow the deviation; the subjective probability that the infraction would be detected. In addition, resistance to deviation was related to several other variables: demographic variables like
age, gender, and race; person variables, such as intelligence and knowledge of moral
rules; and contextual variables, including family background, child rearing practices,
and membership in religious or youth organizations.

Studies on character and on resistance to temptation were motivated by a general interest in moral development. More recently, however, self-control has become
an interesting subject of research for itself, as an independent process and a general
adaptive function. Here one should list the work by Kopp (e.g., Vaughn, Kopp, and
Krakow 1984) with very young children, the longitudinal study by Jeanne and Jack
Block (1980), and the series of studies conducted by Mischel and his collaborators
with children and adolescents (Mischel 1981, 1996; Mischel, Shoda, and Rodriguez
1989). From a different perspective, one should also list the various attempts to determine the central factors operating in self-control and to construct a model of the
process (e.g., Baumeister and Heatherton 1996; Carver and Scheier 1981).

Willpower and moral character

The findings of the large body of research on resistance to temptation and self-
control in general has been reviewed in detail elsewhere (e.g., Harter 1983; Jones 1954;
Mischel 1996; Wright 1971; Zelazo and Jacques 1997). Here I will simply present what
seem to be the clearest conclusions, particularly in relation to moral character.

It seems now clear that self-control is not a result of effort or struggle; willpower
is not a matter of strength (even if the term, ego strength, continues to be used), but

is a result of a set of interlocking skills, mainly cognitive in nature. Among them are: goal setting; the ability to break down goals into hierarchical plans; future time perspective; the ability to keep one's attention focused, but also to mentally manipulate the object of attention; the ability to distance oneself from the concrete present and to keep distant goals in mind; and monitoring one's action and its outcomes. On this point there is a very broad agreement across different research fields and opposite theoretical orientations. Not surprisingly, then, a most consistent finding is significant correlations between measures of intelligence, on one side, and the early measures of character and measures of resistance to temptation, on the other. Models of self-control that have been suggested (e.g., Carver and Scheier 1981) tend to take an information processes approach and organize these skills in an impersonally operating, negative-feedback system. In addition, children already have a degree of sophistication in many of these skills by the age of three (Kochanska 1991; Vaughn, Crop, and Krakow 1984), and the ability to control one's impulses—for instance, to delay gratification—continues to increase with the development of cognitive capacities (Mischel 1996). Finally, self-control skills tend to cluster together: factorial analyses of character measures produced factors that were characterized by delay of gratification, time perspective, and focused attention (Burton 1963; Maller 1934; Webb 1915); and several studies of resistance to temptation indicated a degree of consistency across different tasks (Nelsen, Grinder, and Mutterer 1969; Sears, Rau, and Alpert 1965) and also a relation to self-control skills (Brock and Del Giudice 1963; Grim, Kohlberg, and White 1968; Sears, Rau, and Alpert 1965). Of course, there is another side to the consistency story, namely, overwhelming evidence for a powerful influence of external and situational factors on resistance to deviation. Even so, it is safe to conclude that, as a skill, willpower is a general personality characteristic on which individuals vary. In this respect, willpower can indeed be considered as one basis for character.

But what can one say about the relations between self-control and *moral* character? One thing can be said with certainty: willpower cannot be the essence, or a part of the essence, of moral character. As such, willpower is a skill, and therefore morally neutral. In addition, self-control, perhaps to a limited degree, is already present at an age when the child is not yet capable of moral understanding, and therefore of specifically moral intentions; it is also present in sufficient degree in the large majority of people, whether or not they tend to behave morally. It should be added that, as is frequently understood, willpower has become an impersonal characteristic, an autonomously operating system of self-regulation. In sum, like memory or intelligence, willpower can be used for moral purposes, but it can also be used to pursue pragmatic, or even immoral, goals. We don't need research to arrive at this conclusion; our daily experience is sufficient.

This, however, does not tell us what empirical relations, if any, self-control has with the ability to act morally and, in particular, with the tendency to do so consistently. Self-control may not be sufficient, but is it necessary for moral character? Moreover, could it be that people who identify themselves with moral concerns also tend to develop a higher ability to control their desires? In general, because the ability to control one's desires has widespread effects in people's functioning, we could expect that willpower will also affect the capacity to translate good intentions into action. Unfortunately, not much can be said beyond this general statement. As already mentioned, recent research on self-control was not motivated by questions about morality. The large body of research on resistance to temptation, including Kochanska's long series of studies, was so motivated, but does not yield more information. One of the amazing aspects of this literature is that from it we can learn a great deal about people's motives in yielding to temptation, but next to nothing about people's motives in resisting temptation. The reason, I think, is that these investigators adopted an external, behavioral definition of honesty and dishonesty and of morality in general: cheating is cheating, lying is lying, both are dishonest; vice-versa, resisting the temptation to lie or cheat is the honest and moral response. Children who consistently performed these behaviors across different tasks would be considered to have moral character. The assumptions seem to be that what is a moral rule for the investigators is also a moral rule for children; that children would perceive a prohibition from an authority, as arbitrary as it might be, as having moral meaning; and that the grasp of these situations would essentially be the same for all children. These assumptions are not only too simple, but are unrealistic and inadequate. The assumption adopted here is that morality requires action guided by moral intentions, providing the behavior with moral meaning, within the framework of the agent's understanding of morality. In addition, as we know, children's moral understanding significantly differs from adults', and also from child to child, even concerning the same behaviors.

In general, early studies on character and research on resistance to temptation did not explore whether resisting the temptation to cheat or lie was in fact mediated by a moral understanding of the situations and by a desire to do what is morally right. With regard to studies with very young children, it is doubtful that three- or four-year-old participants were frequently capable of even the most elementary moral understanding and motive. In fact, there is evidence in the studies conducted by Kochanska (1991, 1993, 1995) and her collaborators that the motives behind compliance and self-control had little to do with morality (for a discussion of this body of research, see Blasi 2000). According to the investigators' own account, the children seemed to be fearfully concerned with the consequences of their behavior; the more conscientious among them were those that were more easily distressed and anxious, inhibited, and constricted. Fear and anxiety, however, are not moral motives; neither is the desire to maintain one's parents' good favor nor to gain advantages for oneself. People could become well socialized out of fear; they could consistently comply with the rules out of conditioned anxiety, even when no one else is there to observe their behavior. But, in these people, the will leading to compliance could not be interpreted as moral. As for the children involved in resistance-to-temptation experiments, they were typically older; presumably many were capable of moral understanding and of genuine moral motives. However, information about their specific understanding of the temptations and about the motives behind the decision to comply with the rules is frequently not present.

In several resistance-to-temptation studies an effort was made to assess the moral understanding of the participants and to relate it to resistance to deviation (for a review, see Blasi 1980). Here too, however, it is difficult to arrive at a clear conclusion concerning the moral meaning, from children's perspective, of either yielding to or resisting temptation. One reason is that the investigations are not comparable to each other in overall quality and method, using different measures of resistance to deviation and of moral understanding. But there are two additional problems: First, knowing a person's general view of morality does not tell us how the same person assimilates a concrete real-life situation. Second, there is a difference between moral understanding, general or specific, and caring about morality either in general or concerning the concrete situation. We know that moral motivation does not always match moral understanding; and we also know that many people may view cheating on a test or in a game as morally relevant, but also as morally trivial. It is not our task to determine whether this is a morally defensible attitude (even though it may be our task to find whether this attitude is a result of self-deception). However, it is difficult to estimate the role of willpower in behavioral consistency, if the desire to behave morally is lacking.

It is conceivable, in fact to be expected, that, on occasion, a person may not be able to act according to his or her sincere moral wishes, because of inadequate will capacities; this would lead to inconsistency in action and between action and beliefs, suggesting a lack of moral character. On the other hand, it is also conceivable that strong will capacities are used to successfully carry out pragmatic and evil goals. To my knowledge, only one study, by Grim, Kohlberg, and White (1968), tested and confirmed both of these expectations: these investigators reported that "strong-willed" morally conventional children resisted the temptation to cheat more effectively than "weak-willed" subjects at the same level of moral understanding; however, "strong-willed" preconventional children opted for the cheating option significantly more than "weak-willed" children at the higher moral stage (in this study willpower or ego strength was assessed by combining IQ and focused attention measures). But there is no need of experimental research. One should only think of the level of ego strength and will capacities that were needed to carry out the Holocaust. The conclusion is inescapable: a person can now and then, here and there, behave morally without much of a moral character. However, to be able to consistently guide one's life according to moral aims, one needs the set of capacities that constitute willpower; most important, one needs to put these capacities at the service of stable moral concerns.

THE CORE OF MORAL CHARACTER: THE WILL AS MORAL DESIRES

A conception of the will

If willpower consists of a set of tools, without a specific motivation of its own, then one needs a different kind of will to set willpower in operation and provide it with a specific meaning; what one needs, with regard to moral character, is a will that desires and tends toward the moral good. It may seem inappropriate, indeed paradoxical, to use the term "desire" in the context of moral character; morality, in fact, is frequently conceived as being opposed to desires, and character as being on the side of rigid, unspontaneous duty. But the term "desire" has several advantages over the more technical "motivation": first, "desire" connotes a certain intensity of affect, which fits the notion of virtues as human excellences, and the idea of character as providing stable and effective direction in one's life; second, desires can only belong to a person, a subject, and therefore the term moves us away from the impersonal language of motivation and regulatory system, and from the cybernetic models of self-control; finally, "desire" ties in with Frankfurt's philosophical conception of the will on which I rely.

Over the past thirty years, Frankfurt articulated a very influential theory of the will (several of his papers are collected in Frankfurt, 1988). His views are not uncontroversial, and yet they seem to be so simple and so right at the same time, their implications so deep and pervasive, that they succeeded in capturing philosophers' imaginations.[4] He relied on the basic human capacity not only to have desires (first-order desires), but also to reflect on one's desires and to have desires about them (second-order desires)—that is, desires to have and perhaps nurture or reject one's desires. The will is then conceived as a person's desire that a first-order desire one finds within oneself be effective in producing action. For instance, my desire to smoke becomes the reflected object of another desire, my wish that I did not have the desire to smoke. If I wish that the desire not to smoke be effective, I have a second-order volition, or an act of will. The definiton is simple enough. But a few comments may be useful to appreciate the power of Frankfurt's elaborations.

To have desires about our desires means to distance ourselves from them: that is, to recognize that, as objects, they are external to me as an agent, and that I am free to make them internal, to appropriate them, to recognize them as my own. By doing so, I begin to exercise some control on my desires, and also to construct the boundaries of a certain kind of sense of self.

To grasp the meaning of Frankfurt's move one needs to grasp the crucial difference between the will and unreflected desires—whether they are inborn drives and impulses, or socially conditioned motives and wishes, such as the empathic wish to share or the desire to obey the parents' command. All these desires, if they are unreflected, act like impulses: they are spontaneous responses, with which the agent is totally merged, lacking the minimal distance that reflection introduces. Even though an impulse is clearly mine and is immediately experienced as mine, in the absence of distancing, it is felt as passively surging within me. In its deepest sense, the will is the opposite of an impulse: it requires, and is constituted by, an intervention on oneself whereby the impulse is first separated, made an object, and then is either rejected or accepted, endorsed, and given support and energy by the agent. The dynamically related distancing and appropriation are minimally necessary for the will to be will. For example, a child may experience the empathic desire to share his candies with another child, and may spontaneously act on this desire. Another child, perhaps out of fear or love, may wish to obey his parents' command, and does in fact comply with it. Even though both these actions are intentional, they would not be a result of volitions, if these children did not reflect on their desires, appropriate them, and want to translate them into action.

In Frankfurt's conception, the will is organized hierarchically, according to increasingly encompassing levels of motivation; when, in any situation, different desires are in conflict with each other, second-order desires establish an order of preference, and second-order volitions effectively translate these preferences into action. Volitions may also be in conflict with each other—my will to be loyal to my friend may on occasion be in conflict with my will to be honest in my job. Higher-level volitions bring order in the will and in the way the structured will regulates one's life.

A special case of will structuring, particularly important for moral functioning, is when certain desires are not simply ordered on a quantitative scale of practicality, but are totally rejected, for example, as unworthy and bad, and made external to one's will; they are no longer open to volition, under any circumstances, even as they persist as desires. An even more stringent case is when a person cares so deeply about certain desires and about the special order of one's will that he or she wants to be guided by them also in the future. These commitments may be so decisive that they shape the core of one's identity. At this point it becomes unthinkable to intentionally engage in actions and projects that contradict the essence of one's will and identity.

I should add one note concerning the relations between second-order volitions, the will in general, and the reasons by which volitions and will are justified. This issue is particularly important for the moral will, and has been the object of debate among philosophers. Frankfurt insists that the question about the structuring of the will is different from two other fundamental questions—the epistemological question of what is true and false, and the moral question about what is right and wrong—and consistently avoided making the transition from first-order desires to second- or higher-order volitions depend on judgments about what is true or right. On the other hand, several philosophers (e.g., Watson 1975; Stump 1988, 1996) argued that second-order volitions would not have any special authority unless they were based on an appreciation of values, and value judgments autonomously belonged to the person; in sum, the caring-about by which commitments and identity are established would have no validity unless they were based on a fundamental value system. I think this is right, particularly when it comes to moral commitments and moral character. I also think that the emphasis on value judgments is perfectly compatible with the emphasis on the autonomy of appropriation. Frankfurt probably has been one-sidedly concerned with the autonomy of the will from cognitive determinants. On the other hand, his opponents, in their concern for philosophical justification, may not have sufficiently appreciated the psychological truth of at least two of Frankfurt's points: One is the way appropriations—that's what second-order volitions are—operate to effectively create boundaries in the sense of self, and appropriations do so, whether or not they are informed by valid reasons. The second point concerns the decisiveness, the quasi-finality, of commitments; namely, their power to put an end to the potentially endless inquiry about values, even when a person, in his commitment, remains intellectually open.

Frankfurt's conception may be incomplete and one-sided; several of its details may be problematic. And yet, when considered from a psychological perspective, and particularly from the perspective of moral character, several of its features seem to be very attractive and helpful. In addition to its focus on the will, these include: the understanding of the will as a structure of desires; the hypothesized parallel between the structure of the will and the shaping of a person's sense of responsibility and identity; and the idea that the will, responsibility, and identity are constructed by a person through appropriations. Moreover, Frankfurt's hierarchical design of the will lends itself to articulating developmental hypotheses. Frankfurt is not a psychologist; it was not his intention to analyze the processes by which the will is structured. Moreover his concern is not with morality: as he sees it, the will can be structured equally well by moral commitments and by other kinds of commitments.

In what follows, thinking as a developmental psychologist, I will try to imagine how the moral will and moral character may develop, if they are seen from the perspective of Frankfurt's hierarchical conception. Table 2 sketches a series of hypothetical steps. In constructing them I was aware that the will is one dimension, albeit a central one, in the very complex context of personality; its development cannot occur in isolation from other developmental dimensions. Cognitive development and the development of a motivational system—of the rise and structuring of needs and desires—are particularly important for the will. In particular, the transition from step 3 to step 4 cannot be grasped without hypothesizing certain milestones in these two developmental dimensions. Cognitively, the child constructs categories of actions and experiences. For what concerns the moral domain, labels like "good," "bad," and "nice" are extremely important, even if the corresponding concepts remain undifferentiated and motivationally confusing for some time. In the area of motivation, at some point the child begins to appreciate the intrinsic value—that is, independent of immediate self-interests—of certain aspects of the world: the harmony of music, the beauty of a picture, the sharing involved in playing with others, the goodness of giving, and so on. This experience, no doubt socially and culturally mediated, is the foundation for the understanding of objective values and of their normativity: there are objects that one desires and wants, but there are also objects that are desirable and valuable, and should be desired and wanted also by other people.

The steps presented in table 2 should not be seen as analogous to a Piagetian sequence, where the final stage is universally desirable, the natural goal in the development of the will. Probably the first few steps, leading to the acquisition of stable values, are common to all children: to develop a will and to structure it according to stable desires and values must be seen as a part of normal development. Morality, of course, is necessary to all of us in order to function socially. But there are many other values that people can choose to structure their will and center their sense of self. The other steps of the series, therefore, are meant to reflect the special experience of

TABLE 2. Steps in the Development of the Moral Will

1. The child experiences desires, frequently in conflict with each other; however, he is not capable of distancing himself from them, of choosing among them. His intentional action follows the more immediate or pressing desire. There is no volition.

2. Aided by memories of previous desire satisfactions, the child wishes to replicate one specific experience, to pursue one action rather than another (second-order desire). In making his preferred desire effective, the child begins to form volitions: he appropriates existing desires and brings them under the domain of his agency. His volition is concrete—of this desire as experienced now.

3. The will progresses in extension: it appropriates more and more concrete desires in more and more concrete situations. The child's will is characterized by extreme fragmentation.

4. Categories of actions and desires become objects of volition. The will is somewhat less fragmented. Even so, it does not completely recede from the level of concrete experience, which continues to provide its justification. Moral desires may be present, but would still be local and not well differentiated. Moral volitions are probably rare.

5. Value categories are abstracted from desires of the concretely good, beautiful, etc. In many people, including adults, moral values are accepted alongside other values. Moral volitions are in competition with other volitions, and also with first-order desires. Morality is one among the many self-concepts.

6. Some people want certain specific moral desires to prevail, especially when they are in conflict with rejected desires. Moral desires become genuine virtues and organize aspects of one's life. For other people, several moral virtues are related to each other, regulating larger areas of their lives. These people can be said to have moral character. The emphasis, however, still is in avoiding rejected desires. Therefore, the lives and self-concepts of average adults are still defined by a variety of desires and values. There is no wholeheartedness.

7. In some people, specific virtues or a general moral desire become the basic concerns around which the will is structured. Their "wholehearted commitment" to the moral good produces, at the same time, the core identity, and an undivided will. It becomes unthinkable for them to behave in ways that are not fully moral.

those people who choose morality as the main source of values, and rely on it to completely order their will and to establish the core of their identity.

Moral desire and action in empirical research

What follows is not a review of the literature on moral motivation. It is rather a discussion of a few paradigmatic studies relating moral action and internal moral dispositions in ways that illuminate issues about moral character. My purpose is to relate available research to the previously discussed conception of the moral will and to explore methodological issues in approaching moral character from this particular perspective. The ideal study should provide: (a) information about relatively consistent moral behavior, (b) an assessment of subjects' perception of their behavior in moral terms, and (c) an assessment, independent of behavior, of the participants' general or specific moral concerns and desires. Information about subjects' moral knowledge and understanding may be desirable, but is not necessary, especially if data on (b) are available. Within these parameters, available studies are unfortunately very few.[5] The four discussed here are extremely useful for thinking about moral character, even though some lack the information about the participants' perception of their own behavior. They followed two very different strategies: some studies selected the participants for their clear moral behavior, and then investigated their moral concerns (consequent-to-antecedent strategy); others started by assessing the participants' degree of moral caring, and then related it to moral behavior (antecedent-to-consequent strategy). Each strategy has its advantages and disadvantages: the strength of the former is the clarity and real-life relevance of behavior; the strength of the latter is the ability to form the sample in order to test specific hypotheses.

The first two studies, following the consequent-to-antecedent strategy, were about adults who distinguished themselves for the quality of their actual moral choices: one is the study by Oliner and Oliner (1988) of over four hundred rescuers of Jews in Nazi Europe; the other is Colby and Damon's (1992) study of twenty-three moral exemplars. One advantage of starting with these studies is that they offer us an idea of the *telos* towards which the moral will ideally tends. They also clarify some of the dimensions along which developmental progression should be located.

There is no doubt that the rescuers' behavior is moral, at least from an external viewpoint. Based on lengthy interviews and questionnaires, there is also strong evidence that rescuing actions, in many of the participants, expressed internal moral dispositions: several reported frequent altruistic activities both before and after World War II; more significantly, they related their decisions to values that they had learned from their parents, and also to general ethical attitudes of their own (including openness to other people and tolerance); finally, a good number of them considered morality as being among their deepest and most cherished values. The investigators classified each subject, on the basis of his or her overall interview, according to a tripartite division of central values: 37% focused on the needs of other people and on feeling a direct connection with them ("empathy centered," in the Oliners' terminology); 52% were characterized by a sense of obligation to group norms, for example, family, religious groups, or political organizations ("normocentric"); in 19% of the cases, these norms had been thoroughly internalized, providing the rescuers with a sense of freedom and active independence; finally, 11%, a surprisingly small minority, were classified as "principled," for whom certain values—typically, either universal justice or universal caring—were independently chosen as a result of personal reflection, and seemed to organize their entire life, providing a sense of identity. Even before the rescuing activity, this last group was characterized by a high sense of autonomy, sustained commitment, and remarkable consistency in moral action (the Oliners' conclusions were essentially confirmed by Monroe 1994, and Gross 1994).

The moral attitudes of Colby and Damon's (1992) exemplars, including the less cognitively sophisticated among them, seem to be remarkably similar to the Oliners' principled rescuers. Since the exemplars were selected on the basis of evidence of "sustained commitment to moral ideals" and "dispositions to act in accord with one's moral ideals and principles" (Colby and Damon 1992, 29), the quality of their active engagement is not in question. The lengthy interviews clarify the characteristics of their moral concerns. The investigators did not organize the information according to a coding system, but discussed it according to a number of themes that seemed to characterize the group as a whole. Three are important in the present context: there was a total certainty of moral convictions, not as abstract formulations, but as individually appropriated ideals; these ideals permeated the exemplars' will and determined the core of their identity; actions and commitments, then, felt as necessities about which they had no choice—as many exemplars put it, "I had to do it," "I needed to do it." Exactly the same expressions were used by several of the rescuers in Oliner and Oliner (1988).

One is struck by the difference between these experiences of moral commitment and our stereotypical idea of critical moral decisions as being marked by struggle, inner battles, and hesitations. Here, as it seems, there is no calculation of possible risks or weighing of the consequences, even when the adverse effects of the decisions are noted and regretted. In sum, willpower, like courage, does not seem to have much of a role in these exemplars' everyday moral functioning. Moral desires are so strong and unconflicted, so central in the actors' motivational system, and so identified with their core identities, that moral action follows from a kind of spontaneous necessity (this point is strongly emphasized by Monroe 1994). These are also the characteristics that Frankfurt recognizes in the type of will that is completely structured by those desires about which one cares deeply and with which one identifies: such wholehearted commitment, and such volitional necessity, that acting against one's will is felt to be unthinkable. By comparison with the moral exemplars, many, perhaps the majority, of the rescuers in the Oliners' study seem to be ordinary good people, called by the circumstances to act in extraordinary ways. It is easy to believe that, in normal circumstances, most of these people would have led good but not particularly remarkable lives. The important point for us is that moral character comes in different forms and different degrees of intensity, and is compatible with very different kinds of personality.

The next two studies, Arnold's (1993) and Nunner-Winkler's (1999), focused on younger subjects and raised developmental questions. It would be nice to report that these investigations allow us to trace back in age the moral attitudes that appeared in the study of rescuers and moral exemplars. However, Arnold and Nunner-Winkler followed research strategies and relied on criteria to assess moral motivation that are widely different from those adopted in the studies described earlier of morally committed adults; no direct comparison between the two sets of studies is thus possible. Even so, both studies, conducted with extraordinary care, help us to think developmentally about the vicissitudes of moral desires. Their weak aspect, as in many studies of moral functioning, was the assessment of moral behavior. Arnold relied on teachers' ratings of conventional behaviors; Nunner-Winkler used one or two resistance-to-cheating tasks, and also behavioral ratings from parents and teachers. Neither investigator looked at the ways participants perceived the behaviors on which they had been rated. The focus and the strength of both studies lie in their different criteria and strategies for estimating moral concerns.

Arnold's investigation, covering four adolescent groups between the ages of twelve and eighteen, approached moral motivation as related to the extent to which moral concerns had been integrated in the sense of self. The information was gathered in two steps. First, the participants were asked to select from a list of virtues, moral as well as nonmoral, three virtues that were most central to their sense of self, "without which you would not be you"; and to select one among the three as the most important or crucial. During the following interview the adolescents were asked to explain the meaning of their selections: what it meant for a virtue to be important to the self, why the selected virtues were especially important to him or her. On the basis of this information, the investigator constructed several scales. I will limit my summary to the three that are most useful to grasp the central meaning of the findings. The Moral Identification Scale (from 0 to 5) was based on the number of *moral* virtues that were selected as the crucial one or among the most important to oneself. The Moral Motivation Scale was constructed around the purity of moral motives (by contrast with self-interest or a concern for self-perfection) as justifying the selection of the virtues that are central to oneself: a score of 0 was assigned when no moral motive was mentioned, a score of 3 when only moral motives were mentioned. The Depth of Self Scale (Arnold's label for it is "Conception of Good Self") brings together three themes concerning the selected virtues, *moral as well as nonmoral:* the meaning of their being personally important, the adolescent's active commitment to them, and the emotions that the virtues elicit in the adolescent. Adolescents coded at the lowest level would say, for example, that the chosen virtue is important because they are good at it, that they would make some effort in trying to be a person characterized by the chosen virtue, and that they feel good whenever they act according to the chosen virtue. In sum, here the adolescent identifies with the chosen virtues and constructs self-concepts around them, but he or she understands the nature of the virtues and of the self in essentially behavioral terms. By contrast, adolescents coded at the highest category would speak of the chosen virtues as the core and foundation of the self, as aspects of themselves they cherish and care about and to which they are committed. They say that, in following the chosen virtues they would be true to themselves, to the persons they are. At this level, therefore, Arnold's adolescents speak in the language of Colby and Damon's (1992) exemplars; their wills seem to be constructed around what Frankfurt calls an "identity conferring caring-about."

The findings, in a very simplified summary, were: (a) The Moral Identification and Moral Motivation Scales produced clear individual differences: 20% of the total sample selected only moral virtues, while 16% did not choose any moral virtue as central to the self; in justifying their choices of the central virtues (moral and nonmoral), about 38% of the adolescents relied exclusively on moral motives, but an equal number did not mention any moral motives. (b) These two variables had low correlations with each other and with moral judgment stage (on Kohlberg's interview); neither correlated significantly with age. (c) Moral Identification and Moral Motivation had relatively high correlations with moral behavioral ratings (respectively .46 and .60); together with moral judgment stage, they accounted for approximately 50% of the variance in moral behavior ratings. (d) By contrast, the Depth of Self Scale correlated highly with age (.75) and with moral judgment stage (.69); thus, no adolescent in sixth and eighth grades, 30% of tenth graders, and 40% of twelfth graders were coded in the highest category. (e) The Depth of Self Scale was unrelated to Moral Identification and Moral Motivation, and had a low though significant correlation with moral behavior (.23). This last set of findings should not seem surprising when one remembers that the Depth of Self Scale reflects the degree of integration in personality of the chosen virtues, but the virtues could have been moral or nonmoral. In other words, as Frankfurt suggested, a person's will and identity can be structured according to the values one deeply cares about. The intensity of one's commitment follows the values that one has chosen to structure one's identity, but morality is only one of many possible values.

When we look at this study with our questions about moral character, some points are immediately clear: already by the age of twelve, a minority of adolescents have predispositions to behave morally. Their predispositions are manifested in the simple choice of moral virtues as important to them, a part of their self-concept, and in the justifications of the choices in terms of their concern with justice, altruism, or other moral values. Interestingly, the frequency of adolescents with moral predispositions does not seem to change with age. This study, however, does not tell us whether moral predispositions are relatively permanent, whether they predict consistency in moral behavior, or whether there are age or individual differences in the intensity and the depth of moral commitments (but Hart and Fegley [1995] reported, also among adolescents, a significant relation between the tendency to describe oneself in moral terms and unusual commitment to care for other people). Perhaps we could find the relevant information if we selected the subgroup of adolescents who have a deeper sense of their identities and structure them around their moral values. As Arnold's study shows, this sense of self begins to develop only in middle adolescence, between eighth and tenth grade, and even then is only present in a minority of adolescents. It would be interesting, then, to see how this subgroup relates to moral behavior, but the relevant data were not presented. It could be that the differences from those who identify with moral virtues but have a superficial sense of identity would only appear with different measures of moral behavior, perhaps behavior characterized by consistency, self-sacrifice, or long-term commitment.

The last work I will comment on is Nunner-Winkler's (1999) longitudinal study with children ranging from four to ten years of age. How can one investigate the depth or even the existence of the moral will in five- or six-year-olds? Nunner-Winkler relied on a very sound psychological principle: that emotions reflect whether our needs and desires are being satisfied or frustrated, and therefore are indirect indicators of desires. If a child has moral desires, he will experience negative emotions as a result of his wrongdoing; and if a child is young enough not to be consciously concerned with self-presentation, he will spontaneously attribute positive or negative emotions to other wrongdoers, depending on which of his own desires, moral or nonmoral, he projects on them. Nunner-Winkler, therefore, presented children with four stories involving breaking various moral rules, and asked them to predict which emotions the hypothetical wrongdoer will experience, and also to explain the reasons for their attributions. Moral motivation was inferred by combining these two kinds of information; the number of negative emotion attributions was taken as an indication of the strength of moral desires. This measure did not work well with ten-year-olds, the oldest group in the study, who seemed to filter their attributions through their knowledge of social expectations and of the logic of moral action. With this group the investigator used a different method: interpreting the entire protocols and classifying them according to the moral quality of their concerns, from purely pragmatic and self-interested to exclusively moral.

The findings are complex and can only be presented in the simplest summary: (a) Children between four and seven years of age already have some moral knowledge and understanding; and yet, for the large majority of them, moral motivation is too weak to produce negative emotional attribution or action, at least when moral rules are in conflict with other desires. For these children, the person who breaks moral rules in order to satisfy certain wishes will feel good. These results, as surprising as they might be, were replicated several times, and should be considered a solid finding. (b) On Nunner-Winkler's index, moral motivation increases with age. However, at ten, only about 35% were classified as having a high consistency in moral emotional attribution. (c) There seems to be longitudinal consistency in degree of moral motivation, at least after six years of age: for instance, children who at the age of eight were classified as low, medium, or high in moral motivation, had a probability of (respectively) 0%, 33%, 43% to be classified as high in moral motivation at the age of ten; those who were classified as high at the ages of six and eight had a probability of 57% to be classified as high at ten. (d) The strength of moral motivation (based on the number of moral emotional attributions and on the reasons explaining them) tended to correlate with behavior, both in experimental honesty tasks and in parental and teachers' ratings.

The important, and frequently corroborated, finding of Nunner-Winkler's study is that before the age of six or seven moral desires may be present but are frequently ineffective in the context of other desires, even when the child knows and understands what is right and wrong. Also interesting is the relative consistency of moral motivation starting from middle childhood. It is probably then that moral predispositions are first manifested. However, this study does not answer important questions, particularly from the perspective of moral character. We don't know at what age emotional attributions, as an index of moral desires, is related to the appropriation of moral desires and the structuring of the moral will—whether, for example, they generate effort and perhaps elementary commitments. Therefore we don't know at what point in development the moral will determines consistency in moral behavior and begins to shape moral character. Finally, from this study, we don't know whether consistent moral desires are translated into stable self-concepts, or an elementary structure of identity.

Important questions eventually need to be answered: What produces moral motivation? What factors determine the structuring of a morality based will? What factors determine whether or not morality constitutes the core of a person's identity? Psychology has no answers to these questions. Certain factors—for example, parental examples and values, or religious commitments—seem to be frequently related to moral desires; but, in every case, there are glaring counterexamples. These variables, therefore, seem to play a facilitating, and not an essential role. Probably, as in all instances of the will, the essential ingredients have to do with the perception, based on concrete sensual experiences and on intelligence, of the good of moral actions, and eventually the intellectual grasp of their importance for other people and for the world as a whole. These perceptions are easier to come by and to gain a hold in the person's imagination and will, if one is actually engaged and has real personal experiences with concrete goodness. Later abstractions are necessary, but probably need to be built on this experiential core in order to gain the strength of desire. Perhaps here lies the key for understanding the influence of parents on people's moral motivation.

We need to remember that morality is not the only objective good. There are several objective goods, such as learning and knowledge, or music and art, that have the power of offering visions of transcendence necessary to anchor people's commitments and the structure of the will. Because morality is an objective good, most people can grasp it to the point of wanting it; because there are other objective goods, we can understand why not everybody selects morality to construct his or her will and sense of identity. Why some do but many don't is a difficult question for which there is no answer yet.

A conception

Integrity is on everyone's list of virtues; for some, it constitutes the very essence of character. But this virtue can be understood in widely disparate ways. The conception I follow here goes back to the etymological meaning of wholeness and intactness, a meaning that has the support of many philosophers and is consistent with my overall approach to moral character. In a general sense, I take "integrity" to refer to a person's serious concern for the unity of his or her subjective sense of self, as manifested in consistency with one's chosen commitments. Understood in this sense, then, integrity is not a specifically moral virtue. Whether it is or is not relevant to morality would depend on the concrete commitments around which the sense of self is constructed and on the specific motives for wanting to remain consistent with them. This concept of integrity should be carefully distinguished from other constructs of self-consistency that have a far wider currency in psychology: behavioral and trait consistency; the various kinds of cognitive and logical consistency, including coherence among self-representations; the notion that underlies research on cognitive dissonance; and, finally, the concept of personality integration (Blasi and Oresick 1986). As presented here, integrity is a virtue, that is, always a result of a conscious concern about, and intentional care to avoid, the contradictions between what we say or do and those commitments on which the sense of who we are was constructed.

The psychological basis for integrity lies in the human capacity to construct the sense of self by appropriating one's desires and actions, and then, reflecting on these processes, to relate to and care for not only the objects of one's desires, but also the desiring and acting self. One aspect of caring for one's self is to be concerned about its wholeness and inner consistency. The first step in this process is the construction of the sense of self through appropriation. The appropriations that constitute the subjective self go beyond the immediate, unreflected sense of "mineness" that accompanies every experience of agency in acting and desiring. They also go beyond those appropriations by which desires are taken over by the subject and are transformed into second-order desires and volitions; these, in fact, are still completely oriented to their objects (Blasi 2004).

Soon, however, reflection and affect are also turned to the desiring and willing self. The early development of pride in achievement is a clear example of this process. In Heckhausen's (1984) account, around the age of two-and-a-half to three years a new realization occurs in the context of the child's efforts to master objects and events, and occupies his awareness, namely, that he and his competence effected the changes in the world. The subjective importance of such a realization is manifested in clearly observable expressions of joy and triumph that can only be interpreted as pride; pride, then, according to Heckhausen, becomes the foundation for achievement motivation. In this example and in other similar processes, there are two simultaneous foci of the person's attention, interest, and caring: one is external—the object of one's action and the changes produced in it; the other is internal—one's sense of control and competence, and the pride that derives from it. The child's pride indicates that he appropriated effort and mastery, and made them his own, thus shaping his sense of self and self-definition. The important point is that a person's caring and concern extends from external objects and people to various aspects of the self that derive from his or her relationships with them, including one's desires, the emotions one experiences, beliefs, promises, commitments, and identity. At some point in development one also begins to care about self-consistency and self-inconsistency. Integrity is the conscious, intentional pursuit of this ideal unity.

There are several kinds of self-consistency and inconsistency to which people can pay attention and care about, determining different forms and degrees of integrity. Three are particularly relevant to moral character: the sense of personal responsibility, moral identity, and the concern with self-deception. Here I can only, and briefly, discuss the first two. Responsibility has been studied by psychologists, but not from the perspective of the subjective sense of self and of integrity. Its two most frequent meanings are oriented to social relationships, or external expectations and demands; for instance, as reliable norm compliance and dependability, or as responsiveness to other people's needs in a caring and concerned attitude. As I am using the term here, responsibility refers to a special relation a person has with oneself as having appropriated norms and relations, and the roles and duties deriving from them. When a person's desire of the moral good is extended beyond situational decisions, when he wants to continue to want in the future what is morally good (though not necessarily above everything else) and wants to make it sure that he will, then the person *makes himself responsible* for behaving morally, within the limits of his understanding. To make oneself responsible is to operate on the self and not simply on one's concrete, situation-bound desires and actions; it means to constrain the self and create a kind of permanent necessity for oneself in relation to certain norms and actions. Understood in this way, responsibility is not a concept (even though we have concepts about it) and cannot be explained cognitively. Rather, it is primarily *a desire about oneself* which must be manifested in action. Verbally, responsibility is expressed through the notions of obligation and necessity: I must, I have to. In action, responsibility is expressed through intentional self-control, resistance to temptation, effort, and determination. A different but related aspect of responsibility is accountability, the sense of necessarily owning the actions one performed and the consequences of one's actions. In my view, responsibility is not necessary in order to act morally—for this, moral intentions, even concrete ones, are sufficient. But responsibility seems to be necessary for moral character, as it makes behavioral consistency the object of one's intention and desire.

Like responsibility, identity also is understood in very different ways by social scientists: as social self-categorization, as a more or less organized system of self-concepts, or as particularly salient self-concepts. Not all of these kinds of identity elicit concerns for self-consistency, or the desire for self-consistency may not always be related to the unity and the wholeness of the sense of self. But there is one kind of identity, I think, that is intrinsically related to the highest integrity. This occurs when a person so identifies with his or her commitments, cherished values and ideals, that he or she constructs around them the sense of a central, essential self. This sort of appropriation determines what "really matters" to the person; it establishes such a hierarchy among the person's goals and concerns as to create a sense of subjective unity and lifelong direction, and provides one with a sense of depth and necessity in his being. As Frankfurt (1988) pointed out, under these subjective conditions, behaving in ways that contradict and negate one's central values is no longer felt to be a choice. Compromising one's identity is felt to be unthinkable: it would be experienced as the most serious self-betrayal and as the total loss of one's self or soul. These are expressions that some people use in interviews, when they are asked to imagine what their affective reactions would be in this case of self-betrayal.

In sum, there seem to be at least two forms of integrity related to moral character: the integrity of responsibility and the integrity of identity. They are not incompatible with each other, but present rather different characteristics, and probably are differently related to psychological development. The former does not require an encompassing unity in the sense of self, nor does it touch the core self, when this is present; there may be many responsibilities, perhaps unrelated to each other. Compromising one's responsibility in one area, then, may not produce the sense of a total loss of integrity. The integrity of responsibility, finally, seems to correspond more closely to certain stereotypical ideas of moral character, characterized by struggle, effort, and self-control. By contrast, the integrity of identity touches the intimate self and is therefore indivisible; being built on a structured and unified will, it appears to be more natural and spontaneous. It would be difficult to think of moral character without, minimally, the integrity of responsibility, but the integrity of identity is not necessary either for behaving morally or for possessing a genuine moral character.

Integrity and moral character in empirical research

In relating integrity, in the concept adopted here, to moral character, two sets of questions need to be addressed. One concerns the general psychological characteristics of responsibility and identity: developmental steps and chronology, individual differences and pathologies, and the factors explaining advances, arrests, and malfunctions. The second set of questions would ask why some people, but not others, define their sense of responsibility and identity in moral terms, and how these processes contribute to their intentional striving toward consistency in moral behavior. Unfortunately not much empirical information is available that is relevant to these questions.

Research on the strict obligation aspect of responsibility is particularly meager, probably because responsibility in this sense was thought to be an intrinsic part of moral judgments. By contrast, one can find a great deal of work that is relevant, in various degrees, to the accountability side of responsibility. Most of it concerns the cognitive prerequisites for a sense of responsibility, for instance, the understanding of causality in general and of psychological causality in particular. Some of this work focused on various components of human action: intention, want, decision, effort, ability, reason, interest, motive, and so on. As for accountability proper, interesting studies focused on its negative side, that is, on the various "accounts" and excusing strategies that people use to deny or decrease their responsibility (e.g., Sykes and Matza 1957; Semin and Manstead 1983).

In one study, my collaborators and I worked with samples of first, sixth, and eleventh graders to investigate the development of moral responsibility in its dual aspect of strict obligation and accountability. The data have been only partially analyzed and published (Blasi 1984, 1995). But some conclusions are already clear: First graders understood moral issues and were capable of genuine moral judgments; in most instances, however, their judgments did not generate any kind of moral necessity. Sixth and eleventh graders acknowledged the strict obligation to act according to one's moral understanding; frequently they justified responsibility by relying on different criteria than those used for moral judgments. With age, the criteria for strict obligation became increasingly related to a reflective sense of self. As for accountability, there were clear age shifts in praxeological criteria, based, namely, on a theory of action: first graders, when they did not externalize blame, tended to justify accountability on the basis of physical causation or intentions; sixth and eleventh graders, instead, relied on such internal processes as effort, decision, and self-control; in addition, for many eleventh graders personality traits became both the source and the object of responsibility. In sum, in this age range, there is an increasing sense of ownership, actions becoming more closely related to those processes and characteristics that constitute the subjective self.

All these findings, originating from different studies and different conceptions and methods, do not add up yet to a coherent picture of responsibility; they are like scattered pieces of an ancient mosaic, waiting for the creative insight that reconstitutes the whole. More important, these findings are several steps removed from the issue of moral character. They have to do with understanding and cognitive criteria; only rarely were they related to morality, and practically never were they used to understand the consistency of moral action.

The situation is different for identity. Here too there is no conceptual agreement among social scientists: some understand identity as self-categorizations, or the sum of self-concepts; others, influenced by Erikson, define it as well thought-out commitments to specific life domains, including ideological values; very infrequently is the term taken to refer to the sense of core, or essential, self. Each of these concepts generated a great deal of research. Even so, one cannot say that we understand how the various bodies of data come together in a coherent psychological picture of identity. Perhaps a sensible way of organizing concepts and data is to see them as concentric levels in the sense of self, from the more superficial and fragmented to the most central and structured. The last level, as Frankfurt suggested, would be constituted by long-term commitments to those values and ideals that one deeply cares about.

By contrast with responsibility, there is solid evidence that identity, in practically all of its levels, is related to commitment in moral action. Hart and Fegley (1995) found that a group of middle adolescents, who had been nominated by adults in their community for distinguished and sustained service to needy people or their own families, included moral characteristics in their self-descriptions more frequently than a matched group. As already reported, Arnold (1993) found that those adolescents who selected moral virtues as the most central to their sense of self, and gave moral reasons for why they are important to them, were significantly more likely to be rated by their teachers as high in moral behavior. The most impressive evidence, however, comes from the studies of Oliner and Oliner (1988) and Colby and Damon (1992). According to the latter investigators, a central theme in the interviews with moral exemplars is how moral commitments originate from and imbue their core identity. The same idea was evident in many rescuers interviewed by the Oliners. This is why, as many rescuers and exemplars explained, they felt they had no choice but to do what they had done. Based on similar findings, Monroe (1994) concluded that the rescuers' actions derived from the perception they had of themselves in relation to others: "this perception effectively delineates and sets the domain of choice options perceived as available to an actor, both in an empirical and a moral sense" (219).

ONE LAST CONSIDERATION

I presented a conception of moral character that is articulated on three, mutually related constructs: the moral will, or a will structured around desires for what is morally good; willpower, or the capacity for self-control; and integrity in its various forms. Willpower and integrity are psychological goods, probably necessary to most human functioning, but, in themselves, not specifically moral. The central aspect is the moral will, as it provides moral meanings and motivational drive to the whole of moral character. All three constructs are related to the sense of self, but in different ways: self-control is an agentic self process, having the person as its object; integrity concerns the organized unity in the sense of self; the moral will is the result of appropriations of moral desires, by the self and to the self, leading to the construction of moral identity. Moral understanding does not figure explicitly in this scheme, but is presupposed by it and is required at every step in the growth of the moral self. One cannot formally desire the moral good, unless one has some grasp of morality. Also, it is unlikely that one can appropriate moral desires to form higher-order volitions without understanding, at a certain level of abstraction, the superiority of moral goods over other, also legitimate, goods. The central task of moral understanding, the one that Kohlberg took as the object of his work, is the determination of which issues count as moral. This task, to some extent independent of the constitution of the moral self in moral character, is one source of individual differences in the content of moral character.

This is the general conception. Looking back, from this perspective, at the many years of theoretical and empirical work on moral development, it seems strange that the issues were approached in such a polarized and totalitarian way, and that one could oppose moral understanding, on one side, and virtues and character, on the other. Of course, moral understanding is necessary, even though it is not clear that Kohlberg's account of it is the only possible or even the best one. Of course, moral

understanding alone, in isolation from the rest of personality, is not sufficient to generate moral action. In fact, implicit in this idea, there may be a rather absurd view of
understanding, as actually occurring apart from the person who is its responsible
subject. Understanding always is the understanding of a specific person, one aspect
of a complex psychological organization centered on the agent-subject. But the same
atomization and depersonalization takes place when virtues and character are opposed to moral understanding, or when moral understanding is treated as one of the
many virtues—a position that is rarely explicitly stated, but seems to be frequently implied in the emphasis on character education. It is as if the various virtues—whatever
they are—were self-subsistent entities, and not qualities of a person; as if their being
virtues did not depend on the whole personality in which they are embedded.

The basic problem, common to all rival approaches to moral psychology, is that
we did not succeed in freeing ourselves from the model with which scientific psychology operates. In this model, the task of finding explanations for complex events
is framed in terms of prediction, and is pursued by postulating separately operating
factors and then determining their probabilistic relations with the events in question. Organismic theories, including Piaget's cognitive-structuralism, tried to remedy
the atomism of classical psychology by recognizing that organisms and structures
are primary relative to their elements; however, they too leave no theoretical role for
a subject of responsibility. These models of psychological science are grossly inadequate to approach morality, and also many other human phenomena. Here, explanatory factors are not what medieval scholars called "entities which" act to produce
events, but rather "entities according to which" subjects act to produce events. Explanatory factors, then, are not differentiated from each other by statistical weights,
but in terms of meanings they have for a subject who is morally intent on producing
changes in the world.

NOTES

1. In this chapter, both "virtue" and "vice" are used synonymously with "moral character trait." In addition, unless otherwise specified, the term, "character" refers to moral character.

2. The higher- vs. lower-order distinction overlaps, to some extent, with the distinction between substantive and instrumental or managerial character traits (Pincoff 1986).
Some philosophers argue that instrumental virtues, in themselves, are morally neutral; others, instead, would resist calling certain traits (e.g., courage or patience) "virtues," if they
could be used to achieve immoral goals. Whether this is the case for all higher-order virtues
depends on which traits one includes under this label. Here, the conceptual distinction be-

tween higher- and lower-order virtues is based on a different criterion, namely, the degree of generality and specificity, and not on their being substantive or instrumental.

3. A number of questions about moral character have to do with the use of language and fall outside the purview of psychology and thus this essay: e.g., in order for us to properly speak of moral character, how many and which specific virtues are minimally needed? How dominant should they be relative to other tendencies? Other questions, though psychological, also will not be addressed here, largely because empirical information is lacking: e.g., are there structural psychological bonds among the virtues? To what extent do people feel the need to be consistent across their several virtues? Are there individual differences in people's orientation to specific virtues? How can this sort of specialization be explained?

4. Debates surrounding Frankfurt's conception are centered around several issues. The most important are: whether his hierarchical model necessarily involves infinite regression, how the freedom of the will should be conceived, and whether judgments play any important role in structuring the will (cf., e.g., Stump 1988, 1996; Watson 1975).

5. One can find clear evidence of moral character in a good number of publications, focusing on people who distinguished themselves in a variety of behaviors: conscientious objectors, whistle-blowers, antiwar activists, human rights activists, poverty and social justice activists, soldiers who refused to obey commands that they judged to be immoral, etc. Unfortunately in these reports data were not gathered, or were not presented, in ways that would satisfy psychology's standards.

REFERENCES

Arnold, M. L. 1993. The place of morality in the adolescent self. PhD diss., Harvard University.

Aveling, F. 1926. The psychology of conation and volition. *British Journal of Psychology* 26:339–53.

Baumeister, R. F., and T. F. Heatherton. 1996. Self-regulation failure: An overview. *Psychological Inquiry* 7:1–15.

Blasi, A. 1980. Bridging moral cognition and moral action: A critical review of the literature. *Psychological Bulletin* 88:1–45.

———. 1984. Autonomie im Gehorsam: Die Entwicklung des Distanzierungsvermögens im sozialisierten Handeln [Autonomy in obedience: The development of distancing in socialized action]. In *Soziale Interaktion und soziales Verstehen*, ed. W. Edelstein and J. Habermas, 300–347. Frankfurt am Main: Suhrkamp.

———. 1995. Moral understanding and the moral personality: The process of moral integration. In *Moral Development: An Introduction*, ed. W. M. Kurtines and J. L. Gewirtz, 229–53. Boston: Allyn & Bacon.

———. 2000. Was sollte als moralisches Verhalten gelten? Das Wesen der 'frühen Moral' in der kindliche Entwicklung [What should count as moral behavior? The nature of 'early morality' in children's development]. In *Moral im sozialen Kontext*, ed. W. Edelstein and G. Nunner-Winkler, 116–45. Frankfurt am Main: Suhrkamp.

————. 2004. Neither personality nor cognition: An alternative approach to the nature of the self. In *Changing Conceptions of Psychological Life*, ed. M. Chandler, C. Lalonde, and C. Lightfoot, 3–25. Mahwah, NJ: Lawrence Erlbaum Associates.

Blasi, A., and R. J. Oresick. 1986. Emotions and cognitions in self-inconsistency. In *Thought and Emotion: Developmental Perspectives*, ed. D. J. Bearison and H. Ziml es, 147–65. Hillsdale, NJ: Lawrence Erlbaum Associates.

Block, J. H., and J. Block. 1980. The role of ego-control and ego-resilience in the organization of behavior. In *Development of Cognition, Affect, and Social Relations*, ed. W. A. Collins. The Minnesota Symposia on Child Psychology, vol. 13, 30–101. Hillsdale, NJ: Lawrence Erlbaum Associates.

Brock, T. C., and C. Del Giudice. 1963. Stealing and temporal orientation. *Journal of Abnormal and Social Psychology* 66:91–94.

Burton, R. V. 1963. Generality of honesty reconsidered. *Psychological Review* 70:481–99.

Burton, R. V. 1976. Honesty and dishonesty. In *Moral Development and Behavior*, ed. T. Lickona, 84–107. New York: Holt, Rinehart, and Winston.

Carver, C. S., and M. F. Scheier. 1981. *Attention and Self-regulation: A Control Theory Approach to Human Behavior.* New York: Springer.

Colby, A., and W. Damon. 1992. *Some Do Care: Contemporary Lives of Moral Commitment.* New York: Free Press.

Collini, S. 1985. The idea of character in Victorian political thought. *Transactions of the Royal Historical Society* 35:29–50.

Frankfurt, H. 1988. *The Importance of What We Care About.* New York: Cambridge University Press.

Grim, P. F., L. Kohlberg, and S. L. White. 1968. Some relationships between conscience and attentional processes. *Journal of Personality and Social Psychology* 8:239–52.

Gross, M. 1994. Jewish rescue in Holland and France during the Second World War: Moral cognition and collective action. *Social Forces* 73:463–96.

Hart, D., and S. Fegley. 1995. Prosocial behavior and caring in adolescence: Relations to self-understanding and social judgment. *Child Development* 66:1346–59.

Harter, S. 1983. Developmental perspectives on the self-system. In *Socialization, Personality, and Social Development*, ed. M. Hetherington. Handbook of Child Psychology, vol. 4, 275–385. New York: John Wiley and Sons.

Hartshorne, H., and M. A. May. 1928. *Studies in the Nature of Character*, vol. 1, *Studies in Deceit.* New York: Macmillan.

Hartshorne, H., M. A. May, and J. B. Maller. 1929. *Studies in the Nature of Character*, vol. 2, *Studies in Self-control.* New York: Macmillan.

Hartshorne, H., M. A. May, and F. K. Shuttleworth. 1930. *Studies in the Nature of Character*, vol. 3, *Studies in the Organization of Character.* New York: Macmillan.

Heckhausen, H. 1984. Emergent achievement behavior: Some early developments. In *The Development of Achievement Motivation*, ed. J. Nicholls, 1–32. Greenwich, CT: JAI Press.

———. 1991. *Motivation and Action*, 2nd ed. New York: Springer.

Hilkey, J. 1997. *Character is Capital*. Chapel Hill: University of North Carolina Press.

Jones, V. 1954. Character development in children: An objective approach. In *Manual of Child Psychology*, 2nd ed., ed. L. Carmichael, 781–832. New York: John Wiley and Sons.

Kochanska, G. 1991. Socialization and temperament in the development of guilt and conscience. *Child Development* 62:1379–92.

———. 1993. Toward a synthesis of parental socialization and child temperament in early development of conscience. *Child Development* 64: 325–47.

———. 1995. Children's temperament, mothers' discipline, and security of attachment: Multiple pathways to emerging internalization. *Child Development* 66:597–615.

Kuhl, J., and J. Beckmann. 1994. *Volition and Personality: Action Versus State Orientation*. Seattle, WA: Hogrefe.

Maller, J. B. 1934. General and specific factors in character. *Journal of Social Psychology* 5:97–102.

May, M. A., and H. Hartshorne. 1925. Objective methods of measuring character. *Pedagogical Seminary and Journal of Genetic Psychology* 32.

McClellan, B. E. 1999. *Moral Education in America: Schools and the Shaping of Character from Colonial Times to the Present*. New York: Teachers College.

Mischel, W. 1968. *Personality and Assessment*. New York: John Wiley and Sons.

———. 1981. Metacognition and the rules of delay. In *Social Cognitive Development: Frontiers and Possible Futures*, ed. J. H. Flavell and L. Ross, 240–71. New York: Cambridge University Press.

———. 1996. From good intentions to willpower. In *The Psychology of Action: Linking Cognition and Motivation to Behavior*, ed. P. M. Gollwitzer and J. A. Bargh, 197–218. New York: Guilford Press.

Mischel, W., Y. Shoda, and M. L. Rodriguez. 1989. Delay of gratification in children. *Science* 244:933–38.

Monroe, K. R. 1994. "But what else can I do?" Choice, identity and a cognitive-perceptual theory of ethical political behavior. *Political Psychology* 15:201–26.

Nelsen, E. A., A. E. Grinder, and M. L. Mutterer. 1969. Sources of variance in behavioral measures of honesty in temptation situations: Methodological analyses. *Developmental Psychology* 1:265–79.

Nunner-Winkler, G. 1999. Development of moral understanding and moral motivation. In *Individual Development from 3 to 12*, ed. F. E. Weinert and W. Schneider, 252–90. Cambridge: Cambridge University Press.

Oliner, S. P., and P. M. Oliner. 1988. *The Altruistic Personality: Rescuers of Jews in Nazi Europe*. New York: Free Press.

Pincoff, E. 1986. *Quandaries and Virtues*. Lawrence: University Press of Kansas.

Power, C., A. Higgins, and L. Kohlberg. 1989. The habit of the common life: Building character through democratic community schools. In *Moral Development and Character Education: A Dialogue,* ed. L. Nucci, 125–43. Berkeley, CA: McCutchan.

Ramsey, H. 1997. *Beyond Virtue: Integrity and Morality.* New York: St. Martin's Press.

Roback, A. A. 1928. *The Psychology of Character.* New York: Harcourt, Brace.

Sears, R. R., L. Rau, and R. Alpert. 1965. *Identification and Child Rearing.* Stanford, CA: Stanford University Press.

Semin, G. R., and A. S. R. Manstead. 1983. *The Accountability of Conduct: A Social Psychological Analysis.* New York: Academic Press.

Smout, T. C., ed. 1992. *Victorian Values: A Joint Symposium of the Royal Society of Edinburgh and the British Academy, December 1990.* Oxford: Oxford University Press.

Stump, E. 1988. Sanctification, hardening of the heart, and Frankfurt's concept of free will. *Journal of Philosophy* 85:395–420.

———. 1996. Persons: Identification and freedom. *Philosophical Topics* 24:183–214.

Sykes, G. M., and F. Matza. 1957. Techniques of neutralization: A theory of delinquency. *American Sociological Review* 22:664–70.

Vaughn, B. E., C. B. Kopp, and J. B. Krakow. 1984. The emergence and consolidation of self-control from eighteen to thirty months of age: Normative trends and individual differences. *Child Development* 55:990–1004.

Walker, L. J., and R. C. Pitts. 1998. Naturalistic conceptions of moral maturity. *Developmental Psychology* 34:403–19.

Watson, G. 1975. Free agency. *Journal of Philosophy* 72:205–20.

Webb, E. 1915. *Character and Intelligence.* British Journal of Psychology, Monograph Supplement, 1, no. 3. Cambridge: Cambridge University Press.

Wright, D. 1971. *The Psychology of Moral Behavior.* Harmondsworth: Penguin Books.

Wright, G. H. von. 1963. *The Varieties of Goodness.* London: Routledge and Kegan.

Zelazo, P. D., and S. Jacques. 1996. Children's rule use: Representation, reflection, and cognitive control. In *Annals of Child Development,* vol. 12, ed. R. Vasta, 119–76. London: Jessica Kingsley Publishers.

FOUR

Character, Responsibility, and the Moral Self

Ann Higgins-D'Alessandro and F. Clark Power

CHARACTER IS AN OLD-FASHIONED TERM IN MORAL PSYCHOLOGY. IT appeared frequently in the psychological and educational literature until the early 1930s. Then the term rapidly fell out of use and was replaced by the value-neutral term personality (Power, Higgins, and Kohlberg 1989a). Leming (1997) notes that although the term character was no longer used by psychologists and educational researchers, character education practices, such as grades for conduct, continued throughout the thirties and into the present day. In the 1980s, however, an explicit appeal to character made a comeback primarily through traditionalist educators, such as Ryan (1996) and Wynne (1989), who sought an alternative to Kohlberg's moral developmental approach. The term character education was also embraced by those sympathetic with Kohlberg (e.g., Berkowitz 2002; Lickona 1997). Among psychologists, however, there has been no corresponding move to reappropriate the term character. Why not? The simplest answer is that those educators who resurrected the term were focused on educational practice rather than research. Believing there was an urgent need for character education in the schools, they devoted themselves to establishing programs rather than exploring character as a theoretical or empirical construct.

We find the lack of attention given to the term character to be unfortunate for two reasons. First, apart from the fine applied research undertaken by the Center for Developmental Studies (e.g., Solomon, Watson, and Battistich, 2002), the outcomes of most character education programs have not been rigorously specified or assessed (see Leming 1997). One of us (Higgins) is presently working on an assessment of the Community of Caring program for character education and school change. To date, the evaluation of this program has focused not on its influence on character but on its effect on attitudes toward inclusion of intellectually challenged students. Community of Caring students and teachers demonstrated significantly more positive attitudes than those in schools that had just voluntarily entered the program (Higgins-D'Alessandro, Markman, and Barr 2003). Second, we believe that the psychological study of character is, indeed, worth exploring and long overdue. Rather than use character in a vague and eclectic sense to represent anything from prosocial behavior to perseverance, we propose an approach to character, centered on the notion of responsibility that appropriates Aristotle's theory, that offers psychologists a window into the developing self, and that can inform educational practice.

In this chapter, after a discussion of Aristotle's *Nicomachean Ethics,* we describe how our thinking about character evolved from our reflections on the just-community approach, which we implemented and studied together. We conclude by discussing our current explorations of three constructs that we find central to the notion of character: responsibility, self-understanding, and moral self-worth. In our view, the study of character development should at the very least focus on the development of the self as a morally responsible agent. We believe that such an approach would be both a faithful extrapolation from Aristotle's most fundamental insights into character and consistent with the primary concerns of most character educators today. We hope that at the very least, this chapter will demonstrate the centrality of the notion of responsibility for the moral life and open up avenues of psychological research on how moral responsibility relates to self-understanding and to self-esteem.

ARISTOTLE

Most character educators today appeal to Aristotle's account of character and virtue, even though most do not appropriate his theory in any systematic way. Traditionalists (e.g., Ryan 1996; Wynne 1989) make the most frequent use of Aristotle in an attempt to distinguish their educational approach from Kohlberg's moral-discussion and just-community approaches, which emphasize moral reasoning and decision making. They typically refer to the following passage in Aristotle's (1985) *Nicomachean Ethics:* "Virtue then is of two sorts, virtue of thought and virtue of character. Virtue of thought arises and grows mostly out of teaching, and hence needs experience and time. Virtue of character results from habit" (1103a14–18). Traditionalists criticized Kohlberg for overestimating the role of cognition in children's moral development and for failing to recognize children's need for moral formation. In contrast to Kohlberg's advocacy of moral discussions and participative democracy, they called for the assertion of adult authority and discipline. Implicitly and sometimes explicitly the traditionalists advocated many of the practices endorsed by social learning theory, such as modeling and the use of rewards for desirable behavior.

We argued some time ago in a chapter coauthored with Kohlberg (Power, Higgins, and Kohlberg 1989a) that traditionalists misread Aristotle. Far from believing that virtue does not demand cognition, Aristotle claimed that the practice of virtue demands mature reasoning and judgment. In fact, Aristotle believed that *phronesis*, often translated as practical wisdom, is the intellectual virtue that guides decision making about the good life. Aristotle's account of habituation should be understood in the context of the development of *phronesis*. He believed that children were incapable of making wise ethical decisions on their own and thus required adult formation. Aristotle described a sequence of phases in the acquisition of virtue beginning with an ethic of fear of punishment, progressing to an ethic of shame and conformity, and culminating in an ethic of practical wisdom. Aristotle's sequence bears some semblance to Kohlberg's scheme of moral levels: the pre-conventional, conventional, and post-conventional.

In our view, Aristotle's sketchy comments on habituation should not be understood as contradicting Kohlberg's cognitive developmental theory of moral judgment. We generally support the position taken by Peters (1963) who argued that habituation should be understood as referring to the first of a two-step process of education: "[Children] can and must enter the palace of reason through the courtyard of habit and tradition" (54–5). Peters pointed out that by habit he did not mean automatic behaviors acquired exclusively through imitation, repetition, and reinforcement. Rather, habits can involve complex activities in which deliberation and adaptability are required. The acquisition of athletic and musical skills require such habits informed by reason. Elsewhere in this volume, Lapsley and Narvaez (chapters 1 and 6) suggest some of the psychological constructs that we believe underlie the formation of moral habits acquired in the first step of moral education. Lapsley and Narvaez are making an important contribution to the study of character by pointing out how much of the moral life takes place without reflection or explicit judgment. On the other hand, we maintain that it is crucial for the psychological study of morality to link such subconscious processes with those that are conscious, rational, and deliberative. As Aristotle noted long ago, one of the distinguishing features of virtue is that the agent is in the proper frame of mind when she or he performs the actions (Aristotle 1985, 1105a30). Aristotle elaborated that, among other characteristics, this implied consciousness, intent, and decision.

THE JUST-COMMUNITY APPROACH AND HABITUATION

In our view, the ideal approach to character development in the later childhood and adolescent years should engage the critical and deliberative moral capacities as well as foster prereflective and even preconceptual dispositions supportive of the moral life. Such an ideal approach would involve a carefully structured environment that would promote moral experience on two levels. At the first level, the environment would provide routine patterns of action that are conducive to the awareness, thoughts, and feelings that comprise moral functioning. Such patterns would minimally bring individuals into regular contact around meaningful social events and focus on the common life. Such patterns would also encourage individuals to take into account each other's perspectives and to consider the common good. Finally, such patterns would provide regular experience in democratic decision making. At the second level, the environment would provide opportunities for moral reflection and deliberation by presenting problems and challenges to individuals' assumptions about right and wrong, good and bad.

Although the just-community approach to moral education as we envisioned it with Kohlberg (Power, Higgins, and Kohlberg 1989b) is often understood as emphasizing only the second reflective and deliberative level of moral experience, it provides considerable experience at the first level. At the heart of the approach are weekly community meetings in which the rules and policies governing the discipline and common life of the students and faculty are discussed and decided upon. The community meetings are preceded by small group meetings designed to prepare students and faculty for the large community meeting and fairness or disciplinary committee meetings arranged to deal with infractions of school rules and policies.

The just communities are organized as schools-within-schools or sometimes as programs within the large school. The common denominator of all just communities is that students take at least two classes together in addition to the meetings described above. Direct participatory democracy is crucial for decision making in just communities because this process assures that all students have regular legislative experience and frequent opportunities for democratic leadership.

The goal of the democratic process is to build a group that is both fair and communal. By communal we mean that the members care for each other and the group as a whole. Community, as we use the term, is demonstrated through building shared norms of trust, participation, and collective responsibility. In this sense, a community is to be differentiated from associations that serve purely instrumental purposes. Schools, of course, may be understood as serving the instrumental purposes of fostering student learning and preparing students to take their place in society. The just-community approach recognizes these ends of school but adds to them a concern for the group for its own sake. This focus on community provides a significant opportunity for students to develop sensitivity to others and an interest in their welfare as well as the welfare of the group as a whole. It also encourages students to consider the effects that their actions have on others and on the group.

THE JUST-COMMUNITY APPROACH AND THE DEVELOPMENT OF RESPONSIBILITY

In assessing the just-community approach, we were interested in assessing student behavior as well as student moral judgment. As hypothesized, we found that the just-community approach did bring about changes in student behavior, changes that we attributed to the moral atmosphere of the school and, in particular, to the development of shared norms (expectations) addressing such problems as cheating, stealing, and clique exclusivity. The finding that changes in the moral atmosphere of the school had a salutary effect on behavior is not in itself too surprising, nor is it especially significant from the perspective of moral development theory that assumes development occurs through social interactions. The Hartshorne and May (Hartshorne and May 1928; Hartshorne, May, and Maller 1929; Hartshorne, May, and Shuttleworth 1930) studies of character showed that context has an important influence on some of the behavior that we associate with character, such as honesty and service. On the other hand, changing behavior, while desirable, is hardly a notable educational achievement unless it is anchored within the self or what we would call character.

Our analysis of meeting transcripts and student interviews indicates that membership in a just-community school fosters a sense of student responsibility that appears lacking in conventional high schools (Higgins, 1987; Power, Higgins, and Kohlberg, 1989b). The following examples illustrate the role that the moral atmsophere plays in influencing students' apprehension of their responsibility to act in ways that they and we would regard as moral. Referring to a widely-known case in which a radio was stolen from a locker in their high school, several student leaders in a conventional, large high school told one of us that they would not report the thief or even attempt to persuade him to return it because:

> You can't put pressure on students [to do] . . . that.
> The school is responsible [not us]; we are teenagers.
> The teachers are grown up. . . . They are supposed to control the students in the school. (Power 1985, 235)

It is understandable that these students would feel uncomfortable in dealing with the enforcement of school rules, but it is surprising that some students went further and excused the thief: "If someone is dumb enough to bring something like that into school, they deserve to get it stolen. . . . If somebody is going to steal then more power to them." All of the students said that stealing was wrong, but none of them felt obliged to intervene in any way to see that the rule was upheld (Power 1985, 235).

In contrast, students in the just-community programs told us that they expected their peers to follow the rules and would be willing in the case of stealing to express their disapproval and even report the thief because "we are a community" and "we are supposed to trust and care for each other" (Power, Higgins, and Kohlberg 1989b, 113). Students spoke about having a sense of "ownership" of their school and feeling that they had to work with the teachers to uphold school rules and expectations. The experience of having to make and enforce rules as a group impressed upon most of the students a sense that the welfare of their school depended upon them. They could not credibly claim that control rested solely with the adults in the school.

The question remains, however, whether the students in the just-community programs felt responsible outside of the bounds of their community. Did the just-community approach promote a sense of responsibility for moral obligations generally, or did it lead to an in-group/out-group, split moral consciousness? The evidence is fragmentary and incomplete. The just-community approach is designed to focus on obligations to those within the community and the community itself. This can lead at times to an apparent indifference to those outside the community. For example, in one of the just-community schools, a student was caught breaking into a house in the neighborhood of the school. A teacher asked whether such an infraction ought to be considered an offense within the community. Many students responded that their rule only pertained to in-school behavior, "what you do on your own time is up to you." Note that the students did not argue that stealing was permissible or that students who steal should not be held accountable. They simply believed that the norms of their community should not be extended to include out-of-school behavior. Although they may not have felt a sense of responsibility as community members for not stealing from strangers, many students expressed a sense of personal responsibility not to steal. There were, of course, some students who felt little sense of responsibility for those to whom they were unrelated, and a few of those, new to the school, admitted to stealing from family members.

Our research on the just-community programs indicated that the students who stole and who readily excused stealing reasoned at moral judgment Stage 2 (Power, Higgins, and Kohlberg 1989b). They did not, however, attempt to justify stealing from a Stage Two perspective; rather they excused it with what Gibbs (1991) has called "self-serving cognitive distortions" (98). The most common distortion that we found was blaming the victim for carelessness or provocative behavior (e.g., bringing something of value to school, not locking one's locker, etc.). Why blame the victim? Gibbs (1991) argues that individuals delayed at Stage 2 can develop an egocentric bias that interferes with their empathy and role-taking. Such individuals respond not only to their own immediate desires but seem to assume that others do too. For example, Jill argued in a community meeting addressing a theft of money, "she [the victim] gives you a chance to steal it; if you had it in your arms, wouldn't you be thinking about stealing it?" (Power, Higgins, and Kohlberg 1989b, 113–14). Jill, as we later found out, was describing her own state of mind when she took money from a fellow student's open pocketbook who had gone to the blackboard. It seems she assumed that anyone in her shoes would at least be strongly tempted to take the money. Jill was clearly reasoning at a pre-conventional level of moral judgment—an action can be justified by a strong need or desire. She did not acknowledge that stealing is a violation of an accepted social norm, let alone of the trust expected of a community member. More significant, in our view, than Jill's Stage 2 moral reasoning about stealing is her diminished sense of agency (Blasi, 1990). Jill's stealing seems almost completely out of her control. Giving Jill the opportunity to steal without the likelihood of detection was the irresponsible deed—not her stealing.

Jill stole the money after being in the just-community school only two months. She was surprised by the reactions of some of her peers, who strongly objected not only to her excusing the thief but also to her refusal to support a resolution that everyone in the community chip in to restitute the victim if no one confessed to the stealing. Jill's fellow students called her to a greater sense of responsibility not only for her own actions but for other members of the community who did not think stealing was such a "big deal." The motion for collective restitution passed, putting Jill in the uncomfortable position of seeing the whole Cluster School community make compensation for her act. This is an illustration of how the experience of democratic decision making within the context of a group sharing the ideal of becoming a community can at least provoke questions about one's agency and responsibility.

We suggested with Jill's example that the practice of collective responsibility can lead to a heightened sense of personal responsibility because one becomes responsible not only for one's own behavior but for the behavior of others (Power, Higgins, and Kohlberg 1989b). The practice of collective responsibility may, however, lead in the opposite direction to a diminished sense of personal responsibility. For example, two years following Jill's stealing, three floating docks were discovered to be missing after an overnight Cluster School retreat. The camp owner retrieved two of the docks and charged Cluster $350 for the missing dock. A strongly supported motion called for following what had become a traditional practice of collective responsibility and distribute the financial burden equally across the community. Those who had untied the docks did not confess, and, even if they had, the cost of restitution would have been too high for them to pay. Although there was a general willingness among community members to help out, some faculty and students expressed the concern that simply agreeing to collective restitution would constitute a "coverup" and undermine the acknowledgment of personal responsibility. These students and faculty argued that the community ought to distinguish between those directly responsible for the loss of the docks and the community as a whole. They advanced a proposal that those directly responsible come forward and assume a greater financial burden than the rest. The proposal passed, and after the meeting twelve students confessed that they had untied the docks.

This incident illustrates that the practice of collective restitution can become a convenient way of dodging personal responsibility. On the other hand, when appealed to within the context of an active democracy, the practice can provoke reflection on the relationship between collective and personal responsibility. The community resolved the loss of the docks in a way that retained a sense of collective responsibility, while recognizing the personal responsibility of those involved. In fact, easing the financial burden by agreeing to make some collective restitution made owning up to the loss of the docks much easier.

The best evidence that the just-community approach had an effect on students' development of a sense of personal responsibility comes from Grady (1994), who focused on civic engagement. Grady interviewed a sample of just-community students in Cluster (the first just-community school) ten years after their graduation and compared them with a sample of graduates in the same year from the same city high school. Grady found that more Cluster graduates were interested in politics and national affairs, had voted in local elections, expressed knowledgeable concern for local government decisions, and had worked with others to solve neighborhood community problems. She also found that 63% of Cluster graduates in contrast with 5% of their peers found that their experience in school helped them to feel more effective in socio-political matters. For example a Cluster School graduate said, "I challenged myself to take control of situations in that program and that helped me in life. Cluster was a microcosm of the world I later entered, so I was prepared for real-life situations. I truly learned to become a responsible leader" (146).

Clearly further research is needed to identify the extent to which the just-community approach has helped students to develop a sense of responsibility for behavior that extended beyond their time in school. We believe that simply the context of a close-knit community heightens an awareness of and encourages reflection upon individual responsibility for others. Although such communities may well limit individuals' moral perspective and range of moral responsibility, they also offer the richest opportunities for development in these areas. Young people (ages ten to eighteen) are at a point in their lives when the most interesting and challenging issues and tensions they face are learning to live in more formally structured groups and institutions than the family and peer group. Creating schools as communities supports the goals and efforts to educate and prepare each student while at the same time encouraging each student to develop a sense of responsibility toward themselves, others, and the groups in which they live. Thus, in our view, the question is not whether schools should become communities but what kind of communities schools should become.

The question of what kind of communities schools should become leads us back to a consideration of the aim of character education. Character education presupposes that there is a character that can be educated in the first place—that what we call moral behavior is a function of enduring personal qualities and individual choice and not simply or primarily a function of situation-specific influences. In our view, Kohlberg's cognitive developmental approach to moral development with its structural stage approach provided a starting point for a theory of character development. Kohlberg focused solely on moral judgment and not on the qualities of the moral agent. Our study of the just-community approach has convinced us of the importance of looking beyond moral judgment to moral responsibility and ultimately to that of the moral self. To what extent are we warranted in describing the study of responsibility and ultimately the moral self as the study of character? To respond to this question, we return to Aristotle's understanding of character and to Kohlberg's thinking about the self in relation to moral judgment.

BACK TO ARISTOTLE: CHARACTER AND THE MORAL SELF

The word character is used to translate two Greek words: *ethos,* which ties character to virtue, and *poios,* which means the sort of person one is (see the glossary in Aristotle 1985). In some passages Aristotle seems to imply that the sort of person one is causes one to act in certain ways and not others. Perhaps Aristotle simply meant to refer to the consistency bred through the processes of habituation and tutored judgment. It may be, however, that the person of character is motivated to act consistently out of a consciousness of the sort of person she is. This self-consciousness of the virtuous person should be distinguished from a sensitivity to shame. Aristotle acknowledges that shame motivates persons to do the right thing; but Aristotle associates shame with what a cognitive developmentalist would call a conventional moral motivation, a motivation based on how others would regard the self. Aristotle views the person of character as not only caring about leading the virtuous life but also being the sort of person that leads a virtuous life.

There is no direct way to derive a psychological construct from Aristotle's references to what is translated as character. We can, however, find warrant in Aristotle for using the term character as a way of describing the role the self may play in explaining consistencies between reasoning and behavior across the moral domain. One may object from the outset that there are no such consistencies. Indeed, the Hartshorne and May (1928) research appeared to demonstrate just that. On the other hand, Kohlberg, ourselves, and other cognitive developmentalists have managed to find a fair amount of consistency in the meaning that individuals make of their moral choices both antecedently and consequently. Whether one finds consistency or inconsistency depends to a large extent on where one looks. If one merely observes external behavior, one will be inclined to conclude that behavior depends on the context. If one tries to approach behavior through the intentions of the agent, one will find a surprising consistency in the understanding and values that inform particular actions. This is not to say that individuals' intentions are always discernable or fully conscious. Nor is it to say that individuals consistently act as they intend or as they believe they should. Most people will readily confess that they do not always act as they think they should act. Yet most individuals are quick to point out that their sense of what they should do is important.

In discussing the Hartshorne and May research, Kohlberg and Candee (1984) noted, "empirical studies relating the two [moral judgment and conduct] begin to build a theory of character, rather than such a theory being a starting point for research" (509). Kohlberg's research on the relationship between judgment and action had convinced him that, although moral reasoning played a primary role in influencing moral behavior, other factors were also at work. We can classify these other factors as either primarily psychological or primarily sociological. The psychological factors that Kohlberg identified included responsibility judgments and ego controls, such as attention and IQ. The sociological factors include influence of aspects of the moral culture, such as shared norms and values. Kohlberg did not offer a theory of character, but he pointed out in his philosophical and psychological writings that a phenomenological approach needed to be taken, that behavior can never be studied in isolation from the agent (Kohlberg 1981, 1984). Heinz's stealing a drug out of love for his dying wife is different from an adolescent's stealing a car to go on a joyride with his friends. We have to build a theory of character from the inside by trying to understand how individuals make moral judgments and what they intend in their behavior. In this respect, we support the commitment to what Kohlberg called the phenomenological approach to moral psychology (Kohlberg 1984; Colby and Kohlberg 1987).

For Kohlberg, the consistency that is the hallmark of character comes from the individual's stage of moral reasoning. A moral stage is a cognitive structure or organized pattern of thinking that gives particular moral concepts their meaning. Within a moral stage approach, particular virtues, such as justice, honesty, and love, can only be understood as parts of a general framework of moral reasoning. Each stage may be understood as having its own underlying "logic," which Kohlberg described in terms of socio-moral perspective and justice operations (Colby and Kohlberg, 1987). Following Blasi (1993), we suggest that the subjective, agentic self is a second source of consistency, which is in some sense more fundamental for character than the consistency of moral reasoning.

THE RESPONSIBLE SELF

In his chapter in this volume and elsewhere (e.g., Blasi 1980, 1984, 1993) Blasi maintains that responsibility judgments are rooted in one's sense of self. Individuals must act in a certain way or refrain from acting in a certain way because of who they believe that they are. Blasi argues that individuals are motivated by a desire to maintain consistency between who they believe that they are and how they act. For example, individuals who believe that they are honest will be motivated to act honestly, even at some personal sacrifice, and will be troubled if they act dishonestly. Acting dishonestly in Blasi's view is more than a matter of not following one's moral judgment. It is more than an irrational act or an act of inconsistent moral logic; it is an act against one's self. If one arrives at a moral judgment that acting honestly in a particular situation is the right thing to do not only for the self but for any agent in a similar situation (following the logic of universalization), then violating one's moral judgment should cause some distress. There may, however, be competing nonmoral rewards for violating one's moral judgment. Telling a lie may win one a coveted promotion and thus lead to desired goods for oneself and one's family. The decision to act rests on the importance one gives to one's moral desires and moral identity.

Moral judgments thus appear to go further than rational assessments of the right and wrong of particular actions. Moral judgments seem to extend not simply to actions but to the agent. Individuals desire to be persons who act morally. In this sense, moral judgments involve the self. Failing to act morally may diminish one's sense of self and of self-worth, while acting morally may increase or at least maintain one's sense of self and of self-worth.

Blasi's (1984) concept of moral responsibility had a decisive influence on Kohlberg's understanding of the judgment-action relationship and, as we indicated, on our conceptualization and assessment of the effects of the just-community approach to moral action. Like Blasi, Kohlberg distinguished responsibility judgments from deontic judgments. Deontic judgments concern whether an act is right or wrong. Responsibility judgments concern whether one should act on what one judges to be right. For example, Kohlberg (1984) regarded the Milgram experiments on obedience-to-authority as tapping primarily into individuals' responsibility judgments. When interviewed afterward, the participants in Milgram's experiment thought that administering shocks as a way of teaching was wrong. Their dilemma was whether they should take responsibility for acting on that deontic judgment by refusing to administer the shocks. As we noted earlier, although Kohlberg came to see the importance of responsibility judgments in the moral life, he stopped short of discussing the implications of responsibility judgments for the self. Kohlberg appeared to regard responsibility judgments as the application of moral reasoning to the question of whether one should act in a particular situation. The higher one's stage of moral reasoning, the less likely one would find acceptable excuses to violate one's deontic judgment (Kohlberg and Candee 1984).

Kohlberg was not opposed to Blasi's linking responsibility to the self. In our view, Kohlberg would probably have welcomed our study of the moral self or character.

Kohlberg and Higgins (1984) had, after all, in "Continuities and Discontinuities in Childhood and Adult Development Revisited—Again," acknowledged that development to the post-conventional stages of moral reasoning appeared to involve adult experiences of "sustained responsibility for the welfare of others and . . . irreversible moral choice (492). Kohlberg and Higgins described these as "personal experiences," related to the development of the self. This was Kohlberg's last and our first step towards an approach to the moral self that directly engaged Blasi's theory.

The starting point for our approach of character is the self as a responsible moral agent. Responsibility, as we noted above, ties moral judgment to moral action through the moral self. One of us (Higgins-D'Alessandro 2002) has been exploring responsibility through open-ended interviews about everyday moral living. One of the simplest yet most startling outcomes of this study to date is that the problems that most individuals describe as moral are not whether a particular action is right or wrong but how to act responsibly in a situation with significant consequences for the self and often for others.

In our work together with Kohlberg in the 1970s and early 1980s, we saw responsibility as linked to the moral judgment-action process and deeply influenced by cultural factors. In our more recent work, we have begun to think of responsibility in relationship to the developing moral self or character. Although we have continued to think of responsibility as a way of bridging the gap between judgment and action, we have turned our attention to responsibility as a way of accounting for personal reliability or what the philosopher Walker (1998) calls integrity.

When we speak of a person as having character, we typically mean that one can count on that person, even in very difficult circumstances. In the context of sports, individuals and teams typically display character by not folding under the most intense pressure. The etymological definition of character as a permanent mark or stamp seems to express this sense of steadfastness and dependability. Yet Walker (1998) points out that reliability should not be equated with immovability or rigidity. The reliable person is a responsive person. The reliable person adapts to new challenges and addresses past wrongs and wounds.

Far too little attention in the moral psychology literature has been given to retrospective judgments of responsibility beyond Helkama's (1979) study relating retrospective as well as prospective judgments of responsibility to moral stage. What is needed today is a study of reparative responsibility parallel to Enright's (1994) study of forgiveness. Reparative responsibility addresses the issue of how one should respond to the hurt that occurred as a result of one's action or inaction. How should one respond to one's past? Underlying this question is an even deeper one: how does one understand oneself as an agent, whose past reveals as well as conceals one's conscious control over one's actions.

We are only beginning to understand all that is involved in judgments of responsibility, which may well be at the center of most moral reflection. Certainly this is what Higgins-D'Allesandro's research suggests. In a study of moral responsibility, she asked participants to describe moral dilemmas or moral problems in their recent pasts in which they found it difficult to live up to their ideals. Her sample consisted of males and females from ages ten to eighty. The participants presented a rich variety of incidents from which Higgins-D'Alessandro extracted distinctive facets of responsibility, which are summarized in table 1. It is clear from table 1 that responsibility is a complex process, involving perception, feeling, and understanding. Responsibility can be experienced antecedent to one's action and consequent to it, as in the case of making reparation. Responsibility sometimes involves moral deliberation about right and wrong and sometimes not. More often responsibility judgments involve balancing personal concerns and responding to the needs and expectations of others. People's stories reflect a certain messiness about the moral life. Choices are complicated, outcomes are often uncertain, strong feelings are almost always present. Resolution of responsibility struggles leads to such positive feelings as happiness, satisfaction, and self-acceptance, or negative feelings, such as guilt, shame, and uncertainty. Resolution also leads in most cases to an acceptance of responsibility or ownership for the negative as well as positive consequences of one's action. Those individuals who blamed others for the negative consequences of their actions were the youngest participants in the study (two preteens and a teen).

All of the responsibility judgments in the Higgins-D'Alessandro study evoke a tension between an ideal and real sense of self. Understanding individuals' sense of responsibility requires an understanding of individuals' sense of themselves and the place that they accord to moral values. The kinds of dilemmas that individuals find really difficult are difficult precisely because they reflect on the kind of person one desires to become.

RESPONSIBILITY AND MORAL SELF-WORTH

Higgins-D'Alessandro suggests that there is a relationship between individuals' efforts to resolve issues of moral responsibility and their self-evaluation. As noted in table 1, individuals' actions not only express something about who they are but also contribute to the self that they are becoming. Being responsible for one's behavior

TABLE 1. Facets of Responsibility

1. Being concerned about the effects of one's action.

2. Having feelings, positive and negative, such as desire/avoidance, hope/fear, like/ dislike, love/hate, that can influence one's action and lead to or deter from intended consequences.

3. Having the ability to foresee to some extent the consequences, positive and negative, intended and not intended of one's actions.

4. Recognizing that one's actions are one's own, even when those actions may be influenced by events and forces beyond one's control.

5. Believing that one's decision and action express something about who one is to oneself and to others.

6. Holding oneself reasonably accountable for the foreseen and unforeseen consequences of one's decision and action.

7. Responding to negative consequences with actions to repair relationships and commitments and to re-establish trust and reliability.

8. Having self-evaluative feelings, such as of well-being or happiness, self-acceptance, remorse, guilt, or shame, after determining the effects of one's actions.

9. Becoming one's self through one's actions.

thus entails being responsible for one's self. The resolutions of the moral struggles that Higgins's respondents identified resulted in a positive or negative evaluation of the self. The respondents did not simply assess their actions but themselves as actors. Their resulting feelings depended to a large part on the extent to which they lived up to their expectations for themselves.

One of us (Power) has attempted to explore the process of moral self-evaluation more thoroughly within the framework of the self-esteem construct. In the psychological literature, self-esteem has been the principal way in which the self has been studied; in fact, self-esteem has often been referred to as self-concept. At issue in the study of self-esteem is the role of moral self-evaluation. Both popular and scholarly accounts of self-esteem have tended to equate high self-esteem with high moral functioning, such that self-esteem has been viewed as both a cause and effect of acting morally. Many self-esteem theorists advocate enhancing self-esteem as the primary goal of moral or character education (e.g., Mecca, Smelser, and Vasconcellos 1989). From this perspective, high self-esteem has a causal or at least an enabling role in promoting morally responsible behavior. Low self-esteem, on the other hand, can lead to deviant behavior, as, for example, is predicted by the "frustration-aggression" hypothesis of Dollard et al. (1939) or by Kaplan's (1975, 1980) "esteem-enhancement" model.

Although self-esteem may conceivably be enhanced through antisocial behavior, most theorists think of self-esteem as based (at least in part) on a moral foundation. For example, Schwalbe and Stables (1991) define self-esteem as "a positive affective response to the self deriving from beliefs that one is competent and moral" (159). Coopersmith (1967) and Harter (1988a) identify "moral self-approval" or "virtue" as a basic dimension for evaluating self-esteem (the others are power, competence, and social acceptance). The inclusion of moral self-approval or integrity as a dimension of self-esteem has not, however, led to any systematic exploration of how moral self-approval comes about or how moral self-approval relates to these other dimensions.

The approach taken by Power and his colleagues looks at the appraisal of moral self-worth as a function of the discrepancy between the ideal and the real self and conversely as a function of the congruence between the real and the dreaded self (Power and Khmelkov 1997). This is a common method for understanding judgments of self-esteem. It had its origins in James's (1985) definition of self-esteem as a function of successes over pretensions, and its use continued in the recent research of Harter (1988b) and Strauman and Higgins (1987). Although we may think of judgments of self-worth in the moral domain as similar to judgments of self-worth in other domains, for example in achievement contexts, such as work, school, or sports, the research undertaken by Power and his colleagues indicates that the moral domain is distinctive in at least three important respects. First, pretensions or aspirations in the moral domain are not susceptible to adjustment or to what Harter (1988a) calls "discounting" as are those in other domains. As Kant (1988) noted long ago, moral duties bind categorically; we are not free to disregard those that we fail to live up to. Second, all of us regularly fall short of living up to moral ideals of beneficence, such as helping others and eradicating injustice. One can, of course, attempt to have "realistic" expectations for service to others based on a "realistic" assessment of what one can contribute, but establishing such expectations is difficult given a sober estimation of the needs of others. Honest moral self-evaluation is more likely to lead to humility than to satisfaction or pride. Third, judgments of moral self-worth tend to be preemptive; they tend to take precedence over judgments of worth in other areas. We say "tend to" because moral concerns may not be central to one's self-definition (Arnold 1993) or to one's ideal self (Power and Khmelkov 1997).

Within the construct of character that we have been developing, however, incorporating moral concerns into one's ideal self is necessary if not sufficient. Character depends upon not only having moral ideals but giving moral ideals a priority among one's other aspirations. Character, as we have noted in our discussion of responsibility, also depends upon a living out of one's moral ideals. One may live out one's moral ideals without always living up to them. By that we mean simply that one's moral ideals can provide a direction for one's life but that there will always be a gap between the real and the ideal. Striving to be a moral person inevitably leads to deep humility, but humility is a virtue as long as it is not self-destructive or debilitating.

CONCLUSION

Our work with just-community schools and our research on moral responsibility, the moral self, and moral self-worth suggest that there is, indeed, a place for the study of character in character education. We do not claim, however, that the approach that we have taken to character is complete. In his chapter written for this volume, Blasi suggests how character may be understood in relation to the will as desire, and in their chapter Bredemeier and Shields link character to achievement and to moral fortitude. These are important, theoretically grounded contributions to a more comprehensive research-based approach to character. We welcome such efforts at a time when there is such overwhelming support for character education.

REFERENCES

Aristotle. 1985. *Nicomachean Ethics.* Trans. T. Irwin. Indianapolis, IN: Hackett.
Arnold, M. L. 1993. The place of morality in the adolescent self. PhD diss., Harvard University.
Berkowitz, M. W. 2002. The science of character education. In *Bringing in a New Era in Character Education,* ed. W. Damon, 43–63. Stanford, CA: Hoover Institution Press.
Blasi, A. 1980. Bridging moral cognition and moral action: A critical review of the literature. *Psychological Bulletin* 88:1–45.

————. 1984. Moral identity: Its role in moral functioning. In *Morality, Moral Behavior, and Moral Development*, ed. W. Kurtines and J. Gewirtz, 128–39. New York: John Wiley and Sons.

————. 1990. How should psychologists define morality? or, The negative side effects of philosophy's influence on psychology. In *The Moral Domain: Essays on the Ongoing Discussion between Philosophy and the Social Sciences*, ed. T. Wren, 38–70. Cambridge, MA: MIT Press

————. 1993. The development of identity: Some implications for moral functioning. In *The Moral Self*, ed. G. G. Noam and T. E. Wren, 99–122. Cambridge, MA: MIT Press.

Colby, A., and L. Kohlberg. 1987. *The Measurement of Moral Judgment*, vol. 1, *Theoretical Foundations and Research Validation*. New York: Cambridge University Press.

Coopersmith, S. 1967. *The Antecedents of Self-esteem*. San Francisco: W. H. Freeman.

Dollard, J., L. Doob, N. Miller, O. Mowrer, and R. Sears. 1939. *Frustration and Aggression*. New Haven, CT: Yale University Press.

Enright, R. E., et al. 1994. Piaget on the moral development of forgiveness: Identity or reciprocity? *Human Development* 37:63–80.

Gibbs, J. C. 1991. Sociomoral developmental delay and cognitive distortion: Implications for the treatment of anti-social youth. In *Handbook of Moral Behavior and Development*, vol. 3, *Application*, ed. W. M. Kurtines and J. L. Gewirtz , 95–110. Hillsdale, NJ: Lawrence Erlbaum Associates.

Grady, E. A. 1994. After Cluster School: A study of the impact in adulthood of a moral education intervention project. PhD diss., Harvard University.

Harter, S. 1988a. The construction and conservation of the self: James and Cooley revisited. In *Self, Ego, and Identity: Integrative Approaches*, ed. D. K. Lapsley and F. C. Power, 43–70. New York: Springer-Verlag.

————. 1988b. Manual for the self-perception profile for adolescents. Unpublished manual, University of Denver.

Hartshorne, H., and M. A. May. 1928. *Studies in the Nature of Character*, vol. 1, *Studies in Deceit*. New York: Macmillan.

Hartshorne, H., M. A. May, and J. B. Maller. 1929. *Studies in the Nature of Character*, vol. 2, *Studies in Self-control*. New York: Macmillan.

Hartshorne, H., M. A. May, and F. K. Shuttleworth. 1930. *Studies in the Nature of Character*, vol. 3, *Studies in the Organization of Character*. New York: Macmillan.

Helkama., K. 1979. *The Development of the Attribution of Responsibility: A Critical Survey of Empirical Research and a Theoretical Outline*. Research Reports of the Department of Social Psychology, 3. University of Helsinki.

Higgins, A. 1987. The idea of conscience in high school students: Development of judgments of responsibility. In *Conscience: An Interdisciplinary View*, ed. G. Zecha and P. Weingartner, 117–33. Salzburg, Austria: D. Reidel.

Higgins-D'Alessandro, A. 2002. Moralizing our selves and taking responsibility: Personality or character. Paper presented at the annual meeting of the Association for Moral Education, Northwestern University, November.

Higgins-D'Alessandro, A., L. Markman, and T. Barr. 2003. Report on teachers' views of social inclusion of students with intellectual disabilities. Evaluation report to the Community of Caring organization, Washington, October.

James, W. 1985. *Psychology: The Briefer Course.* Notre Dame, IN: University of Notre Dame Press. (Orig. pub. 1892.)

Kant, I. 1988. *Fundamental Principles of the Metaphysics of Morals.* Trans. T. K. Abbott. Buffalo, NY: Prometheus Books. (orig. pub. 1785.)

Kaplan, H. B. 1975. *Self Attitudes and Deviant Behavior.* Pacific Palisades, CA: Goodyear.

———. 1980. *Deviant Behavior in Defense of Self.* New York: Academic Press.

Kohlberg, L. 1981. *The Philosophy of Moral Development.* Essays on Moral Development, vol. 1, San Francisco: Harper & Row.

———. 1984. *The Psychology of Moral Development.* Essays on Moral Development, vol. 2. San Francisco: Harper & Row.

Kohlberg, L., and D. Candee. 1984. The relationship of moral judgment to moral action. In *The Psychology of Moral Development,* L. Kohlberg, 498–581. San Francisco: Harper & Row.

Kohlberg, L., and A. Higgins. 1984. Continuities and discontinuities in childhood and adult development revisited—again. In *The Psychology of Moral Development,* L. Kohlberg, 426–497. San Francisco: Harper & Row.

Leming, J. S. 1997. Research and practice in character education: A historical perspective. In *The Construction of Children's Character,* ed. A. Molnar. Ninety-sixth yearbook of the National Society for the Study of Education, Part 2, 31–44. Chicago: University of Chicago Press.

Lickona, T. 1997. Educating for character: A contemporary approach. In *The Construction of Children's Character,* ed. A. Molnar. Ninety-sixth yearbook of the National Society for the Study of Education, Part 2, 45–62. Chicago: University of Chicago Press.

Mecca, A. M., N. J. Smelser, and J. Vasconcellos. 1989. *The Social Importance of Self-esteem.* Berkeley: University of California Press.

Peters, R. S. 1963. Reason and habit: The paradox of moral education. In *Moral Education in a Changing Society,* ed. W. R. Niblett, 46–65. London: Faber.

Power, F. C. 1985. Democratic moral education in a large high school: A case study. In *Moral Education: Theory and Application,* ed. M. Berkowitz and F. Oser, 219–40. Hillsdale, NJ: Lawrence Erlbaum Associates.

Power, F. C., A. Higgins, and L. Kohlberg. 1989a. The habit of the common life: Building character through just community schools. In *Moral Development and Character Education: A Dialogue,* ed. L. Nucci, 125–44. Berkeley, CA: McCutchan.

———. 1989b. *Lawrence Kohlberg's Approach to Moral Education.* New York: Columbia University Press.

Power, F. C., and V. T. Khmelkov. 1997. The development of the moral self: Implications for moral education. *International Journal of Educational Psychology* 27 (7): 539–51.

Ryan, K. 1996. Character education in the United States: A status report. *Journal for a Just and Caring Education* 2 (1): 75–84.

Schwalbe, M. L., and C. L. Staples. 1991. Gender differences in sources of self-esteem. *Social Psychology Quarterly* 54 (2): 158–68.

Solomon, D., M. S. Watson, and V. A. Battistich. 2001. Teaching and schooling effects on moral/prosocial development. In *Handbook of Research on Teaching,* 4th ed., ed. V. Richardson, 566–603. Washington, DC: American Educational Research Association.

Strauman, T. J., and T. E. Higgins. 1987. Automatic activation of self-discrepancies and emotional syndromes: When cognitive structures influence affect. *Journal of Personality and Social Psychology* 53 (6): 1004–14.

Walker, M. U. 1998. *Moral Understandings: A Feminist Study in Ethics.* New York: Routledge.

Wynne, E. 1989. Transmitting traditional values in contemporary schools. In *Moral Development and Character Education: A Dialogue,* ed. L. Nucci, 19–36. Berkeley, CA: McCutchan.

FIVE

Can Sports Build Character?

David Light Shields and Brenda Light Bredemeier

WE'VE ALL HEARD THE CLICHÉ: SPORTS BUILD CHARACTER. BUT IS IT TRUE? Scientific answers to the question of whether sports build character are unlikely ever to be conclusive. Character itself is an elusive construct, sport experiences are widely varied, and in any given sport experience, there are a myriad of potentially conflicting influences. While the question cannot be answered when asked in such general terms, it does lend itself to empirical investigation when addressed through the lens of more specific questions. In this chapter, we address a number of questions about the relationship between sports experience and character development both empirically and conceptually.

The word *character* comes from the Greek meaning "distinctive mark." As we use the term, character has a moral center. It refers both to the content of a person's moral convictions and to the psychological competencies, orientations, and attributes that mediate between those convictions and how they are lived out in action. Moreover, we understand character to be a group phenomenon as well as an individual one. Drawing from Durkheim (1961) and the later work of Kohlberg and his colleagues (see Power, Higgins, and Kohlberg 1989), we posit that groups develop collective norms that give them a "distinctive mark" and influence the moral thinking and behavior of members of the group. Group character and individual character are, no doubt, reciprocally related, with each influencing the other.

For the purposes of this chapter, we will limit our empirical review of the sports literature to the relationship between sports involvement and two aspects of individual moral character: the *development* of moral reasoning and the *form* of moral reasoning used in sports. Thus, in our review of the empirical research, we reword the question of whether sports build character to two related questions: Is sports participation related to moral reasoning development? Do people use similar patterns of moral reasoning in sports as they do in other domains? The rationale for limiting the empirical review to these two questions is as much practical as theoretical. These are questions that have received significant empirical attention.

In the conceptual section of the chapter, we discuss two related issues that will help to broaden our focus. The first concerns an achievement ethic. We suggest that an Aristotelian perspective on virtue can be useful in suggesting how current theories of achievement motivation can shed light on dynamics of moral reasoning in sport contexts. Finally, we close the chapter with a discussion of how sports can be made more conducive to character development. Here, we introduce the idea of promoting sport teams as *communities of character.*

SPORTS AND MORALITY: AN EMPIRICAL REVIEW

In this section of the chapter, we review the literature on the relationship between sports involvement and moral reasoning. By way of preview, we suggest that the relationship between sports participation and moral reasoning development is an ambiguous one, but that when differences between athletes and nonathletes are found, the results do not favor a positive role for sports in character education. With regard to the second question, we suggest that sports tend to elicit a pattern of moral reasoning that is different from the one used in most other contexts.

Sports and Moral Reasoning Development

Sports are socially rich environments that provide participants with many opportunities to interact with others in ways that have moral significance. There are ample opportunities to nurture and practice capacities for role taking, empathy, conflict resolution, and various subskills related to moral judgment. It is plausible, then, that active involvement in sports might provide the kind of cognitive and social stimuli needed to promote moral reasoning development. On the other hand, some would point to the heteronomous way that most sport teams are run and the all too frequent instances of flagrant cheating and aggression to suggest that, rather than promote moral development, sports might actually impede moral growth.

Most of the research that has been done on sports and moral development has utilized one or another theory in the structural developmental tradition associated with the pioneering work of Piaget and Kohlberg (see, especially, Haan 1978, 1983, 1991; Haan, Aerts, and Cooper 1985; Kohlberg 1981, 1984; Piaget 1965; Rest 1979). There are important theoretical differences among these approaches, but they share in common the view that children undergo regular age-related changes in the underlying structure of their moral reasoning, and that with age and appropriate experience comes increasing moral reasoning competence. Progression toward moral reasoning maturity is typically described in terms of a hierarchical sequence of stages, levels, or phases.

For those who look to sports to provide a positive stimulus to moral growth, the research has not been encouraging. Utilizing Kohlberg's interview technique with sixty-five male Division I intercollegiate basketball players, Hall (1986) found that her sample scored lower on moral judgment than reported college norms. Similarly, Bredemeier and Shields (1984b), using Rest's Defining Issues Test, found that their sample of twenty-four male and twenty-two female intercollegiate basketball players scored lower than reported norms of college students. Both of these findings were reported in studies that had other primary research goals, and the negative relationship between sports participation and moral judgment maturity were based on comparing the experimental samples to results reported by others.

In the first study to compare athletes and nonathletes directly on moral reasoning maturity, Bredemeier and Shields (1986c) utilized Haan's interactional model of morality (Haan, Aerts, and Cooper 1985; Haan 1977, 1983, 1991) to assess the moral reasoning of thirty male and female intercollegiate basketball players and ten nonathletes. They found that the athletes had significantly less mature moral reasoning than their peers. However, a follow-up study that added twenty swimmers to the sample concluded that there were no statistically significant differences in moral reasoning development between the swimmers and the nonathletes (Bredemeier and Shields 1986c). In sum, the basketball players, but not the swimmers, scored lower on moral reasoning than nonathlete peers. Since athletes from only two sports were assessed, it was unclear whether the observed differences were due to factors internal to some types of sports (e.g., team sports vs. individual sports, contact sports vs. noncontact sports) or factors extrinsic to the actual sport experience (for example, the study did not control for grade point average).

Similar results were obtained by Stevenson (1998), who employed a measure of cognitive moral reasoning developed specifically for his study of 213 Division I student-athletes and 202 general student peers. Tapping a broader cross-section of sports, he found that the team sport athletes, both male and female, had significantly lower moral judgment scores than did either the nonathletes or the individual sport athletes. Similarly, Priest, Krause, and Beach (1999), in a longitudinal study of 631 U.S. Military Academy cadets, reported a negative impact of sports participation, especially in intercollegiate team sports, on moral judgment. Their study used the Hahm-Beller Values Choice Inventory in the Sports Milieu (HBVCISM) (Hahm, Beller, and Stoll 1989), an instrument that reportedly correlates at .82 with Rest's Defining Issues Test.

Overall, the results from these studies suggest that there is a negative correlation between participation in some sports at the intercollegiate level, especially team sports, and moral reasoning maturity. However, none of these studies controlled for the fact that recruited athletes, on average, enter college with lower academic test scores (Shulman and Bowen 2001). The longitudinal methodology employed by Priest, Krause, and Beach (1999) provides the best evidence of a potential negative effect of sports involvement, but the measure employed in that study has not undergone adequate peer review (see Bredemeier and Shields 1998).

Results are mixed at the high school level. Beller and Stoll (1995) used the HBVCISM in a study of 1,330 male and female high school students, finding that the nonathletes scored significantly higher than the team athletes. However, in the Bredemeier and Shields (1986c) study, mentioned above, no difference was found between high school athletes and nonathletes. Rulmyr (1996) administered the Defining Issues Test to 540 students in southern Arizona high schools and also found no differences between the athletes and nonathletes. Until the validity and reliability of the HBVCISM is further assessed, the Beller and Stoll (1995) results should be treated with caution.

Finally, in a study of children in the fourth through seventh grades, it was found that boys who participated in high contact sports and girls who participated in medium contact sports were significantly less mature in their distributive justice reasoning than children who had participated in other sports or had not participated in any organized sport program (Bredemeier, Weiss, Shields, and Cooper 1986). Level of physical contact may be an important variable because of the type of attributions elicited. Young athletes in relatively high contact sports may believe that opponents are intentionally seeking to inflict pain or harm, even when they are not. Children may have a difficult time distinguishing between aggression and nonaggressive but physically forceful play. This, in turn, may impede the development of conceptions of fairness and just distribution of goods and rewards. That girls in medium contact sports paralleled boys in high contact sports may simply reflect the fact that girls do not have access to high contact sports, and, therefore, may make similar attributions in the highest contact sports allowed them.

Taken together, the results from these studies suggest that it is important not to lump all sport participants together. Though inconsistencies may relate to different methodologies and tools of assessment (cf. Bredemeier and Shields 1998), it is also true that not all sport experiences share similar moral qualities. Not only do the rule structures of the various sports promote different types of social interaction, each sport tends to have its own subculture and implicit moral norms, and each individual sport team develops its own unique moral microculture. Methodologically, it is also important to emphasize that all of the studies reported here, with the exception of the Priest, Krause, and Beach (1999) investigation, were cross-sectional in design, and, therefore, no cause-effect relationships can be inferred. In those cases where athletes were found to be less mature in their moral reasoning, it may be that they were differentially attracted to those sports or, alternately, were selected to participate because of some attribute that itself correlates with less mature moral reasoning (e.g., aggressiveness).

The potential impact of sports on moral reasoning development and/or its differential appeal to individuals with preexisting differences, is far from inconsequential. Within sports, moral reasoning development level has been shown to relate to such important moral variables as aggression (Bredemeier 1985, 1994; Bredemeier, Weiss, Shields, and Cooper 1986, 1987; Bredemeier and Shields 1984a, 1986a; Stephens 2000; Stephens and Bredemeier 1996), sportspersonship (Horrocks 1979), and beliefs about fair play (Stephens, Bredemeier, and Shields 1997).

Sports and Situational Moral Reasoning

The research reported above focused on the relationship between sports involvement and participants' stage or level of moral reasoning. Another line of research relevant to the sports involvement/moral reasoning relationship focuses on how people think about, process, or organize moral situations in sports. Do they do so in the same way, through the same reasoning structures, as they do in other contexts?

Structural developmental theorists have traditionally held that a person's moral reasoning level will remain fairly constant across different types of contents and situations (e.g., Colby and Kohlberg 1987; cf. Krebs et al. 1991). Stages are thought to reflect structured wholes or integrated cognitive systems. While the content of a person's moral thinking may shift from one situation to another, the underlying pattern of reasoning has been said to be relatively constant. This premise of structural consistency across situations, in fact, is central to a stage model of moral development (Kohlberg 1981).

While consistency in moral stage usage across situations is expected, a few highly irregular situations have been shown to significantly alter a person's level of moral reasoning. Research conducted in prisons (Kohlberg, Hickey, and Scharf 1972), for example, has demonstrated that inmates use lower stages of moral reasoning in response to prison dilemmas than when they attempt to resolve standard hypothetical dilemmas. To explain this divergence from theoretical expectations, Kohlberg hypothesized that when a group's collective norms reflect a low stage of moral reasoning the constraining "moral atmosphere" may inhibit more advanced moral functioning, even among those individuals capable of higher stage thought (see Power, Higgins, and Kohlberg 1989). Elsewhere, we (Bredemeier and Shields 1985, 1986b; Shields and Bredemeier 1984, 1995) have hypothesized that sports are among those contexts where moral reasoning is dissimilar to the pattern of reasoning typically employed. This hypothesis was generated in light of two complementary sets of observations, one theoretical, the other empirical.

The theoretical observation draws from a social science tradition that posits that play, games, and sports are often seen by participants and observers alike as "set aside" or "set apart" from everyday life (e.g., Bateson 1955; Firth 1973; Giffin 1982; Handelman 1977; Huizinga 1955; Schmitz 1976). Sports are set apart from everyday life spatially, through clearly marked boundaries, and temporally, by designated playing periods replete with "time outs." A variety of symbols—such as whistles, buzzers, flags, uniforms, and special rituals and ceremonies—are used to create and reinforce the "world within a world" character of sports. The separate world of sports is governed by artificial rules and roles, and sport activities are directed toward goals with no intrinsic meaning or value. Handelman (1977) suggests that entry into this separated realm requires "a radical transformation in cognition and perception" (186). Similarly, Schmitz (1976) has suggested that entry into play involves participants in a world with new forms of space, time, and behavior, "delivering its own values in and for itself" (26). Given this literature, it seemed reasonable to hypothesize that moral reasoning within sports would depart from moral reasoning in everyday life.

The empirical observation comes from several of our studies mentioned earlier. In multiple studies, we used moral interviews that included both standard "life" dilemmas and a second set of "sport" dilemmas. When we analyzed moral reasoning maturity scores, we found that the "life" scores were significantly higher than the "sport" scores (Bredemeier and Shields 1984a). This finding was quite robust, holding for athletes and nonathletes, swimmers and basketball players, college students and high school students, males and females.

Similar analyses were conducted with 110 girls and boys in grades four through seven (Bredemeier 1995). It was found that sixth and seventh graders' "sport" reasoning was significantly lower than their "life" reasoning, and that this life-sport reasoning divergence was significantly greater than that for the younger children. The children below grade six did not demonstrate context-specific reasoning patterns. Selman (1980) suggests that it is roughly during the sixth and seventh grades that children develop the capacity to take the generalized perspective of a third party which may be a prerequisite skill to adopting a context-specific reasoning pattern. It was also the case that the younger children were predominantly preconventional in their everyday life moral reasoning, leaving little room for a drop in moral reasoning level in response to sport dilemmas.

Game Reasoning

Based on these findings, we proposed a theory of "game reasoning" (Bredemeier and Shields 1985, 1986a, 1986b; Shields and Bredemeier 1984, 1995). The theory holds that the context of sport elicits a temporary adaptation in moral reasoning such that egocentrism, typically the hallmark of immature morality, becomes a valued and acceptable principle for organizing the moral exchange. In terms of moral reasoning, we hypothesized that sports offer contexts for a "legitimated regression" (Bredemeier and Shields 1986b; Shields and Bredemeier 1984) to a form of moral reasoning that is similar to less mature moral reasoning. It is important to emphasize, however, that the term *regression* is not meant literally. Individuals in sports do not lose touch with their everyday moral capacities, and the egocentric reasoning that flourishes in sports is not identical to the preconventional reasoning of young children. It is playful egocentrism more than genuine egocentrism. This point needs further elaboration.

Sports, in our view, allow for the temporary suspension of the typical moral obligation to equally consider the immediate interests of all parties, in favor of a more lenient, egocentric style of moral engagement. Most of the time, this egocentric reasoning reflects an implicit consensual agreement among the participants, and there is, thus, an informal social contract allowing for it. Game reasoning can serve as an enjoyable and nonserious moral deviation that is consensually embraced.

There may be several reasons why such a moral adaptation is culturally sanctioned and viewed as appropriate within the limits of sports. First, competition is premised on each party or team seeking self gain. There is little room in sports for equally considering the desires, goals, and needs of opponents. While competition demands a degree of egocentrism, the unique protective structures of sports function to legitimate it. The carefully planned and rigorously enforced rules protect participants from many of the negative consequences that would typically ensue from egocentric morality. Furthermore, the continual presence of officials and coaches allows for the temporary and partial transference of moral responsibility.

The theory of game reasoning adds one more level of complexity. The theory holds that sports may encourage two types of moral "regression." Thus far, we have been addressing a legitimated regression in which an egocentric morality is embraced. But, of course, sports are not devoid of moral concerns. Players remain people and moral responsibility cannot be completely set aside. To remain legitimate, one can only play at egocentrism. When the play character of game reasoning is lost, sports can (and too often do) deteriorate into breeding grounds of aggression, cheating, and other moral defaults. Thus, game reasoning can take the form of an "illegitimate regression."

The criterion of internal consistency can be used to distinguish legitimate from illegitimate forms of game reasoning (Bredemeier and Shields 1986b). Two examples can serve to illustrate. First, since game reasoning is itself legitimated by the set aside character of sports, game reasoning ceases to be legitimate if used to justify actions with game-transcending implications. For example, the use of egocentric morality to justify injuring another person is no more legitimate in sports than elsewhere. Second, game reasoning ceases to be legitimate if it is used to justify actions that undercut the contest structure of sports. Thus, game cheating represents an illegitimate regression. Again, to use the egocentric quality of game reasoning to justify cheating behavior is self-contradictory since cheating undermines the conditions that allow for game reasoning in the first place.

The elaboration and validation of the theory of game reasoning awaits future research, and at this point we can only speculate about potential implications for the theory. If sports do elicit their own special form of moral reasoning, it may help to shed light on some of the earlier findings. Consider, for example, the finding that for some college athletes participation in sports is associated with lower levels of moral reasoning maturity. Perhaps for some college athletes game reasoning may begin to lose its set aside character and have undue influence on moral reasoning beyond the

bounds of sports. Several factors may account for why this is more true for participants in some sports than in others. Participation in elite sports, particularly those for
which professional opportunities are available, often include external rewards contingent on performance. The infusion of "daily life" rewards (e.g., money or educational opportunity) into sport experiences may encourage a blurring of the distinction between sports and everyday life. Additionally, some sports allow for a high level
of physical contact which is inherently ambiguous with regard to moral significance.
Was the low block accidental or a cheap shot? Was the opponent trying to hurt me or
just play hard? High levels of investment in these sports may habituate a moral attribution pattern that is difficult to leave behind once the game is over.

SPORTS AND CHARACTER: A CONCEPTUAL FRAMEWORK

We noted earlier that character is a multidimensional construct. In our view, morality
is central to what is meant by character. But the development of moral judgment is
only one dimension of character. In addition, character involves harnessing such nonmoral skills as emotional regulation and persistence for moral aims. In addition, character involves conceptions of the good, as well as the right. To further flesh out the
concept of character, we have found Rest's Four Component Model of moral action
to be a useful starting place (Bredemeier and Shields 1994; Shields, Bredemeier, and
Power 2002).

Rest (1983, 1984) hypothesized that every moral action necessarily entails the
activation of four conceptually distinct but interrelated sets of processes: moral interpretation (which draws upon moral sensitivity), moral judgment (which draws upon
moral reasoning), moral choice (which reflects moral motivation), and moral implementation (which reflects self-regulation skills). In later works, Rest gave the word
"character" to the fourth component of the model (Rest et al. 1999).

The model is quite useful for identifying psychological processes tethered to
the production of moral behavior. What the model lacks, however, is an integrative
core. It lacks any conception of personal agency that can animate the processes and
give them coherence and coordination. We have proposed (Shields, Bredemeier, and
Power 2002) that the concept of character is centered in what Blasi (1983, 1984, 1985,
1988) refers to as the "moral self," and that it serves as the integrative, agentic center
out of which the moral processes come.

What sports help make clear is that the concept of character, while tethered to
the moral, is not limited to the moral narrowly conceived. Character also connotes

virtues that stem from pursuit of the good, as well as the right. This ties character to the area of achievement and pursuit of worthy goals. Typically in sports, the athlete with character is thought of as the athlete who does not give up, who persists regardless of difficulties or odds, who endures and perseveres. A sport team that has character exemplifies teamwork and courage, loyalty and dedication. To account for these dimensions of character, we have developed the concept of an achievement ethic. In the next section, we elaborate on this concept and relate it to our previous discussion of game reasoning.

AN ACHIEVEMENT ETHIC APPROACH TO GAME REASONING

We noted above that sports tend to encourage a more egocentric style of moral reasoning. This game reasoning can take two forms: a playful, legitimated regression or an illegitimate regression. The consequences are dramatically different for the two. Playful game reasoning may enhance the enjoyment of sports by providing an experience of freedom and release. On the other hand, under the cloak of play, egocentric moral reasoning can, metaphorically speaking, break loose from its moral moorings and justify an "anything goes" morality. This would seem to be implied, for example, in a comment by former heavyweight boxing champion Larry Holmes. In a *60 Minutes* interview, he was asked how he mentally prepared for a fight. In response, he said, "I have to let all the good out and bring all the bad in, like Dr. Jekyll and Mr. Hyde" (quoted in Bredemeier and Shields 1985). Comments such as Holmes's are frequent in the world of sports. As yet we do not understand well what causes a person to employ an illegitimate as opposed to a legitimate form of game reasoning. One avenue that we are pursuing relates to what we are calling an "achievement ethic" (Bredemeier, Power, and Shields 2002).

Sports are achievement contexts. They are goal-directed activities involving competition and a quest for excellence or mastery. They are contexts in which success matters. Psychologists have generally avoided treating achievement issues in ethical terms. In this, they differ markedly from Aristotle (1985) who, in his classical treatment of ethics, located the striving for excellence at the heart of virtue and drew on sports as well as the crafts to illustrate his theory. Aristotle posited that humans achieve happiness when they exercise their capacities, physical and intellectual, to the fullest. Sports provide a rich opportunity for individuals to excel and to experience the happiness intrinsic to excelling. From an Aristotelian view, the ethical value of sports is not that sports participation leads to the rewards associated with success, but that sports participation brings with it, potentially at least, the happiness intrinsic to human striving. Correspondingly, the great danger in sports is that the emphasis on winning can undermine what makes sports virtuous in the first place—the desire to develop one's capacities in pursuit of worthy ends.

Aristotle's ideas can be connected to contemporary achievement motivation theory. Over the past two decades, Nicholls (1984, 1989) and Duda (1987, 1989, 1993, 1996) have proposed that individuals adopt one of two orientations toward achievement—task or ego. While all people are motivated to develop and display competence, people differ with regard to how success is understood. The person who has a *task* orientation feels successful when he or she meets or exceeds self-referenced goals. In contrast, the *ego* oriented person evaluates success through social comparison; thus, an ego oriented person feels competent only to the extent that his or her performance is better than that of peers. Research conducted in the U.S. has provided support for the existence of task and ego orientations in the educational domain (Nicholls et al. 1989; Nicholls et al. 1990; Thorkildsen 1988), as well as in sport contexts (see Duda and Whitehead 1998, for a review).

Nicholls explicitly linked the task and ego motivational orientations to moral motivations. He suggested that a high task orientation would lead to greater weight being given to moral concerns. The focus on performance outcome, in Nicholls's view, will lead to less concern for the moral dimensions of achievement experiences (Nicholls 1989). Evidence within sport domains supports this contention of a link between motivational orientation and moral priorities (Duda, Olson, and Templin 1991; Dunn and Dunn 1999; Guivernau and Duda 1998; Kavussanu and Ntoumanis 2001; Kavussanu and Roberts, forthcoming; Stephens and Bredemeier 1996). However, the two orientations are not mutually exclusive, and high task orientation does not necessarily imply low ego orientation.

Blasi (this volume) has suggested that experiences of intrinsic value (whether of music, of art, of relationship, etc.) are likely precursors to the development of moral desire. An achievement ethic suggests that intrinsic value inheres within striving for excellence. Learning to take pleasure in striving toward excellence in worthy pursuits is itself part of character development. Placed in the context of contemporary achievement motivation theory, we suggest that a task motivational orientation, because it is focused on the intrinsic value of striving within achievement contexts, is to be preferred to an ego orientation.

Though the empirical evidence is not yet available, we hypothesize that a task motivational orientation is closely associated with the legitimated regression of game reasoning and that an ego motivational orientation is linked to illegitimate regression.

As noted earlier, a legitimated regression can enhance the intrinsic quality of the sport involvement by allowing for an experience of freedom and release. When connected with the multidimensional quest for excellence (excellence of performance, excellence of character), this experience of freedom and release is placed in the service of an experience of "the good." The appreciation of the intrinsic good within sports keeps the moral "regression" from straying into illegitimate forms. In contrast, the focus on defeating others that is the hallmark of an ego motivational orientation does not contain a limiting element that would keep the moral regression within legitimate bounds. The only limiting element is an external one—what one can get away with—and does not carry moral force.

SPORT TEAMS AS COMMUNITIES OF CHARACTER

In our view, character encompasses what is usually meant by morality as well as an achievement ethic. Character is an "ethical self" that reflects moral and achievement virtues, integrating them into a coherent sense of self. When we say a person "has character" we mean that they have a coherent sense of themselves, together with those personal competencies that enable them to act consistently with regard to moral and achievement virtues. Moral reasoning is related to character and, in fact, provides the touchstone for the moral dimension. But character involves virtues and reasons beyond the moral. Character entails a view of the good, as well as a commitment to the right.

For coaches and sport educators, the question becomes how to create a sport environment that facilitates the development of character. Clearly, this is a highly complex question, but we think a good starting point is to ask two related questions: How can sport experiences be made conducive to the development of moral judgment? How can they be made conducive to the adoption of a task motivational orientation?

Though the literature reviewed above suggests that sports may not be good contexts for promoting moral reasoning, several studies have also demonstrated that sport experiences can be designed effectively to promote moral growth (Bredemeier, Weiss, Shields, and Shewchuk 1986; Romance, Weiss, and Bockoven 1986; Wandzilak, Carroll, and Ansorge 1988). Thus, when moral development is adopted as an explicit goal and appropriate strategies are implemented, sport experience can stimulate the development of moral reasoning.

In our own work, we seek to incorporate insights from the just-community approach to moral and character education in the schools (e.g., Power, Higgins, and

Kohlberg 1989), together with insights stemming from our research on game reasoning and a motivational ethic. We have labeled our approach a "communities-of-character" approach to character education through sports.

The communities-of-character approach recognizes that people develop their character in the context of social relations and that the shared norms and values of the group are important influences on what the individual comes to value and how they act. Those sport teams, for example, in which collective norms are lenient when it comes to the use of aggression are more likely to have players who accept aggression as legitimate (Guivernau and Duda 1998; Shields, Bredemeier, Gardner, and Bostrom 1995; Stephens and Bredemeier 1996).

The communities-of-character approach to sports has two critical dimensions. First, it attempts to build a sense of community within the team that features shared norms for ethical behavior. From a pragmatic standpoint, the heart of the approach is democratic leadership exercised through the team meeting. In team meetings, rules and goals are established, strategies are taught, and performances are assessed, all with the aim of accentuating the moral dimension of the sport experience. The communities-of-character approach requires that players participate to the fullest extent possible in such meetings by discussing and deciding upon disciplinary rules and punishments and offering suggestions and feedback about strategies and performances. Participation in such team meetings should help players to develop shared norms that express and realize ideals of cooperation, fair play, and respect for officials and opponents. In team meetings, players learn the democratic skills of self-expression, listening, and deliberating about the common good.

A second critical element of the communities-of-character approach is the promotion of a mastery-oriented achievement climate. A *mastery climate* encourages or augments task motivation, in contrast to a *performance climate,* which encourages or augments ego motivation. Mastery climates are associated with participants' use of effective learning strategies, preference for challenging tasks, positive attitudes, and the belief that effort leads to success (Ames 1992; Ames and Archer 1988; Burton 1989; Hall 1988; Newton 1994; Newton and Duda 1998; Seifriz, Duda, and Chi 1992; Treasure 1993; Treasure and Roberts 1994, 1998; Walling, Duda, and Chi 1993). Mastery climates nurture an achievement ethic that places value on the intrinsic quality of the experience.

Pedagogically, coaches can learn to develop mastery climates by paying careful attention to the structuring of the environment and adopting a communication style that focuses on relationship and process (Ames 1992; Duda 1987; Epstein 1988, 1989; Nicholls 1989; Nicholls and Miller 1984). Mastery climates can be created through attention to Task, Authority, Recognition, Grouping, Evaluation, and Timing or the TARGET framework (Epstein 1988, 1989). Though initially developed for educational settings, the framework is readily adaptable to sports. In brief, to create a mastery climate, tasks need to entail variety and diversity; authority should be shared; recognition ought to focus on effort; groupings for drills should be varied and heterogeneous; evaluation should be based on improvement, participation, and effort; and the allotment of time for skill development needs to be flexible and adaptive.

Fortunately, promoting a mastery climate is very congruent with forming a sense of moral community. By emphasizing mastery goals, each participant is empowered to be an active participant in the community and the deleterious effects of an overemphasis on social comparison is mitigated. As a sport community develops its own unique character, rooted in morality and conceptions of the good, it can make a positive contribution to the character development of each of its participants. Future research will determine whether this and/or other models of character education through sports can be efficacious in benefitting our youth.

REFERENCES

Ames, C. 1992. Achievement goals, motivational climate, and motivational processes. In *Motivation in Sport and Exercise,* ed. G. Roberts, 161–76. Champaign, IL: Human Kinetics.

Ames, C., and J. Archer. 1988. Achievement goals in the classroom: Students' learning strategies and motivation processes. *Journal of Educational Psychology* 80:260–67.

Aristotle. 1985. *Nicomachean Ethics.* Trans. T. Irwin. Indianapolis, IN: Hackett.

Bateson, G. 1955. A theory of play and fantasy. *Psychiatric Research Reports* 2:39–51.

Beller, J., and S. Stoll. 1995. Moral reasoning of high school student athletes and general students: An empirical study versus personal testimony. *Pediatric Exercise Science* 7:352–63.

Blasi, A. 1983. The self and cognition: The roles of the self in the acquisition of knowledge, and the role of cognition in the development of the elf. In *Psychological Theories of the Self,* vol. 2, ed. B. Lee and G. Noam, 1–25. New York: Plenum.

———. 1984. Moral identity: Its role in moral functioning. In *Morality, Moral Behavior, and Moral Development,* ed. W. Kurtines and J. Gewirtz, 128–39. New York: John Wiley and Sons.

———. 1985. The moral personality: Reflections for social science and education. In *Moral Education: Theory and Application,* ed. M. Berkowitz and F. Oser, 433–44. Hillsdale, NJ: Lawrence Erlbaum Associates.

———. 1988. Identity and the development of the self. In *Self, Ego, and Identity: Integrative Approaches,* ed. D. K. Lapsley and F. C. Power, 226–42. New York: Springer-Verlag.

Bredemeier, B. J. 1985. Moral reasoning and the perceived legitimacy of intentionally injurious sport acts. *Journal of Sport Psychology* 7:110–24.

———. 1994. Children's moral reasoning and their assertive, aggressive, and submissive tendencies in sport and daily life. *Journal of Sport and Exercise Psychology* 16:1–14.

———. 1995. Divergence in children's moral reasoning about issues in daily life and sport specific contexts. *International Journal of Sport Psychology* 26:453–63.

Bredemeier, B, F. C. Power, and D. Shields. 2002. Sports teams as communities of character. Workshop offered at the American Alliance for Health, Physical Education, Recreation, and Dance convention, Cincinnati, OH, April.

Bredemeier, B. J., and D. L. Shields. 1984a. Divergence in moral reasoning about sport and life. *Sociology of Sport Journal* 1:348–57.

———. 1984b. The utility of moral stage analysis in the investigation of athletic aggression. *Sociology of Sport Journal* 1:138–49.

———. 1985. Values and violence in sport. *Psychology Today* 19:22–32.

———. 1986a. Athletic aggression: An issue of contextual morality. *Sociology of Sport Journal* 3:15–28.

———. 1986b. Game reasoning and interactional morality. *Journal of Genetic Psychology* 147:257–75.

———. 1986c. Moral growth among athletes and nonathletes: A comparative analysis. *Journal of Genetic Psychology* 147:7–18.

———. 1994. Applied ethics and moral reasoning in sport. In *Moral Development in the Professions,* ed. J. Rest and D. Narvaez, 173–87. Hillsdale, NJ: Lawrence Erlbaum Associates.

———. 1998. Moral assessment in sport psychology. In *Advances in Sport and Exercise Psychology Measurement,* ed. J. L. Duda, 257–76. Morgantown, WV: Fitness Information Technology.

Bredemeier, B., M. Weiss, D. Shields, and B. Cooper. 1986. The relationship of sport involvement with children's moral reasoning and aggression tendencies. *Journal of Sport Psychology* 8:304–18.

———. 1987. The relationship between children's legitimacy judgments and their moral reasoning, aggression tendencies and sport involvement. *Sociology of Sport Journal* 4:48–60.

Bredemeier, B., M. Weiss, D. Shields, and R. Shewchuk. 1986. Promoting moral growth in a summer sport camp: The implementation of theoretically grounded instructional strategies. *Journal of Moral Education* 15:212–20.

Burton, D. 1989. Winning isn't everything: Examining the impact of performance goals on collegiate swimmers: Cognitions and performance. *The Sport Psychologist* 2:105–32.

Colby, A., and L. Kohlberg. 1987. *The Measurement of Moral Judgment,* 2 vols. Cambridge, MA: Harvard University Press.

Duda, J. L. 1987. Toward a developmental theory of achievement motivation in sport. *Journal of Sport Psychology* 9:130–45.

———. 1989. Goal perspectives and behavior in sport and exercise settings. In *Advances in Motivation and Achievement*, vol. 6, ed. C. Ames and M. Maehr, 81–115. Greenwich, CT: JAI Press.

———. 1993. Goals: A social cognitive approach to the study of motivation in sport. In *Handbook on Research in Sport Psychology*, ed. R. N. Singer, M. Murphey, and L. K. Tennant, 421–36. New York: Macmillan.

———. 1996. Maximizing motivation in sport and physical education among children and adolescents: The case for greater task involvement. *Quest* 48:290–302.

Duda, J. L., L. K. Olson, and T. J. Templin. 1991. The relationship of task and ego orientation to sportsmanship attitudes and the perceived legitimacy of injurious acts. *Research Quarterly for Exercise and Sport* 62:79–87.

Duda, J. L., and J. Whitehead. 1998. Measurement of goal perspectives in the physical domain. In *Advances in Sport and Exercise Psychology Measurement*, ed. J. Duda, 21–48. Morgantown, WV: Fitness Information Technology.

Dunn, J. G. H., and J. C. Dunn. 1999. Goal orientations, perceptions of aggression, and sportspersonship in elite male youth ice hockey players. *The Sport Psychologist* 13:183–200.

Durkheim, E. 1961. *Moral Education*. New York: Free Press. (Orig. pub. 1925.)

Epstein, J. 1988. Effective schools or effective students? Dealing with diversity. In *Policies for America's Public Schools*, ed. R. Haskins and B. MacRae, 89–126. Norwood, NJ: Ablex.

———. 1989. Family structures and student motivation: A developmental perspective. In *Research on Motivation in* Education, vol. 3, ed. C. Ames and R. Ames, 259–95. New York: Academic Press.

Firth, R. 1973. *Symbols Public and Private*. New York: Cornell University Press.

Giffin, H. L. N. 1982. The metacommunicative process in a collective make-believe play. PhD diss., University of Colorado, Boulder.

Guivernau, M., and J. Duda. 1998. Integrating concepts of motivation and morality: The contribution of norms regarding aggressive and rule-violating behavior, goal orientations, and the perceived motivational climate to the prediction of athletic aggression. *Journal of Sport and Exercise Psychology* Supplement:13.

Haan, N. 1977. A manual for interactional morality. Unpublished manuscript, Institute of Human Development, University of California.

———. 1978. Two moralities in action contexts: Relationship to thought, ego regulation, and development. *Journal of Personality and Social Psychology* 36:286–305.

———. 1983. An interactional morality of everyday life. In *Social Science as Moral Inquiry*, ed. N. Haan, R. Bellah, P. Rabinow, and W. Sullivan, 218–50. New York: Columbia University Press.

———. 1991. Moral development and action from a social constructivist perspective. In *Handbook of Moral Behavior and Development*, vol. 1, *Theory*, ed. W. Kurtines and J. Gewirtz, 251–73. Hillsdale, NJ: Lawrence Erlbaum Associates.

Haan, N., E. Aerts, and B. B. Cooper. 1985. *On Moral Grounds: The Search for a Practical Morality.* New York: New York University.

Hahm, C. H., J. M. Beller, and S. K. Stoll. 1989. *The Hahm-Beller Values Choice Inventory in the Sport Milieu.* Moscow: University of Idaho, The Institute for ETHICS.

Hall, E. R. 1986. Moral development levels of athletes in sport-specific and general social situations. In *Psychology and Sociology of Sport: Current Selected Research*, vol. 1, ed. L. Vander Velden and J. H. Humphrey, 191–204. New York: AMS Press.

Hall, K. H. 1988. A social-cognitive approach to goal setting: The mediating effects of achievement goals and perceived ability. PhD diss., University of Illinois at Urbana-Champaign.

Handelman, D. 1977. Play and ritual: Complementary frames of meta-communication. In *It's a Funny Thing, Humour*, ed. A. J. Chapman and H. C. Foot, 185–92. Oxford: Pergamon Press.

Horrocks, R. N. 1979. The relationship of selected prosocial play behaviors in children to moral reasoning, youth sports, participation, and perception of sportsmanship. PhD diss., University of North Carolina, Greensboro.

Huizinga, Johan. 1955. Homo ludens: *A Study of the Play Element in Culture.* Boston: Beacon Press.

Kavussanu, M., and N. Ntoumanis. 2001. Participation in sport and moral functioning: The mediating role of ego orientation. Paper presented at the Tenth World Congress of Sport Psychology, Skiathos Island, Greece, May.

Kavussanu, M., and G. Roberts. Forthcoming. Moral functioning in sport: An achievement goal perspective. *Journal of Sport and Exercise Psychology.*

Kohlberg, L. 1981. *The Philosophy of Moral Development.* Essays on Moral Development, vol. 1, San Francisco: Harper & Row.

———. 1984. *The Psychology of Moral Development.* Essays on Moral Development, vol. 2. San Francisco: Harper & Row.

Kohlberg, L., J. Hickey, and P. Scharf. 1972. The justice structure of the prison: A theory and intervention. *The Prison Journal* 51:3–14.

Krebs, D., S. Vermeulen, J. Carpendale, and K. Denton. 1991. Structural and situational influences on moral judgment: The interaction between stage and dilemma. In *Handbook of Moral Behavior and Development*, vol. 2, *Research*, ed. W. Kurtines and J. Gewirtz, 139–69. Hillsdale, NJ: Lawrence Erlbaum Associates.

Newton, M. 1994. The effect of differences in perceived motivational climate and goal orientations on motivational responses of female volleyball players. PhD diss., Purdue University.

Newton, M., and J. L. Duda. 1998. The interaction of motivational climate, dispositional goal orientations, and perceived ability in predicting indices of motivation. *International Journal of Sport Psychology* 29:1–20.

Nicholls, J. G. 1984. Achievement motivation: Conceptions of ability, subjective experience, task choice, and performance. *Psychological Review* 91:328–46.

———. 1989. *The Competitive Ethos and Democratic Education.* Cambridge, MA: Harvard University Press.

Nicholls, J. G., P. C. Cheung, J. Lauer, and M. Patashnick. 1989. Individual differences in academic motivation: Perceived ability, goals, beliefs, and values. *Learning and Individual Differences* 1 (1): 63–84.

Nicholls, J. G., P. Cobb, T. Wood, E. Yackel, and M. Patashnick. 1990. Assessing students' theories of success in mathematics: individual classroom differences. *Journal for Research in Mathematics Education* 21:109–22.

Nicholls, J., and A. Miller. 1984. Development and its discontents: The differentiation of the concept of ability. In *Advances in Motivation and Achievement: The Development of Achievement Motivation*, ed. J. Nicholls, 185–218. Greenwich, CT: JAI Press.

Piaget, J. 1965. *The Moral Judgment of the Child*. Trans. M. Gabain. New York: Free Press. (Orig. pub. 1932.)

Power, F. C., A. Higgins, and L. Kohlberg. 1989. *Lawrence Kohlberg's Approach to Moral Education*. New York: Columbia University Press.

Priest, R. G., J. V. Krause, and J. Beach. 1999. Four-year changes in college athletes' ethical value choices in sports situations. *Research Quarterly for Exercise and Sport* 70:170–78.

Rest, J. R. 1979. *Development in Judging Moral Issues*. Minneapolis: University of Minnesota Press.

———. 1983. Morality. In *Cognitive Development*, ed. J. Flavell and E. Markman. Manual of Child Psychology, 4th ed., vol. 3, ed. P. Mussen, 556–629. New York: John Wiley and Sons.

———. 1984. The major components of morality. In *Morality, Moral Behavior, and Moral Development*, ed. W. Kurtines and J. Gewirtz, 356–629. New York: John Wiley and Sons.

Rest, J., D. Narvaez, M. Bebeau, and S. Thoma. 1999. *Postconventional Moral Thinking: A Neo-Kohlbergian Approach*. Mahwah, NJ: Lawrence Erlbaum Associates.

Romance, T. J., M. R. Weiss, and J. Bockoven. 1986. A program to promote moral development through elementary school physical education. *Journal of Teaching in Physical Education* 5:126–36.

Rulmyr, R. 1996. Interscholastic athletic participation and the moral development of adolescents in Arizona high schools. PhD diss., Northern Arizona University.

Schmitz, K. 1976. Sport and play: Suspension of the ordinary. In *Sport in the Sociocultural Process*, ed. M. Hart, 35–48. Dubuque, IA: W. C. Brown.

Seifriz, J. J., J. L. Duda, and L. Chi. 1992. The relationship of perceived motivational climate to intrinsic motivation and beliefs about success in basketball. *Journal of Sport and Exercise Psychology* 14:375–91.

Selman, R. 1980. *The Growth of Interpersonal Understanding: Developmental and Clinical Analyses*. New York: Academic Press.

Shields, D. L., and B. J. Bredemeier. 1984. Sport and moral growth: A structural developmental perspective. In *Cognitive Sport Psychology*, ed. W. Straub and J. Williams, 89–101. Lansing, NY: Sport Science Associates.

———. 1995. *Character Development and Physical Activity*. Champaign, IL: Human Kinetics.

Shields, D., B. Bredemeier, D. Gardner, and A. Bostrom. 1995. Leadership, cohesion and team norms regarding cheating and aggression. *Sociology of Sport Journal* 12:324–36.

Shields, D., B. Bredemeier, and F. C. Power. 2002. Moral development and children's sport. In *Children and Youth in Sport: A Biopsychosocial Perspective,* 2nd ed., ed. F. Smoll and R. Smith, 537–59, Indianapolis, IN: Brown & Benchmark.

Shulman, J., and W. Bowen. 1991. *The Game of Life: College Sports and Educational Values.* Princeton, NJ: Princeton University Press.

Stephens, D. 2000. Predictors of likelihood to aggress in youth soccer: An examination of coed and all-girls teams. *Journal of Sport Behavior* 23:311–25.

Stephens, D., and B. Bredemeier. 1996. Moral atmosphere and judgments about aggression in girls' soccer: Relationships among moral and motivational variables. *Journal of Sport and Exercise Psychology* 18:158–73.

Stephens, D., B. Bredemeier, and D. Shields. 1997. Construction of a measure designed to assess players' descriptions and prescriptions for moral behavior in youth sport soccer. *International Journal of Sport Psychology* 28:370–90.

Stevenson, M. J. 1998. Measuring the cognitive moral reasoning of collegiate student-athletes: The development of the Stevenson-Stoll social responsibility questionnaire. PhD diss., University of Idaho.

Thorkildsen, T. 1988. Theories of education among academically precocious adolescents. *Contemporary Educational Psychology* 13:323–30.

Treasure, D. C. 1993. A social-cognitive approach to understanding children's achievement behavior, cognitions and affect in competitive sport. PhD diss., University of Illinois at Urbana-Champaign.

Treasure, D. C., and G. C. Roberts. 1994. Cognitive and affective concomitants of task and ego goal orientations during the middle school years. *Journal of Sport and Exercise Psychology* 16:15–28.

———. 1998. Relationship between female adolescents' achievement goal orientations, perceptions of the motivational climate, belief about success and sources of satisfaction in basketball. *International Journal of Sport Psychology* 29:211–30.

Walling, M. D., J. L. Duda, and L. Chi. 1993. The perceived motivational climate in sport questionnaire: Construct and predictive validity. *Journal of Sport and Exercise Psychology* 15:172–83.

Wandzilak, T., T. Carroll, and C. J. Ansorge. 1988. Values development through physical activity: Promoting sportsmanlike behaviors, perceptions, and moral reasoning. *Journal of Teaching in Physical Education* 8 (1): 13–22.

SIX

The Psychological Foundations of Everyday Morality and Moral Expertise

Darcia Narvaez and Daniel K. Lapsley

THE COMMON IMAGE OF THE MORAL AGENT IS ONE WHO *MAKES DECISIONS*. Moral decisions are the product of vast calculation. Principles are discerned, judgments are formed, rules of application are weighed. The requirements of duty, the probative force of outcomes and consequences, and the adjudication of competing claims are all fairly transparent to the rational, deliberative agent who engages in extensive cognitive effort in order to resolve dilemmas, make choices, and justify actions. Indeed, the costly investment of cognitive resources into moral deliberation is thought to underlie the very notion of moral autonomy. Moral freedom is grounded in the rational capacity to discern options, make decisions, and enact intentions.

We are not merely reactive to external contingencies; we are, indeed, liberated from "stimulus control" *because* of our ability to bring our behavior under the explicit guidance of rational deliberation.

This image of the moral agent has dominated psychological research on moral development for nearly five decades. Indeed, the cognitive developmental tradition assumes that the child is a "naïve philosopher" whose moral perspective becomes progressively transformed along a developmental path of increasing philosophical and psychological adequacy (Kohlberg 1981, 1984). Moral development is discernable in the conscious deliberations and choices made by individuals as they wrestle with the moral quandaries of hypothetical dilemmas. The quality of explicit judgments and the developmental sophistication of conscious reasoning have been the target of inquiry in the cognitive developmental tradition (Colby and Kohlberg 1987; Rest 1979; Turiel 1983).

Moreover, this tradition insists on the "principle of phenomenalism" (Kohlberg, Levine, and Hewer 1983) to define the domain of inquiry. This principle asserts that the phenomenological perspective of the moral agent is crucial for determining the moral status of behavior (Blasi, this volume). That is, according to this view, a behavior has no particular moral status *unless it is motivated by an explicit moral judgment.* Hence no matter how praiseworthy a commitment, prosocial a line of action, or heroic the display of virtue, none of these has any distinctly moral significance unless the agent is motivated by an explicit moral judgment. A moral behavior is something undertaken for moral reasons, known to the agent. A moral behavior is one that is motivated by an explicit recognition of the prescriptive force of moral rules. It is behavior beleaguered by the weight of moral duty. Consequently, the subjective intention of the rational moral agent is the object of inquiry in moral development research just because, in the absence of explicit judgments or rational deliberation, there can be no distinctly *moral* phenomena in the first place (Lapsley and Narvaez, this volume).[1]

The principle of phenomenalism is the background assumption even of moral development research programs that agree on little else. It is endorsed, of course, by proponents of Kohlberg's stage theory, but also by advocates of domain-based social reasoning who place stricter boundaries around the moral domain (e.g., Turiel 1983). Larry Nucci (2000), for example, in his presidential address to the Jean Piaget Society, wondered about the moral significance of prosocial behavior attributed to "moral exemplars" who were nominated for study on the basis of renown for their moral commitments (see, e.g., Hart and Fegley 1995; Hart, Yates, Fegley, and Wilson 1995; Colby and Damon 1992). "It is not clear," he notes, that the actions described constitute moral conduct. If, for example, I volunteer to work in a soup kitchen because it will increase my chance of getting into my college of choice, is my volunteerism moral? If I volunteer because it will make me feel good about myself, rather than because I feel compelled to volunteer in order to alleviate the suffering of others, is my action moral? *Without knowing why I volunteered, one cannot know to what extent I either did or did not engage in moral deliberation.* (emphasis added)

And absent moral deliberation, one cannot warrant moral conduct.

We contend that an uncritical reliance on the principle of phenomenalism has had three untoward effects on moral psychology. First, the principle unacceptably narrows the range of behavior that can be the target of legitimate moral psychological inquiry. Decisions made outside of consciousness and actions taken without deliberation—in other words, most human behavior—are disqualified from analysis and explanation.

Second, the principle of phenomenalism isolates moral psychology from the theoretical and empirical literatures of other relevant domains of psychological research. It requires that the field of moral psychology ignore advances in a number of otherwise relevant psychological domains—including cognition, social cognition, and personality—if this research reveals models of functioning at variance with the principle. Adhering to the principle leads to vast systems of explanation about situations and phenomena that are rare, specialized, and largely hypothetical. It ignores the commonplaces of everyday moral life, or else rules them out-of-bounds by fiat and by definitional preferences. This a priori constraint on legitimate lines of inquiry cuts off moral psychology from strong integrative possibilities with these literatures, and instead encourages theoretical isolation, atrophy, and irrelevance.

Third, as a result of its narrow focus and theoretical isolation, the principle of phenomenalism gravely distorts and truncates psychological explanation of moral functioning. Indeed, psychological research has much that could inform research in moral psychology, though it has not yet done so. In fact, the principle of phenomenalism violates the contemporary understanding of human action held by cognitive psychologists. For example, in a series of articles John Bargh presents compelling evidence that much of the activity of our daily lives is governed by cognitive processes that are preconscious and automatic (e.g., Bargh 1989, 1990, 1996, 1997; Uleman and Bargh 1989). This literature would seem to radically undermine the psychological foundation of the principle of phenomenalism and to pose a significant challenge to the traditions of developmental research that accept it as a premise, notably moral psychology. Bargh and Ferguson (2000) noted, for example, that "higher mental processes that have traditionally served as quintessential examples of choice and free will—such as goal pursuit, judgment, and interpersonal behavior— have been shown recently to occur in the absence of conscious choice or guidance" (926). If automatic cognitive processes govern much of the behavior of everyday life, very little human behavior stems from deliberative or conscious thought and far less receives moral deliberation. Behavior driven by moral decision making becomes a rare, unusual occurrence, pushed to the margins of human activity. If moral conduct hinges on conscious, explicit deliberation, then much of human behavior simply does not qualify.

In our view, moral psychology is better served by jettisoning starting points that are motivated more by philosophical than by psychological considerations (Lapsley and Narvaez, this volume). Rather than a "moralized psychology" whose parameters and terms of reference are set by certain philosophical goals (e.g., defeating ethical relativism), we opt instead for a "psychologized morality" that attempts to study moral functioning within the framework of contemporary psychological theories and methods. After all, literatures that are rich with data and insight about psychological functioning are not irrelevant for understanding moral functioning. Advances in cognitive science, learning, motivation, and personality are not irrelevant for understanding moral rationality, moral socialization, and the formation of moral identity. We advocate enriching moral psychology with these perspectives, not reinventing moral psychology from the ground up. It should also be said that advances in research in moral psychology can also provide important insights for other domains of psychology.

In this chapter we begin the work of steering moral psychology toward the mainstream of psychological theory and research. We first describe a number of cognitive realities that moral psychological theory will have to integrate, illustrating how cognitive science literatures can further our understanding of moral functioning. We briefly review research on expertise because it is a notion that is gaining ground among those who study intelligence (Sternberg 1998, 1999), learning (Reber 1993), and decision making (Ericcson and Smith 1991; Hogarth 2001). Specifically, we propose that the expertise literature can provide rich insights into the psychological development of moral character and conduct. We apply these findings to the ethical domain and to moral education.

AUTOMATICITY AND SOCIAL BEHAVIOR

It is now clear that much of human behavior is governed by cognitive systems that are characterized by varying degrees of automaticity. Traditionally, automaticity is inferred if cognitive processes are engaged unintentionally, involuntarily, with little or no expenditure of attention or cognitive resources, without effort, and outside of conscious awareness. Automaticity is typically contrasted with controlled cognitive processes that are flexibly under intentional control and conscious awareness. Yet the distinction between automatic and controlled processing is not a rigid one, nor does the designation of automaticity require the co-occurrence of all of the traditional criteria. Indeed, Bargh (1989) argues that awareness, attention, intention, and control are somewhat independent qualities that co-occur in different combinations, elicited under specific enabling circumstances. Moreover, the ascription of automaticity to behavior (e.g., walking, driving, reading) does not necessarily imply that the behavior is not intentional, or that it cannot be controlled or halted (Logan 1989).

Three varieties of automaticity can be distinguished in social information processing. *Preconscious automaticity* describes the involuntary activation of social constructs (e.g., schemas, scripts, plans, stereotypes, prototypes) outside of conscious awareness, as a result of a triggering event. Preconscious activation of chronically accessible (frequently activated) constructs exerts a pervasive interpretive influence over social information-processing and underwrites social judgments of all kinds. Moreover, Bargh (1989) suggests that preconscious automaticity is responsible for our strong feelings of certainty or conviction regarding our social judgments. That is, just because our interpretations and evaluations are generated preconsciously, and without any awareness of inferential activity or cognitive effort, they are trusted as valid and accurate. "Thus, these interpretations are not questioned, but are seen as undoubtedly valid sources of information, and are as a result a prime source of judgments and decisions" (11). Of course, the degree to which our *moral* convictions are similarly the result of preconsciously activated social constructs has not been explored.

A second variety of automaticity, *post-conscious automaticity*, operates after a recent conscious experience or recent deployment of attentional resources, "the nonconscious consequences of conscious thought" (Bargh 1989). That is, a triggering event induces conscious awareness or attention, but has "post-conscious" cognitive consequences that are generated automatically and outside of conscious awareness (Bargh 1989). For example, the conscious activation of a moral concept can reverberate throughout the cognitive system to automatically influence the threshold for social perception of other related concepts. Moreover, evaluative affect can have a residual effect after encountering social stimuli for which one has a strong attitude. This suggests a reciprocal influence: accessible social categories can automatically activate affective reactions and mood states can influence category accessibility. Hence, post-conscious automaticity describes a reverberation effect, or spreading activation, of related social constructs, judgments, and affects. Post-conscious automaticity is also illustrated by priming effects (Higgins and Bargh 1987; Higgins, Bargh, and Lombardi 1985). For example, activation of a social construct (e.g., "hostile") in one context can nonetheless be available and utilized for social information-processing in other, unrelated contexts, even after the triggering event has long left conscious awareness. In other words, a primed construct (including more elaborate mental representations, such as decision rules and the self-concept) can have a residual effect on subsequent information-processing.

Finally, a third kind of automaticity is "goal-dependent," and requires both conscious processing and a particular processing goal. Bargh (1989) draws attention to two forms of *goal-dependent automaticity*, one whose outcomes are *intended* and one whose outcomes are *unintended*. One example of unintended goal-dependent automaticity is when one forms spontaneous personality trait inferences as a side effect when performing a task under a different processing goal (e.g., memorization). This suggests that "an automatic and unintended way in which people understand and encode social behavioral information is in terms of personality trait dimensions, even when they are processing behaviors for purposes unrelated to their social aspects" (21). In other words, extracting dispositional information is an unintended side effect of cognitive processing engaged for some other purpose. Another example is when impressions and evaluations of others, or interpretations of events, are unintentionally influenced by the *intentional* activation of related social categories. "Subsequent evaluation of and behavior toward that person or event may then proceed in line with the context-driven evaluation, even when there is other information present that might lead to a different conclusion" (23).

Intended goal-dependent automaticity is evident as a consequence of skilled or expert performance (Bargh 1989). Well-learned situational scripts or highly routinized action sequences typically operate autonomously, with little need of conscious control or significant attentional resources. Skilled behaviors fall within this category of automaticity, as well as procedural knowledge that has become autonomous of conscious control as a result of frequent practice or application (e.g., driving a car).

What implications do the three varieties of conditional automaticity have for moral psychology? Although the large social psychology literature on automaticity does indeed have implications for understanding social cognition, perception, and evaluation, these implications are rarely drawn for purposes relevant to moral psychology. Yet it is our view that the "morality of everyday life" must be governed necessarily by cognitive processes categorized as various forms of conditional automaticity. To put it differently, the intersection of the "morality of everyday life" and the "automaticity of everyday life" must be large and extensive, suggesting promising new lines of productive, integrative research.

For example, we have already noted the possible linkage between preconsciously activated social constructs and the felt certainty that attaches to our moral convictions (see Haidt 2001). In addition, we have suggested that the chronic accessibility of moral schemas and other knowledge structures may be critical to the functioning of moral character, indeed, may even define what it means to possess a moral personality (Lapsley 1999; Lapsley and Narvaez 2004, this volume). Accordingly, one has a moral character to the extent that moral schemas are chronically accessible for social information processing. One advantage of this theory is that it readily accounts both for the automaticity by which individuals of exemplary moral commitment reach their judgments and for their felt conviction that their judgments are appropriate, justified, and true. As Colby and Damon (1992) have shown, individuals who display extraordinary moral commitments rarely report engaging in an extensive, agonized decision-making process. Instead, they "just knew" what was required of them, automatically as it were, without controlled processing, without the experience of wrestling with intractable quandary. Indeed, any theory of moral character, any theory that attempts to explain the exemplary behavior of "moral saints" along with more prosaic forms of moral identity necessarily requires a specification of the social-cognitive sources of preconscious automaticity (Lapsley & Narvaez, this volume).

The literature on post-conscious automaticity also holds much promise for understanding moral functioning. For example, the reverberatory effects associated with spreading activation can help us understand how moral perception and moral emotions are linked. The literature on priming effects offers surprising insight on a common practice of character education programs that attempt to teach a virtue of the week or month by prominently posting the trait word (e.g., "honesty") or its example around the classroom or school. Although the efficacy of this practice in bringing about moral character is doubted (Kohn 1997; Nash 1997), its real function may lie in its ability to prime the accessibility of virtue-relevant social constructs, which are made available to interpret, appraise, and evaluate social information long after the trait-term has left conscious awareness. Indeed once social constructs (in this case, virtue-constructs) are built in the mind of the child, they are available for social information-processing, either *chronically* as an individual differences variable or as a result of situational priming. Both chronic and situational priming may be rich sources of insight for character development education.

Finally, goal-dependent automaticity, the automaticity that attaches to scripts, routine action sequences, and highly skilled performance, is a source of integrative insights concerning moral conduct. Moral character may depend upon a kind of socialization that inculcates highly routinized action sequences, scripted interpersonal procedures, and patterns of discrimination and judgment. Indeed, such automaticity is "a well-practiced procedure that one intentionally employs in social judgment or pattern discrimination or as part of a complex skilled action" (Bargh 1989, 20).

These three types of automaticity—preconscious, post-conscious and goal-dependent—are representative of a vast area in psychology that has rarely been tapped by moral psychologists: that of tacit or implicit processing and knowledge. Tacit automatic responses expend energy efficiently in obtaining necessary information and facilitating rapid responses to information (Abernathy and Hamm 1995). Increasingly, researchers are pointing out the predominance of tacit processing and decision making (Hogarth 2001; Reber 1993).

THE DOMINANCE OF TACIT PROCESSING

Tacit processing often has been labeled "intuition." Hammond (2000) defines intuition as cognitive activities that somehow produce an answer, solution, or idea without the use of a conscious, logically defensible, step-by-step process. Intuition occurs automatically, happens quickly, yet weighs multiple pieces of information in a wholistic manner.

Robin Hogarth (2001) summarizes a host of findings that indicate that intuitive responses are reached with little apparent effort, typically without conscious awareness, and with little or no conscious deliberation. Hogarth describes three levels or systems of automatic information processing that underlie intuitive processes that take place across domains, from physical causality to social practice. The three systems are termed basic, primitive, and sophisticated. These three levels of automatic information processing represent primitive, default processing systems that share commonalities such as robustness when explicit systems are damaged, low variability among individuals, age and IQ independence, and commonality of process across species.

The first system, the *basic unconscious,* consists of instinctive behaviors that regulate life, such as the feeling of hunger precipitated by a drop in blood sugar that results in the conscious desire to seek food. The second system, the *primitive unconscious,* is involved in basic information processing largely devoid of meaning or interpretation, including subsymbolic processing of environmental stimuli (Rumelhart and McClelland 1986), ranging from mechanistic registration of the frequencies and covariation of events to inferring the implicit rules of systems that are encountered (e.g., grammar). For example, everyone can respond with a rough idea of the number of times in the last six months that he or she has been to a favorite store or has seen a particular friend. This kind of tallying occurs automatically without awareness. These types of processes are considered phylogenetically older because they do not vary according to motivation, education, or intelligence (Hasher and Zacks 1984). The primitive system learns implicitly and without effort and, like the basic system, it is possessed by many animals (Reber 1993).

The third system, the *sophisticated unconscious,* guides perceptual processing, attending to meaning and affect. Introspective reports indicate that meaning is perceived prior to the details in a stimulus array (Neisser 1976). Neisser argues that in a normal environment, individuals perceive meaningfulness or "affordances" without effort. An affordance is the reciprocity of the organism and the environment, that is, the offerings of the environment and the way the organism (through evolution and through experience) can use the resources (Gibson 1966). Perception guides action and action informs perception. The organism balances the environmental supports available and its own dynamic capacities for action. Perceiving an affordance is to perceive the relationship between environmental support and personal capacity. Affordances that are easily detected include apprehending the drift of an argument, noticing the location of an exit door in a hall, or picking up on the undertone or feeling in a comment (Neisser, 1976). What we often call "understanding" belongs to the sophisticated unconscious and is "a cognitive state that remains largely implicit but that goes beyond merely being able to correlate variables" (Wilson and Keil 2000, 97). The sophisticated unconscious has many operations including the three types of automaticity mentioned previously—preconscious, post-conscious, and goal-dependent.

Inasmuch as most of what we learn and know involves these three intuitive systems, most of what we learn and known is tacit. The perceived regularities picked up by the primitive system may or may not activate linguistic centers and, as a result, may or may not be accessible for verbal description (McCloskey and Kohl 1983). The meaningful understanding of how things work (the sophisticated system) may be more evident by behavior than by any kind of verbal explanation. As a result, it is misleading to characterize knowledge solely in terms of the ability to provide explanations. Humans know a great many things that they cannot put into words. Both children and adults know far more than they can explain. Keil and Wilson (2000) distinguish between a basic explanatory set of schemas, evident even in infants, and more advanced explanatory schemas that include statements of principles and are evident through verbal performance. Thus, to characterize knowledge solely in terms of the ability to provide explanations leads one to underestimate what is known, and renders a poor measure of knowledge and understanding.

Converging psychological evidence suggests that most human decisions are made without deliberative thought (Hammond 2000; Hogarth 2001). The sense that we consciously make most of our decisions is epiphenomenal and not empirically supported (Cotterill 1999; Damasio 1999; Libet 1985; Wegner 2002). A person may think he or she is deliberately making decisions because the chain of processing events— sensory registration to activation of neurons to matching patterns with stored patterns in memory—occurs in milliseconds (e.g., Cotterill 1999). Wegner and Wheatley (1999) demonstrated that people mistakenly believe that they intentionally acted when in fact they were led to think about the act just prior to being forced to take the action. Wegner and Wheatley suggest that people commonly assume conscious, willed choice when they associate their thoughts with their actions, even when the movement toward action precedes the thought (Libet 1985). Instead, many decisions are based on simple decision rules such as recognition of familiar configurations that evoke routinized responses governed by one of the intuitive or tacit systems. For example, Damasio (1999) contends that we are often driven by emotion without awareness:

> However, although many important choices involve feelings, a good number of our daily decisions apparently proceed without feelings. That does not mean that the evaluation that normally leads to a body state has not taken place. . . . Quite simply, a signal body state or its surrogate may have been activated but not been made the focus of attention. Without attention, neither will be part of consciousness, although either can be part of a covert action on the mechanisms that govern, without willful control, our appetitive (approach) or aversive (with-drawal) attitudes toward the world. While the hidden machinery underneath has been activated, our consciousness will never know it. (184–85)

We believe that much of moral functioning is similarly "intuitive," is similarly governed by tacit processes. In other words, psychological processes that are not and cannot be accessed explicitly guide everyday behavior. Indeed, individuals have more moral knowledge than they can express. Although moral psychology should be expected to give some account of tacit moral knowledge, the field has neglected to do so because of a bias toward the principle of phenomenalism.

Further, just because much of our moral behavior—like all of our behavior—is governed by implicit, tacit processes does not mean that it cannot be the object of education, development, or training. Indeed, one could argue that the whole point of moral education is to educate moral intuitions so that moral action is not always beleagured by moral deliberation. We do not want our children to have to torturously sort through a vast decision-making calculus in order to come to some basis for action.[2] Moreover, the tacit processes of educated moral intuition that we strive for is similar to what experts do. Experts across domains use intuitive, automatic decision making as a matter of course. This suggests that a study of expertise might provide important clues for understanding the process by which educated moral intuitions might be inculcated in children. Hence we turn to the expertise literature for insights relevant to moral education.

THE NATURE OF EXPERTISE

In order to study how information processing and knowledge develop, it has become fashionable to study the continuum of learning within a domain. Human learning proceeds along a continuum between novice status and expert status (e.g., Sanderson 1989). In comparison to a novice, an expert is more experienced and has developed a more complex understanding of the domain in terms of conceptual associations, action skills, and conditional knowledge (Abernathy and Hamm 1995; Sternberg 1998, 1999).

Experts differ from novices in several systematic ways. First, experts have a different set of representations. According to Sternberg (1998), experts have large, rich, organized networks of representations (schemas) containing a great deal of declarative knowledge about the domain, and well-organized, higher interconnected units of knowledge in the domain. They also have conditional knowledge that guides them in the application of declarative knowledge. Novices, in contrast, have smaller, less organized, shallower knowledge networks.

Second, experts see the world differently (Johnson and Mervis 1997; Myles-Worsley, Johnston, and Simons 1988). Because they have more and better organized knowledge in a domain, experts perceive things differently than do novices. They perceive different affordances. Perception of affordances is highly influenced by the amount of experience that one has with similar situations. Neisser (1976) contends that "information can be picked up only if there is a developmental format ready to accept it. Information that does not fit such a format goes unused. Perception is inherently selection" (55). Whereas a novice is overwhelmed by the information array, the expert quickly and automatically apprehends information that facilitates the goal at hand. Thus, the affordance that one perceives depends on one's level of experience or one's level of expertise in a domain. Experts, for example, possess more relevant schemas, which permit detection and encoding of more domain-relevant information. Experts in morality, like experts of all kinds, can be expected to perceive and act upon the world in a markedly different way than do moral novices. For example, experts in moral sensitivity are able to more easily pick up on the morally relevant affordances in the environment (e.g., What is my role in this situation? What should I do? What am I capable of doing? What does the context allow?).

Third, experts have a different set of skills. Expertise is comprised of more and better content and processes built from extensive experience in the domain. Expert decision making focuses on the critical features in the problem space, initially seeking to define the problem. The expert tries to match the problem with problems held in memory. Problem solving is schema driven and goal oriented. Unlike novices, experts know *what* knowledge to access, *which* procedures to apply, *how* to apply them, and *when* it is appropriate. In other words, experts have a greater amount of conditional knowledge. Experts apply complex rules and heuristics in solving a problem and use automatized routines. Their tacit knowledge or intuition is well trained and complements their explicit knowledge. In contrast, non-expert decision making is shallow and superficial, value-driven and opportunistic. Novices use simple heuristics, applied step by step. They try to solve the problem immediately instead of first defining the problem (Abernathy and Hamm 1995).

One of the clear behavioral differences between and experts and novices is that experts often make decisions rapidly and automatically, whereas novices proceed deliberatively and slowly. Experts use automatic, intended, goal-dependent processing, seeing meaningful information where novices do not. An expert presented with a domain problem can come up with an effective solution relatively quickly by accessing appropriate knowledge and by applying appropriate procedures to the degree and at the time they are needed. A novice presented with the same problem will likely come up with a solution that is superficial and ineffective, based on an incorrect understanding of the problem and/or a misapplication of procedures (Gijselaers and Woltjer 1997; Novick 1988). In short, experts have a richer declarative and procedural knowledge base that increases processing speed, directs attention and perceptual pickup, and triggers automatic, goal-dependent skill usage. Vicente and Wang (1998) point out that the memory of experts is facilitated by prior knowledge in part because it provides goals, constrains what they look for, and limits the complexity of what they see (the "constraint attunement hypothesis"). Ignoring information irrelevant to the current goal, experts use automatic, goal-dependent processing.

Experts demonstrate how all humans can routinize repeated behaviors that subsequently operate beneath consciousness. With much practice, experts become more automatic and less aware of the processes they use in decision making (Ericcson and Smith 1991). Indeed, to study how far humans can develop in skill and knowledge in any domain, we must study experts. This should be as true for moral psychology as for any other domain. Hence we advocate the study of expertise in all aspects of morality—sensitivity, judgment, motivation, and action. Moreover, we advocate using expertise development as a fundamental framework for character development education.

EDUCATING EXPERTS

We have noted what every individual effortlessly does with stimuli through interaction with the environment: she finds contingencies and regularities, creates representations and schemas, and forms a huge base of tacit understanding. The majority of nonschool learning occurs in this way, that is, according to "nonintentional, automatic acquisition of knowledge about structural relations between objects or events" (Frensch 1998, 76). The effects of prior experiences are manifest in a task even though previous learning is not consciously evident to the performer. In other words, implicit learning is "phenomenally unconscious" (Buchner and Wippich 1998). School learning, on the other hand, is predominantly phenomenally conscious. This contributes to the feeling of effort that imbues schoolbook learning in contrast to most learning about the rest of life.

For all learning, interaction with the social and physical environment plays a large role in what is learned. In the words of Hogarth (2001), the environment provides "learning structures" (the characteristics of the task in which we learn from experience), which shape our intuitions. For example, the social environment provides feedback, coaching, mentoring, and zone-of-proximal development interactions. Through direct experience, people learn content and rules, and develop "cultural capital." The associations and contingencies rewarded or punished through relationships encourage memories for some associations and responses to others. From positive and negative outcomes, the person develops expectancies (Kirsch 1999; Mowrer 1960) and assumptions about the world that mold memories, perceptions, and judgments (Bransford, Brown, and Cocking 1999). From interactions with the environment, individuals form action and reaction schemas—behaviors that are triggered by contextual cues. These sets of action and reaction schemas form memories and constitute most learning for most people (Hogarth 2001). Interestingly, most experts have a different sort of education.

How do experts become expert? First, experts learn from interaction or education that has three characteristics: (1) they learn in situations that reward *appropriate* behaviors—behaviors that lead to success in the domain; (2) they learn explicit theory as they build tacit knowledge, in other words, strategy instruction and metacognitive coaching; (3) they experience extensive, focused practice (Hogarth 2001). Unlike most novices, experts learn their skills in favorable (well-structured) environments, interactive situations that provide mentoring from experts, who offer precise feedback on whether they are learning what works to solve problems in the domain and guide them with one-on-one coaching appropriate to their level of skill.

Second, experts become experts in part because they learn to use explicit theory developed by previous generations of experts in their profession. Mentors of experts-in-training explain to their charges how theory relates to the underlying structures of domain problems and why certain choices or responses are better than others. Experts-in-training learn to make decisions in an explicit, deliberate way in the context of explicit theory and explanation (Abernathy and Hamm 1995). Early on they learn to embed explanations in a theory that drives understanding and action.[3] Thus, along with the implicit learning that comes from immersion in a situation, experts-in-training are given theoretical tools with which to "see" the domain (Hinds, Patterson, and Pfeffer 2001). These tools steady them through the process of solving domain problems. For example, experts in moral judgment have learned moral theory from various perspectives and are able to apply the framework of a perspective to a particular domain problem without personal concerns impeding their performance. As a person moves from less-expert status to more-expert status, they get better not only at performing and solving problems in the domain (Kuhara-Kojima and Hatano 1991; Sternberg 1998), but at explaining their action choices.

Third, experts put in a lot of time and focused practice in the domain. Experts in moral judgment have spent countless hours wrestling with and developing solutions to moral problems. Experts are able to sustain interest through tedious hours of focused effort. Some argue that this is the key to expertise and that it takes about ten thousand hours or ten years of focused practice (Ericsson, Krampe, and Tesch-Roemer 1993). In fact, after lengthy practice these skills can become so automatic (Ericsson and Smith 1991) that some experts are unable to instruct others in what they do (Kihlstrom, Shames, and Dorfman 1996).

In sum, experts benefit from an education that differs from that experienced by most novices. Experts are immersed in well-structured environments. They explicitly learn theory, and they spend a great deal of time on focused, deliberative practice developing appropriate intuitions. Unlike the lay person, experts have the benefit of learning tacit knowledge and explicit knowledge in tandem. They have networks of schemas linking their tacit and explicit knowledge banks. They develop a whole set of skills including reflective, deliberative skills, routines, and superior processing capabilities. Taking into account what we know about expertise and its construction, what does expertise in morality look like and how should we teach it?

EDUCATING ETHICAL EXPERTISE

Narvaez (forthcoming-a; forthcoming-b) has recently articulated an expertise model of character development and education, called Integrative Ethical Education (IEE).[4] IEE elucidates both *character* education and character *education.* According to this model, character is a set of component skills that can be cultivated to high levels of expertise. This is not a new idea. Plato believed that the just person is like a craftsman who has specific, well-developed skills that have been cultivated through training and practice (Plato 1974). In *The Republic,* Plato repeatedly draws an analogy between the practice of professional skills and the practices of a just person. Plato describes the skilled artisan as knowledgeable and effective in an art. A just person is one who has particular, highly cultivated skills, namely, is knowledgeable and effective in ethical "know-how" (*techne*). Accordingly, character development can be described as a skill-developing activity in which one becomes more expert through practice and apprenticeship. Of course, ethical expertise encompasses more than judgment and decision making. Effective ethical know-how is dynamic and responsive in real time to events in the world. True ethical expertise requires concurrent, competent interaction with the challenges of the environment using a plethora of processes, knowledge, and skills.

Based on a follow-up of Rest's (1983; Narvaez and Rest 1995) review of social development research, Narvaez has identified the characteristic skills of persons with good character (Narvaez, Bock, and Endicott 2003; Narvaez, Bock, Endicott, and

Lies forthcoming; Narvaez et al. 1999). These skills extend Rest's four psychologically distinct processes (ethical sensitivity, ethical judgment, ethical motivation, and ethical action) by outlining a set of social, personal, and citizenship skills. The four process model provides a wholistic understanding of the moral person, who is able to demonstrate keen perception and perspective taking, skilled reasoning, moral motivational orientations, and skills for completing moral action (Narvaez 2002, forthcoming-a, forthcoming-b).

Experts in the skills of Ethical Sensitivity, for example, are able to more quickly and accurately "read" a situation and determine what role they might play. These experts are also better at generating usable solutions due to a greater understanding of the consequences of possible actions. Experts in the skills of Ethical Judgment are more adept at solving complex problems, seeing the crux of a problem quickly, and bringing with them many schemas for reasoning about what to do. Their information processing tools are more complex but also more efficient. Experts in the skills of Ethical Focus take responsibility for others, prioritizing the ethical ideal. Their motivation is directed by an organized structure of moral self-identity. Experts in the skills of Ethical Action are able to keep themselves focused and take the necessary steps to get the ethical job done. They demonstrate superior performance when completing an ethical action. The IEE approach suggests seven ethical skills, each with three suggested subskills, for each of the four processes (see table 1).

Not only *character* education, but character *education* should be based on psychologically valid research. The pedagogy used in IEE is based on the expertise paradigm that has gained prominence among educational researchers (e.g., Sternberg 1998, 1999) and provides a map for instruction. Adopting a cognitive approach to learning and teaching that assumes that children actively construct representations of the world (Narvaez 2002; Piaget 1952, 1965, 1970), IEE offers guidelines for helping children move along a continuum from novice to expert in each ethical skill that they study. Best practice instruction provides opportunities for students to develop more accurate and better organized representations and the procedural skills required to use them (Anderson 1989). In order to do this, children must experience an expert-in-training pedagogy for each ethical skill that they learn.

The three aspects to an expert-in-training pedagogy, mentioned previously, are a well-structured environment, simultaneous learning of theory and skill, and focused practice. Throughout the process of learning a skill, students must participate in at least one well-structured environment (e.g., school) that rewards the target ethical skill. In order for the school to be a well-structured environment, teachers must adopt an intentional, deliberative approach to structuring the school, its classrooms,

TABLE 1. Four Processes, Their Skills, and Subskills

SENSITIVITY	JUDGMENT
ES-1: Understand Emotional Expression	*EJ-1: Understanding Ethical Problems*
Identify and express emotions	Gathering information
Fine-tune your emotions	Categorizing problems
Manage anger and aggression	Analyzing ethical problems
ES-2: Take the Perspectives of Others	*EJ-2: Using Codes and Identifying*
Take an alternative perspective	*Judgment Criteria*
Take a cultural perspective	Characterizing codes
Take a justice perspective	Discerning code application
	Judging code validity
ES-3: Connecting to Others	
Relate to others	*EJ-3: Reasoning Generally*
Show care	Reasoning objectively
Be a friend	Using sound reasoning
	Avoiding reasoning pitfalls
ES-4: Responding to Diversity	
Work with group and individual	*EJ-4: Reasoning Ethically*
differences	Judging perspectives
Perceive diversity	Reason about standards and ideals
Become multicultural	Reason about actions and outcomes
ES-5: Controlling Social Bias	*EJ-5: Understand Consequences*
Diagnose bias	Choose your environments
Overcome bias	Predicting consequences
Nurture tolerance	Responding to consequences
ES-6: Interpreting Situations	*EJ-6: Reflect on the Process and Outcome*
Determine what is happening	Reasoning about means and ends
Perceive morality	Making right choices
Respond creatively	Redesigning the process
ES-7: Communicate Well	*EJ-7: Coping*
Speak and listen	Apply positive reasoning
Communicate nonverbally	Managing disappointment
and alternatively	and failure
Monitor communication	Developing resilience

TABLE 1. Four Processes, Their Skills, and Subskills (*cont.*)

FOCUS	ACTION
EF-1: Respecting Others Be civil and courteous Be non-violent Show reverence	*EA-1: Resolving Conflicts and Problems* Solve interpersonal problems Negotiate Make amends
EF-2: Cultivate Conscience Self command Manage influence and power Be honorable	*EA-2: Assert Respectfully* Attend to human needs Build assertiveness skills Use rhetoric respectfully
EF-3: Act Responsibly Meet obligations Be a good steward Be a global citizen	*EA-3: Taking Initiative as a Leader* Be a leader Take initiative for and with others Mentor others
EF-4: Be a Community Member Cooperate Share resources Cultivate wisdom	*EA-4: Planning to Implement Decisions* Thinking strategically Implement successfully Determine resource use
EF-5: Finding Meaning in Life Center yourself Cultivate commitment Cultivate wonder	*EA-5: Cultivate Courage* Manage fear Stand up under pressure Managing change and uncertainty
EF-6: Valuing Traditions and Institutions Identify and value traditions Understand social structures Practice democracy	*EA-6: Persevering* Be steadfast Overcome obstacles Build competence
EF-7: Develop Ethical Identity and Integrity Choose good values Build your identity Reach for your potential	*EA-7: Work Hard* Set reachable goals Manage time Take charge of your life

and the activities that take place therein. Too often, school-based learning environments are poorly structured, resulting in children learning the wrong things. The primary redundancies, patterns, and rewards in the school environment that children pick up and learn are commonly the insubstantial accoutrements of schooling, such as standing in a straight line or sitting still. Frequently, the most redundant reward system is built around crowd control techniques. Instead of learning the usefulness and practical application of conflict resolution, for example, students learn about such things as writing neatly, being quiet, and waiting. Moreover, schooling generally is hit-or-miss in regards to character skill development—in part because teachers (and parents) do not like to think that teachers are teaching values. Nevertheless, teachers are teaching values by what they emphasize and reward, too often without deliberation and rather haphazardly. In a superior well-structured environment, all adults at the school are committed to the enterprise of maintaining an ethical climate and all adults model and coach the skills and behaviors students are to learn (see Baum and Gray 1992).

Besides immersion in a well-structured environment, students must experience instruction that mirrors that of experts-in-training. For novices and experts, tacit knowledge forms the rich base of practical intelligence within any domain (Sternberg 1998). But for expertise development, tacit knowledge development must be accompanied by the learning of theory and metacognitive strategies. How do educators begin to foster in students the vast network of tacit and explicit schemas that make up a domain's practical intelligence? According to Marshall (1995), there are several levels of knowledge in a fully developed conceptual network or schema, from less to more complex. Starting with the big picture, the student learns to identify basic aspects of the domain, building *identification knowledge* from many different kinds of experiences in the domain. Complexity is added when the teacher begins to draw attention to the details of problems and patterns, helping students build *elaboration knowledge.* The next layer of understanding involves extensive practice solving problems in the domain, allowing students to build *planning knowledge* by accessing and implementing identification and elaboration knowledge. Finally, students begin to integrate their knowledge across contexts and build their *execution knowledge* in the domain. In summary, students learn to solve domain problems through explicit instruction in "seeing the big picture" of the skill domain, attending to facts and specific detail in the domain, learning specific sets of procedures in the domain, and integrating skills across contexts. In this way they learn theory in tandem with the intuitions that develop in a well-structured environment. Many more years of practice

---

TABLE 2. Levels of Ethical Skill Instruction

Level 1: Immersion in examples and opportunities. In this initial phase, attention is drawn to the big picture and to the recognition of basic patterns in the skill domain. Accordingly, the teacher plunges students into multiple, engaging activities. Students learn to recognize broad patterns in the domain and begin to develop gradual awareness and recognition of elements in the domain (comprising identification knowledge).

Level 2: Attention to facts and skills. In this phase of development, knowledge is built through a focus on detail and prototypical examples. The teacher focuses the student's attention on the elemental concepts in the domain in order to build more elaborate concepts. Skills are gradually acquired through motivated, focused attention (comprising elaboration knowledge).

Level 3: Practice procedures. At this level, one sets goals, plans the steps of problem solving, and practices skills. The teacher coaches the student and allows the student to try out many skills and ideas throughout the domain to build an understanding of how skills relate and how best to solve problems in the domain. Skills are developed through practice and exploration (comprising planning knowledge).

Level 4: Integrate knowledge and procedures. At this level, one executes plans and solves problems. Deliberate practice at this level over a long period of time can lead to expertise. The student finds numerous mentors and/or seeks out information to continue building concepts and skills. There is a gradual systematic integration and application of skills and knowledge across many situations. The student learns how to take the steps in solving complex domain problems (comprising execution knowledge).

---

may lead to expertise in the domain. Table 2 contains a more detailed explanation for each of the four levels that were developed for the Minnesota Community Voices and Character Education project (Narvaez et al. 1999; Narvaez, Bock, and Endicott 2003; Narvaez, Bock, Endicott, and Lies forthcoming).

Finally like the expert, students learn to master the defining features and underlying structures of a domain through practice that is focused and coached (Ericsson and Charness 1994; Ericsson, Krampe, and Tesch-Roemer 1993). The educator provides authentic learning experiences that are structured according to what we know about levels of apprenticeship (Marshall 1995; Rogoff et al. 1995), providing students with opportunities for coached practice in many contexts and with many contents.

CONCLUSION

In this chapter we attempted to show how a consideration of contemporary psychological research paradigms open up promising lines of research in moral psychology. In particular we argued that cognitive processes that are tacit, implicit, and automatic govern much of human functioning, and that a suitable moral psychology must take account of this fact. We tried to show how varieties of automaticity might play out in forms of moral behavior and suggested resulting implications for explaining some common features of character education pedagogy. Indeed, we took up the issue of how to inculcate moral intuitions, appealing to the expertise literature as an orienting framework. To this end we examined the Integrative Ethical Education approach developed by Narvaez as a prominent example of how an expertise approach to moral character can be applied with profit to the curricular challenges of middle school character education. We suggested that moral education should encourage students to develop multiple skill areas to higher levels of expertise in order to encourage the formation and application of moral intuitions.

NOTES

1.   Intention is considered a critical feature of motivation. Perhaps this is why verbalization and deliberative processing have been the focus of moral psychology. However, as pointed out by Blasi (in a personal communication), intention does not need to be explicit or consciously held. Intention has to do with the goal the actor has in mind, whether conscious or not. The examination of unconscious motive is certainly ripe for research in moral psychology. It is time to accept the importance of the unconscious in moral behavior and begin to study it in a scientific and rigorous way.

2.   However, we must point out that deliberative reasoning has its place. The trick is to know when to trust intuition and when to deliberate. Both systems are goal driven, but it is impossible to deliberate on many actions/decisions, and so one must make sure that intuitions are appropriate. Intuition is not precise but approximate, so its errors are usually slight. On the other hand, although the deliberative system can be more precise, its errors are large and damaging. Further, deliberating on an intuitive process can result in less optimal performance (Beilcock and Carr 2001).

3.   Gradually, however, with practice and experience, their decision-making processes become automatic as well. In fact, most experts become unable to explain their decision-making processes (e.g., Kihlstrom, Shames, and Dorfman 1996).

4.   The IEE model was built upon the work of Narvaez and colleagues at the University of Minnesota in partnership with the Minnesota Department of Children, Families, and Learn-

ing, during the Community Voices and Character Education Project, funded by the U.S. Department of Education (USDE OERI Grant # R215V980001).

REFERENCES

Abernathy, C. M., and R. M. Hamm. 1995. *Surgical Intuition.* Philadephia: Hanley & Belfus.

Anderson, L. M. 1989. Classroom instruction. In *Knowledge Base for the Beginning Teacher,* ed. M. C. Reynolds, 101–15. Oxford: Pergamon Press.

Bargh, J. A. 1989. Conditional automaticity: Varieties of automatic influence in social perception and cognition. In *Unintended Thought,* ed. J. S. Uleman and J. A. Bargh, 3–51. New York: Guilford Press.

———. 1990. Auto-motives: Preconscious determinants of thought and behavior. In *Handbook of Motivation and Cognition,* vol. 2, ed. E. T. Higgins and R. M. Sorrentino, 93–130. New York: Guilford Press.

———. 1996. Principles of automaticity. In *Social Psychology: Handbook of Basic Principles,* ed. E. T. Higgins and A. Kruglanski, 169–83. New York: Guilford Press.

———. 1997. The automaticity of everyday life. In *The Automaticity of Everyday Life,* ed. R. S. Wyer, Jr. Advances in Social Cognition, vol. 10, 1–61. Mahwah, NJ: Lawrence Erlbaum Associates.

Bargh, J. A., and M. J. Ferguson. 2000. Beyond behaviorism: On the automaticity of higher mental processes. *Psychological Bulletin* 126:925–45.

Baum, B. E., and J. J. Gray. 1992. Expert modeling, self-observation using videotape, and acquisition of basic therapy skills. *Professional Psychology: Research and Practice* 23 (3): 220–25.

Beilcock, S. L., and T. H. Carr. 2001. On the fragility of skilled performance: What governs choking under pressure? *Journal of Experimental Psychology: General* 130 (4): 701–25.

Bransford, J. D., A. L. Brown, and R. R. Cocking, eds. 1999. *How People Learn: Brain, Mind, Experience, and School.* Washington, DC: National Academy Press.

Buchner, A., and W. Wippich. 1998. Differences and commonalities between implicit learning and implicit memory. In *Handbook of Implicit Learning,* ed. M. A. Stadler and P. A. Frensch, 3–46. Thousand Oaks, CA: Sage.

Colby, A., and W. Damon. 1992. *Some Do Care: Contemporary Lives of Moral Commitment.* New York: Free Press.

Colby, A., and L. Kohlberg. 1987. *The Measurement of Moral Judgement,* 2 vols. New York: Cambridge University Press.

Cotterill, R. 1998. *Enchanted Looms.* Cambridge: Cambridge University Press.

Damasio, A. 1999. *The Feeling of What Happens.* New York: Harcourt and Brace.

Ericsson, K. A., and N. Charness. 1994. Expert performance: Its structure and acquisition. *American Psychologist* 49:725–47.

Ericsson, K. A., R. T. Krampe, and C. Tesch-Roemer. 1993. The role of deliberate practice in the acquisition of expert performance. *Psychological Review* 100 (3): 363–406.

Ericsson, K. A., and J. Smith. 1991. *Toward a General Theory of Expertise.* New York: Cambridge University Press.

Frensch, P. A. 1998. One concept, multiple meanings: On how to define the concept of implicit learning. In *Handbook of Implicit Learning,* ed. M. A. Stadler and P. A. Frensch, 47–104. Thousand Oaks, CA: Sage.

Gibson, J. J. 1966. *The Senses Considered as Perceptual Systems.* Boston: Houghton-Mifflin.

Gijselaers, W. H., and G. Woltjer. 1997. Expert-novice differences in the representation of economics problems. Paper delivered at the annual meeting of the American Educational Research Association, Chicago.

Haidt, J. 2001. The emotional dog and its rational tail: A social intuitionist approach to moral judgment. *Psychological Review* 108:814–34.

Hart, D., and S. Fegley. 1995. Prosocial behavior and caring in adolescence: Relations to self-understanding and social judgment. *Child Development* 66:1346–59.

Hart, D., M. Yates, S. Fegley, and G. Wilson. 1995. Moral commitment in inner-city adolescents. In *Morality in Everyday Life,* ed. M. Killen and D. Hart, 317–41. Cambridge: Cambridge University Press.

Hammond, K. R. 2000. *Judgments Under Stress.* New York: Oxford University Press.

Hasher, L., and R. T. Zacks. 1984. Automatic processing of fundamental information. *American Psychologist* 39:1372–88.

Higgins, E. T., and J. A. Bargh. 1987. Social cognition and social perception. *Annual Review of Psychology* 38:369–425.

Higgins, E. T., J. A. Bargh, and W. J. Lombardi. 1985. Nature of priming effects on categorization. *Journal of Experimental Psychology: Learning, Memory, and Cognition* 11 (1): 59–69.

Hinds, P. J., M. Patterson, and J. Pfeffer. 2001. Bothered by abstraction: The effect of expertise on knowledge transfer and subsequent novice performance. *Journal of Applied Psychology* 86 (6): 1232–43.

Hogarth, R. M. 2001. *Educating Intuition.* Chicago: University of Chicago Press.

Johnson, K. E., and C. B. Mervis. 1997. Effects of varying levels of expertise on the basic level of categorization. *Journal of Experimental Psychology: General* 126 (3): 248–77.

Keil, F. C., and R. A. Wilson. 2000. Explaining explanations. In *Explanation and Cognition,* ed. F. C. Keil and R. A. Wilson, 1–18. Cambridge, MA: MIT Press.

Kihlstrom, J. F., V. A. Shames, and J. Dorfman. 1996. Intimations of memory and thought. In *Implicit Memory and Metacognition,* ed. L. Reder, 1–23. Mahwah, NJ: Lawrence Erlbaum Associates.

Kirsch, I., ed. 1999. *How Expectancies Shape Experience.* Washington, DC: American Psychological Association.

Kohlberg, L. 1981. *The Philosophy of Moral Development.* Essays on Moral Development, vol. 1, San Francisco: Harper & Row.

————. 1984. *The Psychology of Moral Development.* Essays on Moral Development, vol. 2. San Francisco: Harper & Row.

Kohlberg, L., C. Levine, and A. Hewer. 1983. *Moral Stages: A Current Formulation and a Response to Critics.* Contributions to Human Development, vol. 10. New York: Karger.

Kohn, A. 1997. How not to teach values: A critical look at character education. *Phi Delta Kappan* 78 (February): 429–39.

Kuhara-Kojima, K., and G. Hatano. 1991. Contribution of content knowledge and learning ability to the learning of facts. *Journal of Educational Psychology* 83 (2): 253–63.

Lapsley, D. K. 1999. An outline of a social-cognitive theory of moral character. *Journal of Research in Education* 8:25–32.

Lapsley, D. K., and D. Narvaez. 2004. A social-cognitive view of moral character. In *Moral Development: Self and Identity,* ed. D. Lapsley and D. Narvaez, 189–212. Mahwah, NJ: Lawrence Erlbaum Associates.

Libet, B. 1985. Unconscious cerebral initiative and the role of conscious will in voluntary action. *Behavioral and Brain Sciences* 8:529–66.

Logan, G. D. 1989. Automaticity and cognitive control. In *Unintended Thought,* ed. J. S. Uleman and J. A. Bargh, 52–74. New York: Guilford Press.

Marshall, S. P. 1995. *Schemas in Problem Solving.* Cambridge: Cambridge University Press.

McCloskey, M, and D. Kohl. 1983. Naive physics: The curvilinear impetus principle and its role in interactions with moving objects. *Journal of Experimental Psychology: Learning, Memory, and Cognition* 9 (1): 146–56.

Mowrer, H. O. 1960. *Learning and Behavior.* New York: John Wiley and Sons.

Myles-Worsley, M., W. Johnston, and M. A. Simons. 1988. The influence of expertise on x-ray image processing. *Journal of Experimental Psychology: Learning, Memory, and Cognition* 14 (3): 553–57.

Narvaez, D. 2002. The expertise of moral character. *Education Matters* 8 (6, July/August): 1, 6.

Narvaez, D. Forthcoming-a. Integrative ethical education. In *Handbook of Moral Development,* ed. M. Killen and J. Smetana. Mahwah, NJ: Lawrence Erlbaum Associates.

Narvaez, D. Forthcoming-b. The neo-Kohlbergian tradition and beyond: Schemas, expertise and character. In *Moral Motivation through the Lifespan,* ed. C. Pope-Edwards and G. Carlo. Nebraska Symposium on Motivation, vol. 51. Lincoln: University of Nebraska Press.

Narvaez, D., T. Bock, and L. Endicott. 2003. Who should I become? Citizenship, goodness, human flourishing, and ethical expertise. In *Teaching in Moral and Democratic Education,* ed. Wiel Veugelers and Fritz K. Oser, 43–63. Bern, Switzerland: Peter Lang Publishers.

Narvaez, D., T. Bock, L. Endicott, and J. Lies. Forthcoming. Minnesota's Community Voices and Character Education Project. *Journal of Research in Character Education.*

Narvaez, D., R. Herbst, S. Hagele, and A. Gomberg. 2003. Nurturing peaceful character. *Journal of Research in Education* 13:41–50.

Narvaez, D., C. Mitchell, L. Endicott, and T. Bock. 1999. *Nurturing Character in the Middle School Classroom: A Guidebook for Teachers.* Roseville: Minnesota Department of Children, Families, and Learning.

Narvaez, D., and J. Rest. 1995. The four components of acting morally. In *Moral Behavior and Moral Development: An Introduction,* ed. W. Kurtines and J. Gewirtz, 385–400. New York: McGraw-Hill.

Nash, R. J. 1997. *Answering the Virtuecrats: A Moral Conversation on Character Education.* New York: Teachers College Press.

Neisser, U. 1976. *Cognition and Reality: Principle and Implications of Cognitive Psychology.* New York: W. H. Freeman.

Novick, L. R. 1988. Analogical transfer, problem similarity, and expertise. *Journal of Experimental Psychology: Learning, Memory, and Cognition* 14 (3): 510–20.

Nucci, L. 2000. The promise and limitation of the moral self construct. Presidential address delivered at the thirtieth annual meeting of the Jean Piaget Society, Montreal, June 3. http://tigger.uic.edu/~lnucci/MoralEd/articles/nuccipromise.html.

Piaget, J. 1952. *The Origin of Intelligence in Children.* New York: International University Press.

———. 1965. *The Moral Judgment of the Child.* Trans. M. Gabain. New York: Free Press. (Orig. pub. 1932.)

———. 1970. *Genetic Epistemology.* Trans. E. Duckworth. New York: Columbia University Press.

Plato. 1974. *The Republic.* Trans. D. Lee. London: Penguin Books.

Reber, A. S. 1993. *Implicit Learning and Tacit Knowledge: An Essay on the Cognitive Unconscious.* New York: Oxford University Press.

Rest, J. 1979. *Development in Judging Moral Issues.* Minneapolis: University of Minnesota Press.

———. 1983. Morality. In *Cognitive Development,* ed. J. Flavell and E. Markman. Manual of Child Psychology, 4th ed., vol. 3, ed. P. Mussen, 556–629. New York: John Wiley and Sons.

Rogoff, B., J. Baker-Sennett, P. Lacasa, and D. Goldsmith. 1995. Development through participation in sociocultural activity. In *Cultural Practices as Contexts for Development,* ed. J. J. Goodnow, P. J. Miller, and F. Kessel, 45–65. San Francisco: Jossey-Bass.

Rumelhart, D. E., and J. L. McClelland, eds. 1986. *Parallel Distributed Processing,* 2 vols. Cambridge, MA: MIT Press.

Sanderson, P. M. 1989. Verbalizable knowledge and skilled task performance: Association, dissociation, and mental models. *Journal of Experimental Psychology: Learning, Memory, and Cognition* 15 (4): 729–47.

Sternberg, R. J. 1998. Abilities are forms of developing expertise. *Educational Researcher* 3:22–35.

———. 1999. Intelligence as developing expertise. *Contemporary Educational Psychology* 24 (4): 359–75.

Turiel, E. 1983. *The Development of Social Knowledge: Morality and Convention.* Cambridge: Cambridge University Press.

Uleman, J. S., and J. A. Bargh, eds. 1989. *Unintended Thought.* New York: Guilford Press.

Vicente, K. J., and J. H. Wang. 1998. An ecological theory of expertise effects in memory recall. *Psychological Review* 105 (1): 33–57.

Wegner, D. M. 2002. *The Illusion of Conscious Will.* Cambridge, MA: MIT Press.

Wegner, D. M., and T. Wheatley. 1999. Apparent mental causation: Sources of the experience of will. *American Psychologist* 54 (7): 480–92.

Wilson, R. A., and F. C. Keil. 2000. The shadows and shallows of explanation. In *Explanation and Cognition*, ed. F. C. Keil and R. A. Wilson, 82–114. Cambridge, MA: MIT Press.

Wyer, R. S. 1997. *The Automaticity of Everyday Life.* Mahwah, NJ: Lawrence Erlbaum Associates.

SEVEN

A Certain and Reasoned Art

The Rise and Fall of
Character Education in America

Craig A. Cunningham

So far as moral character is concerned, education has been merely futile, and not even injurious; the real formative power has been original spiritual nature.... But from this time forth must the education of man be rescued from the hands of this obscure and enigmatical power, and put under the control of a rational art, able to compass its end and in every individual intrusted to it,—or at least fully aware when it has not attained it, and therefore knowing that the task is not yet finished. A certain and reasoned art of forming in man a firm and reliable good will—such is the education I propose, and this is its prime characteristic.

Johann Gottlieb Fichte, *an die deutsche Nation*

EDUCATORS IN THE UNITED STATES HAVE CONTINUOUSLY WORRIED ABOUT the moral quality of American life, and have attempted to use the schools to improve that quality or to protect it against perceived threats. During times of national identity conflict, especially, character education has often become a rallying cry for those seeking a return to traditional visions of what it means to be a human being or to be an American. Yet these periods of national identity crisis are precisely those eras when consensus about character education is most elusive. A repeated historical pattern emerges in which diverse groups turn to "character education" as an ideal and seek to develop programs to promulgate this ideal. Character education becomes, for a time, a "Big Tent" for a wide variety of interest groups—each with its own understanding of the meaning of character and the means to develop it. Eventually, the "nomistic din" within the tent (Geertz 1983, 222)—combined with the effort to destroy consensus by those who are opposed to a frightening vision of coordinated social action by traditionalists—leads character advocates to look for less controversial ways to protect their social interests.

In this essay, I survey this history in terms of the rise and fall of character as a rallying cry among educators. By focusing on the Character Education Movement of the 1920s and 1930s, I seek to understand the possible contours of contemporary trends in character education. My conclusions are that sustained efforts toward character education are impossible without a shared conception of what it is and how it is developed, and that the failure of psychologists and other social scientists to foster a coherent model of the human self that appeals to diverse audiences continues to handicap efforts to make character education an ongoing shared effort.

WHAT IS CHARACTER EDUCATION?

Nearly everyone agrees that one of the most important goals of American schools should be to develop "good character" in their students. Yet this agreement proves to be superficial once the debate gets down to specifics about what this is and how it should be developed. Traditional understandings, fostered by the religious beliefs or ethnic experiences of particular groups, fail to satisfy a broad spectrum of the population. Even commonsensical secular conceptions—such as the early nineteenth-century faculty psychology view that good character results from the repeated practice of good acts fostered by moral persuasion and coercion—have failed to withstand the scrutiny of psychological research, or find themselves repudiated by more liberal notions about the nature of children. The continuing lack of a clear societal consensus on goals and methods has even led James Davison Hunter (2000) to conclude recently that secularized character education in the public schools is impossible. Hunter's view is that without the contextualized stories and ideals of particular communities, moral education becomes devoid of meaning.

The most prominent twentieth-century attempt to create a secularized consensus about the meaning of character was that of John Dewey, who once defined character as: "the interpenetration of habits which can be read through the medium of individual acts" (Dewey 1922, 29–30). According to Dewey, the character of a person is built up by the habits gained through experience; character is *part* of the person's essential nature. Indeed, it *is* the person to a large extent. Habits, for Dewey, are "working adaptations of personal capacities with environing forces" (16) that are operative below the surface of behavior at all times, ready to be expressed given the opportunity. Thus, it is necessary to observe a person in a variety of circumstances in order to see the person's character. The emergence of patterns of response over time becomes the primary evidence of an individual's character.

An education for character would provide educational experiences that would produce certain kinds of desired habits or attitudes and repress others. The broadness of the aims of character education and of the concept of character itself makes it difficult for people to agree on what "character" is and how it should be taught. Perhaps this is why many contemporary empirical researchers and theorists eschew it as a theoretical construct. Character is difficult or impossible to operationalize—to verbalize, to theorize, and to rationalize—and so it has been difficult to study. Educational researchers have concentrated on less encompassing terms: specific traits, such as honesty, self-deceit, or self-esteem; specific behaviors, such as drug use or cheating; specific academic skills; artistic creativity; or physical stamina and prowess.

Despite the lack of consensus about what character is or how it can be operationalized as a research construct, character remains a vital issue for many qualitative education writers (e.g., Grant 1988; Lightfoot 1983). This continued reliance on the term in some circles may be an indication that it articulates a useful concept. Moreover, because of the lack of scientific consensus, character education has been an arena in which the non-scientific lay community—parents, church groups, philanthropists—have been able to remain relevant, especially in local school communities, pushing their programs and approaches without being subject to the careful scrutiny of experts.

CHARACTER EDUCATION BEFORE 1900

Education for character has always been a concern in the United States. After the War of Independence, political figures such as Thomas Jefferson in Virginia and Benjamin Franklin in Pennsylvania were instrumental in founding schools that would add to the intellectual capacities of the emerging states. Together with a concern for increasing intellectual skills was a strong feeling that education could add to what was then called the "moral character" of the larger society.

It was commonly believed in the late 1700s and early 1800s that the child must be protected from his own evil impulses, and that the only way to insure his compliance with the norms of society was through moral training. This training of the child's character away from evil impulses and toward the good was largely based upon Christian beliefs and ethics. For example, the doctrine of original sin led educators to believe that children are by nature disorderly or immoral, and that education must include means for every individual to be trained to overcome his wild, savage impulses through discipline.

Following strict Protestant tradition, and often dominated by harsh discipline, early schools used two basic means for teaching moral character to their students: coercion and exhortation. Coercion was explicit when schoolmasters applied the aphorism "spare the rod, spoil the child," but, perhaps more importantly, coercion was implicit in the tightly knit communities of early America, in which the children often attended the same church as well as the same school, and in which the scorn of public disapproval had a great effect upon children who chose to disobey the accepted norms of behavior. Exhortation was also explicit and obvious in the early schools, through what was then known as "moral suasion." Using the Bible, primers, and other texts, teachers relied upon the common religious and ethical understandings of their pupils and communities to mold the behaviors of their charges.

With the waves of immigration in the 1820s and 1840s, the religious consensus governing early American schools began to fall apart. Eventually, immigration led to an erosion of the homogeneity that had allowed early teachers to rely upon coercion and exhortation. However, it would be decades before educators realized the implications of this changed landscape. Common School advocates such as Horace Mann remained convinced that the schools could rely on innate powers of intelligence and morality to produce "voluntary compliance with the laws of reason and duty" (quoted in Johnson 1980, 42). This faith was bolstered by the prevalent faculty psychology, which held that every person possessed certain innate faculties such as reason, emotion, self-control, and chivalry, and that these faculties could be trained through repeated practice. This is just one example of how psychological theories have supported prevalent modes of character education.

During the period from 1850 to 1880, the view that moral rules and obligations were self-evident laws of nature slowly eroded. The writings of Charles Darwin and Karl Marx began trickling down to the popular imagination as theories that showed that human systems of thought and behavior evolved as the result of contingent and random events, rather than in accordance with the higher purposes of God. Along with this general trend, people in America slowly lost faith in the inherent goodness of human civilization. The sheer brutality of the Civil War and the increasing poverty and hopelessness of growing industrial cities convinced many people that it was not the adults in the society who modeled moral purity, but rather the children who came to be seen as "unspoiled innocents," not depraved original sinners (Gutowski 1978, 36). This view led educational leaders to develop schools that were protective havens staffed by nurturing and loving teachers trained to bring out the best in the children not through constant discipline but through appealing to interest and aesthetic sensibilities.

At the same time that these general philosophical shifts were changing the nature of American schooling, immigration had reached the point where the public schools could no longer assume that their charges would submit to thinly-veiled Protestant theology. This changing landscape is illustrated by two events that occurred in Chicago. In 1875, the city banned the reading of the Bible in public schools. Teachers thus lost the traditional source of their authority for teaching morals and character, the source of the exhortations of the past. This was followed in 1880 by a ban on all corporal punishment in Chicago schools. Thus teachers lost much of their power of coercion.

Without the authority of the Bible, teachers looked for ways to secure the obedience of their children through moral instruction. As a seemingly secular concept, character offered two advantages for moral educators. First, unlike the state of a child's soul, which was inevitably subject to religious doctrines and easily offended sensibilities, character was open to dispassionate analysis. Thus it offered at least the veneer of objectivity. Second, character was taken to offer a universally acceptable educational goal: everyone wanted their children to have good character, and educators seemed to believe that this agreement could somehow mend the ideological and perspectival frictions of America's new pluralism. In addition, character as a collection of traits was consistent with mainstream understandings about how people learn. According to this faculty psychology, good character results from effective training of native capacities for honesty, compassion, leadership, and so forth. But new methods were required; the old techniques—coercion and exhortation—would no longer work in a pluralistic society.

Americans at the turn of the twentieth century were conscious of being at a crossroads with regard to who or what they were or were becoming, leading to a period of deliberation about America's "national character." This angst was made particularly poignant by what was visualized as an increasing "tide" of immigration that was noticeably changing the nature of America's communities and disturbing the sense of identity that had been built up during the first 150 years of the nation by the WASPs (white, Anglo-Saxon Protestants) who conceived of themselves as "native" Americans. This flood of non-Americans threatened to overwhelm what was coming to be seen as the "American character." Most of these newcomers were from areas of Europe that were traditionally underrepresented in America—especially eastern and southern Europe—and "nativists" worried about their uncouth habits and mores. These discomforts were especially felt in the nation's schools: due to changes in workplace and compulsory education laws, the number of children in school skyrocketed (Bowles and Gintis 1976), and by 1920 the percentage of students who were either immigrants or the children of immigrants approached seventy-five percent (Callow 1982, 263).

Even though many of these new immigrant groups displayed remarkable social structures supported by strong codes of morality and fervent religious belief, their behavior differed sufficiently from that of the "nativists" that questions were raised about the underlying "racial character" of these groups, an issue made more volatile by reports that many new immigrants, especially single, young men who had come to America mainly to make money to send home to their families in Europe, engaged in socially pathological behavior (Ward 1982, 275). Especially in urban areas, observers saw much reason to be concerned about the future of the nation.

As the growing diversity of groups in America fought for control of the structures and processes of schooling, issues of moral education became *political.* The character of particular groups was compared to the character of other groups or to a character ideal. Individuals' characters were evaluated and studied in order to develop practical techniques for improving the "national character."

THE CHARACTER EDUCATION MOVEMENT OF THE 1910S AND 1920S

By 1910, character education had become a nationwide movement. Articles on character education and moral education began to flood popular journals and magazines. The discovery that certain wealthy individuals were both using their economic power to form illegal trusts and subjecting the ordinary factory worker to appalling working conditions contributed to an increased perception that the public schools were failing in what had been their primary mission. Articles with titles like "Can Virtue Be Taught?" raised the cry that the public schools were doing a fine job of training in knowledge and skills, but too little in the way of character development: "it hardly sur-prizes [sic] us to see a *magna cum laude* Harvard graduate leading downgrade politics, or a Phi Beta Kappa man handling corruption funds" (Sisson 1911, 264). The roots of this movement can be categorized as social, intellectual, and educational.

Social Roots

In addition to immigration, educators also saw the danger of "rapid physical growth" of large urban centers and their concomitant activities (Lawson 1915, 928). "The lure of the street, the unsavory moving pictures, the yellow journal, the low comedy of so many vaudeville performances—and, be it said, of so many so-called 'comic' journals and supplements—all have their effect" (Taylor 1914, 224). Various character educa-tion advocates spoke of what was called "the modern crime wave" (e.g., Golightly 1926, 20), which was closely connected with both urbanization and the diversification of the cities through immigration. These factors were compounded by a feeling that many parents were not prepared to do their part to train children in character, and that the churches and Sunday schools were reaching an increasingly small minority of children.

These wider social trends were reinforced by changing conditions in the schools. Schooling had become compulsory everywhere in the country, which meant that edu-cators could no longer rely upon expulsion as a disciplinary measure. Enrollments in secondary school were increasing dramatically: in 1890, only four percent of fourteen-to seventeen-year-olds were attending public high schools; by 1930, forty-seven per-cent of these teenagers were enrolled (Bowles and Gintis 1976, 181). The effects of this "massification" of the public school cannot be underestimated: teacher tactics that may have worked with the relatively homogeneous student populations of the nine-teenth century were ineffective with the new heterogeneity. The changing nature of the economy, combined with the previously mentioned breakdown in the traditional con-sensus, spurred educators to create a new institution that would prepare all youth for the multitudinous demands of life, which in their minds went well beyond train-ing in intellectual skills.

Intellectual Roots

These social causes of the emphasis on character were supported by dramatic changes in the ways that psychologists and other intellectuals conceived of morality. In the mid-1800s, there was a fascination with the idea that a person's character was some-

how tied into his biology, and pseudo-scientific theories connecting moral dispositions to bodily "humours" or even to the size and shape of the head abounded. These
theories received additional impetus from the work of Charles Darwin and Francis
Galton, which showed that mental activities—like "purely" biological ones such as
skin color—were genetically determined. When combined with the notion that different "racial" groups had different "characters," this conception of the person provided fertile ground for speculation about the influence of evolution on disposition.

No longer were most thinkers caught up in traditional issues of religious ontology: topics such as the "soul" and the "Christ within" were giving way to "naturalized" concepts such as the will and the dispositions. These constructs were rooted
in the growing belief that cognitive/emotional states were related to biological/
genetic causes. "Character," because it somehow encompassed the sense that a person's behavior was related to underlying psychological conditions, became an increasingly useful way to conceive of the stability thought to exist within the person as the
foundation of her specific choices and activities.

As Darwin's theory found expression in the popular writing of Herbert Spencer
and the experiments of Francis Galton, the issue arose of the extent to which such
dispositions were the effect of *inherited* qualities versus the extent to which they
were acquired. The interplay between inherited and acquired influences on character was explored in order to determine how much hope should be placed on reforming people's characters versus ameliorating the effects of bad character. The eugenics movement sprang up as a response to the notion that if character was primarily
inherited then the "national character" depended upon changing the reproductive
habits of various groups of Americans.

The concept of character also received a boost from developments in the field of
intelligence. The faculty psychology view of the mind as a collection of discrete mental
functions was dealt a severe blow by experiments at the turn of the century that showed
that little "transfer of training" occurred between, say, instruction in Latin grammar
and performance on tests of spoken English. If the mind could not be conceived of as
a set of discrete faculties, then what was it? There were two competing views, which
eventually became the competing ontologies of character as well as intellect.

The first view was to espouse a more extreme view of the faculty psychology
model in which the mind was conceived not as a finite set of easily definable functional units, but as an infinitely large set of functions, in which, for example, a separate and distinct neural connection existed for every single element of learning. This
"neural connectionism" view became the favorite model of empirical psychologists
such as Lewis Terman, John B. Watson, and Edward Thorndike. Thorndike began to

oversee a number of empirical studies on character, based upon his conception (articulated in his 1913 *Educational Psychology*) that original tendencies could be classified, analyzed, and eventually trained, if only they were operationalized in terms of specific behaviors.

The second view was that the mind consisted not of discrete mental faculties but rather as an organic whole that developed its functions in reaction to the impact of its entire environment. This view thought of mind as "pure potentiality," which was actualized in response to specific needs and desires. The primary activity of mind was *will;* thus, this view of psychology has been called "connative" psychology. Its primary champions were William James, John Dewey, and W. C. Bagley.

Educational Roots

In 1917, at the Detroit meeting of the Department of Superintendence of the National Education Association, it was announced that "a certain business man" had provided a five-thousand-dollar prize for the "National Morality Codes Competition." This competition sparked interest among various educators: seventy spent a year writing codes, and fifty-two actually submitted plans. The competition was won by Professor William J. Hutchins of Ohio. This competition brought to light the fact that very little was known about *educating* children in morality or character, so in 1918 the same donor put up a twenty-thousand-dollar prize, to be awarded by the National Institute for Moral Instruction (later the Character Education Institute) to "the best method of character education in public schools." Milton Fairchild, the director of the Institute, said that "this is by far the largest award ever offered in education" (1918, 121). This competition caused educators in almost every state to expend considerable energy on character education; in fact, this prize may be single-handedly responsible for the burst of articles related to character and moral education through the 1920s and into the early 1930s.

That this was more than one anonymous businessman's concern is suggested by the Seven Cardinal Principles of Secondary Education that were promulgated by the National Education Association's Educational Policies Commission in 1918. The Seven Cardinal Principles were: Health, Citizenship, Command of the Fundamental Processes, Vocational Efficiency, Worthy Home Membership, Worthy Use of Leisure, and Ethical Character. The seventh principle, Ethical Character, was called "paramount" (Johnson 1980, 45), and was seen as the fundamental concern of all teachers in all subjects.

The archetypal example of how this goal was expressed in school curricula is found in the Iowa Plan for Character Education. Produced by the Research Station in Character Education and Religious Education and the winning entry in the twenty-thousand-dollar Character Education Institute's competition, the Iowa Plan urged a "complete" education:

> In all fields of education . . . the public schools should strive to be complete in their service, but the national system of public education is not now complete, because while intellectual education is fairly well developed, vocational and physical education are only partially provided, and character education on human motives, covering the wisdom of human experience, although recognized by school authorities and by parents as the supremely important phase of public education, is undeveloped and often neglected. (iv)

Training for character would be focused on practice in good character through engaging in hands-on projects: "One actual ethical situation met and solved is worth more to the child than a dozen imaginary moral questions, selected as topics of discussion. Practice the good life rather than entertain thoughts about it" (1). These projects were to come out of the child's own experience and the needs of the community. For example, in a community where maintaining lawns was a problem, children could make signs such as "Please Help Save The Grass" and "Don't Spoil the Lawn" and put them up around the town (23).

The authors of the Iowa Plan did not seem to have any limits on the goals of their curriculum, which were given in a list as Preparation for Health, Preparation for Life in the Community, Preparation for Civic Relations, Preparation for Industrial and Economic Relations, Preparation for a Vocation, Preparation for Parenthood and Family Life, The Mastery of Tradition, Preparation for the Appreciation of Beauty, Preparation for the Use of Leisure Time, Preparation for Reverence, and Preparation for Creative Activity.

In justifying the schools' involvement with the first of these, Preparation for Health, the authors wrote:

> It is the business of the school, working out into the homes, to know that each child has the right nourishment, invigorating exercise, and habits of cleanliness. . . . Ill health and anemia are the basis of moral delinquency, and are the nation's greatest liability. (6)

As was typical of the plans developed in that era, the Iowa Plan aimed to address the whole child, not just his or her intellectual capacities.

In keeping with the ideology of progressive education, the school was to be democratic: "Student participation forms character—If the students feels himself a responsible agent in the conduct and success of the school, he rises to meet it with a new sense of the dignity of his own personality and of the importance of the program in which he is existing" (12). Teachers were to focus upon the ethos of the schools: "instead of talking about moral qualities it is the business of the teacher to see that the spirit of morality dominates the entire life of the school" (29).

One of the implications of this whole-school approach to character development was increased attention to the "Extra-Curriculum." The 1920s saw a veritable explosion of interest, with a barrage of "how-to" manuals for teachers interested in forming clubs, service organizations, and hobby groups (for a partial list of publications, see Gutowski 1978, 220, note 1). The Junior Red Cross, which had become popular during the war, gave way to bands, orchestras, school newspapers, student governments, and civic, class, homeroom, and self-improvement clubs. This focus was supported by the widespread view of character as a collection of traits, each of which would be developed through both the discussion of ideals and practice in the controlled situation of the classroom or after-school organization.

Emerging disagreements

By the end of the 1920s, character had become such a widely accepted educational goal that several states passed ordinances requiring schools to institute a course of study on character (see Powers 1932, 8). Despite the near-universality of this movement, there continued to be substantial disagreement about the methods of character education. Ruth Shonle Cavan (1927) reported a wide divergence in her study of seventy-two cities' character education programs. Charles A. Brown (1928), superintendent of Birmingham, Alabama, public schools, discussed what he saw as a "sharp division of opinion as to method of approach," claiming that the most pressing question was "shall it be direct or indirect?" (628). Walter H. Adams (1928) complained about the "unorganized and, as a rule, unscientific nature" of much character education (167).

Educators in the late 1920s, along with nearly everyone else in American society, were increasingly in awe of the successes of the "scientific approach" to solving problems in the physical and biological sciences. Early reports of successes in the social sciences—most notably the development of allegedly scientific ways of sorting people according to their intellectual capacities—led many educators, especially those associated with university departments and schools of education, to predict the end of education as an art and the beginnings of an educational science. These calls for a more scientific approach to character naturally caused tension among those who believed that traditional values and practices had already been severely undermined by the scientific attitude toward morality and religion. These tensions are exemplified in the 1928 volume of *Religious Education*, where the debate between the "traditionalists" and the "modernists" raged in articles such as "Is There a Scientific Philosophy of Life?" (McFarland 1928), "Science as Technique of Religion" (Haydon 1928), "The Scientific Attitude in Religion" (Dimock 1928), and "Teaching the Bible in an Age of Science" (Aubrey 1928). The Religious Education Association devoted its 1928 convention to "Education in Religion in an Age of Science," a conference remarkable mainly for the unanimity with which religious and secular educators embraced science as the key to more effective schooling in character and religious attitudes. While attention was paid to the possible conflicts between science and religion (especially concerning the nature of theological belief), the speakers tended to believe that science and religion would, in the end, be perfectly "harmonized," and that science would provide religion with the "facts" to support religious "values," if those values were properly infused with an open mind and "continually . . . rethought and reconstructed with every appearance of new [scientific] facts" (May 1928b, 325).

Essentially what was happening was that science was overtaking religion as the determiner of "truth," and those interested in saving religion were coming to the belief that they must cede this role to science and assume a different role, perhaps concentrating on inculcating the proper motivations—ideal goals and the commitment to reaching them—that would enable people to live well. This task, it was said, would place religion and philosophy as the "art" that would complement the findings of science (Smith 1928).

This debate among religious educators mirrored a similar debate in education, where empirical psychology was said to be producing an increasing understanding of how character was formed, but could not begin to develop a sense of which types of character were "good" versus "bad." Ideals for character continued to be the province of philosophical fiat rather than scientific analysis (although there were those educationists who hoped for a scientific solution to the problem through the techniques of "job analysis" advocated by David Snedden and others). But educational psychologists increasingly saw these ideals as unfounded, and by the late 1920s were prepare to do battle even within the realm of moral values.

The Trait Issue

The most consequential (and problematic) disagreement among character advocates was the question of the generality or specificity of conduct. This had been an important issue in the study of character since at least 1911, when Stanford University's Lewis H. Terman—the inventor of the concept of the "intelligence quotient"—had discussed the "baffling complexity" of character as analogous to the "discreteness of all thinking processes" and "powers of observation" (371). Terman had drawn attention to a "principle of the fragmentariness of morality" (374), which the science of penology had discovered, and expressed some pessimism about ever being able to develop (or study) character efficiently.

Terman's connection of the character issue to the issue of intelligence is commonly seen among those who discussed character. Because work on intelligence had proceeded more quickly than work on character, educators who were interested in character looked to work on intelligence as a template for their own thinking about character. The intelligence issue had occupied a good deal of early empirical psychological attention during the opening years of the century. Edward L. Thorndike had made his reputation through his work (with Robert S. Woodworth, 1901) in the famous transfer-of-training experiments. These experiments had overthrown the notion that the human intellect consists of a limited number of discrete "faculties" that could be developed through various tasks of "mental discipline." Thorndike and Woodworth concluded that there was only *minimal* transfer of training between similar tasks, and that if a teacher wanted a student to learn, say, English grammar, then the teacher needed to teach English grammar explicitly, and not expect it to come about through transfer from work done in Latin (Jonçich 1968). Thorndikian psychologists began developing a new model to replace faculty psychology (Kliebard 1987, 106–10). This new model was based on physiological experiments that had proven that the connections between individual nerve cells were somehow involved in mental functions. It was theorized that any particular unit of learning would somehow correspond to the development of a particular nerve connection in the brain and that therefore schooling needed to develop the specific skills and knowledges that would be needed by each student once he had left school. This "connectionism" was a strong and effective argument against the "general education" that had been urged by educators allied with faculty psychology.

The connectionist model was especially favored by those educators who desired a differentiated curriculum to suit the specific needs and native capacities of individual students. Since the intelligence tests were taken to provide a highly valid and reliable measure of what any individual could do mentally, it was felt by some that general education was highly inefficient: Why teach Latin, it was thought, to some near moron who was likely to spend his life digging coal? Why not teach him what he needed: basic reading, writing, some rudimentary figuring, and perhaps some life skills?

That such differentiation of curriculum, if determined on the basis of intelligence tests, would result in deep segregation in school among those of different cultures, socioeconomic backgrounds, and nationalities did not bother Thorndike or many of his followers. Thorndike had looked favorably upon the aims of eugenics (1913); this was not a man who had any personal compunction against racial or cultural prejudice. Rather, his psychological doctrine supported his nativist tendencies and those of many other educators and public commentators during the period leading up to and immediately following World War I. As we have seen, many Americans (particularly the upper social classes) were disturbed at the effect on American culture of massive immigration and were concerned lest the intelligence of the population be severely undermined by the infusion of obviously less-well-endowed peoples from southern and eastern Europe. These nativist thinkers looked to the data collected on army soldiers in World War I for evidence that intelligence was determined by heredity and therefore, to a large extent, untrainable.

An educational theorist who accepted the basic conclusions of the transfer experiments but rejected many of the alleged implications was William Chandler Bagley. Bagley spent most of the teens and twenties arguing against what he called the "deterministic school of psychology" of Thorndike and Terman (Bagley 1928). Bagley agreed that faculty psychology was faulty, and that "transfer" did not take place under ordinary (i.e., uncontrolled) situations. But he claimed that transfer could be accentuated through an emphasis on ideals:

> It is clear from the experiments [of Thorndike and Woodworth] that transfer which will be wide enough in scope to justify a faith in intellectual discipline is quite unlikely unless the learning is of such a character as to give the learner a confidence in the value of the procedure; hence the writer's insistence, since his first discussion of the problem, that the task of the teacher is to develop, not only clearly conscious ideas or concepts of procedure, but also ideals—ideas with feelings of worth attached to them. (1934, 89–90)

Bagley felt that certain human characteristics, such as "persistence, neatness, ability to concentrate on different tasks" could be taught by first having students go through a series of intellectual endeavors (he favored Latin for everyone), then having a discussion with the students about the key factors in their success, and then progressively generalizing these factors into "conscious ideals that will be explicitly applied as standards in other situations" (90).

This perspective gradually found its own set of adherents. Willerd W. Charters of the University of Chicago became one of the most vocal educators urging teachers to concentrate on the development of certain generalized "traits" or characteristics. Under this theory, people develop certain traits that will determine how they behave in a variety of circumstances. As Charters wrote in his 1927 *The Teaching of Ideals*, "In the field of character, a *trait* may be defined as a type reaction. The trait of courage indicates the fact that the individual who possesses this quality is likely to react according to type in a wide variety of situations. If he does, then we say that he possesses the trait under consideration" (33). Charters believed that the goal of education was to inculcate certain traits and, like Bagley, felt that ideals—defined as traits that have "become the object of desire"—were the surest path to developing these "type reactions" among students.

This view of character is in direct contradiction to the conclusions that Thorndike and Terman took from the transfer experiments. Bagley and Charters were urging that while there may not be such thing as intellectual faculties, there were "character faculties" that would develop during the course of a number of specific experiences and would be used generally to control behavior in the future. As a person acquired more such traits, he developed character: a highly integrated personality in which "traits, habits, and customs [combine] in such a way that the person will act in the light of principles" (Charters 1927, 13). In other words, Bagley and Charters were arguing that there was "transfer" from one situation to the next, if not in intellectual faculties, then in the traits that make up character.

Charters suggested education consisted, then, of three aims:

> These are, first, to develop established traits of character and personality; second, to teach children to think their way through situations which involve these traits, and third, to generate in children an emotional conviction concerning the importance of certain qualities of character to them and to their generation. (Charters 1930, 747–48)

Even among those who agreed that character should be conceptualized as a set of traits, there were disagreements, not the least of which was the problem of agreeing upon which "traits" were most essential. Even if agreement about trait priorities could be had, however, there was little known about how to teach each trait—for example, how does the teacher develop established traits of, say, honesty? While there were some useful ideas for education related to this trait approach (the project method, role-playing, reading stories), educators had trouble implementing this type of character instruction.

Another problem with the trait approach to character development was that it was seen as the purpose of the "whole curriculum" to develop these traits. Teachers could not be held accountable for the development of various traits, because, despite the desire to measure traits, there existed no way to evaluate students' moral development. Making this the task of the whole curriculum was problematic: "Everybody's task soon became nobody's task, as it seems obvious it would" (Johnson 1980, 46). Also, the divorce of traits from reasoning—the belief that traits evolved in response to situations rather than to intellectual development—resulted in a gradual cessation of education in moral reasoning.

By the end of the 1920s, two basic positions were forming on the ontology of character. Educators and university educationists were prone to see character as the sum total of traits that were progressively "integrated" into a person's personality. Empirical psychologists were coming to a view that character, if it existed at all, was the accumulation of specific responses to specific situations. The first view believed that the concept of "character traits" was a useful educational heuristic, and that such traits were best developed by generating the "emotional conviction" to these traits, or ideals. The trait idealists were less concerned with whether these trait concepts correlated with empirical data than with whether curricular activities were successful in creating an emotional conviction to acceptable standards of moral conduct. The empirical psychologists, on the other hand, were laying the groundwork for their claim that character traits were mere illusions; that, in fact, there was no such thing as "courtesy" or "honesty"—there were only habituated responses to specific stimuli. This view would increasingly attack the notion that ideals were of any value in the development of character; preferring to adopt the behaviorist view that responses would only be developed through stimulus training.

These two positions on the ontology of character often carried additional baggage. The trait theorists tended to believe that the successful inculcation of ideals was a greater influence on student's character than inherited capacities and that schools had the responsibility and the power to teach devotion to certain moral norms. The specific response theorists were more likely to believe that the individual's capacity for gaining habitual responses to situations was the primary determinate of character and that schools could do very little to alter the inherited characters of students. The disagreements between these groups set the stage for the Character Education Inquiry (CEI), a research project whose overarching goal—implicitly at least—was to disprove, once and for all, this lingering belief among educators in the transfer of lessons in character.

THE CHARACTER EDUCATION INQUIRY

As more and more people entered the Big Tent of the Character Education Movement, differences of opinion arose on a number of issues about character. By the middle of the 1920s, the argument about whether character was something that could be trained in terms of general traits such as honesty or courage or rather consisted of habitual responses to specific situational stimuli had reached a pitch where the psychologists thought it necessary to resolve the issue once and for all. This resulted in the Character Education Inquiry, a massive empirical and conceptual research project, which was completed during 1925 and 1926, and its results published in 1928, 1929, and 1930.

Toward "A Great New Era"

Along with the increase in interest in character education came a rise in optimism about both the school's ability to develop it in children and science's ability to understand its foundations and development. This scientific optimism was well expressed by the German psychologist William Preyer (1895): "the science of the development of the mind is the indispensable foundation for the theory and practice of education" (preface). This optimism was embodied in America by the child-study movement, conducted under the leadership of G. Stanley Hall, which assumed that education would be more effective the more that psychology was able to unlock the secrets of child development.

British psychologists at Cambridge University had begun exploring J. S. Mill's call in the sixth book of his *System of Logic* (1952) for an "Ethology, or the Science of the Formation of Character." Such a science, it was hoped, would inform a policy of Spencerian social control. Empirical psychologists under Charles Spearman made attempts at character measurement, spurred on by the success of the French in their ratings of intelligence. Spearman's protégé Edward Webb completed one of the first statistical studies of character as his 1915 doctoral thesis, "Character and Intelligence: An Attempt at an Exact Study of Character." Claiming that "the business man's judgments are vitiated by the lack of scientific investigation and knowledge," Webb called for a "scientific analysis of character" that would "enable him to judge character more effectively."

Webb and Spearman developed the view that character was the result of a limited number of "factors" that were heterogeneously distributed in the population. A general factor, g, was somehow related to a person's energy level and was responsible for most of the variation among people's achievements. A second factor, w, was related to "perseveration," "purposive consistency," or "self-control." Spearman and others later added a third factor, c, which related to quickness and originality. It was claimed that these factors could account for virtually all societal variation in character. (Note that none of these terms carries much moral connotation. This is a sign that the psychologists and the educators never really agreed on what character education or character are.)

In the United States, Thorndike had begun to lay the groundwork for a study that would test the proposition that character is the result of differential distribution of a small set of factors. His incorporation of the statistical methods of Pearson and Galton was widely admired (Jonçich 1968), and he and his department head, James McKeen Cattell, had made bold first steps toward measuring character. Thorndike had staked his reputation on the proposition that education, to the extent it would become effective, must become quantitative (Jonçich 1968), and the study of character was just one of the areas of his increasing influence. His *Educational Psychology* (1913–14) had championed the use of empirical measurements and "modern statistical methods" in the study of character. He would provide intellectual leadership for the Character Education Inquiry.

Officially directed by Yale University professors Hugh Hartshorne and Mark May, the Character Education Inquiry purported to put to scientific test the basic notions of the Character Education movement. The results of the study—published in three volumes as *Studies in the Nature of Character*—were both widely publicized and widely discussed. Under the joint sponsorship of the Religious Education Association and the Institute for Social and Religious Research—funded by John D. Rockefeller— the study proceeded under the intellectual and administrative guidance of Edward Thorndike. Working from 1925 through 1930, the authors developed new methods of educational data collection, measurement, and statistical analysis in an attempt to find out the answer to the basic question: whether the primary determinants of character was a general character factor, the accumulation of a set of ideal traits, or the aggregation of specific behaviors.

Mark May threw down the gauntlet in a speech to the Chicago Child Study Association concerning the early results of the study:

It is a matter of much concern to character education which of these is correct. If conduct is determined, even in part, by a general character factor, such as "persistence of motives," as suggested by Webb, or something like "will-power" as suggested by Spearman, then the task of character education is to locate this factor and seek its development. If character is an aggregate or even an integration of traits such as honesty, loyalty, self-control, obedience, and the like then the task of character education is to develop these traits by whatever method seems best. This is the conventional theory and is the one on which most of our character education is now built. But if the third theory is correct, namely that conduct is in all cases specific and a function of the circumstances, then character becomes a much more difficult task. It is most difficult namely because we cannot assume transfer of training from one situation to another. Habits are specific, and they transfer only to situations that have elements in common. (May 1928a, 39)

Thus we see that the stakes were high and also that at least one of the primary investigators believed that the results of the study would overthrow "conventional theory" and practice.

"We are interested in the social functioning of children," the authors wrote in their preface,

And by this we mean that we intend to study social behavior in relation, on the one hand, to the ideas, purposes, motives and attitudes entertained by the individual, and, on the other hand, in relation to the group life within which the observed and tested behavior takes place, including both the systems of behavior or customs of the group and its codes, ideals, and purposes. Furthermore, we think of behavior as a function not only of the group but of the self which is becoming enlarged and organized within itself as well as integrated with its groups in the processes of social interaction which are being studied. (Hartshorne and May 1928, 7)

In other words, they were going to study both behaviors and ideals, both on the personal level and on the social level, in an effort to determine the relationships among these levels of character. Their most important question: what is the relationship between the idealized norms of the social group and the morally charged behaviors of the group's members?

The scope of the Inquiry was enormous. In all, more than 170,000 tests were given to more than 8,000 public and 2,500 private school students over three years. The tests attempted to determine both attitudes and ideals toward character as well as actual behavior. The focus, however, was primarily on the various problems involved in measuring *behavior*. The investigators felt that the crucial factor for improvement of practices of "moral and religious education" was the development of "ways of measuring results" (1930a, 607), and hoped to show that "tests for predicting success in living" (608) could be designed that would allow educators to know whether the curricular experiences they were advocating actually affected student's character.

The results of the study were published in three volumes: *Studies in Deceit* (Hartshorne and May 1928), containing Book 1, reporting results, and Book 2, discussing statistical techniques; *Studies in Service and Self-Control* (Hartshorne, May, and Maller 1929), and *Studies in the Organization of Character* (Hartshorne, May, and Shuttleworth 1930). The major results of the study were also summarized in two articles in *Religious Education* (Hartshorne and May 1930a, 1930b).

The authors reported a number of findings, including:

- Socioeconomic background showed "a very significant relation to honesty and moral knowledge, as it does also to intelligence, but shows a rather low relation to co-operation, inhibition and persistence" (1930b, 759).
- The study found only "general relations" between moral knowledge and conduct and almost no relationship between general knowledge and conduct (1930b, 756).
- "When occupations [of parents] are scaled according to their social levels . . . we find significant differences in honesty between children whose parents are engaged in the professional occupations and children whose parents are unskilled labor" (1930b, 759).
- "We have evidence to show that children probably do inherit something like a low constitutional weakness which, in social life, takes the form of low resistance to temptation" (1930b, 760; see also Hartshorne and May 1928, 230 for detailed study).
- "In the matter of conduct, we find that children of English-born and Scandinavian-born parents are frequently the most honest, cooperative and charitable. Children of Italian and Irish parents usually stood at the bottom of the list" (1930b, 760).

The study's most striking conclusion, and the one that was most picked up on by commentators, was that the children were observed to be quite *inconsistent* in how they reacted to the test batteries. "If we call perfect consistency one hundred and perfect inconsistency zero, the average consistency score of a hundred children already referred to is only twenty. We see that there is very little evidence of unified character traits. *We have collected three main lines of data showing that there is no such thing as a unified trait of honesty residing within an individual.*" (Hartshorne and May 1930b, 755; emphasis added). The specific elements of the circumstance were found to be more determinative of a child's behavior than "any mysterious entity residing within the child" (755). In the authors' words:

> There is no evidence of any trait of goodness or character if what is meant by goodness or character is just what may be observed or measured by conduct. We cannot infer from the conduct tests the presence of a general factor. Any community of conduct is due to factors common to the situations represented in the test and not to an inner organization of habit systems or abilities operating independently of the interrelations of situations. (Hartshorne, May, and Shuttleworth 1930, 173)

In other words, character as a general human quality does not exist. Nor, it seems, do the individual traits that were thought to make up character exist. Even if they do, one cannot make generalizations about whether a child is or will be "honest" or "dishonest"—it depends entirely upon the specific circumstances involved. There is no such thing, Hartshorne and May claimed, in "transfer" of learning about honesty. It is meaningless to talk about a "trait" of honesty, and even less significant to try to teach "honesty" to children. This finding became known as the doctrine of "situational specificity."

Educational Implications

The Character Education Inquiry was perceived to have serious implications for character and moral education. First, the study noted that "such consistency of character as pupils have achieved is the product of experience preceding the fifth grade in school and does not materially increase as they move up through the eighth. It would seem to be implied that radical changes are called for in our prevailing methods of character education" (Hartshorne and May 1930b, 762). The value of teacher exhortations to be honest was particularly undermined:

> The mere urging of honest behavior by teachers or the discussion of standards and ideals of honesty, no matter how much such general ideas may be 'emotionalized,' has no necessary relation to the control of conduct. . . . There seems to be evidence that such effects as may result are not generally good and are sometimes unwholesome. (Hartshorne and May 1928, 412)

Also, and perhaps more importantly, the study concluded that individuals must actually experience each distinct type of situation and be taught in detail how and why certain behaviors are honest and dishonest: "What is learned must be experienced. What is to be experienced must be represented in the situation to which children are exposed" (Hartshorne, May, and Maller 1929, 454). Educators must come to emphasize a "process of conditioning through a skilful [*sic*] manipulation of the situations" to which a student is exposed (May 1928a, 43).

In a speech before the Third Annual Conference on Character Education in 1927, Hartshorne and May summarized their earliest findings in this way:

> The conclusions seem to be warranted that (1) when dishonesty is rewarded, dishonesty is practiced; (2) mere verbal promises to be honest and verbal formulations of the ideal of honesty do not produce general honest habits; (3) fundamental changes in the school procedure which permit the exercise of initiative and self-judgment and change the traditional hostile attitude between pupil and teacher to one of cooperation, may tend to eliminate dishonest practices in schoolwork. (May and Hartshorne 1927, 715)

Every educational reformer is aware that making "fundamental changes in the school procedure" is difficult at best and a mere pipe dream at worst. Without the willingness of school administrators and teachers to make such fundamental changes, it would appear from the findings of Hartshorne and May that teaching honesty in school would be impossible.

One commentator, looking back over the history of the character education movement, wrote in 1936:

> The entire movement of character measurement is still upon the horns of a dilemma: tests which are administratively feasible are of little or no value; tests in actual life-situations which have some validity at least in the specific situation of the test are administratively impracticable. They are expensive to give; involve cooperation of several agencies; and as soon as the child becomes aware that he is being tested, it is no longer a true measure of his ordinary behavior. (Brown 1936, 589)

This commentator bemoaned the fact that "after more then two thousand years [of character education] there is still no agreement either as to method of instruction of the kinds of measurement to be used in determining the effectiveness of such instruction" (ibid.).

One effect of the publication of the study was to undermine the widespread be-lief among educators that they understood what is meant by the term "character." Hartshorne and May were explicit in their criticism: "traditional theories concern-ing what character and personality 'are' have no basis in scientific fact, no matter how correct they may turn out to be upon future investigation" (Hartshorne, May, and Shuttleworth 1930, 214). Without a "basis in scientific fact," these researchers assumed, "character" had no place in the discussion of education.

While at least one observer has suggested that the actual effect of the CEI on public conceptions or practices in character education was limited (Leming 2002), many specific references to the findings bring doubt to this view. For example, in 1933 George Coe, former General Secretary of the Religious Education Association (REA), bemoaned the "present crisis in religious education." He recounted how the REA had gradually come to believe that

> We did not really know how to judge character-forming processes. To a large ex-tent we were relying upon guesses as to cause-and-effect relations. Though some guesses and guessers are better than others, it was imperative to replace guesses with knowledge at crucial points. Consequently there grew up an attitude of self-criticism and inquiry. Research enterprises, some of them of great magni-tude, became part of the movement. (Coe 1933, 181)

Coe related how "in some noteworthy instances"—presumably referring to the CEI—"research has proved the incorrectness of what had seemed to be wisdom, and the total pressure of many researchers is in the direction of revisions of both content and method far more drastic than at first thought necessary" (181–2). Coe traced the "crisis" to what he saw as a large crisis in the Protestant religion, with ministers "by and large, either confused as to the issue involved, fretted by the strain of it, fever-ishly endeavoring to galvanize dying methods, or petrified by the thought of putting out to sea" (185).

Character Education after the Movement

After the publication of the CEI, psychologists increasingly abandoned the notion of character in favor of the more neutral term "personality." This probably re-flected both the conclusions of the Hartshorne and May study and increasing pro-fessional relativism. Personality had been eschewed in the late 1920s by psychologists who saw it as too broad a term, which escaped easy operationalization (e.g., Symonds 1928, 286–87); however, the CEI showed that character, too, was not only not easy to operationalize but may, in fact, have been an illusion. Personality offered a more neutral term, which wasn't so automatically loaded with the values of people who used it.

Educators who read the CEI and who discussed it seemed to reach the most pessimistic conclusions about their efforts in character education. One, who summarized the results for the *Journal of Education*, wrote: "What children are learning of self-control, service, and honesty seems to be largely a matter of accident. There is little evidence that they are being influenced by effectively organized moral education" (Astor 1931, 730).

The only window left open for educators who were interested in teaching character was the possibility of manipulating the peer group to play a significant role in each child's character education. If educators could get the peer group to espouse the same values as the school was espousing, so that each student would get "through cooperative discussion and effort the moral support required for the adventurous discovery and effective use of ideals in the conduct of affairs" (Hartshorne and May 1930b, 762), then children could develop character. This window led to an increased use in the 1930s of the "group discussion" as a tool of character education. This tied in well with the promotion of extracurricular activities, which had been emphasized since the early twenties, and was taken up in many "progressive" curricular reforms through, for example, core courses such as "Social Living."

CHARACTER EDUCATION SINCE WORLD WAR II

After the typical war-time drop in discourse about character and moral issues in education (along with a concomitant increase in discussions of "morale"), discourse about character rebounded slightly in the late 1940s as part of the "life adjustment" model of education. During this trend toward seeing the school as primarily a socialization institution, educators became preoccupied with values and behavior. Wars have a way of making people realize how important these things are, and the atrocities of World War II, which became clear as the Allies began cleaning up the mess in Germany in the late forties, led to a renewed emphasis on what was then known as "moral and spiritual values," an emphasis exemplified in the 1951 report of the Educational Policies Commission of the National Education Association (NEA). Like many recent contributions to character (or more likely "moral") education, the Commission fell back on a notion that

> The values approved in American society today . . . will be better taught if they permeate the entire school than if the instruction is centered in a special course. . . . Evidence now available [not cited] suggests that the procedure most likely to be effective in the teaching of moral and spiritual values is to weave these concepts into the entire life of the school and make them a vital part of all subjects of instruction in the school program. (59)

While the Commission was aware that making the teaching of values "every teacher's business" had the danger of making it "no teacher's business" (60), they espoused a "whole curriculum" approach to the teaching of morals and values in which a school would have a positive ethos. If schools were actually able to meet the Commission's recommendations, then surely character growth would result from a student's involvement in the school community.

Most American schools in the 1950s had enough homogeneity for this to be a realizable goal; in many places, a sense of community and of shared values still pervaded the schools (Grant 1989). This "implicit consensus," which the Commission tried to make explicit in its list of shared values, probably resulted in a strong moral education for many students during this time. However, the implicit consensus was to go through a profound shake-up during the 1950s. New racial tensions, brought on by the Supreme Court's decision in *Brown v. Board of Education* and other cases, would make it clear that all Americans did not share more than a superficial commitment to "common consent," "moral equality," and "brotherhood." Deep religious tensions, particularly between Catholics and Protestants, would surface and make many people suspicious of schools engaging even in the limited discussion of religion that the NEA proposed.

So too, the controversy that erupted in the 1950s regarding communism and the "red scare," led to a reluctance by teachers to get into moral questions: they could lose their jobs if they were not careful. States were adopting laws and procedures, including loyalty oaths and "prohibitions against the teaching or advocacy of 'un-American' or subversive doctrines" (Ravitch 1983, 82), which must have dampened whatever freedom teacher's felt to talk about "soft" issues like values. "By 1950, thirty-three states had adopted legislation permitting the ouster of disloyal teachers. In twenty-six states, teachers were required to sign a loyalty oath" (ibid., 93). This activity certainly affected students and teachers: "the college students of the late 1950s were dubbed 'the silent generation.' It was not that they were intimidated, but that they came to political consciousness in an age that was weary of ideology, skeptical of utopias, and alert to ambivalence (ibid., 112).

This new "ambivalence" toward teaching values and beliefs was, in retrospect, a necessary response to (1) the decreasing American consensus on specific ethical rules, (2) the "new psychology," which led to a pessimistic view of the results of teaching character explicitly, and (3) a new thrust in public concern for academic excellence. Books by Arthur Bestor (e.g., *Educational Wastelands*) and others blasted the progressive legacy in American public schools and urged a new attention to intellectual training. The mood of ambivalence toward values provided a ripe situation for character education to be put on the back burner. When Americans were shocked out of complacency toward their educational preeminence by the launching of Sputnik in 1957, character education suffered further: Sputnik came to be a symbol of the consequences of indifference to high academic standards, which received renewed attention. While no one at this time was advocating a complete end to moral education, the momentum of the academic purposes of education came to push aside concerns for the character and morality of students.

The passage of the National Defense Education Act (NDEA) in 1958 heralded a new era of intellectual emphasis in public schools. As Gerald Grant has written of the era after the NDEA:

> The formal content of the curriculum was stripped of moral justifications, and the schools increasingly reflected the separation between the public and private realms that became common currency in American society. In this division the discussion of religion and morals was classified as personal and relegated to the private realm. . . . There was an absence of moral glue, vision, emotional bonds, and social ties. . . . In many schools, the psychological climate deteriorated markedly. Teachers grew more reluctant to enforce norms against cheating, stealing, or verbal or physical abuse unless they felt they had evidence that would stand up in court, so to speak. . . . The moral order of the typical public school became increasingly legalistic and bureaucratic in its reliance on written rules within a centralized administrative hierarchy and in its formalism, impersonality, and emphasis on legal due process. (Grant 1989, 56–57)

The 1960s and 1970s were periods of many political conflicts in education: desegregation, education for the disadvantaged, a neo-Marxist critique of the schools beginning with Paul Goodman's *Growing Up Absurd* in 1960 and continuing with books such as Ivan Illich's *Deschooling Society* in 1970, the "open classrooms" of the early 1970s, and the "back to basics" movement of the late 1970s. During this time there was decreasing discussion of the importance of moral and character education and very little in the way of consensus. On the whole, this period can be seen as a time of retrenchment, in which schools were fighting for the right to educate student's intellects—never mind their characters.

The most important development in moral education during this time was the "Values Clarification" movement. Based upon the belief that the school had no right to "indoctrinate" children into a certain set of moral beliefs, this movement emphasized reasoning about morals and values to the exclusion of any sort of behavioral training. Sidney Simon, one of the originators of this movement, argued that "none of us has the 'right' set of values to pass on to other people's children" (Simon 1971, 902). Values Clarification thus represents the inevitable result of relativistic notions of morality—the teacher's job is merely to help students discover what their values are, not to attempt to change those values.

This scheme received some modification under the work of Lawrence Kohlberg. Kohlberg (1976) began to develop a sense that children went through stages of moral development and that the teacher could help children by identifying which stage of development the students were at and by prodding them to move into the next stage. This "Moral Development" approach was based on the work of Jean Piaget, who had urged a model of learning that provided educational experiences appropriate for the child's stage of development. Kohlberg's approach received wide circulation in the late 1970s and early 1980s, and became the method of choice for moral education in those schools that are now engaged in this task.

However, most schools in the late 1980s were not engaged in any form of explicit moral or character education. This is not to say that such education was not taking place implicitly. A continuing trend among those interested in moral education is to argue for altering the "implicit" curriculum of schools by developing a "strong positive ethos." Gerald Grant (1989) provides an example of this approach:

> The real alternative is an educational community in which all are bound by some transcendent ideals and common commitments to an articulated sense of the public good for which education exists. This community is one in which the responsible adults honor individual rights and procedural guarantees but do not believe these are adequate to express the ideals toward which the community strives. It is a community in which therapeutic contracts cannot override some kinds of common expectations and in which some values are not end-

lessly open. . . . The adults primarily responsible for a given educational community should be continually in the process of reflecting upon and renewing
their world. There are no shortcuts. Stimulating and guiding such reflection is a
crucial aspect of school leadership. (57–59)

What this means for educators is unclear: Grant implies that there are no
generalizations possible about character and moral education, and that it is up to
the leadership of each school to develop a sense of community. How this process of
community-formation is done is also unclear: it seems to require that each school
have long-term charismatic leadership that is willing to set an example for all teachers and students. That this is possible for the entire educational system is doubtful.
One indication that this topic was receiving less attention than other areas was that
in 1992 there was no Educational Resources Information Center (ERIC) descriptor
for "Character Education"; the reader interested in such issues is advised to look under
"Values Education" or "Personality."

THE NEW CHARACTER EDUCATION MOVEMENT

During the early 1990s, a new groundswell of interest in character education emerged.
This most recent movement seems related to several social and intellectual trends.
First, the 1980s and 1990s saw a huge increase in the numbers of immigrants enter-
ing the United States, with the concomitant worries among nativists about the future of American values. Second, several highly visible incidents of school violence
led many people to call for renewed attention to the moral development of young
people. Third, a new conservativism in religion caused many to believe that the public schools needed to recommit themselves to traditional Judeo-Christian values.
Fourth, a renewed interest among philosophers and ethicists in "virtue ethics" led to
new attention to issues of character education.

   In 1990, the president of the United States, together with the nation's gover-
nors, established a set of six national education goals. Goal six was "By the year 2000,
every school in America will be free of drugs and violence and will offer a disciplined
environment conducive to learning." This goal led to the development of several
programs, including an increase in the number of programs related to character education. By 1995, the U.S. Department of Education was giving large grants to state
departments of education to develop character education pilot projects, under the
Improving America's Schools Act of 1994. In addition, several important books on

character education were published in the 1990s that affected this new movement. Among these were Jacques Benninga's *Moral, Character, and Civic Education in the Elementary School* (1991), Thomas Lickona's *Educating for Character: How Our Schools Can Teach Respect and Responsibility* (1991), and Edward Wynne and Kevin Ryan's *Reclaiming Our Schools: A Handbook on Teaching Character, Academics, and Discipline* (1997).

The new character education movement shares many of the features of the Character Education Movement of the 1910s and 1920s, not least of all disagreement about goals and methods. As an op-ed that appeared in the September 12, 2001 edition of *Education Week* complained, "Unfortunately, too many programs that say they are developing character and call themselves 'character education' are aimed mostly at promoting good manners and compliance with rules, not at developing students of strong, independent character." These programs, the authors say, "may well produce certain limited benefits, such as calling attention to matters of character or bringing some order to a chaotic environment. But they will not yield deep and enduring effects on character. They aim for quick behavioral results, rather than helping students better understand and commit to the values that are core to our society, or helping them develop the skills for putting those values into action in life's complex situations." The authors urge the use of a variety of community-building approaches, woven seamlessly into the school day, to create a "caring and just environment in the classroom and in the school at large" (Schaps, Schaeffer, and McDonnell 2001).

Thus character education has become synonymous with school improvement, losing all pretense that there is anything identifiable or measurable about the students that is referred to by the word "character." The result is most likely to be a gradual fading away of discourse about character education per se, until another generation hits upon character education as a cure to the social and educational problems of the day.

IS PSYCHOLOGY HELPFUL OR NOT?

One of the increasingly common sources of means and understandings for educators has been currently popular theories of human behavior and development. We have seen some of the effects of psychological theories in the discussion given above. Each educational method was supported by a psychological model based on currently popular theory. The "mental discipline through effort" pedagogy of the mid-1800s was supported by the early "faculty psychology" model of George Herbart and others. The "character as the sum of its traits" approach of the 1920s and 1930s received support from the account of human nature produced by John Dewey. The "whole curriculum" approach of the 1940s and 1950s was in line with the emerging "environmentalism" of child psychologist Arnold Gesell. "Values clarification" was supported by Jerome Bruner's "discovery" model, and Kohlberg's stages of moral development reflected the cognitive theories of Piaget.

Each of these psychological models attempted to resolve the mind/body question. Indeed, issues of the relationship between mental and physical are at the heart of character pedagogy. Questions to be resolved by an acceptable model of character include: What is the relationship between thought and action? What does emotion have to do with behavior? Can values be taught implicitly as a course of study, or do children need to discover right values for themselves? How much of character is inherited and how much acquired? Many additional questions arise concerning the ways in which the structure of the human personality can affect pedagogy.

Accepting a certain model of the human personality has direct implications on the ways in which these questions will be answered, and therefore on what kind of character curriculum will be proposed. For example, in the 1930s and 1940s it became unacceptable to teach values explicitly. Hartshorne and May's study combined with behaviorism to inform a theory of development that implied that reason and intellect were not useful tools of morality. This behaviorist model was later discredited, so that in the 1970s it was much more acceptable to talk about moral choices in a rational way rather than trying to inculcate values through experience. By changing their model of the personality, educators have justified a change in their curricular choices.

Recent writers have stressed that a better model of the self and of human development is crucial for character education. In his 1988 overview of issues in character education, Ivor Pritchard of the U.S. Department of Education wrote that "the formulation of an adequate philosophical psychology [is] the primary condition for significant improvement in educational theory and the source of root conflicts between traditional and progressive schools of educational thought" (482). Betty Sichel makes the same assertion in her 1988 book on moral education: "A conceptualization of character needs some view of a coherent self that retains its selfhood through a wide variety of change" (82). Similarly, David Carr (1991) writes:

> My basic view is that *all* the major mistakes about the moral educational role of the teacher with respect to the moral development of others to which people are nowadays inclined are based on *misconceptions* or *misunderstandings* of the nature of moral life which have followed certain failures of nerve concerning the legitimacy of a fairly familiar and informal sort of enterprise. In short,

teachers fail in the task of moral education not primarily on account of their lack of any pedagogical skill or technique or of a coherent curriculum theory, but rather because they have only an uncertain grasp of what moral life actually means. (8)

As we have seen, character education advocates displayed a tremendous lack of certainty and agreement about the proper relationship among the brain, emotions, conscience, and the body. To a large extent, their failure to build continuing consensus can be traced to the failure of psychology's attempt to develop "a comprehensive and generally accepted conception of the nature of man" (Allport 1968, 5). This psychological failure, in turn, can be traced to the failure of a larger societal consensus about the nature of the person—a failure that has resulted in what Judith Shklar calls the social and religious "nonscheme" of contemporary society (1984, 248).

James Davison Hunter believes that psychology cannot fill this void; indeed, that there is no possibility of creating an "inclusive moral vocabulary that is shared by all" in our democratic society (2000, 225), and that the ongoing attempt to do so—relying on psychology, democratic consensus, or other nonparticularized sources or techniques—is doomed to failure. Hunter writes:

> Intending to deepen innate moral sympathies and even build character, moral education takes shape in ways that make that impossible. It is through a strategy of inclusion, which includes the denial of all particularity, that one guarantees the death of all godterms capable of rendering morality authoritative within communities and binding on conscience. The problem is that character cannot develop out of values 'nominated' for promotion, 'consciously chosen' by a committee, negotiated by a group of diverse professionals, or enacted into law by legislators. Such values have, by their very nature, lost the quality of sacredness, their commanding character, and thus their power to inspire and to shame. (225)

Hunter suggests that American society will have to find ways to respect and nurture particularistic differences, rather than continue to seek consensus. This recommendation lends itself to abandoning the notion that common public schools can adequately forge a strong national identity in favor of strong supports for decentralizing education using charter and private schools.

Without the development of an shared view of human nature and of the role of character in personal behavior, American public education will continue to flail about—moving at one time toward an emphasis on the child and at another to the subject—in the attempt to engage the student and create effective schools. Unless psychology can provide a better model of human development which can fill this gap in the philosophy of education, character will continue to receive sporadic and faddish treatment, and the public common school will continue to be undermined. The repercussions of these developments will likely be felt throughout society for generations to come.

REFERENCES

Adams, Walter H. 1928. Education for character in secondary schools. *Education* 49 (3): 167–72.

Allport, Gordon. 1968. *The Person in Psychology: Selected Essays.* Boston: Beacon Press.

Astor, Frank. 1931. Studies in deceit and self-control. *Journal of Education* 113 (27): 730.

Aubrey, Edwin E. 1928. Teaching the Bible in an age of science. *Religious Education* 23 (2): 149–53.

Bagley, William C. 1928. *Determinism in Education: A Series of Papers on the Relative Influence of Inherited and Acquired Traits in Determining Intelligence, Achievement, and Character.* Baltimore: Warwick and York.

———. 1934. *Education and Emergent Man: A Theory of Education in Particular Application to Public Education in the U.S.* New York: Thomas Nelson and Sons.

Benninga, Jacques S., ed. 1991. *Moral, Character, and Civic Education in the Elementary School.* New York: Teachers College Press.

Bestor, Arthur. 1953. *Educational Wastelands: The Retreat from Learning in Our Schools.* Urbana: University of Illinois Press.

Bowles, S., and H. Gintis. 1976. *Schooling in Capitalist America.* London: Routledge and Kegan Paul.

Brown, Charles A. 1928. Character Education. *Proceedings of the National Education Association* 67:628–32.

Brown, Francis J. 1936. Character education—Past and present. *School and Society* 43 (1114): 585–89.

Callow, Alexander B., Jr. 1982. *American Urban History,* 3rd ed. New York: Oxford University Press.

Carr, David. 1991. *Educating the Virtues: An Essay on the Philosophical Psychology of Moral Development and Education.* London: Routledge.

Cavan, Ruth Shonle. 1927. Character education in public schools. *Religious Education* 22 (9): 917–25.

Charters, W. W. 1927. *The Teaching of Ideals.* New York: Macmillan.

———. 1930. *Aims and Methods of Character Training in the Public Schools.* National Education Association Proceedings. Washington, DC: National Education Association.

Coe, George A. 1933. The present crisis in religious education. *Religious Education* 28 (3): 181–85.

Dewey, John. 1922. *Human Nature and Conduct.* John Dewey: The Middle Works, vol. 14, ed. Jo Ann Boydston. Carbondale: Southern Illinois University Press.

Dimock, Hedley S. 1928. The scientific attitude in religion. *Religious Education* 23 (2): 125–31.

Educational Policies Commission. 1951. *Moral and Spiritual Values in the Public Schools.* Washington DC: National Education Association.

Fairchild, Milton. 1918. Character education. *National Education Association Proceedings* 46:120–22.

Geertz, Clifford. 1983. *Local Knowledge: Further Essays in Interpretive Anthropology.* New York: Basic Books.

Golightly, Thomas J. 1926. *The Present Status of the Teaching of Morals in the Public High Schools.* George Peabody College for Teachers Contributions to Education, 38. Nashville: George Peabody College for Teachers.

Goodman, Paul. 1960. *Growing Up Absurd: Problems of Youth in the Organized Society.* New York: Vintage.

Grant, Gerald. 1988. *The World We Created at Hamilton High.* Cambridge, MA: Harvard University Press.

———. 1989. Bringing the 'moral' back in. *National Education Association Journal* (January): 54–59.

Gutowski, Thomas W. 1978. The high school as an adolescent raising institution: An inner history of Chicago public secondary education, 1856–1940. PhD diss., University of Chicago.

Hartshorne, H., and M. A. May. 1928. *Studies in the Nature of Character,* vol. 1, *Studies in Deceit.* New York: Macmillan.

———. 1930a. A summary of the work of the Character Education Inquiry, part I. *Religious Education* 25 (7): 607–19.

———. 1930b. A Summary of the work of the Character Education Inquiry, part II. *Religious Education* 25 (8): 754–62.

Hartshorne, H., M. A. May, and J. B. Maller. 1929. *Studies in the Nature of Character,* vol. 2, *Studies in Self-control.* New York: Macmillan.

Hartshorne, H., M. A. May, and F. K. Shuttleworth. 1930. *Studies in the Nature of Character,* vol. 3, *Studies in the Organization of Character.* New York: Macmillan.

Haydon, A. Eustace. 1928. Science as technique of religion. *Religious Education* 23 (2): 120–25.

Hunter, James Davison. 2000. *The Death of Character: Moral Education in an Age without Good or Evil.* New York: Basic Books.

Illich, Ivan. 1970. *Deschooling Society.* New York: Harper & Row.

Johnson, Henry C., Jr. 1980. *The Public School and Moral Education.* New York: Pilgrim Press.

Jonçich, Geraldine. 1968. *The Sane Positivist: A Biography of Edward L. Thorndike.* Middletown, CT: Wesleyan University Press.

Kliebard, Herbert M. 1987. *The Struggle for the American Curriculum, 1893–1958.* New York: Routledge and Kegan Paul.

Kohlberg, Lawrence A. 1976. The cognitive-developmental approach to moral education. In *Moral Education . . . It Comes with the Territory*, ed. David Purpel and Kevin Ryan, 176–95. Berkeley: Phi Delta Kappa.

Lawson, George B. 1915. Character—The secondary school; Its opportunity. *Education* 35 (10): 628–32.

Leming, James S. 2002. Hartshorne and May: A reappraisal. Paper presented at the annual meeting of the Association for Moral Education, Northwestern University, November.

Lickona, Thomas. 1991. *Educating for Character: How Our Schools Can Teach Respect and Responsibility*. New York: Bantam.

Lightfoot, Sara Lawrence. 1983. *The Good High School: Portraits of Character and Culture*. New York: Basic Books.

May, Mark A. 1928a. What science offers on character education. In *Building Character: Proceedings of the Mid-west Conference on Character Development*, 7–45. Chicago: University of Chicago Press.

———. 1928b. Which is it: Religion vs. science, or religion vs. religion? *Religious Education* 28 (4): 320–26.

May, Mark A., and Hugh Hartshorne, 1927. Experimental studies in moral education. *Religious Education* 22:712–15.

McFarland, Ross A. 1928. Is there a scientific philosophy of life. *Religious Education* 23 (2): 109–19.

Mill, John Stuart. 1952. *A System of Logic: Ratiocinative and Inductive*. London: Longmans, Green, and Co. (Orig. pub. 1843.)

Powers, Francis F. 1932. *Character Training*. New York: A. S. Barnes and Co.

Preyer, William. 1895. *Die Seele des Kindes: Beobachtungen über die geistige Entwicklung des Menschen in den ersten Lebensjahren*. Leipzig: Verlag T. Grieben.

Pritchard, Ivor. 1988. Character education: Research prospects and problems. *American Journal of Education* 96 (4 August): 469–95.

Ravitch, Diane. 1983. *The Troubled Crusade: American Education, 1945–1980*. New York: Basic Books.

Research Station in Character Education and Religious Education. 1922. *The Iowa Plan for Character Education*. Washington, DC: Character Education Institution.

Schaps, E., E. F. Schaeffer, and S. N. McDonnell. 2001. What's right and wrong in character education today. *Education Week* 21 (2 September): 40–44.

Shklar, Judith N. 1984. *Ordinary Vices*. Cambridge, MA: Harvard University Press.

Sichel, Betty A. 1988. *Moral Education: Character, Community, and Ideals*. Philadelphia: Temple University Press.

Simon, Sidney B. 1971. Values clarification vs. indoctrination. *Social Education* (December): 902.

Sisson, Edward O. 1911. Can virtue be taught? *Educational Review* 41:261–79.

Smith, Gerald B. 1928. Some conditions to be observed in the attempt to correlate science and religion. *Religious Education* 23 (4): 304–10.

Symonds, Percival M. 1928. *The Nature of Conduct.* New York: Macmillan.

Taylor, Charles K. 1914. Moral education—The history of an experiment. *Education* 35 (4): 220–30.

Terman, Lewis M. 1911. Some paradoxes of personality, or muckraking in the psychology of character. *New England Monthly* 44 (May): 371–74.

Thorndike, Edward L. 1913. Eugenics: With special reference to intellect and character: A lecture given at Columbia University (in March). *Popular Science* 83 (Aug): 125–38.

———. 1913–14. *Educational Psychology.* New York: Teachers College, Columbia University.

Thorndike, Edward L., and R. S. Woodworth. 1901. The influence of improvement in one mental function upon the efficiency of other functions. *Psychological Review* 8:247–61, 384–95, 553–64.

Ward, David. 1982. The making of immigrant ghettoes, 1840–1920. In *American Urban History,* 3rd ed., ed. Alexander B. Callow, Jr., 268–79. New York: Oxford University Press.

Webb, Edward. 1915. *Character and Intelligence: An Attempt at an Exact Study of Character.* Cambridge: Cambridge University Press.

Wynne, Edward, and Kevin Ryan. 1997. *Reclaiming Our Schools: A Handbook on Teaching Character, Academics, and Discipline.* New York: Merrill.

EIGHT

How Not To Educate Character

Joel J. Kupperman

THIS PAPER WILL BE CONCERNED WITH BOTH BAD PHILOSOPHY AND BAD practice. The philosophical mistakes to be discussed are those of slighting the interpretative and volitional elements in ethical decisions, as well as ignoring the ways in which personal goals and plans of life may or may not serve as a bulwark against bad choices. The bad practice is that of reducing moral education to a process of imprinting a good set of moral messages.

MORAL CODEBOOKS IN THE MIND

It is part of the Judeo-Christian tradition that (a) ethics centers on behavior (that is, on deciding what to do and what never should be done), and (b) that highly general rules tell one all that one needs to know about this. At the root is Exodus, chapter 20 and the Ten Commandments. The lingering influence of this strong emphasis on

202 JOEL J. KUPPERMAN

general formulations as the key to goodness can be found in the ethical philosophy of Kant (and the tradition it gave rise to) and in the features in contemporary common sense that lead us to acclaim a person's virtue by speaking of "a woman (or man) of principle."

There are complications that go a little beyond this simple story. First it is well-known that, in the New Testament, Jesus (after saying in Matthew 5:17, "Think not that I have come to destroy the law . . .") strongly recommends a purification of thought (eliminating anger and lust) that gives modification of one's self a share of the ethical spotlight along with behavior. Further, there is a sense in which ethics is not merely a set of general requirements for everyone: some people may do better than what is generally required. This idea is presented in Matthew 19:21 with the words "If thou wilt be perfect. . . ." It might be argued that there are some anticipations in the Old Testament (e.g., in the book of Job) of these departures from the simple model of ethics.

It also would be too simple to regard Western tradition as entirely dominated by a model of ethics as centering on broad, general rules of conduct. We can appreciate this by keeping in view some of the main philosophical alternatives. First, some major philosophers have argued that many important decisions of how one should behave cannot be arrived at on the basis of general rules. This is at the heart of Aristotle's treatment of "the mean" in Book II of the *Nicomachean Ethics*. To say that a virtue like courage or generosity represents a mean between two extremes is to say that always behaving in the same way (always or never giving money to those who ask for it, always advancing into or retreating from danger) is stupid. Instead, one has to rely on experience to decide what is appropriate for each case.

Aristotle concedes that not all decisions of how one should behave can be understood on this model. There are some things that one simply never should do. His example is adultery: it is not a matter of committing it with the right woman at the right time, he jokes (Aristotle 1962, 1107a44)—rather one simply should not do it. But many important ethical decisions in his view are not so straightforward, and general rules will not provide the answers.

Confucius's view of this was remarkably like Aristotle's, and he claims for himself that he is not inflexible (see Confucius 1938, 18.8, 221–22). There is a Confucian "Doctrine of the Mean." The ethical influence of Confucius on the West is fairly recent, but Aristotle has been regarded for a very long time as important and influential. It is not difficult to find prominent Western philosophers who have not regarded deciding how one should behave as always being able to be determined by means of general rules.

A deeper deviation arises over the principal concern of ethics. It is hard not to regard, say, Plato's *Republic* as a work of ethics. Its central topic is the nature of justice, and it provides an elaborate justification for a view of what should be most important in one's life. But nowhere does it present general rules for behavior, and indeed the main subject of inquiry is what kind of person one should want to become. In short, the development of personhood or soul is what really matters. How we choose to behave certainly also matters, but it emerges as secondary, to a large extent determined by the development of one's personhood or soul. Something like this is also true in general of classic texts of Asian philosophy, despite the variations in the kinds of development of personhood that they recommend (cf. Kupperman 2001a, chapter 9).

In short, the model of ethics as primarily concerned with behavior that should be entirely determined by general rules does not fit all elements within the Western tradition, and fails badly to fit the most important ethical philosophies of ancient Greece or Asia. Nevertheless I want to suggest that it plays a dominant role in contemporary Western common sense. We need to look at its merits, and in particular at its usefulness in the education of character.

The first thing to insist on is that it does have merits. As Aristotle conceded (and Confucius would have agreed) there are some important decisions that follow very straightforwardly from general rules interpreted in uncontroversial ways. Further, even in cases in which this arguably does not hold, familiar general rules can provide the starting points of ethical reflection, helping to orient us in what otherwise would seem a rather chaotic map of relevant factors. As Julius Kovesi (1967) has argued, one function of moral rules is to structure our perception of situations to which they might be applicable.

Also, philosophers who are skeptical of claims that general rules always direct us clearly toward what would be for the best, have sometimes also pointed out the difficulty we inevitably have in being sure what would be for the best. One line of thought runs as follows. An ideal, extremely knowledgeable, and dispassionate moral judge perhaps would not always follow moral rules, instead regarding some cases as providing exceptions to the rules. But none of us is this ideal moral judge. We are all prone to think that cases in which we would very much like to do something that violates a rule are somehow exceptional, so that the rule can be ignored. Because of these human limitations, the safe general policy is to follow the rules, period. (Something close to this line of argument, but considerably qualified, is to be found in G. E. Moore's *Principia Ethica*, 1903, 155–58.)

Perhaps, though, we sometimes can be confident—even discounting possible biases in our own outlook—that a case represents an exception to a traditional moral rule. We should keep promises, in general; but many would agree that sometimes there are unusual circumstances in which it is justifiable and reasonable to break a promise. (Whether there then is a residue of obligation to the person to whom the promise had been made is a separate question.) Similarly, it can be argued, as in effect Lawrence Kohlberg did in his well-known example of the man who can get medicine for his dying wife only by stealing it from an extortionate pharmacist, that there are imaginable cases in which it would be best to steal (see Kohlberg 1981).

A deeper set of problems with the view that ethics centers on general rules of how to behave is this: whatever general rules we work with do not interpret themselves. As Kant (1981, 3) pointed out, we need "a power of judgment sharpened by experience" to connect rules or maxims with a specific case. In most of life this is not a serious difficulty. Normally, it is fairly clear when something would represent theft, promise-breaking, murder, torture, or rape. For each of these categories, though, there are cases (real or imaginable) in which there might be room for doubt.

For most of us most of the time, the interpretative activity that links moral rules with specific cases is invisible. This is because we take for granted the traditional interpretations of the moral categories. This ease of judgment can be very useful in maintaining a smoothly running social order. But it also carries risks, in that the traditional interpretations cannot in every case be assumed to be neutral among the interests of those affected by moral choices. In the era of slavery, it was widely assumed that slaves were property and that removing a slave from the power of his or her master was a form of theft. When gender inequality was a given, there were similarly interpretations that we would now regard as highly questionable of activities that involved or affected women. The transitions that ensue when such interpretations are challenged in a sustained way are very unsettling, not least in undermining many people's sense that they know where they are in the moral universe.

The cases just referred to center on single, large moral issues: slavery or the rights of women. In each, the point is that a transition in moral common sense (e.g., from acceptance to rejection of slavery) required changed descriptions of relevant situations and forms of behavior. Really a change in vision was required. The contestable interpretative elements could be viewed as confined to one area of decision and of experience. Someone who prefers a settled, consensus-based way of seeing what is relevant to morality might well regard the transition as a temporary disruption—akin to wars, plagues, and famine—leading from one kind of stable moral universe to a different kind of stable moral universe.

The experience of living in a pluralistic society however is radically different from this. There may be some central vexed issues (e.g., gender and racial equality, the rights of animals, and responsibility to the environment), but increasingly the central issues radiate outward in ways that affect the interpretation and description of behavior and situations that initially might not have been seen as closely linked to the central issues. Feminism is no longer merely about equal rights, and a similar comment applies to the other issues referred to above. Interpretations of most of life become contestable. Further, in seeming contrast to the older issues of slavery and equal rights, there is no end in sight. One cannot foresee any reestablishment of a stable moral universe.

This sense that much is "up for grabs," that very often descriptions that seem intuitively obvious (and easy) to one person turn out to be challenged by another, is heightened by what might feel to some people like a quickened pace of change in the circumstances of everyday life. Many of us have a feeling that not much in our childhood moral instruction prepared us specifically for some of the moral problems we now confront. One feature of contemporary life for many people is a repeated sense of disorientation, which is connected with rapid technological innovation, social change, and personal mobility. Sometimes this takes the form of disorientation in the presence of what looks like it might be an important moral choice.

Most of us are not at our best in such situations. Among the features of Stanley Milgram's experiments, in which subjects were asked to administer what they thought were electric shocks of increasing severity to someone they thought was another experimental subject (who kept giving wrong answers in what was billed as a learning experiment), was that the situation and the decision it called for must have been unprecedented for all of the subjects. Most of them complied, and administered electric shocks up to a level that (had they been real) would have been highly dangerous. It is quite possible that the tentative description in the minds of many of them for what they were doing was "playing my part in a scientific experiment managed by people who must know what they are doing." Perhaps, if they had had a lot of time to think, most of the subjects would have described things differently. But in real life, ethical choices often are made by people who do not have time to think; and part of the artfulness of the Milgram experiments was that they maintained a fairly rapid pace.

Disorientation can be presumed as a feature of a thought experiment presented by Plato in the final book of the *Republic* (see Plato 1997, St. 614–21, 285–92). This is the Myth of Er, in which Plato imagines the souls of the deceased in the underworld choosing new lives (after which they will drink of the river of forgetfulness and return to the world above). He describes one man, who had led a morally acceptable life in a well-run society, who chooses the life (with its glittering aspects and its crimes) of a tyrant. This poor choice is described by Plato as what one might expect of someone whose previous "virtue" had been a matter of "habit and without philosophy" (St. 619c, 1222). But it is striking also that the tyrant-to-be is described as soon regretting his choice, and implicit in the extraordinary scene is the fact that nothing in the hapless man's previous life would have prepared him for the choice that he had to make.

Running through the *Republic* is the thought that a pattern of virtuous behavior is not tantamount to genuine virtue. There is a similar line of thought in the *Analects* of Confucius: "The honest villager spoils true virtue" (17.13, 213). Confucius's great follower, Mencius, interprets this as based on the idea that "the honest villager" is at heart a conformist, guided only by desire for approval (see Mencius 1970, VII.B.37, 203). In favorable and familiar circumstances, the traditional virtuous choice is also the path of least resistance, and the easy continuation of childhood habits. But if we want to know whether someone is genuinely virtuous, we have to see how he or she behaves in circumstances that are not favorable and familiar. These tests of character are especially revealing if they contain unusual pressures, threats, or temptations.

A real life example is referred to in Plato's *Apology*. The oligarchic Thirty Tyrants temporarily in power in Athens wanted to involve others in complicity with their misdeeds. On one occasion, they summoned five citizens, including Socrates, and ordered them to arrest Leon of Salamis (presumably an innocent man; see Plato 1997, St. 32c–e, 29–30). The others did this; Socrates, risking execution, simply went home. Many choices that were comparable to this confronted citizens of European countries occupied by the Nazis during World War II, and Chinese intellectuals and artists during the Cultural Revolution. One of my students, who was sent to the countryside during the Cultural Revolution, reports that others were ordered to beat up a young man in their group whose father had been a landlord.

Arguably, even if such choices often are made in situations that are highly unusual, it is possible to address them by means of moral rules with which we are all familiar. It is wrong to contribute to the death of an innocent person, or to beat up an innocent person. Poor choices hence cannot be, by and large, regarded as the result of some kind of confusion or misguided interpretation of the facts. In the excitement or stress surrounding the choice, of course, someone can (so to speak) lose sight of the general moral knowledge that should have made it clear that certain things were not to be done. (This clearly seems to have been the case for most participants in the Milgram experiments.) But, alternatively, someone who retains a clear view that something is morally wrong still may do it. This is especially likely if (as in the Leon of Salamis case) there is fear of what will happen if one does not do it, or conversely if something extremely appealing is associated with the violation of moral norms.

One of Plato's thought experiments in the *Republic* concerns a case of great temptation: the ring of invisibility. A Lydian shepherd finds the ring, and with it goes to the capital, seduces the queen, murders the king, and becomes a great tyrant (Plato 1997, St. 359d–360b, 1000–1001). This is a clever example, in part because it presents a temptation that might grow in time. Initially perhaps many people would refuse to use the ring to do anything that they previously would not have countenanced. But one imagines that after a while it would occur to some of them that there were some possible uses that were not too grossly heinous, and this might be the start of a gradual process of corruption. If it is true that power—including this kind of power—corrupts, one should not imagine that the transformation need be instantaneous.

The relevance of the ring of invisibility to the topic of moral knowledge is this. One might think of moral knowledge as like some other forms of knowledge in involving, first and foremost, a capacity to come up with right answers. But someone who helps to arrest Leon of Salamis or to beat up the landlord's son, or who abuses the ring of invisibility, can come up with the right moral answers.

One way of formulating what is lacking is in terms of a good will. Kant's view clearly is that genuine virtue requires not only that we know right from wrong (which he regards as being in many cases rather easy), but also that we have the requisite volitional commitment to do what is right because it is right. Plato's diagnosis I think is more complicated. He would agree with Kant that volitional elements are required for genuine virtue. But his view seems to be that someone who is genuinely virtuous will have internalized the requisite volitional commitments, so that they are strongly implicated in sense of self. For this person virtuous volition is much more than a matter of habit, or of a momentary decision that is supposed to last for all of life. Habits of course can be broken, especially in unusual circumstances, and decisions can be reversed. But commitments that are intimately connected with who we are will not be so easily abandoned.

This is connected with the goals or plans of life that are characteristic of a genuinely virtuous person. Plato seems to intend us to think that, even if most people would abuse the ring of invisibility, Socrates would not. This would follow from the values of Socrates' life, the things that mattered to him. His values and goals focused on the search for knowledge and also psychic harmony. How would the ring of invisibility contribute to these? On the other hand, for someone—even someone whose behavior previously had been consistently acceptable—whose dreams and hopes centered on money, power, and fame, the ring of invisibility would be an overwhelming temptation.

There is a parallel line of thought in the *Analects* of Confucius. To be a truly virtuous person is to have major sources of satisfaction within oneself. Whatever else goes well or badly, one will have the satisfaction of a well-functioning psyche that is securely within one's control. He that is really good, Confucius contends (1938, 9.28, 144), can never be unhappy. Most of the things that most people seem to care most about, on the other hand (e.g., money, power, fame, love relations) are not entirely within their control. Hence the "true gentleman is calm and at ease; the Small Man is fretful and ill at ease" (7.36, 131). Without (true) goodness a man cannot long endure adversity, because he lacks sufficient inner sources of satisfaction; and cannot for long enjoy prosperity, because he soon will be wanting more, and at the same time will be insecure about what he has (4.2, 102).

This brings us back to the question of what the central topic of ethics is. For Plato, Aristotle, and Confucius it is how a person can come to lead a very satisfying life of high quality. How people choose to behave also is important; but it is secondary, being influenced especially in difficult cases, by what people come to see as a satisfying life of high quality. This view of ethics has become increasingly uncongenial in democratic liberal societies. We are uneasy about making judgments of the quality of people's lives, regarding this as something that is not our business (especially if someone has not been violating anyone else's rights). Conversely, there is a more sharply focused interest now in what amounts to social control, and specifically in the role of morality in controlling behavior that might result in direct harm to members of the society.

Social control is important, and any reasonable person will hope that morality fulfils this role well. There is room however for an argument that an ethics whose focus is like that of Plato, Aristotle, and Confucius can engage quality of life issues seriously without intrusive responses to people's lives that run counter to the values of a liberal society (see Kupperman 1999, in progress). There is also room to question how effectively a morality can provide social control over behavior if quality of life issues are entirely ignored.

The next section of this paper will take us to this topic. First, let me sum up the view of this section, of philosophical mistakes to be avoided. If genuine virtue must be reliable (even in disorienting circumstances, or ones that involve severe pressure or great temptation), it is a mistake to think of genuine virtue as merely a matter of having an acceptable moral code imprinted in the mind. Even if we specify further that the agent always murmurs "Yes" at the thought of any element of the code, that still is not enough. At the least there must be a good will. Further, it is a mistake to suppose that a reliable good will is merely the product of a habit of good moral decision. Habits can be broken (under pressure or because of temptation) or can seem irrelevant (if the present situation looks entirely different from anything that went before). Plato and Confucius both provide arguments that reliable willing of good decisions becomes more likely if the agent's virtue is closely implicated in her or his sense of self, and especially if good moral behavior is strongly connected with major sources of satisfaction for the agent (as opposed to the case in which the strongest sources of satisfaction have at best a tenuous connection with good moral conduct).

MISEDUCATION OF CHARACTER

In the dialogues of Plato, whether virtue can be taught is treated as problematic. One can point (as Plato in fact does) to teaching techniques that arguably are likely to work, and in the penultimate section of this paper I will make an attempt of this sort. But the fact remains that it is easier to specify techniques that do not work reliably than it is to specify ones that are more likely to work.

Many people's intuitions about moral education can mislead them. Imagine groups of people who have lost their moral compass. Intuitively it might seem that the crucial thing is to tell them what kinds of things are right and what kinds of things are wrong, and to tell them when they are young enough so that the knowledge will be absorbed. This, one might think, will do the job.

Now in fact what is recommended is not a bad idea. There is no good reason not to do it. Parents need not adopt a stance of moral neutrality, and there is no reason why schools should do so either. Indeed schools need to have their own rules, banning disruptive anti-social behavior, including physical violence and theft; so it would be absurd for a school to avoid taking moral stands.

The mistake is in supposing that what is recommended—telling students what is right and what is wrong—is by itself a reliable method of producing virtue. Schools in Germany under the Weimar Republic, which preceded the Nazi takeover, must have told their students what kinds of things are right or wrong. As we know, this did not produce quite as much widespread virtue as one would have liked.

Some might think that perhaps the Weimar Republic schools should have told more. But what is the added information about right and wrong that would have made all the difference? Perhaps the schools could have gone beyond the usual generalizations about not harming innocent people and could have specified that this especially included treatment of ethnic minorities or of the populations of countries bordering on Germany. But we need to realize how very difficult it is for a moral educator to have an assured sense of what the special moral challenges will be that will confront her or his students. This is not to say that all attempts at anticipation are totally useless. One of the uses of courses in business ethics is that they can familiarize future business people with some of the kinds of moral problems that they might confront, and this might lessen the sense of disorientation that could impair the quality of their responses. Something similar can be said about other courses in professional ethics (medical ethics, legal ethics, etc.).

In any event, however, even someone who has been prepared for a kind of moral challenge can, at a particular moment, forget the training—especially if a different kind of response seems to be expected by everyone around her or him. Educators often assume that what has been learned and memorized has thereby been absorbed and internalized. Sometimes this happens. But experienced teachers know that even ordinary bits of information, no matter how often they are repeated, can be lost in transmission or can be forgotten six months after the teaching has concluded. Moral teaching, which should have such an intimate connection with our volitions and maps of the world, cannot be assumed to remain permanently operative from some secure location in the memory banks.

Why is it then that so many people, including educators, suppose that the key to teaching virtue consists in conveying (and repeating often) generalizations about the kinds of things that are right or are wrong? The short answer is that in favorable circumstances it looks as if it works. By favorable circumstances I mean ones in which an agent's life is experienced as going well in a stable way. These circumstances preclude a major social upheaval, and also significant temptations or pressures from others. If all of the conditions are met, and life goes well, the great majority of people who have been well brought up and educated properly will behave well. This result should not be scoffed at. It contributes greatly to peaceful and secure societies in which large numbers of people are able to feel good about themselves.

However, as the arguments in the previous section showed, this pattern of good behavior (while things go well) does not amount to genuine virtue. To someone who has never experienced bad times, it may seem as if it does. The great majority of the students I teach seem to assume that niceness is equivalent to virtue. This in turn leads to a high estimate of the percentage of the population that is genuinely virtuous. Anyone who has experienced bad times, or is mindful of the kinds of human behavior that emerge in them, would not be likely to make this mistake. Even the microcosm of the Milgram experiments points to the ways in which most people (including many who presumably in ordinary life were "nice") can behave badly while disoriented and feeling under pressure.

There are other risks in moral education that consists largely in imprinting the messages of a moral code. It may make virtue seem dull. This always has been a problem, but it especially is a problem in a culture (like ours) in which the same students who are to have moral messages imprinted on them are also constantly exposed to highly addictive messages of excitement. As many philosophers have argued, genuine virtue is not dull, in part because it is not easy and indeed requires a dynamic reorganization of an agent's mental processes and view of life. There also is psychological evidence that suggests that genuine virtue has a closer relation to happiness than many students will assume, in that typically an important element of happiness is the ability to think well of oneself (Argyle 1987, 124). All of this can be lost sight of when moral education concentrates on memorizing and repeating an established moral code.

There also is the factor of human contrariety, especially among people who are assigned essentially passive roles as recipients of traditional messages. Oppositional subcultures can form, finding more excitement and distinction in being "bad" than in being "good." This is especially a risk if the assigned "good" role does not seem to offer many rewards. It may well be more attractive to be an interesting "bad" person than to be a marginal member of the group of the "good."

The primary problem, though, with the moral education package that consists mainly of imprinting moral messages is that it largely produces the moral counterpart to "sunshine soldiers," people who can be relied upon mainly in stable, favorable circumstances. The problem remains even if the package includes childhood training of habits. Aristotle famously assigned the acquisition of good behavioral habits a major role in moral education. But, in his view, it amounted to the first phase of a two phase process. The second phase included coming to understand the reasons for elements of traditional morality, and also gaining experience and judgment that are required for good decisions in the large number of cases in which we have to pick our way between consistent (and often stupid) extremes. Good habits by themselves (without the second phase that builds on them) do not constitute genuine virtue in his view. There is abundant evidence that good habits by themselves, without additional elements in a person's sense of self or understanding of morality, fall far short of guaranteeing good behavior in difficult or disorienting circumstances.

EFFECTIVE EDUCATION OF CHARACTER

The words "fall far short" in the previous sentence need to be emphasized. The truth, I believe, is that any method of character education falls short of guaranteeing good behavior in difficult or disorienting circumstances. Perhaps there is a psychological element that corresponds to the doctrine of original sin, or maybe one should speak merely of essential human imperfection? There also is the problem that the social sciences, including psychology, are far more successful at predicting behavior of groups or portions of groups than in giving entirely assured (as opposed to probable) predictions of the behavior of individuals. A fortiori we can hardly guarantee anything for each individual case.

Hence, the contrast to be drawn is not between methods of character education that will always work and those that generally will not. Rather it is between methods that fall far short in the sense of being distinctly unreliable and those that will be less unreliable but all the same do not provide guarantees of good behavior. To get an idea of methods that often will work, we need to look at what good character consists of. We also need to avoid any assumption that the sources of good character will be exactly the same for everyone who becomes a genuinely good person.

Here is a very short version of what good character is (for a much longer one, see Kupperman 1991). Character consists in patterns of thought and behavior, especially in the areas of life that are related to morality or to success in personal projects. Good character requires patterns of moral choice that are reliably good. There can be many kinds of good character, but all must have this moral reliability.

"Choice" here has a broad meaning: it applies to anything someone does that she or he could possibly (in some sense of "possibly") not have done. Much choice is immediate and unreflective, and often people make important choices that they are unaware of making. Indeed many of the patterns that distinguish virtuous people from those lacking in virtue have to do with first responses or with what grows out of thoughts that pop (or do not pop) into people's heads.

The moral reliability necessary to good character in turn requires strong character. To have a strong character is to persevere (which in moral matters involves keeping to one's guidelines) despite obstacles, temptations, or confusing circumstances. A morally reliable character by definition is strong, requiring specifically a strong tendency to make morally virtuous choices in cases (such as those involving life and death, or possibilities of acute harm to someone) in which a great deal is at stake.

Here is one further comment on what character is. There is some division, both among philosophers and psychologists who study character, on whether character traits should be viewed as "broad" or as "narrow" (for some recent psychological and philosophical debates relevant to this, see Ross and Nisbett 1991; Funder 1999; Harman 1999; and Kupperman 2001b). A broad character trait involves a consistent pattern of behavior across a variety of contexts. An example would be the combination that includes honesty about money, honesty about what one's feelings are, honesty in sexual relations, and so forth. Another would be courage in the face of physical danger, in giving a public speech for which one is not well prepared, in approaching strangers who may not like you, in submitting writing to a publication that may despise it, and so on. It may be that lay people usually tend to think of character traits as broad. A view that assumes this, though, will look like an easy target for those who are skeptical about the claim that there really are character traits. A great many character traits that we encounter turn out, on investigation, not to hold across a variety of contexts. People very often, for example, are courageous about some kinds of things and not others. The Milgram experiments especially have been cited as a case in which most people can be presumed to have behaved very differently from the way in which they might have behaved in normal contexts.

If character traits are viewed as narrow, on the other hand, they will be specified in terms of how someone tends to behave in a certain type of context. Someone might be described as quite kind when friends need help or money, but often less kind to strangers. Or one could be scrupulous about not causing pain, except when the pain is an essential byproduct of some required activity that has its own value. (This is a character trait that would make a person unreliable in the Milgram experiment, or during wartime conditions.)

Let me suggest that it is far more plausible to expect virtually all of some people's character traits, and most character traits of most people, to be narrow than to think of most of them as broad. This does not preclude, however, the possibility that someone could be, in all contexts, scrupulous about (say) not causing acute harm to an innocent person—which is a major requirement for genuine virtue.

These two topics—weakness of character and the narrowness of character traits—have some connection. Assume for the sake of argument that, at least for the great majority of people, there is a normal tendency to behave differently in different kinds of situations; and that in this sense narrow character traits are the norm. However genuine virtue, as it is usually construed, requires some broad traits. That is, a genuinely virtuous person will strive not to harm innocent people, in any of the variety of ways in which people can be harmed, and in any of the variety of circumstances in which this can occur. The character traits corresponding to justice also should be broad. In other words, genuine virtue requires that an individual's conscientiousness in not harming innocent people, and justice, become consistent over a range of circumstances, despite what might be a normal tendency for such traits to be much stronger in some kinds of situations than in others.

It would seem then that genuine virtue may well require processes of control. An agent will need to be self-monitoring, and to make herself or himself behave in ways that are consistent with the virtue that is at stake. Some might speak here of willpower as central to moral virtue, although what the will is and how it might have power are both difficult and obscure topics. It is safest merely to say that there often need to be habits of mind that control and integrate behavior over a range of circumstances. These habits amount to strength of character, which is required for genuine virtue. It should be noted that, though strength of character is necessary, it is not sufficient for genuine virtue: true wickedness in some cases also requires strength of character, which is one reason why reliably wicked people are in fact rather rare.

In most cases, someone we are educating will look far more likely to develop habits of behaving reasonably well than habits that point toward wickedness. How do we strengthen such a person's character? The problem here is that of integration of self: of creating reliable connections among the moments and fragments of a person's life, including the ability to think at crucial moments "To do that would not acceptably fit the general pattern of my life." In a social world that increasingly is full of distractions and discontinuities, this is a major task.

One method that can be effective is that of creating projects that require real effort over more than a brief amount of time. Acquiring athletic, musical, or artistic skills (and displaying these to advantage) may seem far removed from the domain of character. But the process, organizing one's attention around a set of goals and also overcoming difficulties over a period of time, can create habits of control of one's behavior, and in this greatly strengthen character. This is not to say that such experience guarantees (or even by itself makes likely) good character. The claim rather is that a life in which there have been no comparable experiences—in which all challenges have been easy and none have persisted continuously for a period of time—virtually guarantees weak character.

Strength of character amounts to good character only if it is directed and constrained along morally good lines. What can make this likely? One factor is a connection between morally acceptable behavior and an agent's sense of self. It is hard to imagine really good character that is not to some degree conscious of itself, even if not of all of its manifestations; and this awareness will have a great deal to do with loyalty to standards of behavior.

The connection between virtue and sense of self is particularly strong if the agent has some pride in who she or he is. Projects of the sort described above, in which people have to discipline themselves over a period of time in order to meet long-term goals, can contribute to a sense of pride. Conversely, anyone who has never had to overcome difficult obstacles in a sustained way can be expected to be limited in her or his sources of pride. Pride and a capacity for shame normally go together. Someone who has never had legitimate sources of pride canot be expected to be ashamed of morally deficient behavior, and there cannot be much hope of such a person achieving good character.

Finally, someone who has a sense of what the point of morality is will be much less likely to abandon it than someone for whom it is merely another piece of rote learning. The point of morality, to speak broadly, is to make more likely flourishing lives, ones that are good to have. Because of this, we have at least some obligations to help people make their lives better. However, many of the ways in which people's lives can be wonderful are largely within their own control, in such a way that much of the help they require consists in clearing away obstacles and offering chances. We cannot *make* someone we know have a wonderful life. But often we *can* make such a person miserable and have a rotten life. Hence, most of morality traditionally has been concerned with negatives: forbidding conduct that harms others.

This much can be explained and conveyed by words on a page. But much of understanding the point of morality cannot be intellectualized, and includes affective and perceptual elements. Someone who does not care about other people, or who often is unable to take in ways in which they might be harmed, is deficient in understanding the point of morality.

Many great philosophers—one thinks of Plato, St. Augustine, and Kierkegaard—have made a point very like this: ethical knowledge is unlike most forms of knowledge in that it implies a change in the nature of the person who acquires it. Certainly we cannot be said to know what is good in our own lives and conduct if we coolly choose an inferior way to live and allow ourselves to damage the lives of innocent people. It would count heavily against any claim that Bloggs has a good character if he does not notice that what he is about to do would ruin X's or Y's life, or if he notices but is indifferent.

Because of this, education that has a good chance of producing good character must include promoting sensitivity and concern for others. Let me follow this obvious point with one that is a shade less obvious. If attempts to promote sensitivity and concern consist chiefly of the portrayal of others in an uplifting and sanctimonious way, this teaching is very likely to seem phoney and can turn out to be counterproductive. There is no substitute for developing a broad sense of what it is like to be someone seemingly quite different from oneself. Novels and autobiographies (Richard Wright's *Black Boy* is a good example) can help to accomplish this. Getting inside a different kind of life does not guarantee sympathy; but it can make sympathy more likely, and it also should strengthen the ability to be aware of the kind of impact life's vicissitudes can have on others.

THE HEART OF THE MATTER

Education of character is a complicated business. There are many bad ways to approach it, and more than one kind of good strategy. Two points though in this essay should be central.

First, good character should be thought of as a modification of the self of the person who acquires it, rather than as some fund of information in the memory banks. Knowing some rules of good behavior certainly is part of it, but there has to be much besides. Coming to understand the point of morality, which includes sensitivity and concern for others, will make someone a different person. A sense of self that includes pride, and that carries with it possibilities of shame for moral lapses, also makes a difference. So does a sense of what is most important in a life that will be wonderful to lead.

Second, much inadequate moral education consists largely of the first steps of what could be adequate moral education were it not cut short and simplified. Learning rules of good behavior is useful. However psychological experiments such as Milgram's, as well as experience of how people behave during social upheavals, suggest that learning the rules often will not make virtuous behavior probable. A sense of what justifies the rules, and also of the relation of virtue to a satisfying life, can greatly improve the odds. Childhood acquisition of habits of acceptable behavior also is useful. However such habits are not proof against the disorientation brought on by drastically changed circumstances, or by the feeling that there is a new social order in which old rules do not apply.

REFERENCES

Argyle, Michael. 1987. *The Psychology of Happiness.* London: Methuen.
Aristotle. 1962. *The Nicomachean Ethics.* Trans. Martin Ostwald. Englewood Cliffs, NJ: Prentice Hall.
Confucius. 1938. *The Analects of Confucius.* Trans. Arthur Waley. New York: Vintage Books.
Funder, David C. 1999. *Personality Judgment: A Realistic Approach to Person Perception.* San Diego: Academic Press.

Harman, Gilbert. 1999. Moral philosophy meets social psychology. *Proceedings of the Aristotelian Society* 99:315–31.

Kant, Immanuel. 1981. *Grounding for the Metaphysics of Morals.* Trans. James Ellington. Indianapolis, IN: Hackett.

Kohlberg, L. 1981. *The Philosophy of Moral Development.* Essays on Moral Development, vol. 1, San Francisco: Harper & Row.

Kovesi, Julius. 1967. *Moral Notions.* London: Routledge and Kegan Paul.

Kupperman, Joel J. 1991. *Character.* New York: Oxford University Press.

———. 1999. *Value . . . And What Follows.* New York: Oxford University Press.

———. 2001a. *Classic Asian Philosophy: A Guide to the Essential Texts.* New York: Oxford University Press.

———. 2001b. The Indispensability of Character. *Philosophy* 76:239–50.

———. In progress. *Ethics and the Qualities of Life.*

Mencius. 1970. *Mencius.* Trans. D. C. Lau. Harmondsworth: Penguin Books.

Moore, G. E. 1903. *Principia Ethica.* Cambridge: Cambridge University Press.

Plato. 1977. *Complete Works.* Ed. John M. Cooper. Indianapolis, IN: Hackett.

Ross, L., and R. Nisbett. 1991. *The Person and the Situation: Perspectives of Social Psychology.* New York: McGraw Hill.

NINE

Harness the Sun, Channel the Wind

The Art and Science of Effective Character Education

Matthew L. Davidson

CHARACTER EDUCATION HAS RETURNED TO EDUCATIONAL VOGUE FOLLOW-ing several cycles of surging interest and declining support, transforming one of the oldest educational emphases into one of the fastest growing educational movements in the nation today. Since the late 1980s, public funding and support for character education has steadily grown. The popular interest in character education seems simultaneously a blessing and a curse. Enthusiasm for character education has lead to important changes in educational policy regarding its inclusion: character education requirements are now found at district- and state-wide levels, including at least seventeen states currently addressing character education through legislation. There are new sources of funding for character education: since 1995, thirty-six states and the District of Columbia received a combined total of approximately $27.5 million from the

U.S. Department of Education seed money, allocated through its "Partnerships in Character Education Pilot Projects," with an additional $16 million available for dissemination in Fall 2002 as part of a second wave of "Partnerships in Character Education" projects. Finally, character education has earned bipartisan political support, from both Houses of Congress, Presidents Clinton and Bush, and State Governments across the country (Character Education Partnership 2000), an important accomplishment for an educational topic that, for good or bad, can be a politically charged endeavor (c.f., Purpel 1997). The positive enthusiasm that has propelled character education from small grassroots efforts into a national movement has also left many educators and school districts struggling to implement some form of character education, frequently without the time, training, or expertise necessary for effective program planning and evaluation. It has left researchers and theoreticians struggling to provide clear and concise programmatic recommendations for effective character education across highly diverse developmental and contextual realities.

From the late 1980s up through the present, the character education movement has continued to gain momentum as more and more supporters get behind the idea. But momentum is double-edged: how can it be sustained or increased, and yet prevented from running out of control. Despite the overwhelming public support, character education is certainly not without its critics—both inside and outside the movement (c.f., Kohn 1997; Schaps, Schaeffer, and McDonnell 2001). In general, critics argue that character education is a mile wide and an inch deep, suggesting an inability to access the deeper content and systemic issues required to realize deep and lasting change. It is not as though character education is beyond critique (in fact, I mean to offer several critiques of my own); however, many critics approach character education as if it were monolithic, as if there were just one character education program or approach. Whereas, in reality, differentiation is the rule—developmental levels, environmental contexts, curricular approaches, and myriad other factors render one-dimensional critiques limited, at best. In addition, critics make it seem as if character educators are somehow uninterested in achieving deeper, more rigorous efforts, but those critics rarely, if ever, acknowledge the significant macro-forces (such as school and class size, teacher training, and competing educational initiatives) that render these deeper effects so difficult to achieve. Concerns for greater rigor and consistency must be vigorously pursued, but they must also be balanced by the real-world challenges that accompany character education.

History substantiates a sporadic pattern of political and empirical support for character education, and yet practitioners have seemingly never wavered in their character education efforts. This has at times left practitioners with theories and strategies, such as values clarification, which were later demonstrated to be ineffective (c.f., Leming 1993, 1997). Nevertheless, the sustained practitioner interest in character education suggests a foundation of education that will not go away simply because we haven't perfected the research and development. Character education is a timeless need of all societies and cultures. According to Lickona (1991), education has always had two great goals: to help students become smart and to help them become good. It is not surprising that we find these same, timeless goals at the forefront of current educational emphases that focus on academic standards and character education.

Perhaps the great goals of education haven't changed. It seems, however, that two fundamental things have changed. First, the pressure to achieve these goals has seemingly increased, crystallized by the ongoing threat of school violence and concerns regarding optimal academic achievement. In addition to the pressure to put programs in place to meet the goals of smart and good, there is an urgency to know whether the efforts are "working," which seems simultaneously understandable and misplaced. That is, the pressure to prove effectiveness reduces a life-course process like character education into a tenuous time crunch—as if we would abandon the cultivation of character if students weren't more honest, just, and responsible by fourth, eighth, or tenth grade. Second, it seems that the two great goals, which once seemed of concomitant importance, are now pitted against each other. Teachers and parents routinely ask the question: "Can you prove that character education will improve grades?" (I'm fond of the reply given by educator Chip Wood, who responds: "Can *you* prove that attention to grades will improve character?") The standards emphasis seemingly privileges intellectual development over moral development (pressure is so great to meet the academic standards that there are even reports of *teachers* cheating to help students make the grade). Clearly, the competitive atmosphere of American society generally, and of the standards era specifically, asserts a significant force, which shapes and influences the moral culture of the school. As a senior from an affluent Chicago area high school recently told me, "Students in the school have taken to saying, 'If character counts, show me what it can do for my GPA.'" He said that, for his classmates, the message from the community was pretty clear: getting good grades and getting into the best colleges, *not* necessarily being a good person, is the bottom line in this competitive school.

The fundamental challenge for character education today is to provide an experience that is wide (integrated throughout the structures and content of the school and community experiences) and deep (based upon a fully integrated psychological and educational model capable of addressing the developmental and ecological reality of the complete moral person). As the title of this chapter suggests, understanding and promoting effective character education is a bit like harnessing the sun or channeling the wind, a quest that is nearly as old as our quest to find and convert effective sources of energy. (At least as far back as Aristotle and Plato, one finds concern regarding how to best develop the character of the youth and the general citizenry.) Like the potential power that lies within the sun and wind, the potential for character development is always present. The moral and ethical formation of youth is a timeless endeavor that nearly everyone sees the importance of, even if there is not agreement over how it should occur or who should do it. Whereas the belief in the importance of character education is seemingly stable, what waxes and wanes is our commitment to devoting the time, training, and resources required for effective character education. Why is this? Among a litany of plausible explanations, I present two general reasons for our inability to garner sustained efforts contributing to the science of character education. First, like the sun and wind, it seems that nearly everybody has had some firsthand experience with character education (most educators and parents tend to feel some degree of character education expertise). Thus, while you must have formal training to be a carpenter, teacher, lawyer, or doctor, most people feel qualified to handle character education with little or no formal instruction on the topic. For example, a study on the state of character education in the nation's schools of education (Jones, Ryan, and Bohlin 1999) found overwhelming support for character education by leaders in teacher education (ninety percent agreement that core values should be taught in schools; ninety-seven percent agreement—to a negatively worded statement—that character education is the responsibility of schools). Despite this avowed commitment to character education, however, that same report also cited that less than twenty-five percent of the same respondents indicated that character education is "highly" emphasized within the program's course offerings.

The second reason for the lack of commitment to cultivating the science of character education relates to its pervasive nature. That is, in one form or another character education is occurring at all times and in all places—at home, at school, at work, or at play—either through the formal curriculum of what is taught, through the informal rules and structures, or through the unspoken norms of the hidden curriculum. It is difficult to know what character-forming practices are taking place, how often or with what degree of quality, and by whom. Establishing the relative impact of each character-development influence proves nearly impossible. Therefore, establishing formative control of the character-development "program" proves particularly difficult (which may in part account for some of the struggles to evaluate character education effectiveness). The all-encompassing nature of character education presents a dilemma. On the one hand, character education wants to convince its stakeholders that this isn't some new add-on, that it's as old as education itself, and that it underlies all educational endeavors. On the other hand, character education must convince character educators that there is a new and evolving science for best practice in character education that challenges character educators to reconsider the what, why, and how of character education.

Every time there is an energy crisis we reconsider the potential of resources such as sun, wind, and water, not because these are new resources, but because they are fundamental resources, proven to be available, accessible to nearly everyone, and, if harnessed, capable of having far-reaching positive effects. The same might be said of character education. However, turning to character education while in the throes of a social or educational crisis and expecting miraculous results is at best poor planning, and, at worst, a social catastrophe. There are two critical things that we cannot afford to continuing doing: First, we can't have character education disappear again from the educational policy and research landscape (as it did at least two other times in the twentieth century). Second, we cannot continue to rely on outdated theoretical and scientific knowledge to meet the challenges presented today—knowledge that was unable to meet the challenges confronted in the past. As Lickona argued in the introduction to *Raising Good Children,* "a child is the only known substance from which a responsible adult can be made." To which I would add, responsible adults are the only known substance from which a responsible society can be made. We must, therefore, cease approaching character education as if faced with a decision to preserve or terminate the experiment, approaching it instead with the sense of urgency, concentration, and diligence that has distinguished previous challenges of national importance. This type of effort will require cooperation, communication, and commitment from the various "camps" surrounding the field of character education; it will require open-mindedness and willingness to grow and change from those within character education, as well as sustained commitment from those critics who choose to cast dispersions from the safety of the sidelines rather than attempting to master the messy and difficult reality of schools and communities.

In a field that seems to know very little for certain, there are two fundamental things that we do know. First, character education is taking place in our schools, homes, and communities, and we don't get to choose whether or not that should or will be the case; for even the decision to remain neutral, or avoid altogether character-development issues, impacts the character development of individuals and communities. What, for example, would be the message conveyed by silence regarding naturally occurring moral matters within the content of the curriculum? Regarding academic integrity and its importance? Regarding the structures of education and the responsibilities of individuals for caring for those in their school community, as well as those outside of their community? Second, in the quest to develop character, it is never too late. Intuitions abound regarding the age and circumstances that render positive character development impossible: for example, if not achieved by school-age, or at latest by the close of adolescence, and definitely not if you come from a particular type of home or environment. Granted, character development may be truncated at various times and in various environmental conditions, but the potential for developmental growth remains present throughout the life-course. For example, research on children in violent and traumatic environments records the presence of truncated moral development caused by repeated exposure to chronic danger and trauma. However, this research also indicates that truncated moral development is not irreparably fixated at lower levels and that, when stability is restored, normal moral development resumes (e.g., Arbuthnot and Gordon 1986; Garbarino 1990b; Garbarino, Kostelny, and Dubrow 1991; Gibbs 1991; Garbarino and Abramowitz 1992); it may not, but the potential still remains. Thus, while we approach character education with a sense of urgency akin to immunization of the young—as well we should—nonetheless, our interest and enthusiasm should be paced for a life-course endeavor.

What follows is a theoretical paper based on personal experience assisting schools and communities to plan, monitor, and evaluate comprehensive character education. From that experience, foundational questions emerge that must be continually reconsidered in a reflective process of hypothesis, knowledge acquisition, theory testing, and reformulation with a view to providing practical theory. It is assumed that a developmental perspective mediates all character education processes, although space constraints prevent elaborate discussion of the particular nuances in this single chapter. This chapter will attempt to explore some foundational questions for the field of character education, bootstrapping back and forth between the practical reality and a theoretical ideal by identifying troubling trends and promising theoretical and practical advances in the field of character education. I intend to describe the reality of character education: what it is and what it does. Simultaneously I hope to consider variously *what* is done in the name of character education, as well as *why* these practices are done, their underlying rationale and the overall quality and depth of their implementation. Finally, I want to offer a theoretical synthesis that can help move the field forward in its attempts to create more adequate psychological foundation for character education—theoretically, pedagogically, and empirically.

WHAT, EXACTLY, IS "CHARACTER"?

To begin, discussions of character education assume a shared understanding of the pivotal concept, character. One overarching problem for advancing the science of character education, however, is our inability to adequately define character. If character educators were on trial, they would undoubtedly take their Fifth Amendment rights regarding the question, "What is character?" At the risk of incriminating myself, I want to try and answer this. In its original Greek, *charaktēr* translates as an engraved, enduring, or indelible mark. When describing individuals' (or a community's) enduring or indelible mark, invariably the language of values is utilized, and specifically, we describe action connected with those values (e.g., they are honest, hardworking, trustworthy, caring). Therefore, character might best be defined as "values in action," and character education as "the deliberate attempt to shape the environment and processes for cultivating the knowledge, skills, and commitment required for realizing the goal of values in action." Toward what end? The goal of character education is personal fulfillment or happiness balanced with competent participation in a liberal democracy—whose goal is the realization of a just and civil society. Values are important because they represent the content of character, the tangible outcomes of character education—few would quibble over this. However, questions of knowledge, intent, context, and motivation regarding when and how values are taught and lived out represent the mediating psychological and environmental processes that have captured the interests of so many for so long.

Moral psychologists might say, "Okay, even if I conceded that the end goal of character education was to see values in action, how do we get there? What are the keys to moral functioning that can be understood and taught to achieve this end?" Here's an example that dramatically depicts the challenge: some have argued that if you want to live a good life, work backwards from an image of your funeral, picturing how you would like people to describe you, and begin to shape your values in action so that your distinguishing mark matches that idealized picture of what you would like people to say about you. Sounds reasonable. Here's the problem. Go back to your imagined funeral and answer this question: aside from a concern that they might say unflattering things about the kind of person you were, what is your next biggest fear as you observe your own funeral? Exactly. That the members of your church might compare notes with your colleagues from work, or worse still, that either group might talk to your poker friends. Why does this concern us? Because we are all more or less moral schizophrenics whose character tends to split or change from situation to situation. We like to think of character as a stable compound; but in reality it's quite volatile for most of us, and somewhat volatile even for exemplars. Even when we can neatly define character (values in action) we struggle mightily for comprehensive psychological definitions that capture the personal and environmental processes that mediate positive displays of values in action. Specifically, the display of character (as evidenced by the demonstration of the values) is not meaningfully separated from the cognitive, affective, and behavioral psychological dimensions. It has become commonplace in the current character education paradigm to approach the three dimensions as though they were distinctly separate. Even the oft-echoed notion of "head, heart, and hand" implies the dissection of the moral person as a task no more challenging than the dissection of the physical body.

In one sense, the commonplace belief of character having at least three psychological dimensions reflects progress in the field of character education, because previous moral education theories attempted to reduce the moral person to simply moral behavior or habit (character education of the 1920s), or simply reason (moral reasoning dilemmas), or simply affect (values clarification). Nonetheless, as Rest (1986) has argued, "there are no moral cognitions completely devoid of affect, no moral affects completely devoid of cognitions, and no moral behaviors separable from the cognitions and affects that prompted the behavior" (4). In the end, there is an important tension between the three dimensions, a connectedness that, fully understood, might offer crucial insights for the field. In fact, it is precisely the inability of character education to adequately address the interconnectedness or wholeness of the three dimensions that has prevented a fully integrative theoretical rationale for its various practices.

MORAL IDENTITY: THE BRIDGE

One of the distinguishing features of character education (as compared to other moral education efforts) is the focus on values (suspending for another day discussions regarding the distinctions between values and virtues). Character education has spent considerable time and attention on values, under the assumption that values represent the content of character. And yet, in this approach, character education has struggled with two key features: consistency of character across domains and bridging the gap between moral knowledge and moral behavior (c.f., Hartshorne and May 1928; Hartshorne, May, and Maller 1929; Hartshorne, May, and Shuttleworth 1930). In his work on moral identity, Blasi (1984) argues for the importance of moral identity as a key factor in bridging moral action and moral cognition, because moral identity unites cognition and motivation (e.g., when I know the moral dimension as the core of my being, I am motivated to consistently act in ways that support this belief). Moral identity, I believe, is the missing piece of the character education puzzle, a theoretical concept that pulls the constituent pieces of character education practice into a coherent whole—even at elementary levels where identity formation isn't an active developmental reality, the idea of moral identity offers a sense of direction and purpose, a reason for existing, for character education practices. Moral identity includes the extent to which a person: sees their moral self as the core of their being; feels compelled to do things they feel are right; feels a sense of betrayal when they do something other than what they feel is right; and has a conscience that is independent of social pressure to believe or act in a way that is contrary to their beliefs (Blasi 1984, 1988; Shields and Bredemeier 1995). Returning to the funeral analogy used above, an individual with a strong moral identity, a sense of morality as the core of their being, would more likely manifest consistent values in action (character) across domains because to do otherwise would be to violate the essence of who they are. Whereas an individual who cares about the perceptions of others, who would like to seem honest, responsible, and so forth, but does not see these concepts as the core of her being, is more likely to demonstrate inconsistency in putting her values in action. Plato may have captured the essence of identity in his statement "You must be what you want to seem." To realize this vision from a moral perspective, we must assume that individuals have a vision of who they want to be, morally speaking; that they see the moral dimension of their self as something intrinsically desirable. And we must assume that they have the composite skills required to consistently live out the vision.

Character education has focused its attention on the component dimensions of character through knowledge acquisition, development of reasoning, cultivation of intrinsic motivation, and providing opportunities for lived moral experiences like mentoring and service learning. It has focused on the specific character attributes or values exhibited by exemplary individuals who consistently display values in action. At the elementary level (the level where character education is most prominent and arguably most effective), these practices may in fact provide a reasonably effective approach in the short term. At the middle and high school levels, however, character education has been only marginally effective at putting the component parts of character into a coherent whole, one that adequately captures the psychological essence of moral functioning. In other words, I would suggest that character education has broken character down into its composite elements, but has failed to present an adequate vision of character in its wholeness—especially for pre-adolescents and adolescents who require a deeper rationale of what it is and why it's important. If character (values in action) is ultimately a function of moral identity, then character education is about at least two primary functions: First, it is about providing an environment that supports and guides individuals in the construction of their moral identity, a view of the moral dimension as an essential part of who they are. Second, it is about providing the processes that facilitate self-reflection regarding the construction and consistent application of a coherent moral identity. From these two primary purposes, let me discuss specific character education practices, and offer some justification for their inclusion and some critiques on how they are currently utilized.

CREATING ENVIRONMENTS THAT SUPPORT AND GUIDE THE CONSTRUCTION OF MORAL IDENTITY

The Zone of Proximal Moral Development

In character education, the people are the program. I know of no program or curriculum specifically designed to achieve greater gains without instructors than with them. Whether it's in the classroom, on the sports field, or at home, adults are given opportunities to create environments that support or detract from the construction of character. The nature and degree of adult involvement for optimal effects is a point of considerable theoretical, practical, and empirical discussion for character education. What seems clear is that adults bear primary responsibility for creating the environment where character is developed. The core of morality is respect (Lickona 1983, 9), which requires character education that is done *with* students, not *to* them. This requires character educators (a term used generically to describe all types of primary adult educators—parents, coaches, and teachers) who strive to meet students at their current developmental level, and then structure an environment and related experiences designed to expand students' developmental functioning and overall capacity. Character education is a process whereby individuals are constructing character through the interaction of their existing cognitive structures, novel experiences, and the influence of those around them. Character education is essentially a quest to identify and dwell in what Vygotsky (1978) referred to as the "zone of proximal development" (ZPD), which he defined as "the distance between the actual developmental level as determined by independent problem solving and level of potential development as determined through problem solving under adult guidance or in collaboration with more capable peers" (86). Character educators are striving to create an environment that proactively structures moral problem solving opportunities where individuals can grow through the assistance of teachers, parents, or peers. They are attempting to create the zone of proximal moral development, an "optimal" environment that balances the need for development with the need for competence. In essence, character education is about creating optimal moral development environments.

In creating a zone of optimal moral development, character educators are attempting to create a culture that lives and breathes the content it wishes to convey—no small task, for certain. However, Tappan (1998) argues that from a Vygotskian perspective moral functioning is a socio-cultural activity that is "mediated by a vernacular moral language that fundamentally shapes the ways in which people think, feel, and act. . . . [T]his vernacular moral language, moreover, is shared by persons who share the same activities, who are engaged in similar social/moral practices" (148). This is a critical insight into character education practices that attempt to shape the environment through the consistent use of moral language—specifically, values. To be certain, the role and nature of values in character education theory is an issue that has generated more heat than light. It lies at the heart of the mantra uttered first and foremost by character education skeptics, namely, "Whose values will we teach?" This connects to the concern that character education is tantamount to indoctrination. Similarly, the emphasis on values is reminiscent of Lawrence Kohlberg's famous quip referring to character education as the "bag of virtues," suggesting that for any virtues that one might choose to throw into the bag, countless others are omitted for no apparent logical reason. Finally, from a practical perspective, core values act as a lightning rod since determining shared values is where most schools generally begin the character education process. Values receive the most frequent attention from the developers of prepackaged character education curricula and resources, leading critics to assume—in some instances rightfully so, and in other instances not—that the sum of character education rests in identifying, advertising, and celebrating the values. Nevertheless, we have to ask ourselves, "Is there a psychologically valid role for identifying, promoting, and celebrating manifestations of shared community values?"

While many remember Lawrence Kohlberg's irreverent quip characterizing character education of the 1920s as "the bag of virtues," few recall that within the development of the just-community approach, Kohlberg actually came to see the importance of promoting his own particular bag of virtues. In describing the just-community schools, Kohlberg argued, "the teachers in this school go beyond Socratic moral dialogue to advocate the virtues of justice and community" (Power, Higgins, and Kohlberg 1989, 2). And, according to Power, their experience with the just-community schools led them "to focus on particular norms such as trust, respect for democratic authority, integration, caring, participation, and collective responsibility" (174). These values were descriptive of the approach, but were also explicitly advocated. Let me acknowledge that many schools engaged in character education still rely on what Philip Jackson (1993) refers to as "bumper-sticker morality . . . whose pithy phrases and eye-catching designs seemed patterned for quick consumption by passerby rather than being intended as a subject matter for reflection and discussion" (9). To be certain, the public awareness approach to values can be legitimately critiqued for what it *doesn't* do; posters on the wall and words of the month that are not connected to deeper pedagogical processes are missing out on authentic character-development potential. I'm certainly not suggesting that "bumper-sticker morality" is the highest realization of character education's potential. Again, if the goal of character educators is to create a zone of optimal moral development, then posting core values is the equivalent of a basketball coach simply rolling out the balls before practice; obviously, there must be more. Nevertheless, we shouldn't be too glib or hasty in dismissing every poster on the wall or attempt to proactively structure the shared moral language of the community.

What if we consider the practices of identifying, studying, and celebrating prosocial values with some different twists of the theoretical rationale? First, the practice of promoting particular values is an attempt to create and define the environment, an essential task in the process of defining who *we* are as a community, not unlike school mission statements, songs, or cheers. Promotion of values is a form of identity development whereby individuals essentially "try on" particular values as they attempt to define themselves (a process that is obviously more complete with guided reflection). Second, as Tappan (1998) argued, promotion of values is about creating vernacular moral language that mediates moral functioning. As Dewey (1972) has argued, society exists by transmission; he states "the chief business of the school is to transmit [information and skills] to a new generation" (17). Finally, consistent representation and framing of moral terminology may contribute to the easy (or chronic) accessibility of moral terminology and functioning (Lapsley 1996). For example, a colleague[1] recently provided a powerful example of how language and concepts become chronically accessible and why the identification, promotion, and celebration of positive values is an important first step in effective character education. He told of an exercise done with students where he asked them to complete a series of popular advertising slogans, which they did quite easily. He would say, "You deserve . . ." and students quickly responded, "a break today." He said, "Just . . ." and students said, "do it." Their access to these marketing concepts was extensive, including food, alcohol, and numerous other categories. Then he asked them to complete some other presumably well-known phrases like, "Any job worth doing . . ." He received no or few responses. "If at first you don't succeed . . ."—again, no or few responses. From this experience and others like it, my colleague concluded that character education is partly about reserving some space for the moral domain—its language, ideas, and exemplars—on the cognitive "hard drives" of youth.

As schools and students struggle to define themselves, we ought not feel uneasy about making moral language and concepts chronically accessible for students. We know that nature abhors a vacuum, and that if we aren't filling the airwaves of our community with discussion of prosocial values, then something else will rush in. On the one hand, it is vitally important that teachers model and structure a culture or experience that exemplifies the values they wish to teach (allowing character to permeate the lived experience), while simultaneously labeling the actions of good character and the values they exemplify (providing an opportunity to explicitly teach the nuances and rationale). This practice of "induction" holds particular importance for parents and teachers. According to Lapsley (1996), "Parents who use induction, that is, who draw the child's attention to the consequences of his or her misconduct on others, accompanied by an appropriate rationale for the norm or standard in question tend to have children who internalize moral standards, who feel appropriate levels of guilt for misconduct and empathy for victims, and who accept responsibility for behavior" (190). Through induction there is integration between the norms of the community and the lived experience thereby developing deeper understanding and commitment to the shared moral vernacular. It suggests the importance of the adult role in scaffolding the thoughts, feelings, and actions of the individual and the moral norms or core values of the community, a process that requires Socratic dialogue to discern what exactly students know, feel, and are capable of doing. The induction process, however, is not confined simply to the content—the moral norms or values. As Lickona (1983) has argued, educators must "practice what they preach, but also preach what they practice." Too often character educators assume that students simply catch character by participating in a particular experience (e.g., service, classroom meetings, etc.), that students understand why experiences are structured a certain way, and why these experiences are important. In fact, character is both caught through the experience and taught through the metacognitive sense-making both of the experience itself (through explanation and discussion) and of how the experience represents and fulfills the norms of the classroom or school. Student buy in to character education depends on their interactions with the intended goals and processes of character education.

Much work is still to be done in understanding the optimal role and functioning of values in character education. For example, there is clearly a tipping point where commonly used language begins to have a backlash, where concepts get blocked out or overlooked by people's radar. There are certain values that draw individuals into the discussion and others that push people away (and these change with developmental level, context, and exposure). Nevertheless, in the quest to create an optimal zone for moral development, shaping the environment is an important first step— it's not the only one, but it's a doable, psychologically valid first step.

The Ecology of Character Development

The quest to create an optimal zone for moral development requires coequal emphasis on developing character and community. Unfortunately, the ecology of character education is frequently overlooked, or at least undervalued. Critics such as Kohn (1997) argue that character education takes a "fix-the-kid approach," one that means to simply change the knowledge, disposition, and behaviors of students, with no attention to the moral life of the school, its structures, policies, and their resulting influence on the development of student character. Well-intentioned character educators can become overly concerned with fixing kids, instead of working on the developmental assets of the community itself. On this point I should be very clear: character education must attend to the development of the individual *and* the community. Character education is about creating a zone (or environment) of optimal moral development, one that fosters maximum development in the individual.

Character educators are only just beginning to understand the empirical power of the moral atmosphere, despite the intuitions and experience of major theoreticians such as Durkheim, Dewey, and Kohlberg. The power of the school atmosphere is among the most impressive, and little touted, keys to effective character education. Pioneered in the just-community approach to moral education (Power 1988; Power, Higgins, and Kohlberg 1989), character education is still working toward realizing a coequal emphasis on the development of the individual *and* the community (the failure to fully meet such a goal is due in part to the time, training, and commitment required for school-wide change and development—especially in larger, economically and academically challenged schools). Nevertheless, there is a growing body of research empirically substantiating the importance of community. The Child Development Project, for example, perhaps the most impressive sustained character education effort of the past twenty years, has produced research demonstrating that a sense of the school as a caring community is a leading predictor of a number of positive character qualities, including:

> Greater liking for school, greater enjoyment of class, greater empathy towards others' feelings, greater concern for others, greater enjoyment of helping others learn, stronger motivation to be kind and helpful to others, more sophisticated conflict resolution skills, more frequent acts of altruistic behavior, higher general self-esteem, higher academic self-esteem, stronger feelings of social competence, less feeling of loneliness in school, less use of tobacco, alcohol, and marijuana, fewer delinquent acts, less victimization. (Schaps, Watson, and Lewis 1996, 43)

In this research we see the sense of the school as a caring and supportive community mediating nearly all of the outcomes that character educators might hope to see if effective. Experiencing the school as a caring community requires that character education fulfill Kohlberg's exhortation to "change the life of the school as well as the development of the individual" (Power, Higgins, and Kohlberg 1989, 20).

In practice, much of character education is about the process of developing a caring community, a place where individuals are known and needed, safe and cared about, and where they have authentic opportunities for shaping their environment. The experience of community is our fundamental human need to be a part of something bigger than ourselves; it's about who *we* are and how what *we* do defines *us*. Class meetings, democratic participation, group problem solving, and other cooperative learning strategies provide the essential practices for cultivating the sense of community. We know very little about the origins of school violence witnessed in recent years; however, nearly every example displayed the two sides of community attachment. Students have a fundamental human need to be known, needed, and cared about, and whether it's with the "trench-coat mafia" or the football team they will find that experience. And frequently communities show who they are by showing how others are not like them. The so-called, "jock-acracy" is about defining yourself by attaching to a group (a healthy developmental milestone) by excluding those from other groups (a divisive and limiting process). From an ecological perspective we are reminded as character educators that the moral habitat is not inconsequential, but rather is essential to the character-development process. Human development does not take place in a vacuum; it is a dynamic process of interaction between the organism and its environment. Garbarino (1990a) argues that the habitat of children includes "family, friends, neighborhood, church, and school, as well as less immediate forces that constitute the social geography and climate (e.g., laws, institutions, and values), and the physical environment" (78).

At the heart of an ecological approach to character education is an ongoing examination of the dynamic relationship between organisms and their multiple microsystems (e.g., families and schools), the interrelationship between the microsystems (family, peer groups, school, church), as well as the impact of macrosystems (including broad ideological and demographic patterns like the standards push and the ever-increasing size of schools). Clearly, character education must attend to developing the assets of the school community; in addition, character education must involve the home and community in the process. Optimal development for the individual requires sustained presence in the zone of proximal moral development, not just in school but also across moral domains. Consider, for example the 1997 National Longitudinal Study of Adolescent Health, which interviewed twelve thousand students (grades seven to twelve) from eighty schools about their experience in eight high risk areas including violence, suicidal tendencies, emotional distress, use of alcohol, marijuana, and tobacco, sexual activity, and pregnancy. They found only two factors that were clearly protective against teen involvement in nearly all of these activities: (1) family connectedness, feeling close to and cared about by parents and other family members—the more connected students were the less they were involved in risky behaviors—and (2) connectedness to school, feeling close to people at school, feeling fairly treated by teachers, feeling part of one's school (Resnick et al. 1997). This research suggests that the cultivation of character and community in the home is co-equal in importance with cultivating character and community in the school. Changes in social, economic, educational-policy, and familial structures leave schools today being asked to do more than ever before; it is essential that schools enlist the support of the home and community in the development of character.

CREATING PROCESSES THAT FOSTER SELF-REFLECTION REGARDING THE CONSTRUCTION AND CONSISTENT APPLICATION OF MORAL IDENTITY

Character education is not a program, but rather a process, a process that seeks to proactively structure practices that both foster self-reflection regarding the construction of moral identity and develop the skills for consistently living out that identity. Aside from developing community assets that support the development of moral identity, what are the theoretical and practical processes utilized by character education? Through knowledge acquisition, discussion, debate, demonstration, role-play opportunities, and lived experiences like service learning, mediated by guided reflection from teachers and peers, character education attempts to facilitate self-reflection on the following critical questions: Who am I? What skills are required to consistently live out who I want to be? Why be good?

As discussed above, answering the question, "Who am I?" is virtually inseparable from the question, "Who are we?" That is to say, an important part of how individuals determine who they are is through their interactions with the communities where they live and dwell (home, peers, school, etc.). Through attention to prosocial values, interactions with historical and literary stories, identification of moral exemplars, and participation in applied activities, character education seeks to create fertile soil for optimal development. Ultimately, as others have argued, "character is an inside job" that individuals must construct and maintain for themselves, which is especially important in the middle- and high-school years when students are constantly questioning who they are. While younger developmental populations generally do not engage in metacognitive reflections on the consonance between their individual identity and the identity of their community, adolescents do. Thus, across the developmental spectrum, character education is attempting to structure activities that help students to positively approach questions of identity—specifically, character educators are attempting to have students integrate moral identity as an important feature of the "Who am I?" question.

In the quest to develop practices that cultivate a sense of moral identity, the zone of optimal moral development is not established by simply doing activities. Once again, as discussed above, the role of the character educator is not simply to provide an experience, but also to facilitate the development through guided reflection. For example, many character educators advocate the use of literature as a character education strategy, but they frequently fall short in its optimal use as such. Clearly, literature is a deep source of moral identity development material that provides students with characters and situations to reflect upon and "try-on" through various role-plays; but, optimal moral development requires more than simply reading the stories. Research by Narvaez (2001) exploring moral theme comprehension in grade school children found that "reading moral stories to children does not guarantee that they will understand the moral message or theme as intended by the author" (483). Rather, there were several mediating processes requiring active guided reflection to achieve desired developmental gains. Similarly, service learning is an activity that many schools utilize to provide authentic opportunities to live out the community's values and norms. It is through active, guided learning that service learning is able to realize its full potential, not simply through the service alone. Research has suggested that service learning provides key experiences that lead to resiliency and help develop a sense of social responsibility (Berman 1997). Recent research compiling evidence from the past ten years on the impact of service learning indicates that service learning helps develop students' sense of civic and social responsibility and citizenship skills, improves school climate, increases respect between teachers and students, and improves the interpersonal development and ability to relate to diverse groups (Billig 2000). The impact of service learning clearly relates to the experience; however, the learning part of service learning is the part that involves discussion of important themes, and an inductive meta-reflection on why service learning is important for understanding and living out the norms or core values of the community.

The development of identity is fundamentally a question of self-consistency. It is a process of defining oneself, and then attempting to live in a way that is consonant with that vision. Putting values in action consistent across domains is the goal of character education. How we make sense of inconsistency is key for character education (e.g., students are respectful in my classroom but not in the hallway, bus, or playground—why?). Too often as character educators we resort to exhortation or coercion: "Please be good, and if you do, here's what I'll give you." Celebrating those "caught being good" isn't necessarily a problem, unless you offer the celebration itself to others as self-evident description of the means. For example, if you were a new basketball coach who wanted a highly skilled basketball team, you wouldn't show them a video of the ticker-tape parade for the NBA champions. Instead, you might break down the victories (or losses) along the road to the championship into their component parts. One promising practice in the field of character education integrates the fields of character education and social and emotional learning. For any value that we might want students to embody, there are nearly infinite nuances and particulars, especially when factoring in age, development, and contextual factors. The identification of particular social and emotional skills helps transform and extend instruction beyond exhortation, by breaking down the general concept into skills that can be taught, practiced, and evaluated. For example, respect is a value that most would agree character education should teach; however, respect is a composite of numerous skills—nearly infinite if one considers individual development and social context—including active listening, appropriate interrupting, ignoring, and apologizing, to name a few. Living out the realities of justice—giving each person their due—requires particular problem-solving skills, as well as skills for taking different perspectives, negotiating, and myriad others; the skills are infinite because age, development, and context dictate different skills. The development of emotional skills lies at the heart of positive displays of values in action: self-control over anger, desires, and passion; courage in the face of fear, self-doubt, and peer pressure. A skills-based approach renders the concepts teachable and the outcomes measurable.

The famous "Marshmallow Test" research of Walter Mischel and colleagues at Stanford University found that social skills such as self-control (specifically, delayed gratification in four-year-olds) were predictive of numerous academic and social outcomes. In particular, the third of the children who waited as compared to those who grabbed the marshmallow were: more likely to take initiative, more trustworthy and dependable, better able to cope with stress, more likely to persevere in the face of difficulty, more eager to learn, more capable of concentrating, more academically competent (on the average, their SAT scores were more than 100 points higher than those of the children that grabbed the marshmallows), and still more capable of delaying gratification in the pursuit of a goal (Shoda, Mischel, and Peake 1990). In addition to providing ways to develop self-control, additional research from the field of social and emotional learning supports the effectiveness of self-control in promoting a more caring classroom atmosphere, skills for conflict resolution and democratic participation, more prosocial behavior, more empathy, and numerous other positive outcomes. These outcomes are very powerful, as many of them represent the particular outcomes that character educators would like to see when they advocate values such as perseverance, responsibility, and work ethic. Obtaining similar results, however, requires a highly specified articulation of program goals and outcomes, an identification of the specific skills required for the display of particular values, and an explicit connection of the skill to the related overarching values.

How is it that cultivating social and emotional skills facilitates the development of moral identity? The development of social and emotional skills leads to moral competence, or the ability to translate your ideal self into your actual self. One certainly need not be perfect or without fault to be competent. It is unlikely, however, that one could maintain strong moral identity—that is, viewing the moral dimension as the core of your identity—without the basic requisite skills for moral functioning. (Just as it would be unlikely to have an identity as an athlete without minimal skills of strength, stamina, and coordination.) The development of social and moral skills render abstract concepts accessible for further development and reflection. With competence comes an internal motivation and locus of control—an essential piece of the character education puzzle.

Why Be Good?

The integration of social and emotional skills has powerful implications for character education because it integrates the three dimensions of character—cognitive, affective, and behavioral—particularly through its essential connections to the motivation orientation literature. In general, the literature on motivation orientation might be described as examining the self in relation to others. It suggests that an ego (or performance) orientation is one where a person is motivated to show competence in relation to others by showing superiority in the task at hand (e.g., by winning, by getting the most right, by being able to list the most kind things done to others), whereas a task (or learning) orientation is where a person competes against self-referenced personal achievement (e.g., a better time than before, more right on this test than last time, less unnecessary interruptions of the class today than yesterday). In addition to numerous positive performance outcomes (academic, athletic, and other), a task orientation tends to promote self-reflection and awareness, to support strong intrinsic motivation, and to reduce helpless response to failure (Nicholls 1984; Duda and Nicholls 1992; Harackiewicz and Elliot 1993; Molden and Dweck 2000). Achievement motivation is particularly important to character education since it provides the most compelling and integrated access of the affective dimension of character; in particular, it provides a pedagogical pathway for developing intrinsic motivation. Promoting a task orientation requires that the overall goal (the development of character) be broken into self-referenced particulars, which are the values and their particular social and emotional skills described above. These tasks can be practiced and monitored over time, simultaneously promoting competence through cognition and habit. In particular, cognition is developed when students learn to assess moral breakdowns or failures. Both student attributions regarding the cause of the breakdown and guided reflection with character educators help students to feel a sense of control over their ability to change. As students set goals, monitor their progress against those goals, and acquire skills to accurately attribute the antecedents of success and failure, they grow in their intrinsic motivation, another important aspect of character education and a critical piece of the "Why be good?" question.

Intrinsic motivation is an important topic for character education because it gets to the heart of the question "Why be good?" According to Ryan and Deci (2000), "the phenomenon of *intrinsic motivation* reflects the primary propensity of organisms to engage in activities that interest them and, in so doing, to learn, develop, and expand their capacities. Intrinsic motivation is entailed whenever people behave for the satisfaction inherent in the behavior itself" (16, original emphasis). This definition simultaneously identifies the importance of promoting a task orientation through a skills approach (in order to learn, develop, and expand), and the challenge of identifying intrinsic motivation (since it is difficult to determine for certain that an individual is performing the behavior for the satisfaction inherent in the activity, and not for other reasons like the recognition, the reward, etc.). The difficulties inherent in identifying intrinsic motivation in some pure form represent a challenge wedded closely to the field of character education; because they both seek to identify an autonomous morality or motivation for being good (as opposed to a heteronomous one). Aside from its relationship to achievement motivation, the development of intrinsic motivation is perhaps most closely linked to rewarding practices. Clearly, the devil is in the details when it comes to rewarding practices and their supportive or detrimental effects on the development of character. Another troubling trend in the field of character education, however, is a persistent use of extrinsic motivators—stickers, stars, gum, and other forms of behavior inducements. Forms of extrinsic motivation are not inherently evil. As Damon (1995) states, "The notion that intrinsic and extrinsic motivation are incompatible, and that educators must choose between them in formulating their strategies for working with students, is just another myth based upon a false dichotomy" (207). Nonetheless, a greater cause for concern is the absence of consistent school-wide philosophies of motivation. That is to say, schools where the affective domain, and intrinsic motivation specifically, are not conscientiously and proactively addressed, but are rather left to the whims of good fortune.

There are certain dangers related to the use of extrinsic rewards, and frequently schools display no knowledge of, or at least indifference to, these dangers. For example, a recent meta-analysis by Ryan and Deci (2000) compiled hundreds of studies to clarify the relationship between intrinsic and extrinsic motivation. Their findings suggest that tangible extrinsic rewards for controlling behavior tend to *undermine* intrinsic motivation and self-regulation, that extrinsic rewards are less detrimental if they are not used contingently and if the social context is oriented more toward support control, and that verbal rewards conveying information and feedback or affirming competence tend to maintain or enhance intrinsic motivation. The practical implications from this finding suggest that extrinsic rewards used to control student behavior (a practice that is most often witnessed in difficult or at-risk schools) is likely to undermine character development, and that verbal feedback may be a safer pedagogical strategy. Bandura (1991) argues that "successful socialization requires gradual substitution of symbolic and internal controls for external sanctions and demands" (54). In other words, Bandura presents a theoretical notion of meeting the individuals at their current level, and gradually inducing them toward the next level in their development. Once again, however, the inductive process connecting pedagogical practices and their connection to school norms would mediate the experience by acting as the verbal feedback.

THE CHARACTER EDUCATION OPERATING SYSTEM

Effective character education is as much a process as it is a product. As argued throughout this paper, character education is about creating the optimal zone of moral development, the distance between the independent development and the potential development derived from adult or peer collaboration. Creating the environment and practices that establish the zone is where the art and science of character education meet. It is precisely the process of planning, delivering, monitoring, and reflecting on individual and community development that drives effective character education. By way of comparison, it is said that for every airline flight there is an ideal path for getting from point A to point B in the most efficient way; however, most flights don't stay on the path, but must repeatedly pull the plane back to it. Pilots are equipped with instruments, gauges, and other observational tools (including aviation centers on the ground who monitor every flight) that help to bring the plane back on the path in order to reach the intended destination. The character education process is closely akin to this, and when properly conceived, evaluation can guide the process. Patton (1986) states that "program evaluation is the systematic collection of information about the activities, characteristics, and outcomes of programs for use by specific people to reduce uncertainties, improve effectiveness, and make decisions with regard to what those programs are doing and affecting" (14). This definition of evaluation comes close to describing the type of process that underlies the effective design and delivery of character education. And yet the history of character education demonstrates evaluation done after the trip, so to speak, with little or no communication of crucial data to the pilots before or during the trip. A so-called crash like the Hartshorne and May research didn't end flights, it just ended help for the pilots; and data from the flight recorder weren't examined in-depth until fifty or sixty years after the fact, when it was too late to make much difference.

In character education, the most important question is not "Did it work?" but rather questions such as: What worked? What might have worked better? Where do we go from here? For character education to be effective, character educators must become reflective practitioners possessing sophisticated tools for planning and monitoring character education practices. On the macro level, character education planners must utilize data to drive the organization of programs and to determine the developmental and environmental needs of the community (including focus groups, needs assessments, and existing archival data). On a micro level, character education practitioners need more diverse tools for day-to-day planning and monitoring of progress (including questionnaires, rating scales and checklists, interview protocols, and observation instruments). Tailor-made character education programs derived from rigorous planning and sophisticated monitoring of implementation is not necessarily a new idea; it was a prominent feature in Kohlberg's just-community approach, where common principles were modified to meet the specifics of each school. The data driven interplay between content and process is akin to the action-research approach described in the social science literature, specifically the cyclical intertwining of theory and practice where knowledge is gathered, a theory is developed, the theory is tested and revised, and then tested again and again in a systematic and ongoing process. Action research is so vital to character education precisely because it involves practitioners and researchers working together in a common endeavor—a critical void in character education today. In this regard, collaborative action research is pragmatic and useful, increasing the likelihood that the results inform practice. Action research is a theory-driven form of evaluation that gathers outcome-data based on a theory, but this data is part of ongoing theoretical reformulation and subsequent modification of the intervention. At the whole-school and classroom level, action research is the process for determining the zone of proximal moral development. Action research is the process for going beyond intuition to determine what students know, feel, and do—critical elements in guiding them to the next level of development. Action research does not rule out the need for rigorous longitudinal research in the field of character education; however, it does increase the likelihood that rigorous longitudinal research would find positive outcomes.

MOVING FORWARD

It should be clear that the commitment required to do character education well is significant; and, the desire to see fast results from character education is generally not matched by a concomitant commitment of time and resources. In particular, as indicated by the *Teachers as Educators of Character Report*, teachers receive very little training (Jones, Ryan, and Bohlin 1999). Systematic training in cooperative learning, classroom discipline, democratic education, teaching values through the curriculum, facilitating moral discussions, and the creation of community are not acquired in a one-day in-service. Teachers need time—time for dialogue, time to develop concrete pedagogical strategies, time to share, and reflect, and learn from each other. In the absence of committed resources, character education is overly dependent on the super-teacher, the teacher that intuitively or through time-honed skills can foster character development. But no single, or even a few, super-teachers are capable of overcoming the systemic challenges presented to educators today. Character education requires skilled practitioners capable of creating environments that support and guide individuals in the construction of their moral identity; they must implement practices that develop knowledge, skills, and motivation for competent and consistent moral functioning.

In attempting to grapple with the complexity of character education, theoreticians and practitioners alike might seek the wisdom of the principle of parsimony, or Occam's Razor. Many remember the principle of parsimony as essentially arguing that a good hypothesis is one that is as simple as the circumstances warrant; however, few remember the theoretical antithesis known as "Kant's Shaving Bowl," which argues that a good hypothesis should be complex enough to explain the observed facts. This is precisely where character education evaluation has historically run aground: research has focused on results or facts, but it has failed to provide an adequate understanding of the process that produced the observed facts. These are the in-depth insights into the process that are sorely needed by the field. Whether the problem is actuating the potential from energy sources like the sun and wind, or actuating the full potential of character education, the challenge is the same: creating practical and useful theories simple enough to implement and complex enough to adequately capture reality—a challenge as much art as science.

NOTE

1. I'm grateful to W. Ben Hill of the Community Character Project (Brewton, AL) for sharing this insight with me.

REFERENCES

Arbuthnot, J., and D. A. Gordon 1986. Behavioral and cognitive effects of a moral reasoning development intervention for high-risk behavior-disordered adolescents. *Journal of Consulting and Clinical Psychology* 54 (2): 208–16.

Bandura, A. 1991. Social cognitive theory of moral thought and action. In *Handbook of Moral Behavior and Development*, vol. 1, *Theory*, ed. W. M. Kurtines and J. L. Gewirtz, 45–103. Hillsdale, NJ: Lawrence Erlbaum Associates.

Berman, S. 1997. *Children's Social Consciousness and the Development of Social Responsibility.* Albany, NY: SUNY Press.

Billig, S. 2000. *Service-learning Impacts on Youth, Schools and Communities: Research on K-12 School-based Service Learning, 1990–1999.* Denver, CO: RMC Research Corporation.

Blasi, A. 1984. Moral identity: Its role in moral functioning. In *Morality, Moral Behavior, and Moral Development*, ed. W. M. Kurtines and J. J. Gewirtz, 128–39. New York: John Wiley and Sons.

———. 1988. Identity and the development of self. In *Self, Ego, and Identity: Integrative Approaches*, ed. D. K. Lapsley and F. C. Power, 83–90. Chicago: University of Chicago Press.

Character Education Partnership. 2000. *Questions and Answers about CEP and Character Education.* Washington, DC: Character Education Partnership.

Damon, W. 1995. *Greater Expectations: Overcoming the Culture of Indulgence in Our Homes and Schools.* New York: Free Press.

Dewey, J. 1972. *Experience and Education.* New York: Collier Books.

Duda, J. L., and J. G. Nicholls 1992. Dimensions of achievement motivation in schoolwork and sport. *Journal of Educational Psychology* 84 (3): 290–99.

Garbarino, J. 1990a. The human ecology of early risk. In *Handbook of Early Childhood Intervention*, ed. S. J. Meisels and J. P. Shonkoff, 78–96. Cambridge: Cambridge University Press.

Garbarino, J. 1990b. Youth in dangerous environments: Coping with the consequences. In *Health Hazards in Adolescence*, ed. K. Hurrelman and F. Losel, 193–218. New York: Walter de Gruyter.

Garbarino, J., and R. H. Abramowitz. 1992. The ecology of human development. In *Children and Families in the Social Environment*, ed. J. Garbarino, 11–33. New York: Aldine de Gruyter.

Garbarino, J., K. Kostelny, and N. Dubrow. 1991. What children can tell us about living in danger. *American Psychologist* 46 (4): 376–83.

Gibbs, J. C. 1991. Sociomoral developmental delay and cognitive distortion: Implications for the treatment of antisocial youth. In *Handbook of Moral Behavior and Development*, vol. 3, *Application*, ed. W. M. Kurtines and J. L. Gewirtz, 95–110. Hillsdale, NJ: Lawrence Erlbaum Associates.

Harackiewicz, J. M., and A. J. Elliot. 1993. Achievement goals and intrinsic motivation. *Journal of Personality and Social Psychology* 65: 904–15.

Hartshorne, H., and M. A. May. 1928. *Studies in the Nature of Character*, vol. 1, *Studies in Deceit.* New York: Macmillan.

Hartshorne, H., M. A. May, and J. B. Maller. 1929. *Studies in the Nature of Character*, vol. 2, *Studies in Self-control.* New York: Macmillan.

Hartshorne, H., M. A. May, and F. K. Shuttleworth. 1930. *Studies in the Nature of Character*, vol. 3, *Studies in the Organization of Character.* New York: Macmillan.

Jackson, P. W., R. E. Boostrom, and D. T. Hansen. 1993. *The Moral Life of Schools.* San Francisco: Jossey-Bass.

Jones, E. N., K. Ryan, and K. E. Bohlin. 1999. Teachers as educators of character: Are the nations' schools of education coming up short? Research report published by the Character Education Partnership, Washington, DC, April.

Kohn, A. 1997. How not to teach values: A critical look at character education. *Phi Delta Kappan* 78 (February): 429–39.

Lapsley, D. K. 1996. *Moral Psychology.* Boulder, CO: Westview Press.

Leming, J. S. 1993. *Character Education: Lessons from the Past, Models for the Future.* Camden, ME: The Institute for Global Ethics.

———. 1997. Whither goes character education? Objectives, pedagogy, and research in education programs. *Journal of Education* 179 (2): 11–34.

Lickona, T. 1983. *Raising Good Children: From Birth through the Teenage Years.* New York: Bantam.

———. 1991. *Educating for Character: How Our Schools Can Teach Respect and Responsibility.* New York: Bantam.

Molden, D. C., and C. S. Dweck. 2000. Meaning and motivation. In *Intrinsic and Extrinsic Motivation: The Search for Optimal Motivation and Performance,* ed. C. Sansone and J. M. Harackiewicz, 131–59. New York: Academic Press.

Narvaez, D. 2001. Moral text comprehension: Implications for education and research. *Journal of Moral Education* 30 (1): 43–54.

Nicholls, J. G. 1984. Achievement motivation: Conceptions of ability, subjective experience, task choice, and performance. *Psychological Review* 91: 328–46.

Patton, M. Q. 1986. *Utilization Focused Evaluation.* Beverly Hills, CA: Sage.

Power, F. C. 1988. From moral judgment to moral atmosphere: The sociological turn in Kohlbergian research. *Values and Counseling* 32 (3): 172–78.

Power, F. C., A. Higgins, and L. Kohlberg. 1989. *Lawrence Kohlberg's Approach to Moral Education.* New York: Columbia University Press.

Purpel, D. E. 1997. The politics of character education. In *The Construction of Children's Character,* ed. A. Molar, 140–53. Chicago: National Society for the Study of Education.

Resnick, M. D., P. S. Bearman, R. W. Blum, K. E. Bauman, K. M. Harris, J. Jones, J. Tabor, T. Beuhring, R. E. Sieving, M. Shew, M. Ireland, L. H. Bearinger, and J. R. Udry. 1997. Protecting adolescents from harm: Findings from the National Longitudinal Study on Adolescent Health. *Journal of the American Medical Association* 278:823–32.

Rest, J. 1986. *Moral Development: Advances in Research and Theory.* New York: Praeger.

Ryan, R. M., and E. L. Deci. 2000. When rewards compete with nature: The undermining of intrinsic motivation and self-regulation. In *Intrinsic and Extrinsic Motivation: The Search for Optimal Motivation and Performance,* ed. C. Sansone and J. M. Harackiewicz, 13–54. New York: Academic Press.

Schaps, E., E. F. Schaeffer, and S. N. McDonnell. 2001. What's right and wrong in character education today. *Education Week* 21 (2 September): 40–44.

Schaps, E., M. S. Watson, and C. C. Lewis. 1996. A sense of community is key to effectiveness in fostering character education. *Journal of Staff Development* 17 (2): 42–47.

Shields, D. L., and B. J. Bredemeier 1995. *Character Development and Physical Activity.* Champaign, IL: Human Kinetics.

Shoda, Y., W. Mischel, and P. K. Peake. 1990. Predicting adolescent cognitive and self-regulatory competencies from preschool delay of gratification. *Developmental Psychology* 26 (6): 978–86.

Tappan, M. 1998. Moral education in the zone of proximal development. *Journal of Moral Education* 27 (2): 141–60.

Vygotsky, L. 1978. *Mind in Society: The Development of Higher Psychological Processes.* Cambridge, MA: Harvard University Press.

TEN

A Postmodern Reflection on Character Education

Coming of Age as a Moral Constructivist

Robert J. Nash

A NOT-SO-RELAXED DINNER PARTY AMONG COLLEAGUES

A short time before writing this chapter, I attended an end-of-semester dinner party with several academicians from my own and other universities—mostly philosophers, theologians, and educationists—along with their partners. The occasion was meant to be a relaxed, somewhat festive, chance to get to know one another as real persons in a pleasant setting far from the academy. I found myself sitting next to a fellow ethicist and highly respected character educator who obviously had a bone of contention he had been wanting to pick with me over something that I had said a few months earlier in a public symposium on moral education at his Catholic college. What he took issue with was the following statement of mine, that, I admit, on second thought, was probably a bit more provocative in tone than if I were to assert it publicly on a Catholic campus today:

> I guess I would call myself a postmodern character educator. What do I mean when I use the term "postmodern"? Simply this: there is no objective, context-independent standard—either "in here," "out there," "up above," or "down below"—to confirm once and for all what we call "truth," "reason," or "good." Too often, metaphysical bottom lines function mainly as conversation-stoppers rather than consensus-generators. In the matter of character education, I believe none of us can ever prove conclusively that our preferred moral virtues are the ones that everybody else will need in order to conduct their affairs in the most praiseworthy manner. It is impossible for any one of us to step outside of our personal histories, cultural contexts, and interpretive frameworks in order to gain a "God's-eye" view of the perfect way to live our lives. At most, we can only teach our students to respect each others' moral truths by trying to understand them on terms other than their own. This exercise—what Wilhelm Dilthey called *verstehen* (empathic understanding)—may actually be an insurmountable challenge for faculty and students, however, given our individual differences in tribal upbringing, talent, training, timing, taste, and temperament. Thus, I question whether an impartial, empathic understanding of morality is ever truly possible.

What I am suggesting is that we need to think about character education on the college level as a project that goes beyond the imposition of those pet religious, political, educational, or moral virtues that we are frequently tempted to call "absolute" or "universal." Educating for and about character in a college setting means putting aside any preconception of an objectivist grounding for values and virtues. In contrast, I believe that the kind of character education that ought to go on in the secular academy is one where no single person, institution, or text is ever seen as having an irrefutable corner on moral or ethical truth. The ideal for all of us in higher education is to help students to settle their moral differences without having to thrust their metaphysical or political absolutes upon one another.

Character education, in my estimation, is most effective whenever it emerges from an honest exchange of opposing points of view in a free and open encounter. I believe that all of us—professors and students—must learn to live with the fact of moral plurality and with the understanding that we ought never to demand absolute validity in our ethical conversations with one another. I can say with some assurance that in thirty-plus years of experience teaching courses in moral education, applied ethics, and character education to students of a variety of ages and backgrounds, I have never found an absolute moral validity that everyone could unanimously agree on. Nor, in truth, would I ever want to. Therefore, let a thousand, or even a million, approaches to character education bloom. Who can say for sure that any single one is unimpeachably right?

What concerned my colleague about this little outburst of mine was, in his words, my "indefensible philosophical stance as a moral educator." How was it possible, he asked, to teach ethics or character education "without adverting to objective moral principles or universal moral laws?" To him, I was simply another "postmodern relativist" whose moral position in the classroom verged on an irresponsible and dangerous nihilism. From his view, teaching for and about character made sense only if I had a "firm moral ground" on which to stand. All other approaches, but especially a postmodern approach, were "arbitrary, ungrounded, and woefully expedient."

It did not take long for several of the other dinner guests to register their enthusiastic support for his critique of my position. Much to my chagrin, I found myself the unwanted center of attention at the dinner table that evening, because I was being put in the position of expressing a very unpopular, almost renegade view on character education. Even the gracious dinner host had her say: "I do not know how anyone can call himself a character educator and be a postmodernist. It sounds to me as if this is another one of those pathetic little, politically correct oxymorons that we hear so much about in the academy."

One guest, a longtime associate in my own department, accused me of being intellectually incapable of issuing any kind of strong moral censure against Timothy McVeigh's bombing of the Oklahoma City federal office-building, lethal student violence on public school campuses, or sexual harassment in the workplace because of my "subjectivist," "anti-principle" leanings. Another colleague upped the ante. She said that "some things are good or evil in themselves, because they are inherent in any objective view of morality and ethics." Her argument was that unless good and evil were somehow located in Kant's "autonomous will," or grounded in Aquinas's natural law, or established by reference to God's inerrant biblical Truth, or verified by reason in the form of the scientific method or logic, then I could never condemn such atrocities as the "holocaust, genocide, rape, and mass murder."

For good measure, one of my closest colleagues at the university added this fillip:

I am sorry, but if you do not become an unequivocal moral compass for your students, then you are deliberately sending them the message that it is okay to become wishy-washy *bricoleurs* of right and wrong, patching together a moral code based on whether one thing or another feels good to them at any given moment. For God's sake, even the politically impotent, morally neutered United Nations constructed a Declaration of Human Rights in order to put itself on record as denouncing violations of human dignity.

Never mind that I sounded very defensive that evening. My responses, I am sure, grew increasingly flippant the more I felt my colleagues were piling on. I found myself referring to Richard Rorty's comment that, no matter how desperate we are to believe it, there is no "built-in, moral reference point" that all human beings share.[1] I heard myself asking, somewhat snidely, why on earth they believed that we needed a metaphysical "back-up" before we could assume a strong, committed position against all the moral evils they took such smug pleasure in enumerating.

Because I believe, like Rorty, that there is nothing good or evil in itself, but only as we use language, consensus, pragmatism, and socialization to define it as so, this does not, therefore, make me an amoral subjectivist or a relativist. I strongly believe that I too can stand passionately for what I think is right, without the need for metaphysical underwriters. Neither does my moral constructivism make me, heaven forbid, a "subjectivist," someone who expresses opinions or attitudes about right and wrong based only on his gut feelings, as one of my colleagues charged.

Somewhat vindictively, I pulled out my doomsday weapon with an intention to deliver the death blow to the prevailing objectivist argument that evening: What do we do in a secular pluralist democracy when one so-called "objective" moral truth is in irreconcilable conflict with another one? Don't pro-life and pro-choice advocates in the abortion debate, or supporters and critics of same-sex marriages and capital punishment, for example, rest their cases on some "ultimate version" of objective moral truth? Moreover, I declared, didn't Hitler believe that his conceptions of the Third Reich, "usurious Jewry," "final solution," and "master race" were grounded in "objective" truths of blood, race, ethnicity, geography, history, destiny, nationalism, and politics? Whose "objective" moral truth, therefore, is most "objective"? According to whose, and what, criteria? What truth ought finally to carry the day? In the end, isn't truth all about who uses the tools of persuasion most effectively?

To complicate matters, how do we convince the loser of the moral argument to gracefully accept defeat and withdraw, chastened yet transformed, from the conversation? Alas, the more I talked that evening the more my colleagues were convinced that I had gone off the deep end of postmodern moral skepticism, and perhaps I had. Little did I realize then that my nagging afterthoughts about that provocative dinner party would provide me with a number of compelling reasons for writing this chapter.

It took me a few days to understand that what the heated dinner-party conversation was really about was a frank difference of opinion between two distinct views in the academy on character education. The pivotal question amounted to this: Which is the best *philosophical* place to start in order to teach for and about character education—*from a position of constructivism or one of objectivism?* Is teaching morality mainly about finding truth "out there" or constructing meaning from "in here"? Or is it somehow a dialectical combination of both approaches that, in the end, might be complementary in some ways rather than contradictory?

No longer is the question whether we in the American university ought to go about the business of inculcating values and virtues. Even a quick glance at a number of representative college mission statements will demonstrate that the question has already been answered in the affirmative. Every college in the United States, in some form or another, has gone on record as declaring that helping students become better human beings is a major aspect of the educational mission. Parents, boards of trustees, and the public-at-large expect no less. Besides, whether we admit it or not, we are always inculcating values and morals. This, in fact, is what we do as professors: We *profess* a strong belief in the worth or worthlessness of some things, either explicitly or implicitly. How could it be any other way?

Consequently, I have two interrelated purposes I hope to achieve in the sections below. First, I want to present my thinking within the framework of a professional narrative explaining why moral constructivism rather than moral objectivism has worked well for me as a character education professor over a period of thirty-plus years. In fact, however, while I think of myself as a strong moral constructivist, I am also someone who has been on a three-decades-long journey to set reasonable limits to my constructivism. Second, I want to develop a rationale for taking a postmodern approach to character education in the academy, and, by implication, in the public schools as well. This will mean talking about such philosophical concepts as objectivism and constructivism, emotivism, incommensurability, indeterminacy, the postmodern virtues, democracy, dialogue, and the disappearance of grand moral narratives.

I hope to do all of this with appropriate caution and humility, but most of all with considerable respect for those of differing philosophical perspectives who will inevitably oppose my position. If, as I truly believe, there is no possible way ever to have the final, indisputable word on matters of morality and ethics in the academy, then, to be consistent, I must acknowledge that my word is but one of many that deserve a fair hearing. Thus, I make no claims for universal or absolute moral truth in any of the statements that follow. In fact, I am on a career-long quest to fashion a view of character education that is both defensible and honest.

MY COMING OF AGE AS A MORAL CONSTRUCTIVIST

Plato, in the *Meno,* raises the one question that has guided my work for all the years I have been in the academy. *What is the best way to teach the virtues?* How should we teach people to be good human beings? During my darker moments in the classroom, and like the young Thessalian nobleman in the *Meno,* Menon, I often wonder whether teaching people to be good is even something achievable, because it might simply be in their natures to be either good or bad, regardless of the kind of moral education they receive. Earlier in my career, at times I reluctantly agreed with Socrates that perhaps moral education and character development were indeed all about "divine allotment": some people were "incomprehensibly" blessed by the gods to be good and some were not.[2]

If this were true, I reasoned, maybe we needed to spend more time "searching out what virtue [was] in itself"; that is, perhaps we needed to be looking for some objective grounding, what Plato called *eidos,* a world of "innate ideas" or "forms," for those qualities of character that were admirable in and of themselves. Plato, Aristotle, Augustine, Aquinas, and Kant, each in his own way, were moral essentialists— believers in immutable, eternally perfect, moral norms. I thought that if this was good enough for these thinkers, considered by many to be the nonpareil character educators of all time, then it would have to be good enough for me. My students taught me otherwise, however.

In 1970, I created one of the first applied ethics courses ever offered in a college of education in this country. I subsequently wrote a book, *"Real World" Ethics: Frameworks for Educators and Human Service Professionals,*[3] describing the process and the content of this course, one that I have now taught over one hundred times to both undergraduates and graduates who represent a variety of human service professions. In the mid-1970s, I also created a moral education course, the first of its kind in my state, which eventually evolved into a character education seminar. Hundreds of students have since enrolled in the course, and I tried to capture the unique challenges posed by a seminar of this type in my book, *Answering the "Virtuecrats": A Moral Conversation on Character Education.*[4]

Finally, in response to those students who wanted to explore in a deeper way the religious and spiritual bases for moral development and character formation, I created another first-of-its-kind course for my university, "Religion, Spirituality, and Education." I went on to write two books on this topic, *Faith, Hype, and Clarity: Teaching About Religion in American Schools and Colleges,*[5] and *Religious Pluralism in the Academy: Opening the Dialogue,*[6] that urged educators to take seriously the religio-spiritual component of character education, particularly in secular school settings.

As I struggled throughout the last three decades to define myself as a character educator, both in my courses and scholarship, my journey from a mild but uneasy form of moral objectivism to a strong yet qualified form of moral constructivism intensified. I became increasingly aware of the presence, and, at times, the irreconcilability, of genuine moral difference and conflict in all my courses. If objectivism is the view that moral truth exists independently of language, culture, socialization, personal taste, temperament, and history; and, furthermore, that it is possible for one to find and know this independent, context-free moral truth; and that, once discovered, this truth must then become the unassailable foundation for all human conduct, then, as a teacher, I was clearly incapable of holding a position of moral objectivism. Whether in my ethics courses or in my character education seminars, it was well-nigh impossible ever to secure even a modicum of agreement from all of my students on those moral absolutes that Plato, Aquinas, or Kant, despite their significant philosophical differences, considered to be universal, unchangeable, and exceptionless.

For example, the so-called unquestioned law of God was out as a moral foundation because so many of my students were confirmed atheists or agnostics. Thus, where did this leave the idea of divinely grounded norms? The so-called inexorable law of human nature was also out because students had such very different takes on whether human nature was even a coherent concept, given its extraordinary plasticity and multiple social constructions. Consequently, how could we ever refer to a universal human essence to validate our preferences for particular moral beliefs and virtues? The so-called ironclad laws of nature, reason, and science were likewise out because a conception of each of these is so intricately context-dependent and driven by self-, cultural, and political interests. Therefore, what is left to confirm the indubitable truth of a particular way to live?

Philosophically, for better or worse, most of my students today are anti-realists regarding issues of morality and character: as they learn to be fluent in the language of postmodern theory, I find that they are less willing to accept the assumption that there are unchallengeable moral facts, truths, and virtues that possess a "real" life of their own, that exist totally separate from personal and social biases. Many of today's college students, particularly those majoring in the humanities and social sciences, are instinctual Nietzscheans, even if they have never read one original word of this philosopher's works. They endorse, almost unquestioningly, Nietzsche's observation that "objectivity" is actually a figment of the scientist's, philosopher's, or priest's imagination. They agree with Nietzsche that, in the end, objectivity is reducible to the "will to power."

For many of my students, being moral, knowing the virtues, and forming character are all about what Nietzsche calls "perspective"; and, for him, the more perspectives "we allow to speak about one thing . . . the more complete will be our 'concept' of objectivity."[7] Most of my Generation-X students are zealous constructivists on moral matters. Some of them insist that, at the very most, any notion of morality must be aesthetically and psychologically pleasing to them. Some ask for nothing else except that a theory of the virtues be pragmatic, coherent, and consensually agreed upon.

Others hold that propositions about what constitutes "good" moral character be recognized for what they are: location-, time-, and person-bound. They are quick to point out that Aristotle, for example, appears to have advanced a notion of moral character less interested in questions of access, rights, entitlements, liberties, and obligations than in constructing a gentlemanly moral code for the Greek aristocrat. Moreover, these students become suspicious whenever contemporary "virtuecrats" like William J. Bennett, William Kilpatrick, and Alan Bloom appear to privilege such compliant virtues as submissiveness; deference to authority, religion, and tradition; and obedience and acquiescence, while ignoring the more robust and assertive political qualities necessary for a rich participatory life in a democracy. To these students, whom I call "liberationists" in my book, *Answering the "Virtuecrats"*, it is no coincidence that virtuecrats like William Kilpatrick[8] usually end up advancing a very conservative political agenda: one that openly blames Nietzsche and other postmodernists for "evils" as far-ranging as Western relativism, nihilism, fascism, Nazism, anti-Semitism, radical feminism, rock music, values clarification, self-esteem education, and environmental fanaticism.

Today's students, with many important religious and political exceptions, are constructivists by temperament, as am I. They know, almost intuitively, that talk about moral character is always a social construction representing a particular thinker's or group's pet beliefs and attitudes. They understand all too well that John Rawls's "impartial" or "ideal" moral observer does not exist in the nitty-gritty, self-interested world that they inhabit.[9] They realize that if character is the sum total of a person's virtues—including behavior, likes, dislikes, capacities, dispositions, potential, values, and even thought patterns—then, in their opinion, a far more complex theory of cognitive, moral, and personality development is required than the one that the classically oriented virtuecrats propose.

They also understand that the virtues are character traits that have no autonomous existence of their own, as some virtuecrats suggest. Rather, the virtues are always a concrete development of particular cultural traditions, upbringings, psychological states, and philosophical, political, or religious inclinations. Thus, there can never be a definitive, meta-situational declaration of a standard of human flourishing, or of the virtues that would lead to its ultimate achievement. Neither can there ever be a foolproof method for resolving the dilemma that occurs when the virtues are in conflict.

Shaping character in the schools and colleges, as in the home and church, is a complicated and demanding intellectual undertaking. In a society where there will always be competing conceptions of what is true and right, and in a culture where, to a large extent, the major shapers of moral character are the family, the popular media, the peer group, the shopping mall, the internet, MTV, video games, the athletic playing fields, and the workplace, my students have learned to become discerning "crap-detectors." They do not suffer gladly the simplistic objectivist solutions to complex social problems that they find in so many of the virtuecrats' writings. They are quick to agree with Warren Nord that:

> For better or worse, the moral character of students is shaped to a great extent by their families, by our culture, and by that predisposition to self-centeredness . . . that lies in the hearts of everyone. It would be naïve to think that public education can solve the moral crisis in our culture. It falls well beyond the competence of schools to eliminate the violence and drugs, the narcissism and psychopathology, of children raised in dysfunctional families and a corrupt culture.[10]

IS IT POSSIBLE TO RECONCILE CONSTRUCTIVISM AND OBJECTIVISM IN CHARACTER EDUCATION?

I often wonder whether it is truly possible to be a moral constructivist, yet still be able to eschew a self-referential, incoherent moral relativism. For example, any declaration of moral relativism, on the face of it, usually presents itself as *universally* true rather than *relatively* so. This appears to be a blatant, indeed logically fatal, contradiction.

Also, I wonder if it is possible to hold the view that even though expressions of moral principles and virtues do in fact differ in many cultures and social subgroups, this fact alone does not preclude the possibility that there very well might be a core morality that, though not *absolutely* valid, is at least *universally* applicable to very different social and cultural situations. In other words, could a character educator be a "dominant" moral constructivist with "recessive" objectivist leanings, without collapsing completely into philosophical incoherence? My dinner party confreres, whom I mention in the first section, were obviously concerned that somehow I had fallen irretrievably into a bottomless pit of moral nihilism. I must confess that, at times, I feel some students in my courses have fallen into the same hole, and this disturbs me very much.

A prominent moral perspective, featured among a particular cadre of college students today, is what Alasdair MacIntyre disapprovingly calls "emotivism." Based on my own teaching experiences, I believe that MacIntyre is prone to over-exaggerate the depth and breadth of emotivism among students, but I think he does make an important observation. Emotivism is the belief that "all moral expressions are nothing but expressions of preference, expressions of attitude or feeling, insofar as they are moral or evaluative in character."[11] Consequently, for emotivist students, moral prescriptions are tantamount to saying nothing more than "What makes me feel happy and satisfied is good. Hooray! What makes me feel unhappy and unsatisfied is bad. Boo!"

According to MacIntyre, emotivists draw the conclusion that there is simply "no established [objective] way of deciding between [competing] moral claims" regarding questions of right or wrong.[12] Therefore, because the moral talk of character educators and other authorities is really personal-preference talk, then such talk must always be taken, if not with a grain of salt, then at most with a wink and a nod. Why then, my emotivist students ask, should anyone get so worked up about talk that, in MacIntyre's rueful words, is always "rationally interminable"? The next logical step for some of these students is to become moral cynics and nihilists.

In opposition to these emotivists, I have gradually come to the conclusion, after three-plus decades of teaching a number of axiologically related courses, that I am *not* a moral relativist if relativism implies that I think all the virtues and vices are of equal moral worth, or that all the virtues and vices are merely arbitrary expressions of idiosyncratic preference. The empirical facts of cultural variance and individual difference throughout the world do not ipso facto validate a belief in moral equivalence or moral nonjudgmentalism. The twentieth century atrocities committed in the Nazi death camps, the mass slaughters at My Lai, Hiroshima, and Nagasaki, the continuing practice of slavery and genocide throughout the world, and the imposition of a system of apartheid on South African blacks, completely destroy the pretensions of those who advocate a nonjudgmental, morally equivalent relativism. In this respect, Jonathan Glover's powerful and sweeping *Humanity: A Moral History of the Twentieth Century* is must reading for absolute moral relativists.[13] I have taught long enough to be fairly confident that some ethical decisions are more defensible than others, that some virtues and vices require decisive approbation and censure, and that some character education theories are more functional and sustainable than others.

I *am* a relativist, however, if the only alternative to relativism is what I occasionally see as an extreme form of moral absolutism among some students and colleagues. I am not speaking here only about religious absolutists. I am also referring to those political, educational, and virtue absolutists who reside on both the right and left ends of the moral spectrum. Moral absolutists believe in Background Truths that are presumed to be free from variability and error, that are underived, complete, and universally binding, that are, in Richard Rorty's words, "unwobbling in their pivots."[14] In my seminars, I find that conservatives, liberals, and radicals of various moral-political stripes are equally capable of resorting to absolutist displays of certitude. Unfortunately, they sometimes do this as a stratagem to short-circuit open-ended, moral inquiry by trying to foster a sense of guilt among those of us whom they consider to be "heretics" and "naysayers." Whenever this occurs in my classes, free and undominated conversation about morality and character gets stopped dead in its tracks.

Having said this, however, I must admit that I greatly respect those students and colleagues whose moral beliefs are rooted in some type of metaphysical or political ultimacy. They can be torridly passionate in their moral convictions, and, at times, I admire them for this. I have met far too many blasé or jaded Gen Xers and cynical baby boomers who think that possessing strong moral convictions worth fighting, even dying, for is an illness to be cured rather than an ideal to be celebrated. The challenge for character educators, in my opinion, is two-pronged: to encourage the absolutists to passionately articulate their most cherished moral beliefs to the rest of us; but also to help them learn to make their case in languages and stories that speak effectively to those of us who might come from contrasting philosophical places.

In the next section of this chapter, I will talk about a postmodern character education aimed at cultivating those conversational virtues that I believe are necessary for active participation in a pluralistic democracy. These virtues include, among others, capaciousness, compassion, flexibility, resiliency, narrative ingenuity, interpretive creativity, empathy, rapport, nonmanipulation, self-critique, confrontation, negotiation, openness to otherness, respect for plurality, patience, tolerance, and an inexhaustible sense of irony and humor.

However, at this point, the pivotal philosophical question still remains: is it possible, or even worthwhile, to reconcile the contradictions that exist between constructivist and objectivist perspectives in teaching for moral character? For my part, I believe that reconciliation is possible but, at best, always tenuous. Moreover, I cannot think of anything that would enliven the conversation on character education better than a healthy, no-holds-barred dialogue on the strengths and weaknesses of constructivist and objectivist perspectives on right and wrong, good and bad, virtue and vice. Actually, there is a moderate philosophico-educational view that stands between absolutist expressions of relativism and objectivism, between emotivism and absolutism, and it is the one to which I subscribe, at this particular stage of my career. Let me describe it as a *character education that strives for pragmatic moral consensus through genuine dialogical encounter.*

I start with the assumption that, though I am dubious (but open-minded) about the existence of a universal human nature (I do accept a universal human biology, however), or a beneficent Divine Being who alone is the Author of all morality, I still believe that people share much in common, despite their obvious cultural, philosophical, religious, and political differences. What most moral codes throughout the world seem to agree on is that the best way to create the good life for everyone—what philosophers call the promotion of human flourishing—is to display a respect for self and others; to practice compassion; to act responsibly; to work with, and on behalf of, others; and to insist on social justice for all.

These are universal moral ideals, not because they are emblazoned in some kind of natural law or inscribed in one sacred book or another, but because they are useful and life-sustaining. They actually confer survival benefits on human beings, as a number of respectable sociobiologists and evolutionary psychologists such as Edward O. Wilson[15] and Robert Wright[16] have argued. These moral ideals are pragmatic in that they set the stage for people to live together productively, happily, and peacefully. Louis P. Pojman has gone so far as to say that "it may turn out that it is not science or technology, but rather deep, comprehensive ethical theory and moral living that will not only save our world but solve its perennial problems and produce a state of flourishing."[17]

Our moral obligations to keep our word, tell the truth, respect the rights of others, prevent harm, honor due process, act responsibly, and strive for social justice are the inescapable, evolutionary requirements for constructing mutually fulfilling social orders. These are the moral principles that, despite their abrogation in many cultures, serve to forge a common bond among all human beings. Stripped to their basics, these ideals provide the moral groundwork, in Rorty's words, for "diminishing human suffering and increasing human equality, increasing the ability of all human children to start life with an equal chance of happiness."[18]

From another front, however, and unlike many character educators, I do not believe that ethical- and moral-stage theorists like Lawrence Kohlberg[19] or William G. Perry[20] succeed in resolving the more glaring contradictions between objectivism and constructivism. These theorists' "universal moral ideals"—justice and commitment— are too abstract and restrictive to be of much concrete help in fashioning character education programs bent on "diminishing human suffering and increasing human equality." In Kohlberg's view, adolescent, white, middle-class, American boys, ages ten to sixteen, pass through "pre-conventional," "conventional," and "post-conventional" stages of moral development. These stages are hierarchical, invariant, and universal. The highest moral stage for Kohlberg, the "post-conventional," is when the individual embraces, and attempts to live out, such principles as justice, autonomy, integrity, and empathy. In Perry's case, late adolescents progress from "dualism" to "relativism" to "commitment." The highest stage for Perry, "commitment," is when the individual develops a view of morality that is complex, situational, and based on a "pledge" to something larger than the self. Perry's stages of ethical development are "wavelike," less linear than Kohlberg's, but still presented as all-embracing, even, at times, as absolute.

As a character educator, I find moral development theory to be too pat and formulaic, too hierarchical and excessively linked to age and gender. I have a built-in bias against those character education programs predicated on an assumption that one size fits all, that proceed step-by-step to an appropriation of the virtues wherein some are presented as "higher" and others as "lower." Many of my students think that developmental moral stages too often act as self-constraining traps and self-fulfilling labels. They strenuously resist being forced to slot themselves at various points along a preestablished, moral plotline. I agree wholeheartedly with them. Most students are quick to recognize that these theories, falsely presented as the product of rigorous scientific research, merely reflect the moral biases of their creators—themselves highly educated, white, middle-class males who studied subjects whom they hoped would grow up to value what they did. Thus, moral development theory comes off to most of my students as being far more subjective than scientific; and much more prescriptive than descriptive. How could it be otherwise?

The trick for all of us who do character education is to resist the seductive temptation to locate once and for all some "highest" stage of moral development, one that alone contains the most "preferred" moral virtues. This is the classical objectivist approach to forming moral character. As a constructivist, I do not believe that there is a "highest" stage of moral formation that justifies the imposition of a sacrosanct bag of virtues. There is simply no moral frame of reference that is beneath or beyond the impress of our personal histories, languages, hermeneutics, cultures, and tempera- ments. O that it were so! This does not mean, of course, that some virtues are not preferable to some vices in particular situations. Neither does this mean that as a character educator I am incapable of teaching the conversational virtues because I am resolutely agnostic as to their ultimate origins or to their absolute validity.

TEACHING THE POSTMODERN VIRTUES: SEEKING MORAL CONSENSUS THROUGH DIALOGUE

I intend to lay my own moral cards faceup in this section. Democracy, despite its grave defects, is, for me, the most humane form of government the world has ever known. I say this because, at least in theory, it thrives on freedom of individual expression and on the near-inviolable rights of self-determination and equal treatment. Democracy functions best when "truth" is considered to be nothing more than the unencumbered, nonmetaphysical outcome of a free and open encounter of equals who represent con- trasting beliefs and goals. The kind of secular pluralist democracy I am talking about is what John Dewey saw as a vibrant experiment in cooperative living, a calculated risk that some early Americans took in order to avoid tyranny and to satisfy their needs for individual liberty and social justice. Thus, for me, the responsibility is great for all citi- zens in a democracy to learn to deliberate effectively in order to make morally defen- sible decisions on those controversial issues that affect their lives.

The best way to resolve conflict, I believe, is to talk openly about differences, to see things from contrasting points of view, to have more diverse resources from which to draw in order to solve complex personal and social problems. Therefore, the best char- acter education is the one that helps citizens to dialogue with each other compassion- ately, peacefully, and productively. All of this, I submit, is a postmodern agenda re- quiring a set of distinctive virtues that will lead to a capacity for thoughtful deliberation with others, a tolerance for their rich complexity and difference, and a willingness to engage in highly creative problem solving. Finally, I believe that a constructivist approach to character education is the ideal one for preparing students to live ef- fectively in a secular, pluralist democracy. Constructivism puts the onus on citizens themselves—not on governments, militaries, churches, despots, or gods—to create and shape a world, that, in Richard Rorty's words, is most likely to "diminish human suffering and increase human equality." How to get there, for the constructivist, is a matter of continual negotiation and conversation, and the end is always up for grabs.

I will go even one step further than Rorty, though: I believe that there *is* an ideal core morality (unlike Rorty, I do not mind using such a term), and it is the one that I believe ought to undergird life in a secular pluralist democracy. I have already alluded to the contents of this core in the previous section. I will only add here that this common core ought to display a public moral language that is *nonfoundational:* one that is ungrounded in particular, self-evident principles that everyone must accept. It should feature a moral language that is *multifunctional:* one that is useful to all individuals and interest groups, regardless of their competing conceptions of the good. Finally, it must be a public language that is *nonexclusionary:* an inclusive lingua franca usable by everyone, regardless of difference, one that patches together relevant ideals, principles, and virtues from a number of diverse, sometimes conflicting, moral vocabularies.

A nonfoundational, multifunctional, and nonexclusionary public moral language is a key to promoting reconciliation and healing division not just in a classroom or seminar, but in a democracy as well. In the words of Edward Tivnan, this type of language is the one best suited to helping us "listen to the other side of the story." This public moral language is pragmatic and dialogical. Its primary aim is to solve problems, to serve as a tool to work out our differences with each other. It seeks to construct consensus out of discord.

It continually reminds us that character education ought to be an unending and open-ended conversation "about how we can keep from stomping on one another's special projects of self-improvement."[21] The kind of character education that I am advocating regards morality, and all the virtues that accompany it, as both the process and product of a to-and-fro, consensus-seeking dialogue. This is a dialogue bent on reaching agreements between and among specific groups about what the content and purpose of character education ought to be. But it also recognizes that, on some occasions, moral consensus may be impossible to achieve. The dialogue I am advocating is always pluralistic in tone and devoid in content of ultimate moral and ethical trumps, as well as final, unimpeachable moral high grounds.

While agreement and consensus are certainly important, character education dialogue also looks to achieve other worthy objectives. Diana Eck advocates a "culture of dialogue" in higher education that comes close to what I am promoting here:

> We do not enter into dialogue with the dreamy hope that we will all agree, for the truth is we probably will not. We . . . enter into dialogue . . . to produce real relationship, even friendship, which is premised upon mutual understanding, not [only] upon agreement. . . .

... '[A] culture of dialogue' ... create[s] a context of ongoing relatedness and trust in which self-criticism and mutual criticism are acceptable and valuable parts of the ... exchange.[22]

We need to set the rules beforehand that factitious agreement or fractious debate have no place in classroom dialogue. Rather, we are seeking mutual understanding, clarification, and the type of conversation that might result in self-criticism of our own strongly held moral views. We need to acknowledge at the outset that respectful, carefully conceived criticism is both acceptable and desirable.

Most significant, however, we must understand that genuine moral dialogue, built on a foundation of respect, trust, and mutual exploration, of necessity invites candor and critique. It does this because it conveys the message that a "value-neutral" approach really does not take the other's point of view very seriously. Conversation about morality and character is superficial without criticism and challenge. In my classes, it is frequently the moral absolutists (of all political and religious stripes) who are unable to tolerate honest criticism in dialogue. I have found that dialogue about morality without the opportunity to engage in critical questioning (I do not mean contrarian academic carping or sniping) narrows rather than widens the search for a moral truth each of us can live by.

There are no conversation *stoppers* in the classroom dialogue I am proposing, only conversation *starters*. Teaching the postmodern virtues presents a formidable challenge, because students must learn a whole new way of thinking about morality, truth, and communication. I would argue that only when teachers are able to construct a dialogical environment in the classroom, one that fosters a spirit of respectful, open-ended moral inquiry, have we really begun to teach, and do, character education. We are exemplifying the democratic virtues that we are explicating. What follows, then, is a brief account of what I consider to be the paramount postmodern virtues, along with an equally brief description of the dialogic process necessary to produce them.

1. A tolerance for the uncertainties and ambiguities entailed by the postmodern worldview, along with a willingness, nevertheless, to persist in educating for a democratic character. As I have been arguing throughout this chapter, the constructivist perspective assumes the absence of a common moral standard with which to evaluate the worth of a plethora of competing moral vocabularies, traditions, practices, and frameworks. Philosophers refer to this condition as "incommensurability," by which they mean that there is no objective and transcendent moral criterion that can finally and forcefully settle all of our disagreements over values. The problem with most current approaches to character education, as I understand them, is that each attempts to advance a particular moral vocabulary and a set of preferred moral virtues, as if both of these were part and parcel of a "grand narrative" accepted by, and normative for, everyone.

Unfortunately, grand *moral* narratives in the postmodern era have gone the way of most grand *religious* narratives: no matter how compelling and consoling to some people, all grand narratives break down at the local level. There is just too much philosophical, religious, political, and lifestyle difference among individuals and groups in communities throughout the United States for any moral meta-narrative to carry the day for all. Alan Wolfe, a sociologist, has spent years talking to Americans who prefer to live what he calls lives of "moral freedom." His exhaustive research documents the fact that most Americans seek to determine for themselves just how they will achieve a good and virtuous life. Unlike their pre-baby-boom predecessors, they are no longer willing to look to authoritative religious figures or institutions for easy answers to complex moral questions. For them, a life of integrity is all about exercising their autonomous rights to make moral choices consistent with their values.[23]

Having said this, however, neither Wolfe nor I intend thereby to lay the groundwork for a despairing moral relativism or a narrow moral subjectivism. Instead, I am recommending just the opposite: character educators must proceed to teach the democratic virtues with a renewed humility and caution. We might try, for one, to get our students involved in helping to define those virtues that are most likely to encourage a better quality of democratic life for everyone. This entails, of necessity, that all of us, students and teachers alike, learn to work with, and integrate, a number of conflicting moral languages and stories in order to advance one major, democratic goal: the common good. The right of all individuals to pursue their diverse conceptions of the good life in their own best ways—what Wolfe calls "moral freedom"—is the basic tie that binds citizens in a liberal democracy. It is America's uncommon common good, and instead of destroying communal ties and responsibilities, Wolfe's research demonstrates that it has actually strengthened a sense of solidarity and commonality among all the people he interviewed.

It is my hope that, even though moral incommensurability is an inevitable fact of life in the postmodern world (despite persistent efforts by a number of religious, political, and educational leaders to resist or to deny it), people can still find a way to come together to build better lives for themselves, their neighbors, and their fellow humans everywhere. Alasdair MacIntyre, and others of his Thomistic ilk, does not think that this is possible without some transcendent moral standard that we can all agree on. I, on the other hand, am convinced that it *is* possible. Despite the persistence of moral incommensurability in the post-Enlightenment world, I believe that we can still be profoundly committed to the elimination of human suffering and to the advancement of human flourishing for all people regardless of their differences. A good place for character educators to start is to recognize that conversation, critique, persuasion, and negotiation are the virtues that must replace imposition and indoctrination in the classroom—the classical forms of character training—along with the guilt-mongering and sermonizing that so often accompany the latter.

2. *A capacity for engaging in moral dialogue that is open-ended, dialectical, compassionate, but, above all, humble and generous.* In my work as a character educator, I always insist that students rely less on pontification and oratory in their conversations with each other and more on an honest give-and-take, a patient back-and-forth exchange of moral points of view. Tivnan, the author I quoted earlier, tells us that "conversation is more likely to continue if we can imagine the world from the other side of the barricade." His point for character educators is to avoid narrowing the dialogue to one-way declarations of our unassailable moral beliefs. It is to realize that no matter how different our views, "we are all bundles of opinions and beliefs, of theories and prejudices about how we and our world are or ought to be."[24] This is simply to say that what we all have in common as we go about the project of teaching for and about moral character is the fact that our views are at one and the same time true and false, whole and partial, strong and weak, each in their own ways. Thus, we need to listen to others as we would be listened to. We need to question and challenge others as we would be questioned and challenged. Finally, we must pontificate to others only under the condition that we want others to pontificate to us.

I contend that, whether we are objectivists or constructivists, we are each unique bundles of moral meanings, looking frequently to express them, hoping to find others to confirm them, and wanting to live our lives in a manner that is consistent with them. Mark R. Schwehn proposes that four virtues in particular—humility, faith, self-denial, and charity—are necessary for respecting, rather than changing, the meanings of others.[25] *Humility* presumes that we attribute at least a modicum of wisdom and insight to others. *Faith* means trusting that what we hear from others is worthwhile in some way. *Self-denial* suggests that, at some point, we need to consider the possibility of abandoning at least a few of the meanings we cherish in the name of intellectual integrity and honesty. Finally, *charity* is all about attributing the best motive and being willing to respond to serious differences of moral opinion with generosity and graciousness.

None of this, however, is to suggest that moral truth is an illusion, or that every view of moral truth is equally true or equally false. Rather, students need to understand that what might represent definitive or inerrant moral truth for some may represent just the opposite for others. Defective intellects, moral characters, or religious convictions (or lack of them) have little or nothing to do with why people actually reject one or another version of moral truth. Usually, a repudiation of a particular moral view has more to do with personal interpretation, socialization, and unique perspective than with a willful recalcitrance, ignorance, or sinfulness on the part of the gainsayer. The conclusion for character educators is inescapable: in order to engage in empathic moral dialogue, we must always work hard to detect even a little bit of truth in what at first might sound like the biggest bunch of nonsense. What constitutes "truth" and "nonsense" depends, of course, on *our* perspective, just as it does on *theirs*.

3. A heightened understanding that we do not live in a world where there are actual moral certainties. Rather, we live in a world where we actually construct stories that may or may not include moral certainties. It is self-evidently true, of course, that we live in a real moral world that we must negotiate every day. Ethical dilemmas abound—at home, at work, and at play—and they need to be resolved. At times, we are duty-bound to call some actions bad, some good; some dispositions virtuous, some vicious; and some decisions ethical, some unethical. However, this is a long way from saying that because we must make moral judgment calls with some definitiveness, even at times as though we possess a sense of moral certainty, that, therefore, moral certainty exists as an objective fact. If we are honest with ourselves, we will acknowledge that our conception of moral truth is largely a product of the way we were raised to think and feel about morality.

Most important for character educators, however, is the understanding that our moral truths unavoidably take the shape of particular stories that enchant us. What we might find narratively enchanting, others might find revolting, or merely vapid. It is unlikely that there will ever be a High Ground of Absolute Moral Truth for all to follow, because there will never be an All-Enchanting Moral Narrative that will appeal to everyone. In today's postmodern world, it is no longer acceptable to superimpose a religious exclusivity onto anybody's unique religious journey. So too it is unacceptable to superimpose a moral exclusivity onto anybody's unique moral journey.

The challenge for character education, then, is not to surrender to the lure of moral skepticism or cynicism. Rather, it is to approach narratives about character education with curiosity, modesty, caution, and, when fitting, with a sense of humor. It is to realize that nobody ever makes moral judgments outside of a particular narrative. It is to listen carefully and to learn how to exchange moral stories with each other with sensitivity, curiosity, and, when appropriate, with respectful criticism. Regarding the latter, it seems patently true to me that some moral narratives are more defensible, more desirable, even more ethically obligatory than others. I would argue, for example, that American democracy is a far more defensible, and moral, form of government than the German Third Reich or a political system of South African apartheid.

However, even though I would fiercely defend the morality of my preferred system of representative government, I must also acknowledge that all moral narratives, no matter how desirable, are infinitely contestable, because they are infinitely interpretable. Their meanings will always be indeterminate, with some people's moral "bottom lines" continually bumping up against other people's "bottom lines." The result is that no people can ever claim to have spoken the final word on any moral issue. Stanley Fish is right: interpretation and perspective do indeed "go all the way down."[26] One person's zero-level, nonnegotiable moral premises are what another person might very well think of as begging all the really fundamental moral questions. Therefore, the question persists: whose moral "down" down there is truly determinate?

I must also acknowledge that every moral narrative contains serious internal contradictions. After all, it was the American system of government—what many virtuecrats and I believe to be the most principled political narrative the world has ever known—that for decades condoned slavery, prevented blacks and women from voting, and established so-called "separate but equal" educational institutions for blacks and whites, along with a set of shameful Jim Crow laws in a number of other social settings.

Moreover, during the Second World War, the American government was the first government to use nuclear weapons against an enemy, resulting in the deaths of hundreds of thousands of innocent Japanese civilians in the cities of Hiroshima and Nagasaki. To this day, the United States still engages in extensive arms trading and builds huge nuclear stockpiles. What better opportunity for character educators to model the postmodern virtues in authentic give-and-take dialogue with students than to open up a frank discussion on the internal contradictions of democracy, or, for that matter, of religion, character education, or capitalism?

PARADOXES IN CHARACTER EDUCATION

There are at least *three* troubling paradoxes in character education that we must acknowledge honestly and publicly if we are ever to improve the work we do as moral educators. *One is that character educators need to continue teaching the virtues they cherish even though, in the end, there is the likelihood that these virtues may simply be unteachable.*

Unfortunately, there is not a lot of empirical evidence that didactic teaching methods such as preaching, shaming, demanding attendance at church, assigning virtue books, requiring community service, posting clever moral aphorisms on the walls throughout a school or college, or designing extensive courses in character education or applied ethics have much effect on the actual formation of students' characters and subsequent moral behavior.[27] Merely telling students in settings where they are captive audiences how they ought to behave both inside and outside school and college walls is hardly enough to conduce them to be people of good moral character. If this were true, then no student who comes from a good family, church, or school would ever go wrong. There would be no drug-experimentation, sexual promiscuity, unwanted pregnancies, school shootings, gang violence, income-tax cheating, or bullying.

The second paradox is that the less calculated character education is, the more effective it might actually be. Educators as various as Aristotle, Jean Jacques Rousseau, Mary Wollstonecraft, and John Dewey, each in their own way, have warned us that, while moral character certainly counts, its formation is incredibly complex and unpredictable. Dewey himself said that "moral education is practically hopeless when we set up the development of character as a supreme end . . . or when it is reduced to some kind of catechetical instruction."[28] To the teacher's dismay, some research suggests that when moral education takes place in isolated family, church, school, and college settings, dramatic transformations of character are infrequent to nonexistent.[29]

More influential in the shaping of character, however rare they might be, are those social settings where the values of school, college, family, and community form an almost-perfect, intersecting web. This web is one that is mutually reinforcing, consistent, clear, and supportive, such as in military families, and in some highly selective, private academies and elite universities attended by many generations of the same family. However, even when this interconnecting moral web exists, there is no guarantee that the virtues will be taught or caught in the precise ways that educators would like.[30]

The third paradox is that a character education most suitable for a democracy might not be one that teaches a bag of predetermined dispositions but rather one that grows out of an indeterminate, democratic dialogue demanding continual compromise and consensus. Democracy, for all its participatory, decision-making advantages for citizens, can frequently be contentious, messy, and frustrating. Thus, citizens need to know how to work well with others who might think differently from them about how to achieve their shared ends. In the event that shared ends are absent, then people need to engage in what philosophers call "deliberative discourse," whose purpose is to create a democratically sovereign society that is fair, free, and compassionate.[31] To this end, all of us must learn to temper our strong moral convictions—even those regarding the worth of both democracy and sovereignty—with a readiness to compromise whenever we find our best intentions thwarted by others. The painful irony of democracy is that, like us, our strongest opponents are also motivated by their own best intentions.

The simple truth in a democracy (as in a classroom) is this: we cannot always get what we want, no matter how noble our goals. An indeterminate, democratic dialogue is one that proceeds to wherever the participants wish to take it, and it requires a particular type of moral character to engage constructively in it. It calls for commitment and conviction, to be sure, but it also calls for sacrifice, patience, empathy, tolerance, and generosity. It asks us, at least initially, to put the best construction on the contributions of others to the dialogue. It obliges us to find the truth in what we oppose and the error in what we espouse, before we go in search of flaws. The paradox in this dialogical process is that, when it goes well, regardless of its outcomes, it teaches the virtues of self-respect, hope, confidence, courage, honesty, and, above all, friendship and trust. When it does not go well—when participants refuse to attribute the best motive to others—it teaches those vices that can endanger democracy: suspicion, self-contempt, hopelessness, powerlessness, cowardice, dishonesty, and, saddest of all, enmity and mistrust. These are the vices that, if left unchecked, guarantee the death of the democratic dream.

NOTES

1. Richard Rorty, *Contingency, Irony, and Solidarity* (New York: Cambridge University Press, 1989), xiv.

2. Plato, *Great Dialogues of Plato,* trans. W. H. D. Rouse (New York: Mentor, 1956).

3. Robert J. Nash, *"Real World" Ethics: Frameworks for Educators and Human Service Professionals* (New York: Teachers College Press, 1996).

4. Robert J. Nash, *Answering the Virtuecrats: A Moral Conversation on Character Education* (New York: Teachers College Press, 1997).

5. Robert J. Nash, *Faith, Hype, and Clarity: Teaching About Religion in American Schools and Colleges* (New York: Teachers College Press, 1999).

6. Robert J. Nash, *Religious Pluralism in the Academy: Opening the Dialogue* (New York: Peter Lang, 2001).

7. Friedrich Nietzsche, *On the Genealogy of Morals,* trans. W. Kaufmann and R. J. Hollingdale (New York: Vintage, 1989).

8. William Kilpatrick, *Why Johnny Can't Tell Right from Wrong: Moral Illiteracy and the Case for Character Education* (New York: Simon & Schuster, 1992).

9. John Rawls, *A Theory of Justice* (Cambridge: Harvard University Press, 1971).

10. Warren A. Nord, *Religion and American Education: Rethinking a National Dilemma* (Chapel Hill: University of North Carolina Press, 1995), 350.

11. Alasdair MacIntyre, *After Virtue*, 2nd ed. (Notre Dame, IN: University of Notre Dame Press, 1984), 12.

12. Ibid., 11.

13. Jonathan Glover, *Humanity: A Moral History of the Twentieth Century* (New Haven: Yale University Press, 1999).

14. Richard Rorty, *Philosophy and Social Hope* (New York: Penguin, 1999), 15.

15. Edward O. Wilson, *Consilience: The Unity of Knowledge* (New York: Alfred A. Knopf, 1998).

16. Robert Wright, *The Moral Animal: Why We Are the Way We Are* (New York: Vintage, 1995).

17. Louis P. Pojman, *Ethics: Discovering Right and Wrong* (Belmont: Wadsworth, 1995), 17.

18. Richard Rorty, *Philosophy and Social Hope* (New York: Penguin, 1999), xxix.

19. Lawrence Kohlberg, *The Psychology of Moral Stages* (San Francisco: Harper & Row, 1984).

20. William G. Perry, *Forms of Intellectual and Ethical Development in the College Years* (New York: Holt, Rinehart, & Winston, 1970).

21. Edward Tivnan, *The Moral Imagination: Confronting the Ethical Issues of Our Day* (New York: Simon & Schuster, 1995), 250.

22. Diana L. Eck, *Encountering God: A Spiritual Journey from Bozeman to Banaras* (Boston: Beacon, 1993), 197, 225.

23. Alan Wolfe, *Moral Freedom: The Search for Virtue in a World of Choice* (New York: W. W. Norton & Company, 2001).

24. Tivnan, *The Moral Imagination*, 250.

25. Mark R. Schwehn, *Exiles from Eden: Religion and the Academic Vocation in America* (New York: Oxford University Press, 1993).

26. Stanley Fish, *The Trouble with Principle* (Cambridge: Harvard University Press, 1999).

27. J. S. Leming, "In Search of Effective Character Education," *Educational Leadership* 51 (1993): 69.

28. John Dewey, *Democracy and Education* (New York: Macmillan, 1916), 101.

29. Gerald Grant, "Schools That Make An Imprint," in *Challenge to American Schools: The Case for Standards and Values*, ed. J. H. Hunzel, 127–46 (New York: Oxford University Press, 1985).

30. Ibid.

31. Amy Gutmann and Dennis Thompson, *Democracy and Disagreement* (Cambridge, MA: Harvard University Press, 1996).

ELEVEN

The Interpersonal Roots of
Character Education

Marvin W. Berkowitz and Melinda Bier

THE BOTTOM LINE OF CHARACTER PSYCHOLOGY AND CHARACTER EDUCATION is child development. After all, what we are really proposing to do is leverage the school context to foster the psychological development of children. As the title and contents of this book suggest, character is a psychological construct. We define character as *the composite of psychological characteristics that serve to promote moral agency.* Within this composite, or "moral anatomy," are included such psychological characteristics as behavior, values, affect, reasoning, self-concept, personality, and so on (Berkowitz 1997). Clearly, as Blasi (this volume) points out, the development of character is a matter of psychological development. Furthermore, it is multifaceted and complex.

If this is so, if indeed character education is grounded in child development, then it behooves us to explore how character develops in children in order to optimally stimulate its growth and flourishing in schools (and elsewhere). This volume provides numerous insights into this process. This chapter is not intended to rehash all of what we know about character development. Rather the goal here is to explore one central cluster of developmental processes that serve as the foundation for effective character education, namely, positive social bonding (alternatively called connectedness, attachment, relational trust, sense of belonging, or sense of community).

In this chapter, we will argue two major (and interrelated) points. First, the core of effective character education is built not upon curricula nor upon finite programs, but rather upon the social relationships that pervade a school's culture. It is the social and emotional bonding of individuals to other individuals and to the school and classroom as social systems that undergird the development of character in students (Berkowitz 2002). Character education comes from how people treat each other more than from what people tell each other. But at a much deeper level, character education comes from the motivation to be good emanating from a sense of belonging.

Second, character education construed in this way ultimately is comprehensive school (or, sometimes, classroom) reform. It implies a basic change in the way a school functions. It means altering policies, processes, and even structures. For to truly change relationships and nurture social bonding, schools must be different kinds of places than they currently are (Bryk and Schneider 2002).

Neither of these themes is unique to this chapter. They pervade this volume, whether they are represented in the psychology of character development, the role of character education in civics and citizenship, the role of character and sports in building community, or in other ways. Nor are these insights particularly new. We don't claim them as novel. Rather we claim them as essential and therefore worth reiterating and exploring more deeply. If effective character education truly depends upon the reshaping of the social structure and climate of schools, then ignoring that fact leaves us where much of character education has floundered for decades: enthusiastically implementing ineffective programs and curricula and having little or no meaningful impact on the development of students' character.

CHARACTER DEVELOPMENT AS GROUNDED IN SOCIAL BONDING

The development of character, as noted above in the concept of the moral anatomy (Berkowitz 1997), includes a diverse set of psychological processes. From the perspective of developmental psychology, these processes tend to be heavily, if not exclusively, impacted by the nature of a child's relationships to others, most notably parents, other caretakers (such as teachers), and peers. Because this chapter is not intended to explore psychological development in depth, we will only offer a few examples to support this contention (for lengthier descriptions of the role of parenting in the development of children's character, see Berkowitz and Grych 1998; or Damon 1988).

Perhaps the most central component of a child's readiness for healthy character development, in addition to her willingness to struggle with the demands of character education and development, is her fundamental social orientation. We know clearly that such an orientation comes from the earliest experiences of parental nurturing (Bowlby 1969; Stayton, Hogan, and Ainsworth 1971). This model, called *attachment theory*, suggests that children who have experienced sensitive and reasonably consistent nurturing in which parents both set appropriate boundaries and expectations and support the child's efforts to meet their parents' expectations develop a positive sense of themselves as effective social agents. Perhaps more importantly, they also develop a positive and secure sense of the world as benevolent and desire relationships with other people (Watson 2003). On the other hand, children who do not experience reasonably consistent, sensitive, nurturing, demanding, and supportive parenting see themselves as unworthy of others' positive regard and see others as threatening. Magid and McKelvey (1987) have labeled such children "trust bandits" for the way that they prey upon others. Blakeney and Blakeney (1987) refer to their distorted senses of self, others, and relationships as "moral madness." Watson (2003) has demonstrated how such children assume that adults will not act in their best interests and rigorously test adults (including teachers) to, in essence, confirm their negative hypotheses about the world. For a teacher to be an effective character educator with such a child, she needs to "pass" the test and remain nurturing throughout the behavioral challenges the child poses. Then, and only then, will the child be open to connecting to the teacher, classroom, and school in a way that can foster character development. By documenting the gradual transformation across two years of several initially untrusting students, Watson (2003) demonstrates the possibility and the power of forming trusting student-teacher partnerships with even highly untrusting and disruptive students.

One can readily imagine that fostering character is rather difficult with students who do not trust, for they are unwilling to bond to the school or the people that populate it. They are resistant to the messages of the school, disconnected from its values, and untrusting of the goodwill of those who are trying to help them. No matter how glossy one's posters, how articulate one's exhortations, how catchy one's ditties, nor how seductive one's rewards, such children will not internalize the positive character messages of the school and will not develop the values, behavior, personality, affect, or reasoning that comprise moral character.

The development of conscience is another example. Kochanska (1993) has provided powerful empirical evidence that conscience is a developmental process and that it depends heavily on the relationship between parent and child. Parents who negotiate rather than dictatorially mandate, for example, have children who develop healthier consciences.

The mature capacity to take others' perspectives and to reason about moral problems and make effective moral judgments stems in large part from the experience of "grappling" (Sizer and Sizer 1999) with peers over social and moral disagreements and dilemmas (Berkowitz 1985). This process applies well beyond the moral sphere of schools, to the content of the academic curriculum as well. Social peer grappling with issues embedded in the academic curriculum is a powerful pedagogical tool (Berkowitz and Simmons 2003).

Another example concerns some of the core educational processes of character education. Character education is most effective when schools incorporate educational processes that provide respect for children and their competencies (existing or potential). Cooperative learning, for example, is a powerful form of character education, especially when it explicitly incorporates social development as a goal alongside whatever the curricular goal of the cooperative learning lesson might be (Developmental Studies Center 1999).

Promoting democratic processes in schools and classrooms is another way of promoting character development in schools (Berkowitz 2000). Empowering students is a form of respect, and respect is one of the most commonly cited goals of character education. As Lickona (1983) argued, respect for children engenders their development of respect for others. It is difficult to nurture respectfulness in children when they do not experience being treated with respect themselves. And giving children autonomy, the experience of authentic "voice," is a primary way of showing respect for children. For instance, a common finding in the service-learning literature is that such programs are more effective when students have responsibility for and decision-making power in designing and implementing the programs (Morgan and Streb 2001).

CHARACTER EDUCATION AS SOCIAL BONDING

Given the dependence of character development upon the positive social experiences of children, it seems likely that educational initiatives designed to foster such development must focus on social processes. This is not new to character education in particular or to education in general. Seminal theorists like Dewey (1944), Durkheim (1973), and Piaget (1965) have all argued that the social environment of the school is the heart of character development. Philip Jackson (Jackson, Boostrom, and Hanson 1993), Lawrence Kohlberg (Power, Higgins, and Kohlberg 1989), and Rheta De-Vries and Betty Zan (1994) focused heavily on the social climate of schools as foundational for the social and moral development of students.

What is so striking about character education is how much this long-standing perspective and scientifically supported information (Berkowitz 2002) is omitted from educational policy and practice. This is particularly striking given the nearly ubiquitous nature of this social bonding construct in the education literature, for example, in effects on student academic performance, character education, social-emotional learning, violence prevention, drug prevention, and even professional-educator community development.

Many years ago, Lawrence Kohlberg told the story of a visit he made to a high school that was implementing his moral dilemma discussion strategy for promoting moral reasoning development. He was touring the school with the principal and both of them were observing a class discussing a hypothetical dilemma. When the discussion of the dilemma petered out, the teacher asked the students if they had any real dilemmas to discuss. One student, knowing that Kohlberg and the principal were in the room, described a rule recently imposed by the principal as an example of a real moral dilemma. There had been a rash of thefts from lockers and the principal has subsequently mandated that students bring personal locks for their lockers (which until then had had no locks on them). The student argued that if it was their property that was at risk, it should be up to them to decide if they wanted to spend the money for a lock to protect it. The principal did not enter the discussion, the bell rang, and the class departed. A bit later the principal told Kohlberg that he did not see the value of such discussions because he had real problems in his school, such as vandalism, substance use, theft, and teen pregnancy. He wanted to know what would help with that. Kohlberg replied that if he wanted to affect such issues, he needed something more ambitious than hypothetical dilemma discussions, something that affected the governance structure and climate of the school. Kohlberg also claims that he was fortunate that the principal did not take him up on this challenge, as he was not sure how to accomplish it. However, his intuitions later reached fruition in the founding of his just-community school model (Power, Higgins, and Kohlberg 1989).

THE EMPIRICAL EVIDENCE

Recently, there have been many studies corroborating the theoretical relationship between school and classroom social climate and students' character development and academic achievement. Furthermore, these studies span the entire prekindergarten through high school spectrum. Only a few key studies will be reviewed here, but extensive literature reviews are offered by Osterman (2000), Najaka, Gottfredson, and Wilson (2002), and Wang, Haertel, and Walberg (1993).

Preschool evidence. In the field of education, status is typically accorded to those educating the oldest and most competent students (e.g., doctoral students at a prestigious university). The lower down the food chain one goes (e.g., early childhood educators), the less status one is accorded. In the field of character education, this general principle gets turned on its head. Those who are most clearly understood as appropriate and effective character educators are those who teach the youngest and least competent students. Early childhood educators tend to understand their professional roles as inextricably interwoven with issues of promoting character development, whereas secondary teachers and college professors tend to think that they "teach mathematics, not students." So it is not surprising that (1) there is appreciable evidence on the relation of teacher-student relationships to preschool students' social and emotional growth and (2) that most of this research makes a very explicit analogy between teaching and parenting. Howes and Ritchie (2002) offer an excellent review of this perspective and the evidence supporting it, relying heavily on attachment theory. Howes, Matheson, and Hamilton (1994), for example, found that for one- to four-year-old children, teacher-student relationships were a better predictor of social development than were mother-child relationships. Children with secure attachments to their teachers were more positive and gregarious, and engaged in more complex social play, than other children at both twelve months and four years of age. Furthermore, they showed more ego resiliency at four years. Howes and Smith (1995) found that preschool students' cognitive activity was significantly predicted by positive interactions with and attachment security to their teacher.

Elementary school evidence. The most relevant research on the issue of school bonding to elementary school student development comes from the Child Development Project (www.devstu.org; Solomon, Watson, and Battistich 2001). Following the work of Deci and Ryan (1985), the Child Development Project (CDP) posits three fundamental needs of children: autonomy, belonging, and competence (Dalton and Watson 1997). It is belonging which is most relevant to this discussion. Belonging is promoted in various ways in the CDP: First, class meetings are used to turn each classroom into a caring community of learners. Second, cross-age systematic "buddying" is used to build whole-school relationships. Third, homework assignments linked to the home are used to build home-to-school relationships. Fourth, school-wide functions are designed to build whole-school community. Solomon, Watson, and Battistich (2001) report that students' perceptions of the school as a "caring community" are the gatekeepers between character education implementation and student character, behavior, and academic outcomes. In other words, the effectiveness of character education is directly linked to the degree to which students come to perceive their classrooms and schools as caring communities, in other words, places where they are accepted, safe, and feel that they belong. In an analysis of twenty-four schools in six school districts, Solomon et al. (1997) report that students' sense of the classroom as a community is significantly related to teachers' emphasis of cooperative strategies and focus on prosocial values.

Hawkins et al. (2001), in their study of the Seattle Social Development Project (SSDP) in elementary schools, examined the longitudinal path of school bonding from SSDP elementary schools through high school. They found that students in full-implementing SSDP schools were more bonded to school. Furthermore, this bonding continued, even increased, in high school. More significantly, SSDP also produced a broad range of desirable character and academic outcomes.

Middle school evidence. The middle school evidence focuses more on teacher-student relationships than on bonding to school in general. Ryan and Patrick (2001) found that students' perceptions of teacher support for respectful student interactions are linked to increased academic self-efficacy and increased self-regulatory capacities. Similarly, Wentzel (2002) studied teacher behavior as analogous to parenting. Her interest was in whether middle school teacher behavior could be understood using the same elements that characterize positive parenting. She found that teachers who promote character development and academic achievement are teachers who (1) set high expectations for students, (2) are nurturing and avoid negative feedback messages, (3) are fair, using democratic communication, (4) model motivation for learning, and (5) do not set many behavioral rules. As a composite, this describes a pattern similar to what Baumrind (1971) calls "authoritative" parenting, which itself has been linked to an extensive set of positive psychological outcomes for children. More particularly, the nurturing aspect of teaching is critical for promoting positive relationships and bonding. It also was linked to all the outcome variables: academic achievement, prosocial behavior, prosocial and school motivation, sense of internal control, and reduced irresponsible behavior.

High school evidence. Resnick et al. (1997) examined data from a national representative sample of seventh- through twelfth-grade students in order to understand what reduced risk behavior of a variety of sorts. They concluded that there were two main protective factors: attachment to family and attachment to school. Adolescents who had positive affective bonds to their families and to their schools were significantly less likely to engage in risk behaviors. McNeely, Nonnemaker, and Blum (2002) and Bonny et al. (2000) analyzed the same data to understand what promoted such bonding to school. They concluded that positive classroom management, tolerant (non-harsh) disciplinary practices, involvement in extracurricular activities, smaller schools, good physical health, and avoidance of cigarette smoking were the main predictors of attachment to school. Power, Higgins, and Kohlberg (1989) studied the just-community-school project and discovered that a deliberate school reform model aimed at promoting a sense of justice and a community within the larger high school successfully promoted the establishment of shared prosocial norms and the individual development of more mature moral reasoning capacities.

Additional Evidence. In a very extensive review of research on school effectiveness, Wang, Haertel, and Walberg (1993) found that sense of membership in one's classroom and school is fostered by the frequency and quality of teacher-student and student-student interactions in the classroom. They also report that classroom climate, which includes frequent cooperative interactions and cooperative goals, is related to academic achievement. Najaka, Gottfredson, and Wilson (2002), in a literature review of school-based prevention efforts from kindergarten through high school, report that bonding to school was the strongest variable in mediating the effects of school-based risk prevention efforts.

THE QUANDARY

When educators are asked what promotes character, they tend to generally understand the centrality of social bonding and connectedness. They mention relationships and school climate as critical aspects of effective character education. However, when they try to implement character education they tend to be much less likely to actually incorporate elements that promote such bonding, relying instead on extrinsic rewards and recognition along with exhortation in the form of posters, slogans, and quotes (Kohn 1993). The challenge, therefore, for quality character education is to get educators to take what they understand about effective practice and to translate it into actual policy and practice (Schaps, Schaeffer, and McDonnell 2001).

Toward this end, we need to establish a "science of character education" (Berkowitz 2002). In other words, we need to examine what empirical research already exists, draw conclusions, and support future research to fill the gaps and clear up the ambiguities.

TWO HEADS, HEARTS, AND HANDS ARE BETTER THAN ONE

Scientific knowledge about what works to promote character development in students (Berkowitz 2002) alone is not enough to transform schools so that they optimally foster such development. The second necessary ingredient in this formula is technology transfer. The Character Education Partnership (www.character.org) has largely adopted the framework proposed by Ryan and Lickona (Lickona 1983, 1991; Ryan and Lickona 1987) that character is comprised of understanding, caring about, and acting upon core ethical values. Alternatively this is described as the "head, heart, and hands" of character. This framework has almost exclusively been applied to outcome or to students; in other words, effective character education must impact the thinking, motivation, and behavior of students. That is quite accurate.

What is missing from this formula, however, is that we cannot impact the head, heart, and hands of students if we do not impact the head, heart, and hands of educators. "The challenge . . . is to find ways of reestablishing [the teacher's] psychological connection to her work: her motivation and her emotional investment" (Pianta 1999, 126).

As we have seen in this chapter, character is impacted most strongly by relationships with significant others. In the case of schools, this most centrally includes relationships with the adults in the school. Many educators already understand this, but some do not. Many of those who do understand it, however, do not effectively act on it. Sometimes this is because they do not know how to do so, and sometimes because they are not committed to it enough to act on it. It is essential for effective practice for educators to understand ("head"), care deeply about ("heart"), and know how to implement ("hands") quality character education.

The centerpiece of such a comprehensive grasp of character education is understanding that building positive relationships with students, creating a caring community in the classroom and school, and fostering students' sense of belonging to such a community is where character education must position itself if it is to effectively impact on the development of character in students. The remaining issue is how best to accomplish this.

EFFECTIVE EDUCATION FOR BELONGING AND CHARACTER

In examining the research on school bonding and belonging, some researchers have studied the predictors of such bonding. This research is not extensive, nor systematic, but at this point in time it does offer some ideas about the basis for students developing a sense of connectedness to school. Cumulatively, we can identify twelve factors that have been empirically related to the promotion of school bonding, while still recognizing that this body of research is far from complete:

- Positive classroom management practices
- Democratic, cooperative classroom communication and practices
- Non-harsh, tolerant disciplinary policies
- Less rule setting by classroom teachers
- High expectations for student performance
- Less negative feedback to students
- Adult modeling of academic motivation
- Focus on prosocial values
- Participation in extracurricular activities
- Smaller schools (secondary level)
- Student physical health
- Non-cigarette smoking students

These findings suggest some very different but potentially influential policy recommendations.

Reforming behavior management and discipline practices. Certainly it is important to maintain safety and order in schools. It would be difficult to sustain an effective learning environment in the face of threat, danger, and chaos. The question is how to do so. This is not that different from the question of how to prevent risk behavior in students. The findings cited here suggest that school bonding is most likely to occur when nonpunitive, proactive, tolerant, and flexible strategies are employed to promote positive behavior and reduce undesirable behavior. As Hawkins (1997) has noted, "Intervention studies have shown that teachers can learn to use proactive classroom management methods and that their use produces less student misbehavior in class and more on-task academically focused behavior" (188). Emmer and Evertson (Emmer, Evertson, and Worsham 1994; Evertson, Emmer, and Worsham 1994) have reviewed the research on classroom management and identified teacher behaviors that are effective in the classroom, including teaching prosocial behavior and establishing classroom rules and procedures.

Conversely, schools often assume that setting many clear rules and clamping down on violations is the most effective way to reduce misbehavior. Wentzel (2002), however, found that reducing middle school student misbehavior was most effectively accomplished by the exact opposite pattern of teacher behavior: fair, democratic classroom communication and fewer rules. Sometimes the counterintuitive path is the effective one. Programs like Responsive Classroom (www.responsiveclassroom.org; Brady et al. 2003) and the Child Development Project (www.devstu.org; Watson 2003) are predicated on such a proactive approach to positive classroom management. Both of them help teachers use forms of democratic class meetings, for example, to create fewer but more meaningful rules with logical consequences.

Promoting healthy lifestyles. This is not a strategy that is typically invoked in the service of character education, although it is an outcome that is often included in character education initiatives. The research suggests however that there is a circular relationship here. McNeely, Nonnemaker, and Blum (2002) and Bonny et al. (2000) report that less cigarette smoking and better student health predict school bonding. On the other hand, Solomon, Watson, and Battistich (2001) and Najaka, Gottfredson, and Wilson (2002) report that school bonding promotes student health behavior and reduces risky behavior. As Blum, McNeely, and Rinehart (2002) conclude from an analysis of the National Longitudinal Study of Adolescent Health, "when middle and high school students feel cared for by people at their school and when they feel like they are part of school, they are less likely to engage in unhealthy behaviors" (5). These findings suggest that promoting healthy student lifestyles may both be a result and a cause of student bonding to school. Clearly this relation needs further research to be understood better.

Encouraging students. The findings that both a reduction in negative feedback to students and setting high expectations promote bonding to school suggests that schools that encourage, and support, students are more likely to promote character development in students. The call for higher expectations (Damon 1995) has been sounded widely in the fields of education and parenting. The literature on parenting is very clear that setting high expectations is linked to child character development (Berkowitz and Grych 1998) and this has been directly linked to teacher behavior (Berkowitz and Grych 2000; Wentzel 2002). In fact, the composite of positive feedback (nurturing) and high expectations is highly parallel to what Baumrind (1971) calls authoritative parenting, a parenting style that has been shown to promote a wide array of desirable psychological outcomes including many aspects of character (Damon 1988). It is important to note that the setting of high expectations requires that the expectations are possible and that support is provided for meeting them (e.g., scaffolding).

Empowering students. Research on bonding to school demonstrates the power of student empowerment in building a sense of belonging (Power, Higgins, and Kohlberg 1989; Wentzel 2002). Schools historically are highly hierarchical organizations where students have little control or input. They are largely powerless in officially impacting the school systems and structures that have so much influence on their lives. As Parker Palmer (1998) has stated, "Implicitly and explicitly, young people are told that they have no experience worth having, no voice worth speaking, no future of any note, no significant role to play" (45) and "only when people can speak their minds does education have a chance to happen" (75). Experiments in school democracy and student empowerment, such as Kohlberg's just-community schools (Power, Higgins, and Kohlberg 1989), demonstrate the power of giving students "voice" in school matters. Programs like the CDP (Solomon, Watson, and Battistich 2001) rely heavily on promoting student autonomy. They do so by increasing shared governance and decision making in the elementary classroom through regular respectful class meetings in the same way as the just-community schools do for the whole high school through regular student-led community meetings (Power, Higgins, and Kohlberg 1989). Furthermore, research on the CDP has demonstrated that teachers who rely more heavily on cooperative classroom strategies have students who are more likely to perceive their classrooms as communities (Solomon et al. 1997). When students are given voice and choice in their classrooms and schools, when they are actively involved in formulating and monitoring the rules that govern their own behavior, and when schools show respect for student personhood by empowering and listening to them, then students are more likely to feel ownership of the rules, the classrooms, and the school, and to act more respectfully and responsibly.

Small schools. School bonding ideally is to a school community. This may be a subdivision of the school, such as a classroom, an advisory group, an academy, or a house. Or it may be manifested as bonding to the entire school as a community. The latter is more difficult the larger the school, although an important variable in any school is reasonable student-teacher ratios, for meaningful teacher-student relationships are more likely when the ratio is low, even in a large school. In 2002, the Character Education Partnership recognized five high schools as National Schools of Character (Character Education Partnership 2002). Four of those five were small, experimental, nontraditional high schools. The growing small-school and school-within-a-school movements have responded to the need to reduce the size of America's high schools either by actual downsizing of schools or by subdividing large schools into smaller subunits (e.g., houses within a large high school). Similarly, reducing student-teacher ratios addresses a similar concern. When staff can know every child's name, or better yet when all students know each other, then students are likely to feel more connected to the school. The size of a school has an indirect effect on teachers and students because "a smaller organizational dimension would facilitate personalized social interactions among school members. Teachers who interact more often with fewer students know their students better. By knowing students better, teachers are likely to worry more about their failures, provide more help directed toward improvement, take responsibility for disciplining everyone, and invest more fully in improving the whole school" (Lee and Loeb 2000, 23). Similar findings and conclusions are reached for schools from the elementary (Lee and Loeb 2000) to the high school (Darling-Hammond, Ancess, and Ort 2002; Lee and Smith 1997) levels.

Extracurricular participation. The finding that participation in extracurricular activity is linked to school bonding has more than one face. The more obvious interpretation is that such activity simply involves one more deeply in the school, hence making bonding more likely. It also may be understood as related to the small-school finding. Extracurricular groups often are small, stable groups (clubs, teams) that are conducive to bonding to the subunit and by implication to the school. Finally, as more students come from homes in which all parents work, the time after school becomes both more treacherous and more significant. Extracurricular participation may be an alternative to unsupervised, more risky alternatives, which may directly affect character development.

Adult modeling and advocacy.   Wentzel (2002) found that middle school teachers who model motivation for learning and school have students who show more character outcomes and academic achievement. This fits nicely with the finding that modeling of character by adults is directly related to character development in children (Berkowitz and Grych 1998, 2000). In addition, Solomon et al. (1997) have reported that teachers that promote prosocial values (e.g., by expressing them and supporting them in students) have students who perceive their classrooms as communities. Sizer and Sizer (1999) have made a cogent argument for the power of teacher modeling on the development of student character in general. "We have a profound moral contract with our students. We insist, under the law, that they become thoughtful, informed citizens. We must—for their benefit and ours—model such citizenship. The routines and rituals of a school teach, and teach especially about matters of character" (xviii).

CONCLUSIONS

It is clear that students' bonding to school, its members, and its subunits is a critical element in effectively promoting the development of student character, as well as an effective element in promoting student academic achievement. As Furrer and Skinner (2003) point out, when students feel connected to school they are more fully engaged in school and consequently achieve more. Schools need to pay more attention to those policies and practices that promote such bonding and sense of school as a caring community.

If character development is truly to be a goal of our schools, our families, and the broader communities in which they exist, then we need to pay closer attention to what scientific research can tell us about the development of community in school and the promotion of student connectedness to school. This chapter has presented some of the recent research on the role of student sense of belonging to both character and academic outcomes. Now it is up to the educational community to align implementation with these guidelines and for the research community to add to the knowledge base to better promote character development in our youth in the future.

REFERENCES

Baumrind, D. 1971. *Current Patterns of Parental Authority.* Developmental Psychology Monographs, 4 (1, Part 2).

Berkowitz, M. W. 1985. The role of discussion in moral education. In *Moral Education: Theory and Application,* ed. M. Berkowitz and F. Oser, 197–218. Hillsdale, NJ: Lawrence Erlbaum Associates.

———. 1997. The complete moral person: Anatomy and formation. In *Moral Issues in Psychology: Personalist Contributions to Selected Problems,* ed. J. M. DuBois, 11–42. Lanham, MD: University Press of America.

———. 2000. Civics and moral education. In *Routledge International Companion to Education,* ed. B. Moon, S. Brown, and M. Ben-Peretz, 897–909. New York: Routledge.

———. 2002. The science of character education. In *Bringing in a New Era in Character Education,* ed. W. Damon, 43–63. Stanford, CA: Hoover Institution Press.

Berkowitz, M. W., and J. H. Grych. 1998. Fostering goodness: Teaching parents to facilitate children's moral development. *Journal of Moral Education* 27:371–91.

———. 2000. Early character development and education. *Early Education and Development* 11:56–71.

Berkowitz, M. W., and P. Simmons. 2003. Integrating science education and character education: The role of peer discussion. In *The Role of Moral Reasoning on Socioscientific Issues and Discourse in Science Education,* ed. D. Zeidler, 117–38. Dordrecht, The Netherlands: Kluwer Publishing.

Blakeney, C., and R. Blakeney. 1987. *A Logic to the Madness.* Monographs of the Institute for Clinical Developmental Psychology, 111.

Blum, R. W., C. A. McNeely, and P. M. Rinehart. 2002. *Improving the Odds: The Untapped Power of Schools to Improve the Health of Teens.* Minneapolis: Center for Adolescent Health and Development, University of Minnesota.

Bonny, A. E., M. T. Britto, B. K. Klostermann, R. W. Hornung, and G. B. Slap. 2000. School disconnectedness: Identifying adolescents at risk. *Pediatrics* 106:1017–21.

Bowlby, J. 1969. *Attachment.* New York: Basic Books.

Brady, K., M. B. Forton, D. Porter, and C. Wood. 2003. *Rules in School.* Greenfield, MA: Northeast Foundation for Children.

Bryk, A. S., and B. Schneider. 2002. *Trust in Schools: A Core Resource for Improvement.* New York: Russell Sage Foundation.

Character Education Partnership. 2002. *2002 National Schools of Character: Practices to Adopt and Adapt.* Washington, DC: Character Education Partnership.

Dalton, J., and M. Watson. 1997. *Among Friends: Classrooms where Caring and Learning Prevail.* Oakland, CA: Developmental Studies Center.

Damon, W. 1988. *The Moral Child: Nurturing Children's Natural Moral Growth.* New York: Free Press.

————. 1995. *Greater Expectations: Overcoming the Culture of Indulgence in Our Homes and Schools.* New York: Free Press.

Darling-Hammond, L., J. Ancess, and S. W. Ort. 2002. Reinventing high school: Outcomes of the Coalition Campus Schools Project. *American Educational Research Journal* 39:639–73.

Deci, E., and R. M. Ryan. 1985. *Intrinsic Motivation and Self-determination in Human Behavior.* New York: Plenum.

Developmental Studies Center. 1999. *Blueprints for a Collaborative Classroom: Teacher Educator Guide.* Oakland, CA: Developmental Studies Center.

DeVries, R., and B. Zan. 1994. *Moral Classrooms, Moral Children: Creating a Constructivist Atmosphere in Early Education.* New York: Teachers College Press.

Dewey, J. 1944. *Democracy and Education.* New York: Free Press.

Durkheim, E. 1973. *Moral Education: A Study in the Theory and Application of the Sociology of Education.* New York: Free Press.

Emmer, E. T., C. M. Evertson, and M. E. Worsham. 1994. *Classroom Management for Secondary Teachers,* 3rd ed. Needham Heights, MA: Allyn & Bacon.

Evertson, C. M., E. T. Emmer, and M. E. Worsham. 1994. *Classroom Management for Elementary Teachers,* 3rd ed. Needham Heights, MA: Allyn & Bacon.

Furrer, C., and E. Skinner. 2003. Sense of relatedness as a factor in children's academic engagement and performance. *Journal of Educational Psychology* 95:148–62.

Hawkins, J. D. 1997. Academic performance and school success: Sources and consequences. In *Healthy Children 2010: Enhancing Children's Wellness,* ed. R. P. Weissberg, T. P. Gullotta, G. R. Adams, R. L. Hampton, and B. A. Ryan, 278–305. Thousand Oaks, CA: Sage.

Hawkins, J. D., J. Guo, K. G. Hill, S. Battin-Pearson, and R. D. Abbott. 2001. Long-term effects of the Seattle Social Development Intervention on school bonding trajectories. *Applied Developmental Science* 5:225–36.

Howes, C., C. C. Matheson, and C. E. Hamilton. 1994. Maternal, teacher, and child care history correlates of children's relationships with peers. *Child Development* 65:264–73.

Howes, C., and S. Ritchie. 2002. *A Matter of Trust: Connecting Teachers and Learners in the Early Childhood Classroom.* New York: Teachers College Press.

Howes, C., and E. W. Smith. 1995. Relations among child care quality, teacher behavior, children's play activities, emotional security, and cognitive activity in child care. *Early Childhood Research Quarterly* 10:381–404.

Jackson, P. W., R. E. Boostrom, and D. T. Hansen. 1993. *The Moral Life of Schools.* San Francisco: Jossey-Bass.

Kochanska, G. 1993. Toward a synthesis of parental socialization and child temperament in early development of conscience. *Child Development* 64:325–47.

Kohn, A. 1993. *Punished by Rewards: The Trouble with Gold Stars, Incentive Plans, A's, Praise, and other Bribes.* Boston: Houghton-Mifflin.

Lee, V. E., and S. Loeb. 2000. School size in Chicago elementary schools: Effects on teachers' attitudes and students' achievement. *American Educational Research Journal* 37:3–31.

Lee, V. E., and J. B. Smith. 1997. High school size: Which works best and for whom? *Educational Evaluation and Policy Analysis* 19:205–27.

Lickona, T. 1983. *Raising Good Children.* New York: Bantam.

———. 1991. *Educating for Character.* New York: Bantam.

Magid, K., and C. A. McKelvey. 1987. *High Risk: Children Without Conscience.* New York: Bantam.

McNeely, C. A., J. M. Nonnemaker, and R. V. Blum. 2002. Promoting school connectedness: Evidence from the National Longitudinal Study of Adolescent Health. *Journal of School Health* 72:138–46.

Morgan, W., and M. Streb. 2001. Building citizenship: How student voice in service-learning develops civic values. *Social Science Quarterly* 82:155–69.

Najaka, S. S., D. C. Gottfredson, and D. B. Wilson. 2002. A meta-analytic inquiry into the relationship between selected risk factors and problem behavior. *Prevention Science* 2:257–71.

Osterman, K. 2000. Students' need for belonging in the school community. *Review of Educational Research* 70:323–67.

Palmer, P. J. 1998. *The Courage to Teach: Exploring the Inner Landscape of a Teacher's Life.* San Francisco: Jossey-Bass.

Piaget, J. 1965. *The Moral Judgment of the Child.* Trans. M. Gabain. New York: Free Press. (Orig. pub. 1932.)

Pianta, R. C. 1999. *Enhancing Relationships Between Children and Teachers.* Washington, DC: American Psychological Association.

Power, F. C., A. Higgins, and L. Kohlberg. 1989. *Lawrence Kohlberg's Approach to Moral Education.* New York: Columbia University Press.

Resnick, M. D., P. S. Bearman, R. W. Blum, K. E. Bauman, K. M. Harris, J. Jones, J. Tabor, T. Beuhring, R. E. Sieving, M. Shew, M. Ireland, L. H. Bearinger, and J. R. Udry. 1997. Protecting adolescents from harm: Findings from the National Longitudinal Study on Adolescent Health. *Journal of the American Medical Association* 278:823–32.

Ryan, A. M., and H. Patrick. 2001. The classroom social environment and changes in adolescents' motivation and engagement during middle school. *American Educational Research Journal* 38:437–60.

Ryan, K., and T. Lickona. 1987. Character development: The challenge and the model. In *Character Development in Schools and Beyond,* ed. K. Ryan and G. F. McLean, 3–35. New York: Praeger.

Schaps, E., E. F. Schaeffer, and S. N. McDonnell. 2001. What's right and wrong in character education today. *Education Week* 21 (2 September): 40–44.

Sizer, T. R., and N. F. Sizer. 1999. *The Students are Watching: Schools and the Moral Contract.* Boston: Beacon Press.

Solomon, D., V. Battistich, D. Kim, and M. Watson. 1997. Teacher practices associated with students' sense of the classroom as a community. *Social Psychology of Education* 1:235–67.

Solomon, D., M. S. Watson, and V. A. Battistich. 2001. Teaching and schooling effects on moral/prosocial development. In *Handbook of Research on Teaching*, 4th ed., ed. V. Richardson, 566–603. Washington, DC: American Educational Research Association.

Stayton, D. J., R. Hogan, and M. D. S. Ainsworth. 1971. Infant obedience and maternal behavior: The origins of socialization reconsidered. *Child Development* 42:1057–69.

Wang, M. C., G. D. Haertel, and H. J. Walberg. 1993. Toward a knowledge base for school learning. *Review of Educational Research* 63:249–94.

Watson, M. 2003. *Learning To Trust*. San Francisco: Jossey-Bass.

Wentzel, K. R. 2002. Are effective teachers like good parents? Teaching styles and student adjustment in early adolescence. *Child Development* 73:287–301.

TWELVE

Struggling for Civic Virtue through School Reform

Jeannie Oakes, Karen Hunter Quartz,
Steve Ryan, and Martin Lipton

AMERICANS EXPECT SCHOOLS TO BE VIRTUOUS PLACES, WHERE CITIZENS become educated to effectively participate in civic life and shape the common good, guided by principles of social justice and an ethic of care. Americans also expect schools to promote and protect liberty, enabling individuals' pursuits of their own good life. Deep tensions in public schooling reflect this dichotomy between civic virtue and individual freedom—tensions we argue in this chapter lie at the heart of character education.

Under what conditions, Aristotle asked, is good character formed? We approach this complex, age-old question from the perspective of schools as a whole and the array of comprehensive reforms aimed at making them better places. Public schools are the one social institution in which members of diverse racial and other groups must by law come face-to-face to define individual freedoms and balance them with the common good. Perennial worries that schools fall short of this balance have guaranteed perpetual reform, triggering—in the best cases—collective dialogue and reflection. Therefore, it is in reforming schools where the national struggle to accommodate multiple, culturally shaped meanings of virtue and freedom takes place most surely. Enmeshed in this struggle, all members of a school community—teachers, parents, administrators, as well as students—have the opportunity to learn the social values necessary for democratic life.

Current reform efforts proceed as if there were a strong consensus on the meaning of school reform. Typically, there is not. In spite of political and policy rhetoric calling for school reform that ensures "high standards for all students" and "excellence and equity," these goals lack common understanding. When acted upon, they are often little more than facile catchphrases, riddled with the contradictions and controversies that lie at the heart of American culture. This chapter foregrounds these contradictions and controversies in an attempt to build a stronger consensus that school reform is about cultural struggle—not merely policy implementation. Elsewhere, we have characterized this struggle as betterment, opposed to a technical conception of reforming or repackaging policies and practices.[1] Betterment does not deny that there are important technological changes needed in schools: better ways to organize the school day, better ways to teach mathematics, better ways to increase minority enrollments in college prep classes, and so forth. But betterment also reaches deep into the culture, into history, to keep, as Cornel West advocates, "the best of the past alive" by making schools places of civic virtue.[2]

CULTURAL LORE, CIVIC VIRTUE, AND SCHOOLING

Character education requires far more than helping individuals embrace proper values or make moral choices for their own lives. It requires enabling participation in a democratic public life that encourages citizens to collectively shape a common, public good. As they work to prepare future citizens, schools intentionally or unintentionally engage in four related struggles crucial to democratic public life: to become educative, socially just, caring, and participatory. Each struggle tugs between our allegiances to civic virtue and individual freedom. Each illustrates the enormous challenge facing today's comprehensive school reform initiatives. And each struggle has important historical roots.

Our democratic tradition venerates these four cultural struggles in its portrayals of deeply admired historical figures. We first encounter romanticized ideas and biographies of these figures when we are young schoolchildren. American heroes such as Thomas Jefferson, Abraham Lincoln, Jane Addams, and Martin Luther King, Jr., remain through our adult civic lives as illustrative, if sometimes dormant, emblems of America's ideological foundations. Jefferson's, Lincoln's, Addams's, and King's oversimplified legacies are useful background for understanding Americans' wishes for a society and schools that are educative, socially just, caring, and participatory. Yet, in their own historic times, these figures also faced the manifestations in their own contexts of enormous ideological and personal contradictions. Thomas Jefferson called for a universally educated citizenry for the very purpose of democratic decision making for the collective good, but he also remained fundamentally committed to individual rights and enormously suspicious of government's infringement on individuals' free pursuit of their self-interest. Abraham Lincoln may have emancipated slaves, but he did so only haltingly; and he doubted the capacity of different races to live together on equal terms. Jane Addams's work at Hull House clearly brought to American civic life an institutional model for an ethic of care, but her model was also characterized by a strong dose of noblesse oblige. Martin Luther King, Jr., struggled mightily to teach that ordinary people could take control of their collective well-being, but his own charismatic leadership and American's need for individual heroes often mask the grassroots participation that created the extraordinary power behind the Civil Rights movement.

Of course, none of the "buts" above diminishes either the power of these ideas or the heroic contributions of these historic figures. Given the contexts of their times, Jefferson was more the democrat than the class-bound pragmatist; Lincoln was more liberator than racist; Addams the model citizen will always outshine Addams the aristocrat; and Martin Luther King, Jr., clearly was a champion for the powerless, even if the story we tell about him obscures as much as it reveals. These contradictions are not the revisionist debunking of great persons; they are evident in their writings and daily struggles as they negotiated their civic and reform missions. That they struggled with themselves as well as with their times makes their contributions to a citizenry that is educated, caring, socially just, and activist all that more heroic. In what follows, we elaborate these ideals of American civic virtue—the cultural lore and the contradictions that shape them—that have spawned theories of educational betterment. We offer these brief historical sketches to frame our collective tradition of school reform as a vital context for understanding the struggles that engage our youngest citizens as they develop their identity and their character.

BECOMING EDUCATIVE

In 1779, Thomas Jefferson set public education in motion, defining a vision for good American schools—an educational vision that is foundational for all else that follows. For Jefferson, public schools, perhaps more than any other institution, bore the responsibility for educating Americans with the cultural knowledge and the skills of deliberation that could make possible a public process of determining the common good. He thought that a liberal education was essential to creating public spaces in which free men—each with his own individual, self-interested perspective—could deliberate and forge agreements on how their individual interests might give way to the common good.[3] Through this exercise, civil society could be virtuous.[4] Despite dramatically changed times and schools, many education reforms in the 1980s and 1990s took an essentially Jeffersonian rationale, arguing that schools must, first and foremost, provide all young Americans with the academic knowledge and skills necessary for democratic citizenship and the public good.

Jefferson envisioned that schools would provide all citizens with the tools of literacy and a basic familiarity with Greek, Roman, European, and American history. This education—conveyed in three years of free, publicly provided schooling—combined with powers of reason and an inborn moral sensibility would allow citizens to read the political ideas in newspapers, form their own political values, and make political decisions. Jefferson believed that a public so educated would protect the new republic and help it prosper. Armed with these skills and sensibilities, citizens would be well prepared to be "guardians of their own liberty." For Jefferson, unlike many of his contemporaries, public schooling held the key to ensuring the public good. So much faith did Jefferson place in education that he tried, without success, to persuade the Virginia legislature to build brick or stone grammar schools at one-hundred-acre lot intervals throughout the state and provide public scholarships for poor children.

Much has changed since Jefferson's time, yet much remains the same. Both the length and substance of the education we see as necessary to prepare citizens have multiplied many times. Three years of common schooling have become twelve, with some suggesting that that be raised to fourteen. More significant is that during the past century, most Americans have come to believe that enlightened and productive citizenship requires far more than basic literacy and knowledge of Western history, and far more than the rote teaching and learning methods that characterized postrevolutionary schools. Anticipating, and unquestionably shaping, much current school reform, John Dewey argued more than 60 years ago that democracy requires an education that engages students in active participation with the intellectual and civic ideas that matter. Dewey's view converges with conclusions from contemporary cognitive and sociocultural research on learning and achievement:

> [L]earning which develops intelligence and character does not come about when only the textbook and the teacher have a say; . . . every individual becomes educated only as he has an opportunity to contribute something from his own experience, no matter how meager or slender that background of experience may be at a given time; and finally . . . enlightenment comes from the give and take, from the exchange of experiences and ideas.[5]

Importantly, Jefferson drew no distinction between the common good and individual liberty, and he believed that education could serve both. Drawing on the sentiments he saw within the early colonies and what he wished for the nation to become, Jefferson argued that the new republic depended on a citizenry that was *both* virtuous and free. Virtue would both inspire service to and sustain the public good. Freedom would foster equality and independence. Only through the deliberation of educated citizens who were both virtuous and free, Jefferson argued, could the nation govern itself and safeguard the inalienable rights of all equally created men. This view is apparent in the *Declaration of Independence*, where Jefferson wrote that our inherent and inalienable rights include "the preservation of life, liberty, and the pursuit of happiness." Far from an individual's hedonistic plea for personal benefit, the pursuit of happiness has Aristotelian roots as a collective end that demands the altruistic exercise of virtue.

Much has changed, making problematic Jefferson's view that public education would necessarily foster his dual commitment to civic virtue and freedom. Since the nation's founding, public schools have been guided by their increasing role in the nation's social selection processes. Inherent in this selection is the belief that schools should certify which students will best succeed in their pursuit of individual social, economic, and political benefits because these students also make the greatest contributions and best decisions on behalf of a good society. If these students gain the greatest material, social, and educational benefits, such gains are fair and just because they have earned these benefits by dint of their greater merit. Further, their example will serve the public good by motivating others to aspire for similar gains. Today, this assumed causality that competition and private motives in schooling produce social betterment distracts from and often overshadows schools' role in cultivating both knowledge and a passion for the public good. For example, the principal use of norm-referenced standardized testing is now to distinguish among and rank individuals. Little theory and no evidence have emerged over the past century to support the testers' claims that these tests contribute to a synergistic balance of private gain and public good.

Understandably, the large-scale reforms of the late 1980s and the 1990s did not entirely abandon the view that a focus on individual development would lead to a virtuous citizenry. However, they did recommend abandoning many of the theories and practices that schools utilized to sort and select children "meritocratically" for future educational opportunities and the life chances that follow from them. These reforms, such as heterogeneous grouping or cooperative learning, stood on cognitive and sociocultural perspectives of learning that largely discredit the traditional theories and educational practices. For example, the conventional notion that teaching is the transmission of knowledge from an adult to a child is not consistent with the recommended changes in school organization or practice. Likewise, the idea that differences in what and how much knowledge students learn are determined by their individual differences in intelligence and motivation is a popular but grossly inadequate theory for explaining why some children succeed in school and others do not. Neither did these newer theories support the conventional schooling practices so familiar to those of us educated in the twentieth century—practices including impersonal student-teacher relationships, lack of cohesion across the curriculum, an emphasis on content coverage rather than content depth, and individualistic learning activities in classrooms.

These late twentieth-century reforms were explicitly Jeffersonian in their mission, affirming in the strongest terms that the future of the democracy depends on a public education aimed specifically at preparing citizens to decide together and act on behalf of a collective good. Like Jefferson, most contemporary reforms insist that the pursuit of individual self-interest and the public good are fundamentally compatible goals. However, contemporary school reforms complicate the enactment of that belief. Rather than seeing learning as simply an individual activity, these reforms argue that the development of the intellect is a fundamentally social process. As such, they eschew the traditional individualistic, even competitive, model of teaching and learning that we associate with unconstrained learning opportunities and the freedom for each child to reach his or her full potential. Embedded in schools struggling to make this cultural shift, students experience firsthand the persistent tension between freedom and virtue. They learn that becoming educated in a democracy goes beyond "applying oneself" guided by the exalted American work ethic; it hinges on helping to create a fair and respectful place of learning.

BECOMING SOCIALLY JUST

When Thomas Jefferson wrote, one-fifth of the nation's population was neither free nor equal—a matter that the nation sidestepped for another century, and schools avoided for nearly two. For Jefferson, the idea of the public good was largely compatible with civic participation limited to white and propertied men. Jefferson, for all his democratic faith in an educated citizenry, placed firm boundaries around citizenship that excluded women and people of African descent. His educational plan for Virginia proposed that only those students who showed promise should be provided more than three years of public schooling. At the time, stratification according to wealth and background was generally acceptable, and stratification according to race and gender was both desirable and a matter of law.

It wasn't until 1860 that Abraham Lincoln acted in ways that both altered Jefferson's conception of who should participate in civic life and remained consistent with Jefferson's democratic sensibilities.[6] As pressure from the Abolitionists grew stronger, as the North's military need for manpower heightened, as blacks sensed the possibility of impending emancipation, as southern white opposition to slavery and planter rule mounted, and as the political response of the southern slave states grew more resolute, Lincoln understood the nation's collective well-being was fundamentally threatened by individuals' continued freedom to own slaves.

In the minds of most Americans, Abraham Lincoln stands as the "Great Emancipator," identifying, then ending, the moral evil of slavery and leading a Civil War based on the conviction that "this government cannot endure permanently half slave and half free."[7] Ask any schoolchild. Indeed, by freeing the slaves, Abraham Lincoln changed who could be an American citizen. Those formerly excluded now had a legal, as well as a moral, platform from which to demand full citizenship and schooling. However, for the nation to end slavery when it did was a commitment to civic virtue only in the narrowest sense. Now it was more *possible* to have a good society for all; there were fewer legal barriers to a good society. Left open was the question of which Americans, how Americans, and whether Americans would embrace such a pursuit. Lincoln affirmed the basic humanity of blacks and denounced slavery as an evil institution, but he also supported the private right to act on racist, segregationist beliefs. This tangled racial legacy left us with complicated questions that are still unresolved at the dawn of the twenty-first century: Who is fully American? What does American citizenship bring? And what does a diverse citizenry mean for the national culture and for the transmission of that culture in schools?

As public education developed and spread across the young American nation, laws in the South barred slaves from schooling. In the North, blacks were not legally excluded, although they were typically not welcome. After the Civil War, segregated schooling became the norm, and outside the South exclusionary policies also restricted and segregated Chinese, Japanese, Mexican-American, and Indian youngsters as well. By the beginning of the twentieth century, the U.S. Supreme Court had handed the nation what most took to be a fair compromise. The Court ruled in *Plessy v. Ferguson* that segregation was constitutional as long as separate facilities were equal. The "separate but equal" doctrine held until mid-century, even though people knew that most minority schools were inferior to most white schools—at least in terms of dollars spent on facilities and resources to support learning. In 1946 a U.S. District Court in California ruled in *Mendez et al. v. Westminister School District of Orange County* that the segregation of Mexican Americans had no legal or educational justification, and eight years later, the U.S. Supreme Court ruled in *Brown v. Board of Education* that racially segregated schools are inherently unequal. Efforts to use the courts to desegregate schools have continued throughout the century, with some gains and many disappointments.

Structures that separate Americans by race have proven more persistent than the early NAACP and other civil rights advocates imagined. *Brown v. Board of Education* in 1954 and the Civil Rights Act of 1964 finally removed legal barriers to blacks' civil and voting rights, but fell far short of resolving the larger cultural dilemma those barriers symbolized. Most American children still attend segregated schools—today a reflection of racially segregated residential patterns, rather than law. And in racially mixed schools, racially distinct, "ability-grouped" academic programs and extracurricular activities have increasingly become the norm.

For most of the twentieth century, Americans attempted to balance freedom and virtue around race by pursuing equal opportunity, and, specifically, equal *educational* opportunity. Yet, even as equal opportunity sets the conditions for individuals to act freely, it often presumes racial neutrality. In the educational sphere it requires school structures and procedures to ensure that the system is fair across lines of race and, increasingly, social class, language, gender, and sexual orientation. We use metaphors like being "colorblind" to indicate normative conditions of fairness and creating a "level playing field" to describe these structural efforts to make schools nondiscriminatory.

The two decades between 1954 and the mid-1970s witnessed a flood of educational opportunity policies from government and the courts, including school desegregation, compensatory programs, and special assistance for language-minority and disabled students. But increasingly the struggle moved beyond racial neutrality to a more proactive stance for equality and inclusion. The Civil Rights movement of the 1960s and 1970s yielded landmark court decisions and legislation on behalf of a wide range of excluded Americans. For instance, the federal War on Poverty created programs like Head Start and supplemental compensatory education to equalize opportunities for poor children. Public Law 94-142 required that schools develop Individual Education Plans for handicapped students. Title IX of the Higher Education Act provided for sexual equality in all educational programs supported by federal funding.

In the 1980s, however, the federal government under the Reagan and Bush administrations raised the banner of "excellence" and cast advocacy for equity as a threat to the goal of excellence. As evidenced by texts such as *A Nation at Risk* in 1983 and *Goals 2000* at the century's end, a well articulated campaign by social and political conservatives argued that the quality of the nation's schools—and with it, the efficacy of the nation's economy and the security of its defense—depended on government setting high standards and holding schools and students accountable for attaining them. Counterarguments that government also had a responsibility to guarantee that all children have the opportunity to meet the specified standards fell on ears that had become not only deaf, but disdainful of expensive and, in their minds, intrusive and ineffective efforts to equalize schooling. Thus began a period, running to the present, when successive demands for schools to improve were answered by research and policies that called for low-achieving students to attend schools in which highly qualified teachers had command of up-to-date teaching practices, generous resources, and full inclusion with a demographic cross-section of all the community's children.

Recommendations for more inclusive and socially just practices, if actually implemented in schools and supported by state and local governments, would require breaking down old hierarchies of educational advantage and redistributing power and resources across race and class lines. Attempting to make this shift places school reformers squarely into Lincoln's struggle over the meaning of civic virtue and freedom in American culture. In a system dominated by purported meritocratic indicators designed to sort and stratify individuals, many schools struggle against the grain to unmask common indicators (standardized tests, language proficiency, etc.) as proxies for race and wealth. Caught up in efforts to redistribute opportunities for college-prep classes, highly qualified teachers, and other resources, students become critically aware of the deep and persistent tensions that define social justice in this country.

BECOMING CARING

A century after Jefferson, social reformer Jane Addams came to stand as a symbol for the deeply rooted view that American social institutions, including schools, should be caring as well as educative communities, particularly for those alienated in their work lives or residing in impoverished neighborhoods. In 1889, Addams established Hull House in the midst of Chicago's burgeoning immigrant neighborhoods. Addams and a group of well-to-do young women spent their days there caring for children, teaching, nursing the sick, and helping immigrant families grapple with horrendous problems in their new lives. The education they attempted to provide went beyond the pragmatic "basic skills" of reading and writing, and included what these young women saw as essential cultural tools of mainstream middle-class life and dignity—including the arts, handiwork, discussion, and political action. Addams's work at Hull House exemplifies Americans' desire for social institutions, including schools, to enable people to attend to one another's well-being.

Like other progressive, big-city settlement houses of the period, the Hull House workers viewed the "problem" of immigrants very differently than did many other influential Americans at the helms of industries, newspapers, government, and so on. The prevailing view at the time was that the immigrants themselves were responsible for increasing urban crime, squalor, and unemployment, and must therefore be reformed. Addams, however, believed that the greed and corruption of wealthy industrialists had created the conditions that fostered these social ills. She argued that the solution was not simply to "Americanize" (or, more accurately, to Anglicize) immigrants, but for social institutions, including government, to rebuild communities torn apart by industrialization and provide for the social needs of immigrant families. Addams intended for Hull House "to provide a center for a higher civic and social life; to institute and maintain educational and philanthropic enterprises and to investigate and improve the conditions in the industrial districts of Chicago."[8] In addition to providing education and culture at Hull House, Addams and her colleagues fought for stronger labor laws and health and safety regulations, provided food programs, offered shelter for prostitutes and battered wives, operated a maternity hospital and a nursery, and more.

The settlement-house movement developed an ethic of democratic community that merged social, educational, and political purposes. Addams argued eloquently in public lectures and in her writing that democracy must have a social as well as a political function. Addams helped the nation understand that immigrant Americans living in contained neighborhoods and ghettos could and should be brought into the realm of what political philosopher Benjamin Barber calls the nation's "civic life." Addams and her colleagues' voluntary, nongovernmental public actions on behalf of the poor were first understood as charity, but came to be considered as work on behalf of the common good, or social work. These social reformers, by argument and by deed, wove new threads to connect to the commonwealth the lives of the poor and disenfranchised. They helped the public consider that freedom to act on one's own volition and in one's self-interest, unfettered by public constraints, was not necessarily a manifestation of individual moral character or God's will. Instead, such freedom, measured by how it translates into a range of power and action, is roughly commensurate with one's resources, education, and status. Those who were persuaded by Addams's arguments began to link the previously private and highly individualistic qualities of freedom to one's quality of life, opportunities, and participation in the community.

The ethic of social service that guided these reformers merged political, social, and educational purposes in an organization that was modeled more after an extended family—a community—than a school. Over time, the settlement-house reformers persuaded schools to consider the family/community model. Schools responded with school physicians, classes for handicapped children, school lunch programs, and school libraries in a movement they called "socialized education." John Dewey's friendship with Jane Addams and his support of her work influenced his thinking that schools might themselves become social centers modeled after the community at Hull House.

What a contrast these ideas were to the dominant mode in early twentieth-century schools. Educational historian Herbert Kleibard recounts that in 1913, a factory inspector, Helen M. Todd, surveyed five hundred child laborers to see if they would prefer to go back to school or to "remain in the squalor of the factories." Todd asked them whether, if their families were reasonably well off, they would choose to continue working or go to school. Kleibard notes, "Of the 500, 412 told her, sometimes in graphic terms, that they preferred factory labor to the monotony, humiliation, and even sheer cruelty that they experienced in school."[9] Even as traditional structures persisted, reformers pressed for more human alternatives. Within the first two decades of the century, many city schools followed Addams's and Dewey's lead, offering health and social services, as well as extended community education programs after school and in the evenings.

By the late 1980s, a growing chorus of school reformers was decrying that American secondary school students too often drift through classes without developing stable relationships with teachers and, often, other students. "Departmentalization," once prized as a reflection of teachers' specialized expertise, became seen as limiting teachers' ability to accommodate students' personal and social needs, as they single-handedly managed the large number of students they had for less than an hour of instruction, with virtually no time for personal interactions. While schools have expected individual students to get what they can from this structure, reformers claimed that it embodied norms that favored only the most motivated and highly skilled students and, frequently, only those students with school-savvy parents who guided their children through the formal and informal structures surrounding scheduling and course selection, grading, discipline, and so on.

Echoing Jane Addams, reformers today seek to foster constructive school relationships by making schools more family-like. Just as the settlement houses built close communities around the common goal of children's intellectual, physical, social, and moral well-being, the Coalition of Essential Schools, the Comer School Development project, Carnegie's *Turning Points* Initiative, the growing small-schools movement, and others are challenging schools to reinvent themselves as socially just and caring communities. They ask schools to make structural changes (e.g., schools-within-schools, teams, and advisory groups) that would create "stable, close, mutually respectful relationships with adults and peers [that] are considered fundamental for intellectual development and personal growth."[10] Such reforms highlight the interdependence among students, teachers, and parents, and reinforce that the responsibility for teaching and learning is not meant to fall on a single individual. The school must become a place, in other words, where people are deeply committed to maintaining a strong and positive school community.

This ethic of care[11] represents a considerable shift from the individualistic charity and service ethics that characterize how schools try to meet student and community needs. Typically, schools provide "needy" students with screening, information, or actual basic health and social services, often through the school nurse or health classes. Some schools encourage students themselves to do "community service," to help the "needy" through activities such as holiday canned food drives. However, attending to the needs of "others" who are in desperate straits is not quite the same as meeting needs as an unexceptional condition of living in one's own community. As educational historian John Rogers has noted, "While schools may have become sites for and conduits to an array of services, they have not necessarily become centers for community life."[12] Some scholars like Rogers argue that community-based activists are needed to prompt schools to go through a critical and respectful process of understanding the circumstances that shape students' lives and the conditions in their communities. They stress the relationships inherent in caring (relationships in which something is built and mutually held) over the transactional and service relationships inherent in meeting needs (relationships in which something goes from one to another). In short, caring without empowerment is pity. Engaged in building these constructive, caring relationships, all members of a school community learn firsthand the value of interdependence so crucial to civic virtue.

BECOMING PARTICIPATORY

The contribution of Martin Luther King, Jr., to the American culture is usually encapsulated in his leadership of the civil rights gains of blacks during the 1950s and 1960s. He is well remembered via film footage of whites' violent reactions to protesters' "direct actions," such as sit-ins, marches, and boycotts. Our popular culture has focused on King's inspirational "dream" and his hope that "some day" racial minorities and the poor would achieve civic and economic justice. Like Addams, King was a heroic leader committed to public action, neither from a wish to "do good" for others nor to gain personal benefit, but rather out of a virtuous concern for the common good.

Popular images of King and the Civil Rights movement have obscured the actual participatory processes that characterized the struggle. King's vision and skillful, charismatic leadership, though surely remarkable, tell only part of the story. More significant were the power of the collective, grassroots struggle that was the core of the Civil Rights movement, the negotiations that such participation forced, and the considerable risk and courage it required of ordinary people. The Civil Rights movement confronted, through its extraordinary collective action, America's uneven distribution of power. For King, freedom was not an aggregate of individual rights; rather, it must be the same for different groups and individuals. For example, in his "Letter from the Birmingham Jail," he wrote:

> I am cognizant of the interrelatedness of all communities and states. . . . Injustice anywhere is a threat to justice everywhere. We are caught in an inescapable

network of mutuality, tied in a single garment of destiny. Whatever affects one directly affects all indirectly.[13]

In this letter, King outlined a process of democratic inquiry and action through which ordinary people become powerful enough to transform social and economic arrangements by fact collection, negotiation, self-purification (preparation for nonviolence), and direct action.

Rather than simply attesting to the power of courageous individuals, the Civil Rights movement and other social movements such as the women's movement illustrate the power of a determined community both to sustain individuals and to create actions that are greater than the sum of the individual contributions. Moreover, these movements also demonstrate that participation stands the best chance of advancing civic virtue when diverse, heterogeneous groups of citizens struggle to solve public problems in common with others.

Throughout the nineteenth century, small and often marginalized reform groups worked to make schools instruments of social justice and, therefore, better places than the community at large. Particularly interesting are the efforts of African American women educators, often assisted by black churches and sometimes by liberal white groups like the Quakers, to use the schools to improve the social, economic, and political circumstances of the African American community. These women used their classrooms and their leadership to teach reading and writing not only to their students but to community adults as well—a daring act of social justice in the nineteenth century. For example, teacher Fannie Jackson Coppin organized tuition-free classes for freedmen coming North and founded a school for children of emancipated slaves. Believing that knowledge is power, Coppin intended her teaching to "uplift" the race. Other well-educated black women educators such as Anna Julia Cooper and Mary McLeod Bethune also went far beyond teaching their students technical skills or rudimentary literacy, and attempted to teach in ways that would bring about social and political change. At the root of their efforts was their conviction that education was not about individual gain, but about strengthening the community, a view captured eloquently in the motto of the National Association of Colored Women: "Lifting as We Climb."[14]

In the educational mainstream, first Horace Mann and later John Dewey envisioned schools as agencies of social reform for the further democratization of American society. Dewey stressed that classrooms are a part of life, not merely preparation for it, and to make society more democratic students must participate in classrooms that are themselves democratic societies. Teachers must give students a chance to learn how their actions affect the success or failure of the group. In classrooms, students must develop their sense of civic-mindedness by sharing both the pleasant and un-pleasant tasks that complex group projects require. "Doing one's part" as a member of a classroom group project prepares students to be both leaders and followers. In 1938, John Dewey wrote,

> The realization of that principle [that schools are a part of democratic life] in the schoolroom it seems to me, is an expression of the significance of democracy as the educational process without which individuals cannot come into the full possession of themselves nor make a contribution . . . to the social well-being of others. I said that democracy and education bear a reciprocal relation, for it is not merely that democracy is itself an educational principle, but that democracy cannot endure, much less develop without education.[15]

Later in the century, during the 1960s and 1970s, efforts to make schools more participatory and socially just emerged in the movement for "community control"—most notably, perhaps, in the Ocean Hill-Brownsville neighborhoods in New York City. Black activists seeking community control of schools were more interested in changing institutions than they were in simply gaining greater access to them. They believed that collective action by ordinary people could create school conditions that would enhance the lives of neighborhood children and families. In Ocean Hill-Brownsville, parents and community activists won the right to hire and fire school staff and select curriculum materials. Teachers, feeling as powerless as the parents, were caught between a school administrative bureaucracy that left them few professional prerogatives and citizens who seemed to be grabbing for the few remaining prerogatives. They responded with a two-month strike that ended the Ocean Hill-Brownsville experiment.[16] This quite radical vision of the schools actually belonging to the central-city communities whose children attended them never became mainstream.

The comprehensive reforms of the late 1980s and 1990s sought to change the prevailing structures and the norms that drive them, arguing that more democratic and participatory processes must be a key component of fundamentally restructured schools. Reformers urged that decisions about students' experiences are best made by those closest to students, and recommended that teams of teachers govern their own classroom budgets, space, curriculum, teaching strategies, and scheduling. They also called for committees composed of administrators, teachers, support staff, students, parents, and community representatives to make school-wide policies. They argued that closer relationships between schools and communities would build trust, respect, and common purpose.

These reforms resonate with the work of current participatory democratic theorists who argue that participating in local community projects—as distinct from the more limited form of democratic participation that voting represents—fosters communities that take control over their collective well-being, as well as care about their members. This civic virtue, according to political scientist Carol Pateman, encourages individuals to act as "public as well as private citizens."[17] And, as democratic theorist Benjamin Barber and activist Saul Alinsky both argue, communal bonds and collaborative action give individuals the power to act in ways that can bring social justice to their communities.[18] Growing up in an era of declining civic participation, young people are typically groomed for what Boyte and Kari call secondary roles in public life—those of "consumers, complaining clients, special interest advocates, or volunteers who 'help out' but make few serious decisions."[19] In contrast, as members of schools struggling to become more participatory, students and others can play a pivotal role in the process of democratic inquiry and action King outlined half a century ago.

A POSITIVE PASSION FOR THE PUBLIC GOOD

As these four historical struggles illustrate, the tug between individual liberty and civic virtue—embodied in contemporary school reform—has deep American roots. In his 1996 book, *Democracy's Discontent: America In Search of a Public Philosophy*, Michael Sandel reminds us that

> Central to republican theory is the idea that liberty requires self-government, which depends in turn on civic virtue. This idea figured prominently in the political outlook of the founding generation. "[P]ublic virtue is the only foundation of republics," wrote John Adams on the eve of independence. "There must be a positive passion for the public good, the public interest, honour, power and glory, established in the minds of the people, or there can be no republican government, nor any real liberty."[20]

It is this positive passion for the public good that lies, we believe, at the heart of character education. In our research on reforming middle schools, it was this passion that distinguished meaningful change from reworked versions of the status quo. Engaged in cultural struggles to create more educative, just, caring, and participatory classrooms and schools, heroic educators exemplified core democratic values for their students. In a few schools, this struggle even extended to parents; as one educator told us: "We are trying to empower [parents] so they will demand change. It is threatening, but it makes the school a better place because parents will demand more of us." Demanding more than the status quo allows, struggling to constantly make life better, takes enormous courage and a great deal of passion. Unfortunately, this passion is rarely fueled by the very structures intended to promote change—an edifice we call the reform mill.

Set in motion by Frederick Taylor nearly a century ago,[21] the reform mill grinds out reworked versions of the status quo that do little to address whatever initially motivated the reform. In place of making schools truly educative, the reform mill offers— but rarely delivers—higher standards and improved test scores. Behind the image of social justice, the mill tries to make schools meritocratic through competition, or it creates compensatory programs for those who can't compete. Instead of care, the mill services the needy, doing for them rather than with them. Providing the illusion of democratic participation, the mill gives a vote on a committee. Disappointed with the results of reform, policy makers, the public, and educators themselves judge the reform to be misguided, poorly implemented, or both; and so the next reform, waiting in the wings with new funding or new leadership takes center stage.

Reformers who struggle against this mill engage in practices driven by the goods internal or essential to betterment—self-knowledge, analytic skill, critical stance, collaboration, active participation, and so on. Dwarfing the scepter of compliance and accountability, a positive passion for the public good guides these reformers to become better at what they do each day—helping schools become more educative, socially just, caring, and participatory institutions. To do so demands a collective effort, redefining "reformers" to include all members, including students, of a school community. On this view, character education is not about a specific curriculum or service project; it's about membership. As students learn what it means to be a member of a thriving democratic community, they learn what it means to be part of the democratic tradition. As Cornel West reminds us:

> To be part of the democratic tradition is to be a prisoner of hope. And you cannot be a prisoner of hope without engaging in a form of struggle that keeps the best of the past alive. To engage in that struggle means that one is always willing to acknowledge that there is no triumph around the corner, but that you persist because you believe it is right and just and moral. . . . We are not going to save each other, ourselves, America, or the world. But certainly we can leave it a little bit better.[22]

NOTES

This chapter is adapted from *Becoming Good American Schools: The Struggle for Civic Virtue in Education Reform,* by Jeannie Oakes, Karen Hunter Quartz, Steve Ryan, and Martin Lipton, © 2000 John Wiley. Reprinted with permission of John Wiley & Sons, Inc.

1. Jeannie Oakes, Karen Hunter Quartz, Steve Ryan, and Martin Lipton, *Becoming Good American Schools: The Struggle for Civic Virtue in Educational Reform.* (San Francisco: Jossey-Bass, 2000).

2. Cornel West, "The Moral Obligations of Living in a Democratic Society," in *The Good Citizen,* ed. David Batstone and Eduardo Mendieta (New York: Routledge), 12.

3. Benjamin Barber's essay "Jefferson and Education" offers a clear discussion of the centrality of education in Jefferson's conception of democracy. See his *A Passion for Democracy: American Essays* (Princeton, NJ: Princeton University Press, 1998).

4. In the twentieth century this idea has its modern counterpart in what Jurgen Habermas termed the "public sphere." See his *The Structural Transformation of the Public Sphere: An Inquiry into a Category of Bourgeois Society,* trans. Thomas Burger with Frederick Lawrence (Cambridge, MA: MIT Press, 1991; orig. pub. 1962).

5. John Dewey, "Democracy and Education in the Word of Today," in *John Dewey: The Later Works, 1925–1953,* vol. 13, *1938–39,* ed. Jo Ann Boydston (Carbondale: Southern Illinois University Press, 1988), 296.

6. Again, Barber's 1998 essay is interesting on this point.

7. Abraham Lincoln, from the first debate with Stephen A. Douglas at Ottawa, IL, August 21, 1858. http://www.nps.gov/liho/debate1.htm.

8. Quoted from the Nobel Prize website. http://nobelprize.org/peace/laureates/1931/addams-bio.html.

9. Herbert M. Kleibard, *The Struggle for the American Curriculum, 1983–1958,* 2nd ed. (New York: Teachers College Press, 1992), 6.

10. Quoted from http://rams.nesd.k12.ar.us/~ogms/mgsspi.html.

11. Nel Noddings, *The Challenge to Care in Schools: An Alternate Approach to Education* (New York: Teachers College Press, 1992).

12. John Rogers, "Community Schools: Lessons from the Past and Present" (report to the Charles S. Mott Foundation, University of California, Los Angeles, 1998), 18.

13. Martin Luther King, Jr., *I Have a Dream: Writings and Speeches That Changed the World,* ed. James M. Washington (New York: HarperCollins, 1992), 85.

14. Michelle Knight, "Unearthing the Muted Voices of Transformative Profession" (PhD diss., University of California, Los Angeles, 1998).

15. Dewey, "Democracy and Education," 296.

16. Rogers, "Community Scools."

17. Carol Pateman, *Participation and Democratic Theory* (Cambridge: Cambridge University Press, 1970), 25.

18. See, for example, Saul Alinksy, *Reveille for Radicals* (New York: Vintage Books, 1969).

19. Harry C. Boyte and Nancy N. Kari, *Building America: The Democratic Promise of Public Work* (Philadelphia, Temple University Press, 1996).

20. Michael Sandel, *Democracy's Discontent: America in Search of a Public Philosophy* (Cambridge, MA: Harvard University Press, 1996), 126.

21. See, for example, Frederick Taylor, *Shop Management* (New York: Harper Brothers, 1919).

22. West, "Moral Obligations," 12.

THIRTEEN

College, Character, and Social Responsibility

Moral Learning through Experience

Jay W. Brandenberger

HIGHER EDUCATION HAS UNIQUE CAPACITIES TO FOSTER MORAL MEANING and to channel students' good will, openness to the world, and developing intellectual abilities for the common good. Each fall, thousands of youths begin a journey of higher learning with a mixture of wonder, trepidation, and trust. Students of traditional college age, while negotiating both new freedoms and challenges, also feel the potentials and callings of young adulthood, and search for something of enduring value worthy of their commitment. Concurrently, college and university mission statements emphasize character development and preparing students for productive roles in society. Students are expected to engage—traditionally through texts—with society, its institutions, and its challenges. Whether named or hidden, there is a great deal of moral education taking place in such contexts. And recent pedagogical developments emphasizing service and civic engagement provide enhanced means to foster moral learning.

Yet amid increasing calls for character development and engaged pedagogies, essential theory building and formative research are too often missing in action, so to speak. That higher education has the potential to foster moral learning and social responsibility is obvious to many, but challenges set in quickly. Moral growth does not fit neatly into traditional disciplines. Mission objectives contrast with increasingly specialized areas of expertise. Deep-set assumptions about objective, distant, and passive knowing still dominate. And few faculty receive training or reward for knowledge of student development and moral education.

This chapter addresses such concerns, drawing from developmental theory to examine moral development during the college years, especially through engaged forms of learning. The goal is to explore the intersection of character, college, and pedagogy, providing both a conceptual lens and applicable resources. My hope is to provide a broad review of relevant works and a theoretical mapping that can inform future practice and research.

THE MORAL ECOLOGY OF HIGHER EDUCATION

A focus on moral and civic principles is fundamental to higher education. While early colleges and universities were more explicit in their efforts to influence character and moral development (Mattson and Shea 1997), Schweiker (2001) reminds us that "Moral questions—questions about how we can and should live—are present in some form, no matter how modest, in every human inquiry" (22). Similarly, the moral domain is not limited to religious contexts. Moral is used here broadly to include both public and private concerns (see Ehrlich et al. 2003, for a thoughtful discussion on the essential integration of moral and civic principles).

Thus, higher education represents a moral crossroads for many. Institutions facilitate faculty inquiry into complex historical, social, and technological issues. Individual students confront the (personally expanding) world through courses as well as extracurricular involvements. All such encounters are shaped by changing cultural contexts, or moral ecologies. Terrorism delineates moral differences. Previous ethical certainties become current points of departure. Poverty, environmental challenges, and globalization are all pressing—though sometimes distant—moral concerns.

Amid such challenges, colleges and universities may contribute to the common good through direct institutional efforts, offering faculty expertise and relevant resources as appropriate. In addition, many realize the long-term importance of addressing the moral development of the students who course through higher education. Most leaders and public servants are and will be college graduates. Future institutions, from day care to Wall Street, will be shaped by those whose ability to identify, process, and act on moral concerns was enhanced or left fallow by higher education.

Nonetheless, while colleges and universities may hold a symposium on global warming or publish findings regarding the spread of AIDS, fostering character development among students still appears to many as tangential, impractical, or ineffable (Schwartz 2000; Brandenberger 2002). Is it appropriate for colleges to address character development and expect social responsibility? What pedagogies may facilitate development? Can we define common constructs and measure progress? These and similar questions underscore the need for theory development that can account for individual moral growth among dynamic social contexts and shape institutional initiatives.[1]

ENGAGED PEDAGOGIES: EXPERIENCE AND MORAL GROWTH

A call to involve young persons in social challenges to enhance their moral development is not new. Recall William James's proposal (1995) for a "moral equivalent of war." As an alternative to military conscription, James envisioned enlisting youth in challenging community efforts to promote justice while enhancing their own growth: "The military ideals of hardihood and discipline would be wrought into the growing fibre of the people; no one would remain blind as the luxurious classes now are blind, to man's relations to the globe he lives on, and to the permanently sour and hard foundations of his higher life" (24–25). Similar educational visions were inherent to early conceptions of the Peace Corps (originally conceptualized as an additional fourth year among five overall in college).

Yet the culture of higher education overall and assumptions about pedagogy change slowly. Experiential pedagogies have remained largely on the margin as Germanic models of the university (distancing learners from the phenomena of study) prevailed (see Boyer 1997). Currently, however, there are signs of change: we hear about inquiry-based learning, active pedagogies, and creative links between the academic and residential life, often framed in moral or civic tones. Derek Bok (1982), former president of Harvard, presents an early vision of the socially responsible university. Ernest Boyer (1996, 1997), past president of the Carnegie Foundation, argues persuasively for new and applied paradigms within the academy, and outlines a *scholarship of engagement*. Walshok (1995) and Palmer (1987, 1998) point out that knowledge itself is connected, that we come to know largely though social relationship.

Consistent with such conceptions of higher education, experiential pedagogies, especially those addressing community concerns, are finding new favor and empirical support (Bringle, Games, and Malloy 1999; Eyler and Giles 1999). Many campuses have a center or office that facilitates service learning, integrating service with academic study.

Such initiatives, however, while welcome on many levels, have been built more from intuition and opportunity than social science theory, especially theory delineating the developmental trajectories of college-age youth (see Brandenberger 1998). Recent pedagogical efforts also want for further clarification of relevant processes and expected outcomes. Service learning places individuals in relational contexts; likewise, the term *engagement* is reciprocal in nature. Community-based learning and research address community concerns and potentials collaboratively. Such pedagogies are thus inherently moral (see Mattson and Shea 1997) and may be framed as efforts to build character or promote justice. Yet, too often discussion of inherent, complex processes of moral and prosocial development remains at the implicit or speculative level, with limited reference to what is known within the social sciences about moral development.

While research on engaged pedagogies has begun to catch up with increased activity in the field, most is atheoretical and does not explicitly examine moral and ethical growth. What is the role of experience in morality? How can colleges foster sensitivity to ethical issues and long-term moral commitment through engaged learning, and what developmental challenges and strengths of college youth shape the process? To address such questions, I draw on moral psychology and research, including cognitive developmental theory.

THEORIES OF MORAL AND CHARACTER DEVELOPMENT
DURING COLLEGE

A variety of literatures provide context to examine character and moral development during the college years. Two schools of thought prevail (for a thorough overview, see Goodman and Lesnick 2001). One, often associated with the term *character educa-*

tion, centers on cultural transmission of accepted values and the inculcation of habits through authority and discipline. A second tradition, emphasizing reflective judgment, prioritizes methods that foster understanding of moral principles and cognitive growth. While the forming of moral habits is important—habits are framed as tools in Dewey's work—cultural transmission models have been critiqued for lack of explicit grounding in theories of human development and for susceptibility to indoctrination. The cognitive developmental perspective, building on the work of Dewey, Piaget, and Kohlberg, provides a refined theoretical framework focused on means to address moral development in a diverse society.

Two concepts are central to moral development theory in this tradition: *interaction* and *construction.* For Piaget (see Gruber and Vonèche 1995), intelligence is based on activity, on interacting with the environment to learn. Through such interaction, individuals construct their own understandings of reality. Our cognitive structures are thus, to a significant extent, a product of "'practical' interventions in the world" (Blasi 1983, 187). With respect to pedagogy, Piaget (1970) emphasized the need to build on the constructive activity of each student: "development is essentially dependent upon the activities of the subject, and its constant mainspring, from pure sensorimotor activity through to the most completely interiorized operations, is an irreducible and spontaneous operativity" (40).

Such constructive processes are particularly operable in the moral domain (for further theoretical development and analysis of proposed stage sequences, see Piaget 1948; Kohlberg 1969; and Lapsley 1996). Piaget (1970) argued for "morality in action" as a means to learn justice and "organic interdependence" (180). Through interactions with parents, peers, teachers, and community, youth construct moral hypotheses about themselves, other people, human nature, and social institutions. By college age, the majority of youth have sufficient cognitive abilities to address moral issues abstractly (formally) and a readiness to examine personal implications.

Although the cognitive developmental framework has influenced primary and secondary education (see, for example, DeVries and Zan 1994) more directly than higher education (a notable, early exception is the work of Whitely 1982), it provides a tested foundation for examining the potential for character development during college. And recent theoretical advances in moral psychology (Walker 2002), incorporating, for example, the roles of emotions, meaning, and identity formation, deepen the analysis. Such frameworks challenge the myth that moral development is basically complete though adolescence. The answer to the question, "Can college students of traditional age (and beyond) develop morally and ethically?" is a strong *yes.* The college years are a particularly sensitive period—described by Parks (1986) as "the critical years"—for moral growth. Such a conclusion can be made on logical and empirical grounds, as will be described below.

Moral growth is complex and multifaceted. In the sections that follow I outline overlapping dimensions of moral and character development that may be facilitated through engaged learning during the college years, including: (1) moral reasoning/judgment, (2) moral sensitivity and moral imagination, (3) moral identity, meaning, and purpose, and (4) moral commitment and behavior.[2] I then highlight the importance of examining moral responsibility and moral learning in relation to social change.

MORAL JUDGMENT: A COLLEGE EFFECT

How individuals reason about moral concerns and how thinking may change in scope and style are especially relevant to higher education contexts. Kohlberg's stage sequence recognizes increasing complexity and integration of principles at higher (post-conventional) levels of moral reasoning. Numerous studies have examined the development of moral thinking among college students. Pascarella and Terenzini (1991) and Rest and Narvaez (1991) provide two thorough reviews of such research, both of which document a positive college effect on cognitive moral growth, as measured, most often, by the Defining Issues Test (DIT scores overall are associated with level of education). A recent, comprehensive analysis by King and Mayhew (2002) demonstrates similar results. Overall, researchers have shown that the college effect is robust and distinct from age-related gains (though not all college students reach high levels of post-conventional thought).

That the college experience has a general and lasting effect has been easier to document than discerning what specific components of higher education may enhance moral judgment. This may be explained in part by the common use of undergraduate samples without intentional examination of associated college contexts (King and Mayhew 2002). Among studies that do explore potential contextual factors such as major or institutional type, few clear patterns emerge.

However, King and Mayhew (2002) report that most published studies of interventions designed to enhance moral reasoning show positive results. While this may be partially a result of underreporting of nonsignificant findings (the "file drawer problem"), it may also suggest developmental readiness for moral growth among college-age youth. King and Mayhew emphasize the need for future research examining what successful interventions may have in common and hypothesize that experiential and cocurricular involvements (e.g., community outreach, leadership opportunities) may play a key role in enhancing moral development.

Research by Boss (1994, 1995) is instructive here. She compared participants in two sections of an undergraduate ethics course, one of which was randomly selected to integrate service-learning components. Both classes were taught by the same instructor, incorporated the same readings (including the work of Kohlberg and Gilligan), and used matching examinations. Results showed significantly higher gains on the DIT for the engaged class. Following the semester, over 50% of the service-learning class scored 50 or higher on the DIT (suggesting the use of principled reasoning as a preferred mode) compared to only 13% of the comparison class (the sections demonstrated statistically equal scores at the start). Analyses also showed no differences on pre-test DIT scores by previous community service involvements. Such findings are consistent with the argument that service learning (built on the integration of community involvement with academic reflection) may be more powerful than direct service or class work alone.

Boss hypothesized that while both classes presented ethical challenges and cognitive disequilibrium, the added dimension of social disequilibrium—active role-taking via service involvement—facilitated more advanced (post-conventional) moral reasoning. Consistent with Gardner (1991), Boss suggests that often what is learned in "scholastic" settings becomes bounded and difficult to apply in other, active contexts. Engaged learning provides practice in the transfer of ethical thinking across domains.

MORAL SENSITIVITY AND MORAL IMAGINATION

Moral reasoning does not take place in a vacuum. To respond morally, *moral sensitivity* is also essential (see Rest 1986; Rest et al. 1999). We must notice moral concerns and cognitively situate what we see in a moral context. Such processes are complex and involve both learning and, according to Johnson (1993), imagination.

Certainly, higher education provides significant cognitive content for students to grapple with (or at least remember long enough for the exam), and some faculty are adept at drawing out moral meaning from texts (e.g., challenging assumptions or pointing out the social implications of a dominant metaphor). Yet too often such insights are left at an impersonal level—fact, value, and personal experience remaining separate. Efforts to promote critical thinking among students younger than those they "criticize" may lead to a mistrust of action (see Loeb 1994). Students may read that we are connected by a vast array of interacting forces, from market to environment to media network, but remain unsure of how to maneuver such interdependence. They are expected to assimilate information and give it back while following pre-designed curricular paths. Concurrently, they accumulate meaningful experiences outside the classroom (which are often salient when alumni recount their undergraduate years). The challenge is to facilitate integration of such elements for personal and academic growth, fostering ongoing moral attention. Pedagogies based on experience have much to offer toward this end, exposing students to moral contexts and highlighting inherent ethical concerns.

Support for an experiential sensitivity and understanding of morality is grounded in the work of Dewey. For Dewey, morality begins in experience, and "moral philosophy is thus a function of the moral life, and not the reverse" (Pappas 1998, 103). Moreover, Dewey (1897) suggests that "the best and deepest moral training is precisely that which one gets through having to enter into proper relations with others in a unity of work and thought." He (1996) describes the process of deliberation in relation to a moral encounter:

> Deliberation is actually an imaginative rehearsal of various courses of conduct. We give way, *in our mind,* to some impulse: we try, *in our mind,* some plan. Flowing its career through various steps, we find ourselves in imagination in the presence of consequences that would follow, and as we then like and approve, or dislike and disapprove, these consequences, we find the original impulse or plan good or bad. Deliberation is dramatic and active, not mathematical and impersonal. (135, emphasis in original)

For Dewey, then, moral processes involve both encounter and imagination. Individuals need to develop a willingness to enter into moral situations, trusting their abilities (character) to engage the inherent complexity; each moral situation is a new challenge, requiring an individual to actively address relevant issues in context using past experience as a guide but creating an appropriate original response when needed (Pappas 1998). Engaged pedagogies may prompt and enhance such moral processes in relatively safe contexts.

Mark Johnson (1993) attempts to integrate moral philosophy (including Dewey) and cognitive science, emphasizing the role of moral imagination over moral tradition or reasoning. Johnson emphasizes that "human beings are fundamentally *imaginative* moral animals" (1). While moral mottos may remind us of our values and moral desires, they are insufficient given the complexity of moral matters. And principles, while important, must be applied in context. Johnson argues that "our moral understanding depends in large measure on various structures of imagination, such as images, image schemas, metaphors, narratives, and so forth. Moral reasoning is thus basically an imaginative activity, because it uses imaginatively structured concepts and requires imagination to discern what is morally relevant in situations, to understand empathetically how others experience things, and to envision the full range of possibilities open to us in a particular case" (ix–x). Johnson points out that such imaginative processes begin in experience: "In general, we understand more abstract and less well-structured domains (such as our concepts of reason, knowledge, belief) via mappings from more concrete and highly structured domains of experience (such as our bodily experience of vision, movement, eating, or manipulating objects). Language . . . is based on systems of related and interlocking metaphorical mappings that connect one experiential domain to another" (10). For Johnson, moral reasoning is dependent on "frame semantics." In any context, multiple framings lead to different conclusions. A fetus may be viewed, he points out, as a human being or as an impersonal biological entity. Thus the conceptual metaphors we inherit from our culture, and construct personally through interaction and reflection, significantly impact our moral thinking. Accordingly, Johnson highlights the narrative aspects of morality.

Johnson's emphasis on moral imagination complements the cognitive developmental perspective, especially with respect to understanding the links between moral reasoning and moral action. Inherited moral laws have important instrumental value, but an active, reflective individual must compose moral meaning within relative contexts and envision alternatives. One does this best, according to Johnson, not in abstract isolation but via "communal discourse and practice" (217). Such a model has important implications for college life and is consistent with engaged pedagogies.

Johnson describes the self in experiential, dynamic terms. We look to a variety of resources to build moral meaning and understanding: "ideals, people we regard as morally exemplary, cultural myths, stories of moral conflict and resolution, principles, and our sense of history" (180–81). These are the raw materials of our experience that we use to construct moral narratives that can guide our actions. Since moral imagination develops later than other capacities, the college years are ripe for growth. According to Johnson, youth need to develop a "mature, experientially grounded moral imagination" built on "experience that is broad enough, rich enough, and subtle enough to allow them to understand who they are, to imagine who they might become, to explore possibilities for meaningful action, and to harmonize their lives with those of others" (183). This is the work of college students in the classroom and beyond.

Such developmental change is built, according to Johnson, upon metaphor and narrative. He cites evidence that a majority of "moral concepts—cause, action, well-being, purpose, state, duty, right, freedom and so forth—are metaphorically defined" (193). Such metaphors are built through experience into personal narratives that shape future decision making. Echoing the work of Parks (1986, 2000), Johnson maintains that "Morality is thus a matter of how well or how poorly we construct (i.e., live out) a narrative that solves our problem of living a meaningful and significant life" (180). Toward this end, an intentional college experience, one that integrates meaningful engagement in socially challenging contexts with relevant texts and probing personal reflection (hallmarks of engaged pedagogies), can foster significant student development.

MORAL IDENTITY: MEANING, PURPOSE, AND FAITH

The traditional college years are, of course, a time of identity development and idealism (consider the often displayed photograph of a resolute Chinese student challenging a tank in Tiananmen Square). Identity is an important area of focus here for a least two reasons. First, various theorists (see Blasi 1984, 1993) have in recent years postulated a central, organizing role for moral identity in overall moral functioning; and second, the college experience provides various opportunities to facilitate students sense of meaning and purpose.

Identity development—central to Erikson's psychosocial theory—involves both internal and social processes (Erikson 1975). Identity is complex, dependent on maturing cognitive abilities developed through interactions in social contexts that change over time. Explorations of self in peer, family, career, and moral contexts are important for mature identity formation. Young persons enjoy exploring ideological issues as a means to test their moral wings, though at times they may employ "totalistic" (Erikson 1975, 206) or utopian thinking. There is much in Erikson's work to recommend direct experience and engaged pedagogy as means to explore and refine moral identity (for a brief review, see Brandenberger 1998).

Chickering and Reisser (1993) present the most thorough review of identity development in higher education. They outline seven relevant developmental "vectors" along a trajectory, from (1) "developing competence" to (6) "developing purpose" and (7) "developing integrity," each of which presents challenges and opportunities during the college years. For Chickering and Reisser, integrity is built on humanizing values, moral principles, a sense of purpose and meaning, congruence, socially responsible behavior, and spiritual awareness, all of which are constructed according to individuals' experiences. They cite consistent evidence (see also Pascarella and Terrenzini 1991) that during the college years students show a "movement toward greater altruism, humanitarianism, and social conscience . . . and more social, racial, ethnic, and political tolerance" (Chickering and Reisser 1993, 237–38). Again, we observe support for engaged pedagogies: "Finding meaning in life is a by-product of engagement, which is a commitment to creating, loving, working, and building" (264).

The work of Sharon Parks (1986, 2000) provides a rich and comprehensive view of development during the young adult years. Integrating the theories of Erikson, Piaget, Perry, and others, she describes the journey from adolescence to adulthood with an emphasis on how individuals compose meaning. Meaning is central to human functioning: "we seek pattern, order, coherence, and relation in the disparate elements of our experience" (1986, xv). "To be human," Parks suggests, "is to seek to understand the fitting connections between things . . . [and] to desire relationship" (1986, 14). She describes this basic human "activity of composing and being composed by meaning" as *faith* (for a similar use of the term, see Erikson 1975). This is faith with a small *f*, not necessarily religious in nature. With or without religious tradition, all persons, especially young adults, seek to understand the larger world, examine their potential roles, and learn what may be worthy of their time and talents. This is an active process involving both cognitive and affective change. Parks invokes the metaphor of a journey at sea as young persons push away from the dock (their parents and inherited authority) and examine new worlds (through peers, texts, teachers, mentors, and experience) with a sense of freedom and adventure yet trepidation (is my boat seaworthy? what is my compass, my lighthouse?).

The metaphor captures well the excitement, hope, and ambivalence many college students feel. How they come to compose meaning and what they learn to have faith in (which worldviews, political frames) will have significant impact on their adult moral lives. Parks describes three key aspects in the process: (1) forms of knowing—how individuals learn what to trust as a source of truth and guidance, (2) forms of dependence—how young adults negotiate the challenges of individuation as well as interdependence, and (3) forms of community—how youth form and reform networks of relationship and belonging that they trust to influence them. In each domain, individuals must navigate using evolving cognitive processes in relation to a changing world. Each mooring along the way, each form of faith chosen or developed has implications for the moral life.

Parks, drawing on the work of Marstin (1979), notes that the "character of one's composition of the whole of reality (one's faith) will condition what one finds tolerable and intolerable" (Parks 1986, 67). She concurs with Marstin that "Issues of social justice are essentially about who is to be cared for and who neglected, who is to be included in our community of concern and who excluded, whose point of view is to be taken seriously and whose ignored. As faith grows, it challenges all the established [assumed and conventional] answers to these questions" (Marstin quoted in Parks 1986, 68).

Parks also emphasizes the role of imagination (distinct from fantasy). Young adults begin to name and develop passion for the "ideal," utilizing new critical thinking abilities. "A central strength of the young adult is the capacity to respond to visions of the world as it might become. This is the time in every generation for renewal of the human vision." (Parks 1986, 97). Building on Kant and Coleridge, she describes imagination as a composing activity that "can apprehend transcendent, moral truth" (Parks 2000, 107). Imagination—grounded in experience—is the raw material of faith that subsequently frames moral choices and commitments.

Since many images for life are available, and presented unceasingly by advertisers and media, how do youth avoid a sense of relativism? Parks suggests that the search should be for "right images," positive visions of an integrated, just world informed by a "empathic, moral imagination" (2000, 124). Young adults need mentors and communities that can help them reflect upon and build such visions.

Two qualitative studies have significant relevance here. In *Some Do Care* (Colby and Damon 1992, 1993) and *Common Fire* (Daloz et al. 1996a, 1996b) researchers examined the lives of individuals nominated by others for their sustained moral commitment. Colby and Damon interviewed twenty-three moral exemplars, employing a form of assisted autobiography that welcomed subsequent input from the interviewees after the authors outlined tentative insights. They discovered a number of qualities shared by the majority of exemplars, including a sense of optimism or positivity, the willingness to take personal risks to sustain their work, and a "certainty of response about matters of principle" (1992, 293). However, while exemplars scored reasonably high on measures of moral judgment (though not at the highest level), what most distinguished them was an apparent fusion of self and morality. Often through salient social interactions early in life, the exemplars developed a "steadfast commitment to purposes larger than themselves" (291). Somewhat paradoxically, the majority of the exemplars developed the ability to recruit ongoing social relationships that would challenge, and thus recharge and expand, their moral orientations. The exemplars were consistently collaborative in their moral pursuits, seeking out colleagues who could offer support, critique, and insight.

Most of the exemplars—more than the authors predicted—drew from religious inspiration to sustain their commitments. And those who were less religious exhibited a sense of meaning similar to that described by Parks, a "common sense of faith in the human potential to realize its ideals" (Colby and Damon 1992, 311). This sense of faith sustained the exemplars, providing a "glue joining all the self's systems of action and reflection." The authors suggest that it is the exemplars engagement in moral concerns that fosters the resilient "unity of self" they demonstrate (Colby and Damon 1992, 311).

How may the college experience enhance the integration of self and meaning exemplified by such exemplars? Daloz et al. (1996a, 1996b) suggest that higher education, especially through the social interactions it fosters, can play a key role. These authors interviewed over one hundred individuals who demonstrated a long-term commitment to the common good. Among this group of exemplars the authors found evidence for common "habits of mind," including: (1) an orientation to dialogue as a source of understanding, (2) the capacity for perspective-taking, to see the world from others' point of view, and (3) an ability to think critically and holistically in terms of connected systems (1996b, 12). Such orientations may begin during the college years, especially in an atmosphere where mentoring is common and a "civil space" is created for developmental interactions.

In addition, the authors suggest that the single most important factor found among their sample of committed adults was an experience the authors label "constructive engagement with otherness": "At some point in their formative years virtually everyone in our sample had come to know someone who was significantly different from themselves. This was not simply an encounter, but rather a *constructive engagement* by means of which they could empathically recognize a shared humanity with the other that undercut old tribal boundaries and created a new 'we' from a former 'they'" (1996b, 12; original emphasis). Certainly colleges and universities, through the efforts to promote diversity on campus and engaging students in community-based learning and research outside of campus, can play a key role in prompting such a movement beyond boundaries, one that seems to have lasting effects.

Robert Coles (1993) offers a personal view of identity development and idealism in relation to the "call of service." Coles points out that "idealism and altruism [have] to do with putting oneself in the shoes of others, absorbing their needs, their vulnerability, their weakness, and their suffering, and then setting to work" (205). Drawing from the writings of Anna Freud, Coles suggests that "What [matters is] not so much the various motivations, per se, as the manner in which all the yearnings and vicissitudes and consequences of a person's childhood and experiences . . . are worked into a life" (204). Yet the path of idealism is not always direct. Genuine empathy may mix with personal emotional needs, multiple ambitions, and concrete thinking to form a complex set of ideals in tension. What is needed along the way is time for reflection, the company of supportive peers, and positive mentors.

Overall, experiential learning may be an important form of meaningful "work" for young people (whose main idea of work may previously have been school assignments to complete). An early encounter with the work of making a better world can have far ranging implications for identity and professional development: "to work is first and foremost to make oneself through the act of transforming reality" (Martin-Baro 1994, 39). In a study of individuals known for joining excellence and ethics for "good work," Gardner, Csikszentmihalyi, and Damon (2001) emphasize the importance of early professional experiences in a moral milieu.

FROM THOUGHT TO ACTION: MORAL COMMITMENT AND BEHAVIOR

Morality, of course, is more than cognition and disposition. The gap between moral belief and personal action can be wide and uninviting. Much of immorality, so to speak, is not the lack of moral knowledge but the ignoring of it in action (Blasi 1983). What, then, facilitates moral behavior generally, and social responsibility in particular, and what role does the college experience play? The authors outlined above point to the central role of the moral self. The sense of self as a moral person, poised for commitment and involvement, is a critical factor that predicts behavior, that mediates between moral reasoning abilities (judgments about moral questions) and personal moral behavior or conduct (see Blasi 1993; Goodman and Lesnick 2001; Damon and Hart 1992).

The challenge is to facilitate a movement from (in William Perry's terms) moral relativism to moral commitment, both cognitively and behaviorally, and to foster ongoing moral motivation. How? Pedagogies of engagement have a key role to play. Years before the service-learning movement, Perry emphasized authentic involvement in "the risks of caring" (1970, 200) as the most effective means for students to test and strengthen their commitments (he also stressed that institutions and faculty need to model such risks in their own programming and commitment to social concerns).

Engaged pedagogies present creative opportunities for students to grow cognitively as well as form moral habits, integrating the alternative emphases found in the moral development and character education literatures. Well-designed service-learning and community-based learning initiatives provide opportunities for students to (1) join with and learn from peers in prosocial activities, (2) witness the commitments demonstrated by community leaders who serve as role models, (3) experience social issues both cognitively and emotionally, (4) experience the worldviews and perspectives of others like and unlike themselves, (5) grapple with academic texts in relation to personal experience, (6) test their developing moral thinking in a challenging environment they may otherwise avoid, (7) work in partnership with faculty who also are themselves exploring issues and appropriate responses, and (8) learn how to learn in moral domains.

Experiential pedagogies thus have strong potentials to unite elements too long separated in the academy: thinking and feeling, reflection and action, theory and practice. Throughout, attention to what students are learning about themselves as moral persons is critical. Students often claim, following a service-learning experience, that they learned more than they gave (for research on service learning and self-knowledge, see Eyler and Giles 1999), but faculty, focused on traditional academic outcomes, often do not feel equipped to handle the personal and developmental aspects that emerge. For this and other reasons, multidimensional approaches are warranted. A comprehensive college environment that fosters an integrated ethical ethos may prove to be one of the best means to enhance character development.

It is also important to note that moral behavior is not simply an end point in a process from moral notice through cognition to application (Rest et al. 1999). A student's new behavior of participating in structured service learning may lead to a reconceptualization of identity: "I find myself serving, so I must be a moral person." At some colleges, students who break campus rules are directed to participate in "community service" programs. Such students sometimes later emerge as passionate advocates and leaders in the service domain. How such transformations take place should be a research focus.

Marcia Baxter Magolda (2001) outlines a comprehensive theory of self-development in higher education. She highlights the importance of assisting students in "becoming the author of one's life" and points to three key dimensions: the epistemological (how and what a student believes), the intrapersonal (his or her thinking about self), and the interpersonal (how one relates to others). College is a key period for development in these realms, building on prior cognitive and social gains; and engaged learning may prompt vital discovery. One student in her research described the process using the metaphor of clay: "You've been formed into different things, but that doesn't mean you can't go back on the potters' wheel and instead of somebody else's hands building and molding you, you use your own, and in a fundamental sense change your values and beliefs" (119). To facilitate growth, Baxter Magolda emphasizes "including students' own lived experiences and questions in exploration of knowledge and mutual construction among members of the knowledge community" (329). She also recommends fostering coherence for students through "an integrated cocurriculum" (328).

To the extent that colleges foster such moral self development, lasting behavioral change may develop. Those "whose self-concept is organized around their moral beliefs are highly likely to translate those beliefs into action consistently throughout their lives. . . . Such peoples tend to sustain a far higher level of moral commitment in their actual conduct than those who may reason well about morality but who consider it to be less pivotal for who they are" (Damon and Hart 1992, 445; also quoted in Goodman and Lesnick 2001, 244).

If the college experience in general and engaged pedagogies in particular foster moral development, what evidence do we see among graduates? A variety of studies provide strong confirmation. Using data collected from over three thousand students at forty-two colleges and universities, Sax and Astin (1997) examined the effect of service participation in college on thirty-five potential outcomes, many of them moral in nature. On *each* of the variables, service participants showed significant positive differences compared to nonparticipants, with effects strongest in relation to civic responsibility. Service participants were, for example, more likely to show increases (from freshman data) in their commitment to "influencing social values," "serving the community," and "promoting racial understanding" (28). A second study by the same authors (Sax and Astin 1997; see also Astin, Sax, and Avalos 1999) of twelve thousand college alumni indicates that such changes can be long lasting. Undergraduates who participated in service or service learning were more likely five years after graduation to be civically engaged, and showed greater gains on measures of "helping others in difficulty," "empowerment," and, some will be glad to hear, inclination to donate to their college (Sax and Astin 1997, 30). A study by Hill, Brandenberger, and Howard (2005) employing interviews of service-learning participants compared to nonparticipants ten years later also showed positive long-term effects.

Thus, the college experience, and especially service learning, may have a channeling effect. Students who find their way into the reciprocal relationships and growth experiences of service or social action may develop long-term readiness for similar involvements after college. Character is not a simple matter of adult choice in the moment. The time demands of early career and family may present few realistic opportunities to *begin* prosocial involvements. Foundations need to be laid early and steeled during periods of readiness that to some extent coalesce during late adolescence and youth, when identity and adult habits are in prime development. In Erikson's terms, youth of college age are developmentally poised to find causes and images of the future that warrant their *fidelity* and facilitate "initiative of imagination and action" (1975, 213).

MORAL AND CIVIC RESPONSIBILITY

A discussion of character and moral behavior leads logically, if not always naturally, to issues of social responsibility. In a complex society, morality has increasing collective import. "The basic fact of the modern world" says British author Geoff Mulgan, "is that it is connected" (1998, 19). Mulgan suggests the word "connexity" to signify the escalating ways people are connected by technology, environmental challenges, mobility, and media. Such links have moral implications: "a more connected world brings with it a moral duty to consider the effects we have on others, and a need for moral fluency that goes beyond simply learning codes of right and wrong." Echoing Einstein's dictum at the dawn of the atomic age, Mulgan suggests we "have to think in a different way, understanding the world as made up of complex systems rather than linear relationships, ecologies rather than machines" (11).

Toward such ends, Mulgan finds hope in the new fact of interdependence itself: "Connexity is undoubtedly breaking down many of the barriers and separate identities that have been the main cause of human suffering and war, and nurturing a new, more open type of human being" (29). Yet success is not guaranteed; governments and educational institutions must assist in the process. College students and faculty are in a prime position to explore and discuss such issues. Perry even hypothesizes an advanced Piagetian "period of responsibility"(Perry 1970, 205) potentially overlapping with the college years (see also Flanagan 1998).

Blasi (1993, 2002) provides a conceptual framework for understanding the development of responsibility and its relation to identity. He argues that responsibility develops, in part, through being an agent in the world, experiencing the consequences of one's behavior, and reflectively (though not necessarily explicitly) appropriating perceptions of self during the process. The result is, for some, a personal "ownership" of relevant values, cohering in an identity wherein moral responsibility is salient. Parallels here to engaged learning are apparent. The challenge is to foster experience that leads to authentic ownership of moral values among young persons whose senses of autonomy and identity are being influenced by multiple processes and forces.

In an early, thorough examination of education and responsibility, Romein (1955) notes that perspectives of responsibility are inherently tied to deep questions of human nature, freedom, and community. The "human capacity to be accountable may be fulfilled in response to a rule or to the dictations of a powerful state or to the inner law of the 'ought' or to the divine imperative of love" (xi). Examining a variety of educational traditions—classical, progressive, humanist, and religious—Romein underscores the role of experience in prompting awareness of human connection and commonality.

Schweiker (2001) claims that responsibility, learned through human interaction, is essential to ethics: "Whereas Kantian-style ethics conceives of human beings as under duties, and virtue theory focuses on patterns of self-formation and well-being, the ethics of responsibility pictures humans as dialogical creatures existing in patterns of interaction" (18). Engaged pedagogies build on such interaction. Berman (1997) notes that a focus on "*relationship* shifts the context of our thinking beyond individual maturation and environmental context to the meaning that people derive from their interactions and the receptivity of the environment to the individual" (18). Berman examines how individuals make sense of social challenges and provides a theoretically grounded view of the development of *social responsibility*, defined as a combination of both character and civil/political commitment to promoting the common good.

Berman suggests that the construct of social responsibility integrates and extends the moral voices of justice and care outlined by Carol Gilligan (1982), and incorporates important elements of social learning theory. Social responsibility, he maintains, involves the following: (1) social and political consciousness, (2) a sense of connectedness, (3) acting on ethical considerations, (4) prosocial behavior, (5) integrity of action, and (6) active participation (Berman 1997, 14). These elements have both cognitive and behavioral components that develop through interactive, social processes. Berman outlines a variety of educational strategies, especially at the secondary level, that studies have shown to foster social responsibility, including direct involvement in the social/political domain. In a similar work, Youniss and Yates (1997) examine the development of responsibility among youth, noting, for example, the link between responsibility and personal agency.

A sense of responsibility at the core of self-definition or identity may be a key factor in prosocial behavior (see Lapsley 1996). Further, the concept of responsibility moves us beyond an individualistic framework common to some character education programs (Berman 1997). Too often morality is framed in private terms while institutional influences and systemic inequalities remain unexamined. Service learning and similar pedagogies are oriented toward what can be (Goodman and Lesnick 2001), toward potential solutions for complex social challenges. And student experiences of working in collaboration for the common good may foster lasting notions of *collective responsibility*. Conceptions of individual responsibility, while important, are insufficient in an interdependent world (Romein 1955). Engagement in service and social action is an important balance to higher education's focus on individual achievement and career preparation.

The most comprehensive study of moral and civic responsibility in higher education has been directed by Tom Ehrlich and Ann Colby of the Carnegie Foundation for the Advancement of Teaching. Ehrlich's edited volume (2000) integrates scholarship from many disciplines. And the book by Ehrlich et al. (2003) documents the Foundation's study of twelve exemplary institutions that have developed a campus-wide focus on moral and civic responsibility. Ehrlich and Colby argue that moral and civic responsibility are inherently intertwined, and their focus on responsibility moves the dialogue beyond discussion of means (pedagogies and methods) to positive outcomes framed in public terms. They call for creative responses to current political disinterest among youth and emphasize the need for improved assessment and research within and across contexts.

James Fowler (1992) suggests the need to move beyond essentially cognitive or sociological explanations to "reclaim a more comprehensive understanding of the *moral* in moral development" (234). "Moral" needs to be understood in public not just private terms (an argument consistent with Kolberg's emphasis on social perspective taking and the just-community approach to education). Fowler presents a comprehensive model of the "responsible self" built on cognitive abilities, character virtues, recognition of community narratives, professional accountability, and citizenship obligations. He suggests that the development of morally responsible persons is an integrated process that also is informed by the "theological virtues of faith, hope, and love" (247). Whether built on religious beliefs and identities or on more civil framings, such virtues give context to and reinforce moral principles and commitments. While faith-based institutions may more directly address such theological virtues (see Howe 1995; Byron 2000), many service-learning participants—forty-six percent in a study by Eyler and Giles (1999)—report spiritual growth as an important outcome even though service experiences were framed in secular, not religious, terms.

MORAL LEARNING AND WAYS OF KNOWING

Moral growth is, broadly defined, a learning process.[3] We learn by assimilation as well as adaptation. We emulate models and mentors. Engaged forms of learning often bring to awareness students' own epistemological assumptions and patterns of learning. In a world of shifting social landscapes and complex human systems, the ability to learn about moral issues—to teach oneself what is morally relevant, salient, and worthy—is essential. Peter Vaill (1996) suggests that social flux and change, which he labels *permanent white water,* is the dominant characteristic of our current age.

Such instability can lead to confusion and doubt, and cannot be addressed adequately through "institutional learning" traditions that rely on transfer of static content. Vaill quotes John Gardner on the potential for self-renewal and innovation: "The ultimate goal of the education system is to shift to the individual the burden of pursuing his own education. This will not be a widely shared pursuit until we get over our odd conviction that education is what goes on in school buildings and nowhere else. . . . The world is an incomparable classroom, and life is a memorable teacher for those who aren't afraid of her" (quoted in Vaill 1996, 76). Vaill makes a strong case for "learning as a way of being," which is self-directed, experiential, holistic, and continuous.

The challenge is to make moral sense out of ongoing experience. "Facts do not speak for themselves, for if they did, humans would find it easy to agree," suggests Vaill. "Meanings, implications, significances, and portents are wrested from the flow of events, *wrested* by men and women who have a felt stake in how things are unfolding" (1996, 141). Socialization explains only part of the process. We need comprehensive and dynamic theories of moral learning able to account for individual development within complex, changing social systems. Experiential educators may draw from the learning models described below.

Kolb (1981, 1984), building on Dewey, Piaget, and related cognitive theory, presents an integrated theory of experiential learning incorporating active experience and ongoing reflection. Individuals (and disciplines) exhibit varying learning styles, necessitating means to promote self-awareness with respect to learning assumptions and processes. "Experiential learning," according to Kolb (1981), is not merely an "educational concept" but a "central process of human adaptation to the social and physical environment." Thus, "learning becomes a central life task" for which the individual must develop the abilities "to experience, observe, conceptualize, and experiment" (248). Kolb's emphasis on learning how to learn in varying contexts provides an important counterbalance to the linear transmission models of teaching students often encounter. Through intentional experiential learning, individuals learn "through both intimate involvement and distanced reflection" and consider "how differences between these processes enable us to better understand our complicated world" (Mattson and Shea 1997, 15).

While various forms of engaged pedagogy may broaden conceptions of knowledge, the reciprocal nature of service learning presents unique opportunities for moral growth. In a national survey (Eyler and Giles 1999), over fifty percent of participants identified learning "that people I served are like me" as a most important or very important outcome of service learning; seventy-seven percent indicated learning "how complex social problems are" as most or very important. These and similar reported outcomes have important moral implications.

The focus here on the role of experience does not devalue the role in moral education of authority, generational influence, or learning about the good. Schwartz (2002) cautions that an overemphasis on the primacy of experience can obscure our awareness that much is learned via moral *transmission*. He describes, for example, how college honor codes as well as teaching of maxims—condensed forms of wisdom of how to live—can have positive impacts. He questions the logic of elevating the autonomous self to the highest moral position. Yet a focus on experience does not imply that all moral truth needs to be discovered independently. Piaget's concept of autonomy, for example, is collectively framed, building on perceived mutual interests and respect through peer interaction (see Philibert 1994). Schwartz (2002) and Carver (1997) point out that even Dewey stressed the role of transmission, framed as the "principle of continuity": "every experience both takes up something from those which have gone before and modifies in some way the quality of those which come after" (Dewey 1938, 35). Our previous experiences thus condition, but do not determine, our responses to later events and encounters.

Science itself, which frames much of higher education, is built on experience (see Cromer 1997). Just as scientific theory provides the basis for understanding experience in the lab, an individual's moral "theories" frame how personal experience is interpreted. The challenge is to develop theories of moral learning that both incorporate continuity and change and foster means to learn in a morally dynamic world.

Anthropologist Mary Catherine Bateson (1994) describes the task succinctly: in a changing society, we must learn "to improvise responsibly, and with love" (6). Bateson outlines the importance of "learning along the way":

> Meeting as strangers, we join in common occasions, making up our multiple roles as we go along—young and old, male and female, teacher and parent and lover—with all of science and history present in shadow form, partly illuminating and partly obscuring what is there to be learned. Mostly we are unaware of creating anything new, yet both perception and action are necessarily creative. . . . Men and women confronting change are never fully prepared for the demands of the moment, but they are strengthened to meet uncertainty if they can claim a history of improvisation and a habit of reflection. (6)

Bateson richly describes current learning challenges, with implicit support for engaged pedagogies. "It is hard to think of learning more fundamental to the shape of society," she points out, "than learning whether to trust or distrust others" (41). She emphasizes that we "bring one-another into being" (63), and suggests a more accurate form of Decartes' *cogito:* "You think, therefore I am. I think, therefore you are. We think . . ." (63). She points out that ideas about the self are learned, then easily challenged by change. New experiences are an essential part of learning, but put our ideas of self at risk. So we need to learn how to learn, to trust that "from a sense of continuing truths . . . we can draw the courage for change" (79).

Mentkowski and associates (Mentkowski 2001; Mentkowski and associates 2000) at Alverno College provide a thorough developmental model of "learning that lasts." Research at Alverno confirms the positive impact on moral growth of an integrated overall curriculum that involves experiential learning. Mentkowski points out that during the college years moral growth may be "seeded" as students develop patterns of learning and commitment that last into the adult years. Similarly, experiential educators may draw from the work of Mezirow (2000) on transformational learning among adults.

From an international perspective, the work of Brazilian educator Paulo Freire (1970, 1994) is critical. Freire's analysis of the moral and political assumptions built into all levels of education challenge teachers and learners to proceed with respect and awareness of patterns of power and oppression. Such awareness begins in experience. Freire (1994) describes an early, formative incident that drew him out of the "certainty" of the academy. As he lectured, interestingly for the current paper, about Piaget's work on moral development, he was challenged by a poor worker to experience directly the conditions and perspectives of those living in poverty.

Freire's work also emphasizes that solutions to social inequalities are not often solved by those who create or benefit from systems in place (see Rivage-Seul 1987). Martin-Baro (1994) of El Salvador argues that psychology is too often blind to social structures and that "social context is thus converted into a kind of natural phenomenon, an unquestioned assumption" (37) that may lead to a limited private morality. Martin-Baro builds on Freire's call for *concientización,* or a critical consciousness developed through learning to "read" the word and the world via an ongoing dialogical process. Both Freire (see Escobar et al. 1994) and Martin-Baro (1991) offer well-developed visions of higher education as a means to foster critical awareness and social responsibility. Martin-Baro, for example, provides a prescient vision of community-based research in which both faculty and students apply *conscience* and *science* "to the analysis of reality's structural problems and present viable solutions as well as prepare those who can carry out such solutions" (1991, 240).

Berkowitz and Fekula (1999) outline five potential means for colleges to foster character development and moral learning: (1) teaching about character and morality, (2) displaying character, (3) demanding character, (4) apprenticeship/practice, and (5) reflection (19). Relying on one method would be inadequate. The displayed motto "Duty, honor, and country" serves as helpful reminder of values at West Point, though it may be less salient to students at Notre Dame or Berkeley, and certainly would not be sufficient alone for moral growth. An integrated approach implemented intentionally is warranted (Berkowitz and Fekula suggest ethics audits as a means of comprehensive planning). Service learning and related pedagogies integrate many of the five elements suggested. Quality service learning provides opportunities for learning across the curriculum, interaction with others who are displaying character, involvements that demand positive behavior, ongoing practice and shared governance, and individual and group reflection/analysis.

The above models demonstrate the need and potential for moral learning. Note that the moral exemplars studied by Colby and Damon demonstrated an "active seeking of new knowledge" (1992, 199) and an interest in learning about alternative perceptions of others. Similarly, Thorkildsen (1994) and George Lind (2002, personal communication) outline the interaction between moral perceptions and attitudes toward learning. Further research on such topics is warranted.

FROM THEORY TO PRACTICE: A SUMMARY

Engaged pedagogies, forms of learning emphasizing the integration of experience and reflection, are, then, well suited to foster character and moral development during the college years. Such pedagogies, thoughtfully implemented, are consistent with developmental theory and integrate potentially disparate aspects of moral education (and higher education): habit and experience, theory and action, reasoning and emotion, virtue and analysis, continuity and imagination. They have the potential both to foster character traits and moral identity and to extend frames of moral awareness into the sociopolitical realm, enhancing moral and civic responsibility. They provide opportunities for perspective taking, interaction with moral exemplars, and development of prosocial peer relations and understandings of community. Further, such pedagogies give students important practice in self-directed moral learning in a changing society. And, perhaps most importantly, they seem to have a channeling effect, prompting ongoing awareness and long-term moral commitment.

Engaged forms of learning thus represent new ways of knowing, alternative epistemologies relevant to moral complexities encountered in higher education and beyond.

While the potentials are many, some cautions are important. Not all moral learning takes place through direct engagement, and not all experience leads to moral
growth. Fragmented approaches may yield inconclusive results that can then be used
to fuel counterarguments that character development cannot be enhanced intentionally during college. We must search for integrated models within higher education,
recognizing that one size does not fit all and building on local contexts and strengths.
Educators must avoid fostering a sense of noblesse oblige (Illich 1968) or framing social challenges simply as individual or community deficits (see McKnight 1989, 1995).
Community members need to be welcomed as educational partners.

Fortunately, various recent initiatives provide direction for future development.
In addition to the thorough outline of Ehrlich et al. (2003) and other sources cited in
this review, educators may want to consult *Colleges that Encourage Character Development,* produced by the John Templeton Foundation (1999), and a new electronic
publication edited by Jon Dalton, the *Journal of College and Character.* See also a comprehensive document (and national initiative) written by young adults themselves:
The Content of Our Character (Behr et al. 1999). This manifesto, written by fifty engaged
youth from across the United States and paralleling the Port Huron Statement by
students in the 1960's, presents a stirring vision of ethical leadership for the current
generation.

HIGHER LEARNING: MORAL IMPLICATIONS

What are the implications of this exploration of moral development through experience in the context of social change? I offer the following twelve recommendations
as a start. College faculty and administrators would do well to:

1) Rediscover institutional mission statements, noting the centrality of moral
   and character development and the call to social engagement. Address reward structures accordingly.
2) Identify and question epistemological dualisms and disciplinary boundaries within the academy that may limit integrated scholarship and applied
   learning. Recognize the need for new epistemologies.
3) Prompt moral notice, cultivate habits of reflection on experience, and foster moral imagination of alternatives.

4) Develop learning opportunities that intentionally foster habits basic to character *and* the development of moral reasoning abilities.

5) Attend to the development of moral identity among students (and faculty). Avoid leaving the self out of the learning process.

6) Foster study of and contact with moral exemplars, and facilitate peer collaboration in learning.

7) Frame moral issues in ways that move beyond the personal domain, highlighting social responsibility and attention to social structures. Foster civic engagement and social analysis through attention to political issues and processes.

8) Build on student initiative and foster relevant leadership development opportunities.

9) Be willing to address "transcendent" and spiritual issues that arise when individuals encounter social challenges.

10) Promote self-directed moral learning and learning how to learn (consistent with the concept of discovery at the heart of the academy).

11) Link moral learning to students' professional development to foster preparation for "good work" (Gardner et al. 2001).

12) Foster comprehensive assessment of moral and character development and related institutional efforts.

Such recommendations underscore the need for relevant theory development and research. Let us build integrated scholarship to identify means to enhance moral and civic responsibility. Given the central role higher education plays in developing future leaders and promoting moral learning in a complex, knowledge-based society, much is at stake.

NOTES

1. This chapter serves, in part, to introduce those promoting engaged forms of learning in higher education to relevant theory and research in moral psychology. The terms *character* and *moral* are used broadly. Sources for further conceptual clarification (e.g., of constructs and inherent psychological processes) beyond the scope of this work are cited throughout the text.

2. Here I build on the four-component model of morality outlined by James Rest (1986). See also Rest et al. (1999).

3. The focus here on moral *learning* is meant to emphasize means by which individuals (as well as organizations) may learn proactively to be moral and ethical in a changing world. It presumes a degree of moral motivation and self-direction. Higher education is a fruitful environment for such.

REFERENCES

Astin, A. W., L. J. Sax, and J. Avalos. 1999. Long-term effects of volunteerism during the undergraduate years. *The Review of Higher Education* 22 (2): 187–202.

Bateson, M. C. 1994. *Peripheral Visions: Learning Along the Way.* New York: HarperCollins.

Baxter Magolda, M. B. 2001. *Making Their Own Way: Narratives for Transforming Higher Education to Promote Self-development.* Sterling, VA: Stylus.

Behr, G., M. Finch, W. Dobson, S. Abrams, and C. Brown, eds. 1999. *The Content of Our Character: Voices of Generation X.* Durham, NC: Duke Publications Group. www.contentofourcharacter.org.

Berkowitz, M. W., and M. J. Fekula. 1999. Fostering character on college campuses. *About Campus* 4 (5): 17–22.

Berman, S. 1997. *Children's Social Consciousness and the Development of Social Responsibility.* Albany: State University of New York Press.

Blasi, A. 1983. Moral cognition and moral action: A theoretical perspective. *Developmental Review* 3:178–210.

———. 1984. Moral identity: Its role in moral functioning. In *Morality, Moral Behavior, and Moral Development,* ed. W. M. Kurtines and J. J. Gewirtz, 128–39. New York: John Wiley and Sons.

———. 1993. The development of identity: Some implications for moral functioning. In *The Moral Self,* ed. G. G. Noam and T. E. Wren, 99–122. Cambridge, MA: MIT Press.

———. 2002. The psychology of moral responsibility. Paper presented at the University of Notre Dame, Notre Dame, IN, November.

Bok, D. 1982. *Beyond the Ivory Tower: Social Responsibilities of the Modern University.* Cambridge, MA: Harvard University Press.

Boss, J. A. 1994. The effect of community service work on the moral development of college ethics students. *Journal of Moral Education* 23 (2): 183–98.

———. 1995. Teaching ethics through community service. *The Journal of Experiential Education* 18 (1): 20–24.

Boyer, E. L. 1996. The scholarship of engagement. *Journal of Public Outreach* 1 (1): 11–20.

———. 1997. *Scholarship Reconsidered: Priorities of the Professoriate.* San Francisco: Jossey-Bass. (Orig. pub. 1990, The Carnegie Foundation for the Advancement of Teaching.)

Brandenberger, J. W. 1998. Developmental psychology and service learning: A theoretical framework. In *With Service in Mind: Concepts and Models for Service-learning,* ed. R. G. Bringle and D. K. Duffy, 68–84. Washington, DC: American Association for Higher Education.

———. 2002. The scholarship of engagement: Research and assessment of moral learning and developmental outcomes. Paper presented at the American Association for Higher Education National Assessment Conference, Boston, MA, June.

Bringle, R. G., R. Games, and E. A. Malloy, eds. 1999. *Colleges and Universities as Citizens.* Boston: Allyn & Bacon.

Byron, W. J. 2000. A religious-based college and university perspective. In *Civic Responsibility and Higher Education*, ed. T. Ehrlich, 279–94. Phoenix, AZ: Oryx Press.

Carver, R. L. 1997. Theoretical underpinnings of service learning. *Theory Into Practice* 36 (3): 143–49.

Chickering, A. W., and L. Reisser. 1993. *Education and Identity*, 2nd ed. San Francisco: Jossey-Bass.

Colby, A., and W. Damon. 1992. *Some Do Care: Contemporary Lives of Moral Commitment.* New York: Free Press.

———. 1993. The uniting of self and morality in the development of extraordinary moral commitment. In *The Moral Self*, ed. G. G. Noam and T. E. Wren, 149–74. Cambridge, MA: MIT Press.

Coles, R. 1993. *The Call of Service: A Witness to Idealism.* Boston: Houghton-Mifflin.

Cromer, A. 1997. *Connected Knowledge: Science, Philosophy, and Education.* New York: Oxford University Press.

Daloz, L. A. P., C. H. Keen, J. P. Keen, and S. D. Parks. 1996a. *Common Fire: Lives of Commitment in a Complex World.* Boston: Beacon Press.

———. 1996b. Lives of commitment: Higher education in the life of the new commons. *Change* 28 (3): 11–15.

Damon, W., and D. Hart. 1992. Self understanding and its role in social and moral functioning. In *Developmental Psychology: An Advanced Textbook*, 3rd ed., ed. M. H. Bornstein and M. E. Lamb, 421–61. Hillsdale, NJ: Lawrence Erlbaum Associates.

DeVries, R., and B. Zan. 1994. *Moral Classrooms, Moral Children: Creating a Constructivist Atmosphere in Early Education.* New York: Teachers College Press.

Dewey, J. 1897. My pedagogic creed. *The School Journal* 54 (3): 77–80. http://edweb.sdsu.edu/people/DKitchen/new_655/my_pedagogic_creed.htm.

———. 1938. *Experience and Education.* New York: Collier Books.

———. 1996. *Theory of the Moral Life.* New York: Irvington. (Orig. pub. 1932.)

Ehrlich, T., ed. 2000. *Civic Responsibility and Higher Education.* Phoenix, AZ: Oryx Press.

Ehrlich, T., A. Colby, E. Beaumont, and J. Stephens. 2003. *Educating Citizens: Preparing America's Undergraduates for Lives of Moral and Civic Responsibility.* San Francisco: Jossey-Bass.

Erikson, E. H. 1975. *Life History and the Historical Movement.* New York: W. W. Norton and Company.

Escobar, M., A. L. Fernandez, G. Guevara-Niebla, and P. Freire. 1994. *Paulo Freire on Higher Education: A Dialogue at the National University of Mexico.* Albany: State University of New York Press.

Eyler, J., and D. E. Giles. 1999. *Where's the Learning in Service-learning?* San Francisco: Jossey-Bass.

Flanagan, C. 1998. Exploring American character in the sixties generation. In *Competence and Character Through Life*, ed. A. Colby, J. James, and D. Hart, 169–85. Chicago: University of Chicago Press.

Fowler, J. 1992. Character, conscience, and the education of the public. In *The Challenge of Pluralism: Education, Politics, and Values*, ed. F. C. Power and D. K. Lapsley, 225–50. Notre Dame, IN: University of Notre Dame Press.

Freire, P. 1970. *Pedagogy of the Oppressed*. Trans. M. B. Ramos. New York: Continuum.

———. 1994. *Pedagogy of Hope: Reliving Pedagogy of the Oppressed*. Trans R. R. Barr. New York: Continuum.

Gardner, H. 1991. The tensions between education and development. *Journal of Moral Education* 20 (2): 113–25.

Gardner, H., M. Csikszentmihalyi, and W. Damon. 2001. *Good Work: When Excellence and Ethics Meet*. New York: Basic Books.

Gilligan, C. 1982. *In a Different Voice: Psychological Theory and Women's Development*. Cambridge, MA: Harvard University Press.

Goodman, J. F., and H. Lesnick. 2001. *The Moral Stake in Education: Contested Premises and Practices*. New York: Addison Wesley Longman.

Gruber, H. E., and J. J. Vonèche, eds. 1995. *The Essential Piaget: An Interpretive Reference and Guide*. Northvale, NJ: Jason Aronson.

Hill, T. L., J. W. Brandenberger, and G. S. Howard. 2005. Lasting effects? A longitudinal study of the impact of service learning. Center for Social Concerns, University of Notre Dame, Research Report 8. http://centerforsocialconcerns.nd.edu/faculty/research.

Howe, C. 1995. Not a private matter: Pedagogies and strategies for institutional change. In *Love of Learning: Desire for Justice: Undergraduate Education and the Option for the Poor*, ed. W. Reiser, S.J., 95–103. Scranton, PA: University of Scranton Press.

Illich, I. 1968. To hell with good intentions. Address to the Conference on Inter-American Student Projects, Cuernevaca, Mexico, April.

James, W. 1995. The moral equivalent of war. *Peace and Conflict: Journal of Peace Psychology* 1 (1): 17–26. (Orig. pub. 1910.)

John Templeton Foundation. 1999. *Colleges that Encourage Character Development: The Templeton Guide*. Philadelphia: Templeton Foundation Press.

Johnson, M. 1993. *Moral Imagination: Implications of Cognitive Science for Ethics*. Chicago: University of Chicago Press.

King, P. M., and M. J. Mayhew. 2002. Moral judgment development in higher education. *Journal of Moral Education* 31 (3): 247–70.

Kolb, D. 1981. Learning styles and disciplinary differences. In *The Modern American College: Responding to the New Realities of Diverse Students and a Changing* Society, ed. A. W. Chickering and associates, 232–55. San Francisco: Jossey-Bass.

———. 1984. *Experiential Learning: Experience as The Source of Learning and Development*. Englewood Cliffs, NJ: Prentice-Hall.

Kohlberg, L. 1969. Stage and sequence: The cognitive-developmental approach to socialization. In *Handbook of Socialization Theory and Research*, ed. D. Goslin, 347–480. Chicago: Rand McNally.

Lapsley, D. K. 1996. *Moral Psychology.* Boulder, CO: Westview Press.

Loeb, P. R. 1994. *Generation at the Crossroads: Apathy and Action on the American Campus.* New Brunswick, NJ: Rutgers University Press.

Marstin, R. 1979. *Beyond Our Tribal Gods: The Maturing of Faith.* Maryknoll, NY: Orbis Books.

Martin-Baro, I. 1991. Developing a critical consciousness through the university curriculum. In *Towards a Society That Serves Its People: The Intellectual Contribution of El Salvador's Murdered Jesuits,* ed. J. Hassett and H. Lacey, 220–44. Washington, DC: Georgetown University Press.

———. 1994. *Writings for a Liberation Psychology.* Cambridge, MA: Harvard University Press.

Mattson, K., and M. Shea. 1997. The selling of service-learning to the modern university: How much will it cost? In *Expanding Boundaries: Building Civic Responsibility Within Higher Education,* vol. 2, 12–19. Columbia, MD: Cooperative Education Association.

McKnight, J. 1989. Why servanthood is bad. *The Other Side* 25 (1): 38–40.

———. 1995. *The Careless Society: Community and its Counterfeits.* New York: Basic Books.

Mentkowski, M. 2001. Transforming college curriculum toward moral learning and civic responsibility. Paper presented at Colleges That Care: A National Workshop on Campus Strategies for Fostering Moral and Civic Responsibility in College Students, Florida State University, Tallahassee, February. http://www.collegevalues.org/articles.cfm?a=1&id=605.

Mentkowski, M., and associates 2000. *Learning That Lasts: Integrating Learning, Development, and Performance in College and Beyond.* San Francisco: Jossey-Bass.

Mezirow, J., ed. 2000. *Learning as Transformation: Critical Perspectives on a Theory in Progress.* San Francisco: Jossey-Bass.

Mulgan, G. 1998. *Connexity: How to Live in a Connected World.* Boston: Harvard Business School Press.

Palmer, P. J. 1987. Community, conflict, and ways of knowing: Ways to deepen our educational agenda. *Change* 19 (5): 20–25.

———. 1998. *The Courage to Teach: Exploring the Inner Landscape of a Teacher's Life.* San Francisco: Jossey-Bass.

Pappas, G. F. 1998. Dewey's ethics: Morality as experience. In *Reading Dewey: Interpretations for a Postmodern Generation,* ed. L. A. Hickman, 100–23. Bloomington: Indiana University Press.

Parks, S. 1986. *The Critical Years: The Young Adult Search for a Faith to Live By.* San Francisco: Harper & Row.

———. 2000. *Big Questions, Worthy Dreams: Mentoring Young Adults in Their Search for Meaning, Purpose, and Faith.* San Francisco: Jossey-Bass.

Pascarella, E. T., and P. T. Terenzini. 1991. *How College Effects Students: Findings and Insights from Twenty Years of Research.* San Francisco: Jossey-Bass.

Perry, W. G. 1970. *Forms of Intellectual and Ethical Development in the College Years.* New York: Holt, Rinehart, and Winston.

Philibert, P. J. 1994. The formation of moral life in a mass-mediated culture. In *Mass Media and the Moral Imagination,* ed. P. J. Rossi and P. A. Soukup, 71–84. Kansas City, MO: Sheed & Ward.

Piaget, J. 1948. *The Moral Judgment of the Child.* Trans. M. Gabain. Glencoe, IL: Free Press. (Orig. pub. 1932.)

————. 1970. *Science of Education and the Psychology of the Child.* Trans. D. Coltman. New York: Orion Press.

Rest, J. 1986. *Moral Development: Advances in Research and Theory.* New York: Praeger.

Rest, J., and D. Narvaez. 1991. The college experience and moral development. In *Handbook of Moral Behavior and Development,* vol. 2, *Research,* ed. W. Kurtines and J. Gewirtz, 229–45. Hillsdale, NJ: Lawrence Erlbaum Associates.

Rest, J., D. Narvaez, M. J. Bebeau, and S. J. Thoma. 1999. *Postconventional Moral Thinking: A Neo-Kohlbergian Approach.* Mahwah, NJ: Lawrence Erlbaum Associates.

Rivage-Seul, M. K. 1987. Peace education: Moral imagination and the pedagogy of the oppressed. *Harvard Educational Review* 57 (2): 153–69.

Romein, T. 1955. *Education and Responsibility.* Lexington: University of Kentucky Press.

Sax, L. J., and A. W. Astin. 1997. The benefits of service: Evidence from undergraduates. *Educational Record* 78 (3,4): 25–33.

Schwartz, A. J. 2000. It's not too late to teach college students about values. *Chronicle of Higher Education* (June 9): A68.

————. 2002. Transmitting moral wisdom in an age of the autonomous self. In *Bringing in a New Era in Character Education,* ed. W. Damon, 1–21. Stanford, CA: Hoover Institution Press.

Schweiker, W. 2001. Disputes and trajectories in responsibility ethics. *Religious Studies Review* 27 (1): 18–24.

Thorkildsen, T. A. 1994. Toward a fair community of scholars: Moral education as the negotiation of classroom practices. *Journal of Moral Education* 23 (4): 371–86.

Vaill, P. B. 1996. *Learning as a Way of Being: Strategies for Survival in a World of Permanent White Water.* San Francisco: Jossey-Bass.

Walker, L. J. 2002. Moral exemplarity. In *Bringing in a New Era in Character Education,* ed. W. Damon, 65–83. Stanford, CA: Hoover Institution Press.

Walshok, M. L. 1995. *Knowledge Without Boundaries: What America's Research Universities Can Do for the Economy, the Workplace, and the Community.* San Francisco: Jossey-Bass.

Whitely, J. M. 1982. *Character Development in College Students,* vol. 1, *The Freshman Year.* Schenectady, NY: Character Research Press.

Youniss, J., and M. Yates. 1997. *Community Service and Social Responsibility in Youth.* Chicago: University of Chicago Press.

Concluding Themes and Issues for the Future

F. Clark Power and Daniel K. Lapsley

A NUMBER OF CONSISTENT THEMES EMERGE FROM THIS VOLUME. ONE IS that character psychology, and moral functioning more generally, will profit from deeper integration with other psychological literatures, specifically the literatures of social cognition, cognitive science, personality, and motivation. A second theme is that self-identity, in particular, is foundational to our understanding of moral character and provides a better basis for conceptualizing moral motivation, commitment, and self-worth than traditional trait notions of personality. A third theme is that rich conceptions of character psychology are a prerequisite for effective character education. Moreover, many chapters in this volume converge on a number of specific recommendations concerning the aims and purposes of character education (e.g., democratic citizenship) as well as on matters of pedagogy and instructional practices, including, for example, the cultivation of ethical skills and conversational virtues, the formation of moral communities (classrooms, sport teams), and the requirement of pervasive school reform, among others.

This volume points to five general prospects that we think will serve as a basis for ongoing reflection and research on the question of moral character and the conditions of its formation. The first is that it is quite evident that we are indeed in a "post-Kohlbergian" era in moral psychology. This volume presents a spectrum of perspectives on Kohlberg's contribution to moral development and education, and we are confident that discussion about what to embrace, revise, and discard will continue well into the future.

Second, it is clear that the boundaries between philosophy and psychology are being renegotiated, and that, as a result, numerous integrative questions will preoccupy us for some time. For example, the renewed concern with virtues and moral character has moved the discussion away from a preoccupation on the right to a focus on the good. How do the right and good interact (a question that endures from early Greek philosophy to the present)? The question of "how to live well the life that is good for one to live" will require psychological as well as ethical reflection. But to what extent can moral psychology help us understand the life that is good for one to live in terms of, say, human flourishing? To what extent are psychological constructs, such as adjustment, ego integrity, or identity adequate for a defensible notion of flourishing, of happiness, or of virtue? How are we to understand the traditional notion of moral intentionality and its relationship to moral appraisal in light of psychological evidence of pervasive automaticity in social cognition? In what form can we retain the principle of phenomenalism as a philosophical starting-point in moral psychology? This volume holds out the prospect that investigations that naturalize ethics and psychologize morality will find common cause, and yet how this conversation is to proceed and what it might say about the relationship between morality and human rationality, agency, and personality are questions just now before us.

Third, the relationship between conscious and unconscious psychological processing, between processing that is deliberative and effortful on the one hand and processing that is tacit, implicit, and automatic on the other, is just now being put to the moral domain. This opens up new lines of research into the notion of habits and into the developmental experiences that encourage moral automaticity and the formation of social cognitive units of moral personality, among other questions.

Fourth, the present volume attests to the emerging consensus on the role of self-identity in understanding the moral personality. The work of Augusto Blasi on the subjective self is particularly influential. Future research will undoubtedly address the question as to whether, and how, the self can serve as an organizing construct for character research.

Finally, the present volume suggests that the politically conservative conception of character tends toward highly individualistic notions of "trait possession." What is required is historical (and perhaps sociological and anthropological) analysis to remind us of how situated is our notion of character. Many of the chapters in this volume suggest that more emphasis is required on notions of community, on civic virtues proper to democratic citizenship, and on the interpersonal basis of character and its relational functions. How these recommendations play out in our contemporary culture will require critical examination. We hope that the present volume will have a galvanizing effect on these exciting prospects.

CONTRIBUTORS

Marvin W. Berkowitz is the Sanford N. McDonnell Professor of Character Education at the University of Missouri–Columbia.

Melinda Bier is an Assistant Professor in the Department of Educational Psychology at the University of Missouri–Columbia.

Augusto Blasi is Professor Emeritus in the Department of Psychology at the University of Massachusetts–Boston. He currently resides in Rome, Italy.

Jay W. Brandenberger is the Director of the Experiential Learning and Developmental Research Program at the Center for Social Concerns and Concurrent Associate Professor of Psychology at the University of Notre Dame.

Brenda Light Bredemeier is Associate Professor in the Division of Teaching and Learning at the University of Missouri–St. Louis.

Craig A. Cunningham is an Associate Professor in the Integrated Studies in Teaching, Technology, and Inquiry Program at National-Louis University in Chicago. He was formerly a Research Associate with the Center for School Improvement at the University of Chicago.

Matthew L. Davidson is the Research Director at the Center for the 4th and 5th Rs (Respect and Responsibility) at the State University of New York College at Cortland.

Ann Higgins-D'Alessandro is the Director of the Developmental Program in the Department of Psychology at Fordham University.

Joel J. Kupperman is Professor of Philosophy at the University of Connecticut.

339

Daniel K. Lapsley is Professor and Chair of the Department of Educational Psychology at Ball State University.

Martin Lipton is communications analyst for the Institute for Democracy, Education, and Access (IDEA) at the University of California–Los Angeles.

Christine McKinnon is Professor and Chair of the Department of Philosophy at Trent University, Canada.

Darcia Narvaez is Associate Professor in the Department of Psychology at the University of Notre Dame.

Robert J. Nash is Professor of Education in the Department of Integrated Professional Studies at the University of Vermont.

Jeannie Oakes is Presidential Professor in Educational Equity and Director of the Institute for Democracy, Education, and Access (IDEA) at the University of California–Los Angeles and Director of the University of California's All Campus Consortium on Research for Diversity.

F. Clark Power is Professor in the Program of Liberal Studies and Concurrent Professor of Psychology at the University of Notre Dame.

Karen Hunter Quartz is the Assistant Director of Research at the Institute for Democracy, Education, and Access (IDEA) at the University of California–Los Angeles.

Steve Ryan is Assistant Professor in the Department of Teacher Education at Michigan State University.

David Light Shields teaches in the Division of Teaching and Learning at the University of Missouri–St. Louis.

SUBJECT INDEX